KEITH SISMAN

TRACES OF THE
KINGDOM

First Published in Great Britain in 2010 by
Forbidden Books
PO BOX 1
Ramsey
Huntingdon
PE26 2YZ
United Kingdom

© Traces of the Kingdom, Keith Sisman, 2010
2nd Edition

www.traces-of-the-kingdom.org.uk

Keith Sisman has asserted his moral rights
to be identified as the author.

A CIP Catalogue of this book is available from
The British Library.

ISBN – 978-0-9564937-1-2

Scripture quotations are from the King James Bible, unless stipulated
otherwise.

This Second Edition Printed by:
Forbidden Books
PO BOX 1
Ramsey
Huntingdon
PE26 2YZ
United Kingdom

Dedicated to my wife Sarah and our children, Anna, Thomas, Tabitha and Lois.

Appreciation

Appreciation is given to the many friends who have helped considerably in this project. I needed someone with a secular background to look into the work; Derek Hanssens Birch, a Cambridge academic and legal expert examined my evidence, arguments, and conclusions presented in the book. Much appreciation is extended to him for his guidance and corrections to the presentation of my evidence. In particular, thanks are given to Ken Chumbley and Dan Mayfield for reading the second manuscript for this edition and their kind advice throughout. My appreciation is also extended to several others in the United States for their assistance in preparing the manuscript for printing. Appreciation is also extended to my son, Thomas, who took many of the pictures. He spent many occasions being abandoned at the side of a road to take pictures and be collected later, sometimes wet and bedraggled, whilst I enjoyed the comforts of a warm car. Neither must we forget the many Christians who have stood firm for their faith, dying in the flames of Catholic and Protestant persecution, through whom accounts have come down to us. Without their bravery recorded through the records made by their prosecutors and executors, this book would have been impossible to research.

Foreword

I am happy to have been asked to write the foreword for this second edition of Keith Sisman's excellent work, *Traces of the Kingdom*.

I first became acquainted with Keith Sisman while my family and I were working with churches in my native England. Keith began dating Sarah, a member of the church in Cambridge. As a result he began studying the scriptures and was baptized into Christ by the late Graham Moulton. Later Graham and I officiated at Keith and Sarah's wedding. Since returning to the United States in 1992, I have returned to England at least once a year and have had a close association with the Sisman family.

Keith and Sarah have four children: Anna, Thomas, Tabitha and Lois. Keith is a "flatlander" being born in Ramsey, in the "fens"—the flatlands north of Cambridge extending up to Lincoln. Sarah is a native of Oxfordshire. They live in Upwood, a small village close to Ramsey and about twenty miles from Cambridge.

Since his conversion, Keith has been very active in the church. He currently serves as the preacher for the Cambridge

Church of Christ. By profession Keith trained as a photographer and photographic technician, first working in one of England's top photographic specialists, Campkins of Cambridge. As photographer he has worked for many well known international companies and magazines. His pictures have been published worldwide. He still retains a keen interest in photography along with Thomas, his son who has helped with taking many of the photographs that appear in the book. Later he worked with his father in the motor trade. He has an interest in cars and motorcycles, holding the coveted RoSPA Diploma in Advanced Driving Instruction and is involved voluntarily in road safety. Today Keith and Sarah own a business specializing in school transport employing nearly twenty staff. Sarah takes much of the day to day responsibilities of the business thus enabling Keith to do the other work that he does for the church as well as his research and writing.

After his obedience to the gospel, Keith developed an interest in the history of the Lord's church in England. He knew of some of my research into the efforts to restore New Testament Christianity in Great Britain during the 19th century and of the connection that I had found between one of those churches with an earlier effort to bring about restoration during the 17th century. The work in the Lake District had roots back to the church in Tottlebank, established in 1669 that later apostatized and became a Baptist church but whose records clearly showed that it was established as a church of Christ and not a Baptist church.

In this work, *Traces of the Kingdom*, Keith has been able to combine his skills as a photograph with the intensive research that he has done in order to produce this informative and well-document work. Living close to Cambridge and having contact with some at the University, Keith was able to gain permission to view the archives of historical materials that are housed at the University. Further, he was also able to get into the archives of the British Museum and view documents that are housed there. Through his research he was able to find many records that indicate early efforts to restore New Testament Christianity going back at least to the 11th century. In many instances, the Roman Catholic Church and later the Church of England, actively persecuted all that did not submit to their views and their authority. Later, the writings of those involved, who were often highly educated, were suppressed and even though many of the writings were still in existence, they were not readily available.

As a result of his research, Keith has been able to visit numerous sites around England and gain further information as well as being able to add photographs of the area and, in some instances, the places where they met, which were often well hidden because of the fact that for much of the time period, those who did not follow the "established religion" of the country were not allowed to openly meet. On occasion, while visiting in England, I have been able to spend some time with him in visiting these places. Additionally, Keith has been able to acquire for his personal library some printed copies of early works. Sometimes these are later reprints from a time when such writings could be more freely circulated.

Keith has titled his work, *Traces of the Kingdom,* because all of the records, writings etc., are not available and therefore we only have a partial glimpse into the beliefs and practices of some of those in earlier centuries who sought to restore the Lord's church to its pristine glory. The research materials that Keith has used are well documented. I heartily recommend this book to its readers. I believe that all who have an interest in the Lord's church and its history will find much to interest them. Keith is to be commended for his many hours of research and writing and his good wife, Sarah, is to be commended for all of her efforts that have enabled him to devote the necessary time to this literary effort.

Ken Chumbley, Belvedere, SC
September 20, 2010

Table of Contents

Illustrations, Woodcuts, and Photographs

Photography
by Keith and Thomas Sisman,
using Canon EOS Digital cameras and lenses

Woodcuts - these are from the 1684 edition of Fox's *Acts and Monuments of the Christian Church*, Southwell's Book of Martrys - *The New Book of Martyrs or Complete Christian Martyrology*, Rev. Henry Southwell, 1790 and *The Lollards* George Stokes, 1838.

Front cover, top picture - James Bainham, preacher Bow Lane Church of Christ, London, executed by burning for preaching believers' baptism and that the Lord's Supper is a memorial, 1532.

Lower picture - the little chapel that is on the bridge in St. Ives, Cambridgeshire. For a few months in the 1650s Henry Denne preached believers' baptism for the remission of sins for the church of Christ who met in the chapel, before they moved to house nearby.

Page 62 - Stonehenge, the photograph is taken from the Southeast showing the circle and one of its many associated mounds.

Page 67 - the river Cam (from which Cambridge is named) at Grantchester, a small village a few minutes from Cambridge.

Page 94 - Brent Tor is a tor (rocky hill) on the western edge of Dartmoor, approximately five miles north of Tavistock, West Devon. It rises to 1100 ft above sea level. The Tor is surmounted by the Church of St. Michael of the Rock, the parish church of the village of Brentor, which lies below the Tor. The picture is taken from the west.

Page 95 - Brent Tor.

Page 95 - Roche, Cornwall. Roche is the Norman name for "rock." It lies to the south of the village of Roche. The church dedicated to St. Michael sits on top of a volcanic outcrop, almost impossible to reach.

Page 96 - Roche.

Page 113 - photograph of the hull of a massive Roman ship recovered from Lake Nemi. The hull was destroyed by the Nazis towards the end of WW2. The picture is in the public domain.

Page 125 - a fourteenth century French picture of the Albigensian Crusade. *Albigensian* is a derogatory name used for Christians, along with *Waldensian*. The house is being ransacked after soldiers expelled the inhabitants. © British Library.

Page 140 - Castle Mound, Oxford. The Normans built forts on top of the Gorsedd or parliaments mounds.

Page 163 - The burning of Oldcastle. Woodcut from page 28 of *The Lollards*, by George Stokes, 1838.

Page 168 - the chamber in the Lollards Tower, Lambeth, London, where the Roman Catholic Church held its prisoners. Woodcut from page 231 of *The Lollards*, by George Stokes, 1838.

Page 172 - a typical burning of a "heretic". Woodcut from page 172 of *The Lollards*, by George Stokes, 1838.

Page 178 - Lollards being executed by burning. Woodcut from opposite page 330, Southwell's *Book of Martrys - The New Book of Martyrs or Complete Christian Martyrology*. Rev. Henry Southwell, 1790.

Page 213 - the River Cam at Chesterton, a few minutes from Cambridge.

Page 213 - Downing Place, Cambridge, where in the 1600 and 1700s a church of Christ met.

Page 214 - a Christian being punished in the stocks, to force their penance as a "heretic." Woodcut from page 305 of *The Lollards*, by George Stokes, 1838.

Page 224 - map of the Waldensian heresy.

Page 225 - map of the heresy as reported as Lollardy.

Page 226 - map of the heresy as reported as Anabaptism.

Page 227 - map of the heresy as the church of Christ.

Page 230 - the burning of "heretics." Woodcut from opposite page 246, Southwell's *Book of Martrys - The New Book of Martyrs or Complete Christian Martyrology*. Rev. Henry Southwell, 1790.

Page 248 - The burning of "heretics." Woodcut from page 243 of *The Lollards*, by George Stokes, 1838.

Page 253 - photograph of the Grasshopper Inn, where John Frith was born in the village of Westerham, Kent. Originally called the Sevenoaks Inn; its name was changed to the Grasshopper at an unknown date.

Page 265 - the burning of Andrew Hewet and John Frith. Woodcut from page 163 of *The Lollards*, by George Stokes, 1838.

Page 268 - Tyndale, from the introduction of volume one, *Annals of the English Bible*, Christopher Anderson, 1845. 2 volumes.

Page 271 - Blue plaque marking the former site of the White Horse Inn, Cambridge, birth place of the Reformation in England.

Page 272 - former site of the White Horse Inn, Cambridge.

Page 273 - Kings College, Cambridge.

Page 274 - Kings College.

Page 284 - The Old Baptist Chapel, Tewkesbury, originally a meeting house of the church of Christ.

Page 287 - William Tyndale and the title page of his New Testament, source unknown.

Page 288 - William Tyndale working on his translation of the New Testament, source unknown.

Page 303 - the burning of William Tyndale. Woodcut from Vol. 2, page 305, *Acts and Monuments of the Christian Church*, better known as *Foxes book of Martyrs*, authored by John Foxe (1517-1587). Ninth edition, 1684.

United Reformed Church.

Page 607 - the Lindale Church of Christ was founded in 1873, the building is now a private house.

Page 608 - Askam Church of Christ was founded in 1878, the building is now owned by the Roman Catholics.

Page 608 - Dalton Church of Christ was founded in 1891. The congregation ceased as a church of Christ in 1971, the building now being owned by the Seven Day Adventists.

Page 609 - Great Urswick Church of Christ was founded in 1911. The congregation is now United Reformed.

Page 610 - The Ellers, Ulverston, the picture dating back to the 1920s. Picture supplied by a member of the congregation.

Page 612 - Walter Crosthwaite.

Page 613 - former church of Christ meeting place, Ulverston, in Union Street.

Page 614 - the present building where the Ulverston church of Christ meets.

Page 615- interior of the Ulverston building.

Page 615 - baptismal pool.

Page 631 - David King.

INTRODUCTION

Beloved, when I gave all diligence to write unto you of
the common salvation, it was needful for me to write unto
you, and exhort you that ye should earnestly contend for
the faith which was once delivered unto the saints (Jude
1:3).

It has often been asked whether churches of Christ existed prior
to the nineteenth century American Restoration Movement of Barton
W. Stone and Alexander Campbell. If churches of Christ, built on
Biblical foundations, ceased to exist after the great apostasy of the
second and third centuries, are we to say there were no Christians and
no salvation until the early 1800s? This study will attempt to answer
these questions and show that autonomous congregations, with a
like understanding of the Holy Scriptures, have existed through the
last millennia, continuing in the pattern set by the congregation that
met in Jerusalem on the first Pentecost after the Resurrection.

Some recent teaching is that the churches of Christ are a
development of the Reformation. This teaching states that the
Reformation came first and from that came the churches of Christ.

This study will prove this view to be erroneous. The restorers would have many vestiges to learn from the churches of Christ that predated the Restoration, such as believers' baptism and congregational autonomy, as practised in some denominations, who in turn had learned of such from the churches of Christ in bygone times.

Sometimes records are murky, we are looking back into the mists and myths of time. Most, if not all, we know of the churches of Christ in the Dark and Middle Ages is from their persecutors, the Roman Catholic Church, which has left the only record. From the 1500s information improves as we have witness accounts and their own printed materials that still exist. This is why this work is called *Traces of the Kingdom*. It is just that, finding those traces of Christians who rejected the teaching of men for the scriptural teaching of the first century church.

Questions will include: did they use the identity "church of Christ," or another; did they baptise by immersion for the remission sins, believers, upon confession; and were they congregational, being autonomous with elders and deacons? The answer is yes to all three. A fourth question is, did they exist prior to the Reformation of Martin Luther? Again, the answer is yes.

Churches of Christ did not come into being because of the Reformation, but due to a desire for scriptural understanding and a rejection of the total depravity of Augustine of Hippo (354 –

430). The doctrine of original sin found its way into the developing Roman Catholic theology of the fifth century, and thus universal redemption through Infant Baptism. Augustine also taught individual predestination, but it was John Calvin in the 1530s that developed Augustine's theology into the Protestant system. Luther too followed in the steps of Augustine, but not to the extreme of Calvin and individual predestination as laid out in Calvin's "Institutes."

The reformation was an attempt to reform what previously existed. Reformed churches were Roman Catholic in theology minus the extremes but with additions. The Roman system was grounded not in scripture, but paganism, which has resulted in paganism finding its way into the Protestant system. The infant baptism of the national churches is nothing more than the pagan lustration of the babies of ancient Rome and other nations worldwide.

National churches have temple-based worship at the altar, a clergy, secular support and infant baptism. These are based on the pagan system which remains present in the Roman and Reformed Churches. Churches of Christ through millennia have rejected this system following the scriptural teaching of freewill and individual responsibility to obey God.

Why this book? Well, apart from the questions above, in about 1997 a friend contacted me to ask if I would check out a document in the Cambridge University Library. I live about thirty minutes from the library, and having friends at the University to advise me, I was able to obtain a reader's pass that gave me access to the Rare Books Room. The library is large, having over six million books and many collections which date back centuries. It is one of the world's great resources for history.

The librarians were very helpful in finding old and ancient sources. The document I read was entitled "A Confession of Faith of seven congregations or Churches of Christ in London." It is dated 1646. The title continues, "which are commonly (but unjustly) called anabaptists." The only place where Baptist is used is to refute being called Anabaptist.

I studied the document and later learned it is what various Baptist historians call the second London confession, though some list it with the confession of 1644. No one to my knowledge reproduces the front title page, which is not surprising. These people, while called Baptists today, used no such title! The document is Calvinistic, and later those of this party would become the forerunners of today's Baptist denominations, but more of this later.

I then spent several months with the kindly assistance of the librarians at Cambridge, supported by my wife, Sarah, digging up old confessions, histories, etc. Some of my early findings were reproduced in J.C. Choate's, *The Voice of Truth*; later still, in 2001, my web site, *Traces of the Kingdom,* was started.

Later, I obtained a research pass for the British Library in London, which has over thirteen million books, the oldest manuscripts being about two and a half thousand years old. What I have found since then is that history, whether church history, or world history, neglects some facts and revises others. For example, world history starts at Babel, but historians have neglected this fact revising history with the invention of the stone, bronze and iron ages. It is the same with church history. Most of the massive multi volume or single volume church histories would be better called histories of church apostasy. My second work, *The Devils' Door*, will follow this volume. It will take world history through neglected secular sources back to Babel; it will also prove that the denominational system of the National Church, which has temple-based worship at the altar, the clergy system, secular support and infant baptism, along with human depravity (original sin) and fatalism is pagan in origin. I cannot think of any system more fatalistic than Calvinism.

Many Baptist historians have misplaced early churches of Christ as Baptist Churches. So, what is a Baptist? In the original and broadest sense, a Baptist is a person who practises believers' baptism, which description includes the churches of Christ in this broadest sense. This broad sense allows for the placing of Churches of Christ, who denied Reformed or Augustinian theology, to be placed in Baptist histories as Baptists. Unless this is explained, it

5

must come under the heading of revised history. Neither does it seem reasonable that a person, who holds to Reformed theology, would write about those who denied Reformed theology making them his own. Most denominations hold to one of the many traditions of Reformed or Catholic theology, excluding a few, including the Jehovah's Witnesses, who it seems to me are excellent in running a business not dissimilar to Network Marketing!

So what is the church of Christ? It is those who submit to Biblical authority, the teachings of Christ, rather than the innovations of man. From the third century onwards, innovations came in. Those who appealed to Biblical authority were dismissed as heretics through "ex-cathedra" condemnation and the use of terror to coerce faithful Christians into conformity with evil works. The teaching of the Sermon of the Mount was replaced with "another gospel" (Galatians Chapter 1) of violence and submission. The faith "once given" (Jude 3) was replaced with the earlier pagan system, dressed up in Christian terms but of another foundation, not of Christ – Christianity had been hijacked. The pagan gods Apollo and Jupiter became St. Michael and Diana became Mary. Pagan infant lustration became infant baptism. The pontiffs and popes of the pagan system continued as "Christian" pontiffs and popes.

This history will attempt to redress those revisions and neglected facts by other historians of the Reformed and Catholic traditions.

The Christian system was complete in the first century, given by inspiration, when the church was established. Anything added since is divisive, based on the then pagan system.

Robert Robinson, a minister of a church of Christ meeting in Chesterton, Cambridge in the 1700s wrote:

> On the caution necessary to a reader of ecclesiastical history: It is an old observation, that of all history, ecclesiastical is the worst written. Such a history, beginning with Jesus, and proceeding through successive ages with his disciples, ought to exhibit bright example of virtue. It should show a succession of men contending (if contend they must) for something worth contending for. Instead of this, every century proceeds from worse to worse, each opening with deplorable scenes of all the ills that afflict society, till in the end Christianity itself becomes doubtful to philosophers, while statesmen with too much plausibility consider the procession of it as a matter to be restrained and regulated by government for the safety of the state. The mistake is natural, and the positions of such respectable objectionists may be admitted without injury to Christianity, on condition the subject be properly explained. If Christianity be a revelation of impenetrable mysteries; if the forcing of mankind into a profession of believing them; if such a profession cannot be obtained without secular power; if governments must be modelled so as to discharge some citizens from the honour and pleasure of reasoning, and to oppress others for enjoying and exercising their own understanding; if God be pleased with his creatures for tithing mint, anise and cumin, and offended at the practise of judgement, faith and mercy, when it is not clothed with prescribed forms; if this be Christianity, the philosopher reasons consequently, when he infers it is not divine, and the statesman acts like a true

patriot, when he controls its influence; but if Christianity be a practice of national piety, a course of social virtue, and an inviolable attachment to universal human felicity, it ceases to be objectionable to the wise, or threatening to the great, and it carries along with it a demonstration of its heavenly original. Man and such religion are both the workmanship of one almighty agent, the Father of Lights, from whom comes every good and perfect gift.

Want of precision in ecclesiastical history is one chief cause of the gloom that involves the divine religion of Jesus, and while this confusion remains, a cheat is put on the reader, and a long time elapses ere he discovers that what had been given him for a history of good men, the very disciples of the son of God, was a history of counterfeits, disciples of the world, and regulated only by the maxims of it. Ecclesiastical history may be so written as to serve the interests of parties while the disguise remains: But to serve the cause of truth and virtue at large the covering must be taken off, for either that or the cause must go to decay.[1]

Sometimes in the book I have retained the original spelling when the author has used the term "Baptist," I have often gone along with that usage to keep quotes original. With a work such as this, I may have made small mistakes, but my overall conclusion, from the historical evidence is that churches of Christ practising the Biblical pattern, have existed for two millennia.

I have used many easily found sources for readers to follow up. One of my sources is the sixteenth century historian John Fox. He is famous today for his *Book of Martyrs*, which is the now common name for *Acts and Monuments of matters most special and memorable, happening in the church: With a Universal History of the same.* In the original, it is a heavy, cumbersome, massive three volumes in Latin. The name is normally abbreviated to *Acts and Monuments.* Today this work is mostly called *Foxe's Book of Martyrs*, but as such it is normally an abridged version of an abridged version, in other words, heavily edited. Unfortunately, *Foxe's Book of Martyrs* is used as a generic term for a wide variety of abridgements from the much larger work, first published in 1563. The edition of 1776 was the first to be entitled *The Book of Martyrs*, the title used in many subsequent editions and still used today.

John Fox (or Foxe—can be spelt both ways) was born at Boston, in Lincolnshire, in the year 1516. He died in 1587. Fox was educated at Magdalen School and College, Oxford, under Edward VI. Fox acted as tutor to the children of the recently beheaded Earl of Surrey. Fleeing Queen Mary, Fox settled first in Frankfort, then latter in Basle, Switzerland, before returning to England in 1539 and entering the established church. I am going to guess Fox became a Calvinist whilst in Switzerland, certainly not Boston, where he was born and had contacts. Lincolnshire being a centre for Lollardy and later the Anabaptists, though in my opinion after study both are the same, being derogatory names for the Lord's Church. Throughout *Traces of the Kingdom* where these derogatory names were used by

9

their enemies, it is addressed.

Fox was helped by his old pupil, the Duke of Norfolk, undertaking to write an early edition of his martyrology which dealt mainly with Wycliffism. While in Basle in 1559, he expanded this early work to include persecutions beginning with Wyclif and ending with Cranmer. Returning again to England, he once again expanded his martyrology and published it in 1563 under the name *Acts and Monuments*. A corrected edition was published in 1570. An immediate success, a Convocation of the English church in 1571 ordered that copies of the *Acts and Monuments* be kept in all cathedrals and in the houses of all church dignitaries for public inspection. Two more editions (1576 and 1583) came out during his life and five (1596, 1610, 1632, 1641, 1684) within the next hundred years. Lord William Cecil, 1st Baron of Burghley, was another supporter of Fox along with Queen Elizabeth I.

The version I use and quote from is the ninth edition of 1684, which is in English; it was the last full edition of Fox's history. Like the original Latin, it is a massive three volumes, but with some additions and corrections, by Fox, from his first edition. It also has a history of his life. The ninth edition was printed in London by the "Company of Stationers." It is considered by many the finest edition of Fox's *Acts and Monuments*.

Fox's work is not without fault and his bias towards Calvinism is a serious problem. Nonetheless, he was a valuable witness to many of the events recorded, and he interviewed several of the people persecuted or their relatives. The two problems that reoccur are, 1) He does get his dates wrong on occasion and spelling in that period was not standard. 2) Regrettably, he leaves out valuable information concerning those who baptised believers. Nonetheless, his work remains a valuable resource. As a single resource, his work is of little value to the serious student, but as an eyewitness and one who met those involved in persecution of the sixteenth century, his work has value, but only when used in conjunction with other sources as I have done. Simon Fish's widow in her old age gave a testimony to Fox, who is our witness. Though some of the dates given are wrong, these can be established by other means such as the historian John Strype (1643-1737), who wrote at a time when greater impartiality and accuracy was being demanded and access to documents now lost was possible. Fox's facts are correct, but his dates are sometimes wrong. He misses important facts and he also avoids mentioning Simon Fish's *Summe*, a book that defends believers' baptism.

I have relied on Johann Lorenz von Mosheim (1694-1755), who was a professor of theology at Gottingen, Germany. Mosheim may be considered the first of true modern ecclesiastical historians, and one thing I find with well studied theologians such as Mosheim is that they know nothing of political correctness—such historians can be quite objective. His history, first published in 1726, was originally composed in Latin; Archibald Maclaine made his first of two translations into English in 1764. I have used the six volume edition of 1802. Its full title is *An ecclesiastical history, ancient and modern, from the birth of Christ to the beginning of the present century: In which the rise, progress, and variations of Church power are considered in their connexion with the state of learning and philosophy, and the political history of Europe during that period.* I will call it *Mosheim's Church History* in the footnotes. I have found Daniel Featly's book, *The Dippers Dipt.*, quite amazing, Featly, one of the translators of the King James Bible and an enemy of the Lord's Church, remains a remarkable resource from a witness who wrote about those with whom he disagreed. The edition I have used is the 1646.

Simon Fish's the *Summe* is absolutely remarkable. Fish remains well known, however, when his book is referenced it is often misquoted. I have used the 1529 edition. I know of two copies, one held at the British Library and the other at the Cambridge University Library. This second copy is the one I have used.

Reginald Peacock's (Roman Catholic bishop and leading fifteen century theologian) work, *The Repressor of over much blaming of the Clergy*, was the first theological book to be written in English after the Norman conquest of 1066. The book was written about

1455 against Lollard doctrines. The English is "old" and his purpose was to bring the Lollards back into the Church of Rome. It confirms much of what we learn elsewhere, though I quote from it only once. Peacock's book is a defence of the clergy, but unfortunately does not deal with baptism. It offers a marvellous insight into pre-reformation religious arguments and proves the masses were not as ignorant of Christianity as may be expected for the Middle Ages. The arguments presented by Peacock from the Lollards are what would be expected from Bible people, and confirm, as do other sources, that they understood Biblical authority for matters of faith and practice.

Another source I have used is that of Dr. William Wall (1647 -1728). Wall was engaged with the "anabaptists" with whom he enjoyed good relations. Both sides produced tracts and books over several years, in which they countered their opponents arguments. The topic debated was, did the Great Commission include infants. Wall did not deny believers' baptism and held to immersion as being the correct mode. Wall's work remains highly regarded and is often quoted for those who defend infant baptism. He wrote his first edition of *A History of Infant Baptism* in 1704. Wall was a well respected Anglican priest, but never rose to any great rank remaining vicar of Shoreham, Kent, until his death. He was offered more lucrative positions, but he refused out of loyalty to his parish, which was not far from where he was born. Oxford University awarded him the degree of Doctor of Divinity in 1720 for his work on infant baptism. I do occasionally quote from him. The edition I have used is the second edition four volume set, edited by the Rev. Henry Cotton, Oxford University Press, 1844. I have been disappointed with Wall. He misquotes and I am at a loss as to whether he was dishonest, a poor researcher, or a mixture of both.

Thomas Crosby investigated those who baptised believers in the seventeenth and earlier centuries, which he published in his *The History of the English Baptists* in four volumes in 1738. Crosby, like Fox, does make mistakes. On the other hand he provides information not found in later histories. He wrote forty years after the persecutions ceased and had access to witnesses and information unavailable today. He also wrote at a time when the Baptist denominations were starting, providing valuable witness for that time.

Fortunately, by the 1530s, there were a number of books being produced and widely circulated by brethren that remain to this day. From these books it becomes possible to read what they actually wrote, rather than what their enemies reported. There was in London and Antwerp a much larger group of brethren. It included the famous names—John Frith, William Tyndale, Simon Fish, James Bainham, William Roy, "old father" Hacker and the Yorkshire Lollard, Valentine Freeze. The first three produced many books, and Tyndale was the first to translate the English Bible (NT) from the Greek and to have it printed. Tyndale, Frith, Bainham, Roy and Freeze were all executed by burning, Tyndale being strangled first. Fish died from the plague, but would have been executed had he not died first. Hacker, under torture, revealed many names and congregations to the authorities. He was widely travelled in England. He is possibly the only one to die in his own bed, apart from Fish. Fish's widow married James Bainham, and within a year he too was burned at the stake.

I have tried to use electronic resources, digital books and various internet sites. I am amazed how people copy others work, and others mistakes. Authors are too often misquoted and then that error is promulgated through the internet. Sometimes an author, writing two or more centuries ago, misquotes their source, and thus, through the internet, that misquote becomes in time "fact." Books too are copied and edited, the original mistakes stay as fact, being unnoticed. Another problem is digitised books, too often not the earliest, being abbreviated or late editions, which fail to reflect what the original author wrote. Despite huge advances in electronic resources, I have found it a requirement to use original materials. For historical research, the internet can be a very bad resource for lazy researchers.

From their books, events and association with others, we know the churches of Christ early on separated from the State

Churches, to which entry was via believers' baptism, by immersion, for the remission of sins (Mark. 16:15-16; Acts 2:38, 2:47). Each congregation was overseen by a plurality of elders, which is the same office as pastors, bishops and presbyters. Each (congregation) had deacons and rejected a separate clergy class. That such congregations existed, as evidence shows, is denied by the majority of historians. From that time onwards, it becomes easier to trace the history of such congregations, which were often closed down by the authorities. Leading brethren suffered loss of property, and were tortured and put to death by being burned alive. Thousands died in prison, others had their noses and ears cut off along with other mutilations.

Established historians in this field too often look for churches meeting visibly. Whereas, in actuality, they met privately, in homes, barns or even fields. For a congregation to be active, it needs no more than two people, and meeting in private, they would be invisible to their opponents. Looking for positive affirmation of believers' baptism by immersion is pointless before the reformation (1500s), as all parties held to believers' baptism, and as immersion was the accepted mode in England. It was not believers' baptism but the denial of infant baptism that is the clue. The Romish Church not only held to believers' immersion, however unscriptural it was in practice, they also affirmed infant baptism. Therefore, the clue is a denial of infant baptism. The main charge of heresy was the denial of the real presence (Transubstantiation). This was seen as blasphemy of the worst kind and once proven and not abjured, execution by burning would follow. After the reformation when the reformed churches rejected transubstantiation and other Romish ceremonies, the charge would be rebaptism – Anabaptism. Thus another name came into use, Anabaptist, and the old terms for heretics, of Lollards and Waldensians, would be forgotten.

There is much more information I could have used, but this would have resulted in a multi-volume work which is a venture I shall consider for the future. If that occurs, there would still be the need for a single volume edition, which you are reading now.

> If ye be reproached for the name of Christ, happy are ye; for the spirit of glory and of God resteth upon you: on their part he is evil spoken of, but on your part he is glorified (1 Peter 4:14).

> Salute one another with an holy kiss, the churches of Christ salute you (Romans 16:16).

Keith Sisman,
Upwood, Cambridgeshire, England,
February, 2010

ENDNOTES

[1]Robert Robinson, *Ecclesiastical Researches* (1792) 1st chapter. Robinson, a wealthy businessman, was for a time a minister of a church of Christ meeting in Cambridge, in Hog Hill, now Downing Street or Downing Place. The congregation later moved to St. Andrew's Street. The author died in 1790; the book was published two years after his death.

2

THE EPISTLE OF MATHETES TO DIOGNETUS
Otherwise known as "The Epistle to Diognetus"

And this is love, that we walk after his commandments.
This is the commandment, that, as ye have heard from the
beginning, ye should walk in it (2 John 1:6).

The author of the letter is anonymous, but gives himself the
pseudonym (Mathetes) "a disciple of the Apostles." The letter is a
wonderful post apostolic example of a Christian apologist, against
heathenism. It is possible Mathetes was known to Paul, or more
likely, to one of the apostle's younger associates. It is said by several
historians that his correspondent, Diognetus, was the tutor of the
Roman emperor, Marcus Aurelius Antoninus Augustus (AD161-
180). Aurelius was known as the last of the "good" emperors, who
were not violently opposed to Christianity. There is nothing in the
letter that is inconsistent with it being later than the second century,
possibly about AD130-160.

The letter sets the stage when Christianity is under attack in a
heathen world, the writer advocating the superiority of Christianity
over the ritualism of Judaism and the idolatry of paganism. I have

removed the last two chapters as it is generally agreed they are an addition. This letter offers a wonderful glimpse of post apostolic Christianity prior to apostasy entering and taking over the church.[1]

CHAPTER I
OCCASION OF THE EPISTLE

Since I see thee, most excellent Diognetus, exceedingly desirous to learn the mode of worshipping God prevalent among the Christians, and inquiring very carefully and earnestly concerning them, what God they trust in, and what form of religion they observe, so as all to look down upon the world itself, and despise death, while they neither esteem those to be gods that are reckoned such by the Greeks, nor hold to the superstition of the Jews; and what is the affection which they cherish among themselves; and why, in fine, this new kind or practice [of piety] has only now entered into the world, and not long ago; I cordially welcome this thy desire, and I implore God, who enables us both to speak and to hear, to grant to me so to speak, that, above all, I may hear you have been edified, and to you so to hear, that I who speak may have no cause of regret for having done so.

CHAPTER II
THE VANITY OF IDOLS

Come, then, after you have freed yourself from all prejudices possessing your mind, and laid aside what you have been accustomed to, as something apt to deceive you, and being made, as if from the beginning, a new man, inasmuch as, according to your own confession, you are to be the hearer of a new [system of] doctrine; come and contemplate, not with your eyes only, but with your understanding, the substance and the form of those whom ye declare and deem to be gods. Is not one of them a stone similar to that on which we tread? Is not a second brass, in no way superior to those vessels which are constructed for our ordinary use? Is not a third wood, and that already rotten? Is not a fourth silver, which needs a man to watch it, lest it be stolen? Is not a fifth iron, consumed by rust? Is not a sixth earthenware, in no degree more valuable than that which is formed for the humblest purposes? Are not all these of corruptible matter? Are they not fabricated by means of iron and fire? Did not the sculptor fashion one of them, the brazier a second, the silversmith a third, and the potter a fourth? Was not every one of them, before they were formed by the arts of these [workmen] into the shape of these [gods], each in its own way subject to change? Would not those things which are now vessels, formed of the same materials, become like to such, if they met with the same artificers? Might not these, which are now worshipped by you, again be made by men vessels similar to others? Are they not all deaf? Are they not blind? Are they not without life? Are they not destitute of feeling? Are they not incapable of motion? Are they not all liable to rot? Are they not all corruptible? These things ye call gods; these ye serve; these ye worship; and ye become altogether like to them. For this reason ye hate the Christians, because they do not deem these to be gods. But do not ye yourselves, who now think and suppose [such to be gods], much more cast contempt upon them than they [the Christians do]? Do ye not much more mock and insult them, when ye worship those that are made of stone and earthenware, without appointing any persons to guard them; but those made of silver and gold ye shut up by night, and appoint watchers to look after them by day, lest they be stolen? And by those gifts which ye mean to present to them, do ye not, if they are possessed of sense, rather punish [than honour] them? But if, on the other hand, they are destitute of sense, ye convict them of this fact, while ye worship them with blood and the smoke of sacrifices. Let any one of you suffer such indignities! Let any one of you endure to have such things done to himself! But not a single human being will, unless compelled to it, endure such treatment, since he is endowed with sense and reason. A stone, however, readily bears it, seeing it is insensible. Certainly you do not show [by your conduct] that he [your God] is possessed of sense. And as to the fact that Christians are not accustomed to serve such gods, I might easily find many other things to say; but if even what has been said does not seem to any one sufficient, I deem it idle to say anything further.

CHAPTER III
SUPERSTITIONS OF THE JEWS

And next, I imagine that you are most desirous of hearing something on this point, that the Christians do not observe the same forms of divine worship as do the Jews. The Jews, then, if they abstain from the kind of service above described, and deem it proper to worship one God as being Lord of all, [are right]; but if they offer Him worship in the way which we have described, they greatly err. For while the Gentiles, by offering such things to those that are destitute of sense and hearing, furnish an example of madness; they, on the other hand by thinking to offer these things to God as if He needed them, might justly reckon it rather an act of folly than of divine worship. For He that made heaven and earth, and all that is therein, and gives to us all the things of which we stand in need, certainly requires none of those things which He Himself bestows on such as think of furnishing them to Him. But those who imagine that, by means of blood, and the smoke of sacrifices and burnt-offerings, they offer sacrifices [acceptable] to Him, and that by such honours they show Him respect, - these, by supposing that they can give anything to Him who stands in need of nothing, appear to me in no respect to differ from those who studiously confer the same honour on things destitute of sense, and which therefore are unable to enjoy such honours.

CHAPTER IV
THE OTHER OBSERVANCES OF THE JEWS

But as to their scrupulosity concerning meats, and their superstition as respects the Sabbaths, and their boasting about circumcision, and their fancies about fasting and the new moons, which are utterly ridiculous and unworthy of notice, - do not think that you require to learn anything from me. For, to accept some of those things which have been formed by God for the use of men as properly formed, and to reject others as useless and redundant, - how can this be lawful? And to speak falsely of God, as if He forbade us to do what is good on the Sabbath-days, - how is not this impious? And to glory in the circumcision of the flesh as a proof of election, and as if, on account of it, they were specially beloved by God, - how is it not a subject of ridicule? And as to their observing months and days, as if waiting upon the stars and the moon, and their distributing, according to their own tendencies, the appointments of God, and the vicissitudes of the seasons, some for festivities, and others for mourning, - who would deem this a part of divine worship, and not much rather a manifestation of folly? I suppose, then, you are sufficiently convinced that the Christians properly abstain from the vanity and error common [to both Jews and Gentiles], and from the busy-body spirit and vain boasting of the Jews; but you must not hope to learn the mystery of their peculiar mode of worshipping God from any mortal.

CHAPTER V
THE MANNERS OF THE CHRISTIANS

For the Christians are distinguished from other men neither by country, nor language, nor the customs which they observe. For they neither inhabit cities of their own, nor employ a peculiar form of speech, nor lead a life which is marked out by any singularity. The course of conduct which they follow has not been devised by any speculation or deliberation of inquisitive men; nor do they, like some, proclaim themselves the advocates of any merely human doctrines. But, inhabiting Greek as well as barbarian cities, according as the lot of each of them has determined, and following the customs of the natives in respect to clothing, food, and the rest of their ordinary conduct, they display to us their wonderful and confessedly striking method of life. They dwell in their own countries, but simply as sojourners. As citizens, they share in all things with others, and yet endure all things as if foreigners. Every foreign land is to them as their native country, and every land of their birth as a land of strangers. They marry, as do all [others]; they beget children; but they do not destroy their offspring. They have a common table, but not a common bed. They are in the flesh, but they do not live after the flesh. They pass their days on earth, but they are citizens of heaven. They obey the prescribed laws, and at the same time surpass the laws by their lives. They love all men, and are persecuted by all. They are unknown and condemned; they are put to death, and restored to life. They are poor, yet make many rich; they are in lack of all things, and yet abound in all; they are dishonoured, and yet in their very dishonour are glorified. They are evil spoken of, and yet are justified; they are reviled, and bless; they are insulted, and repay the insult with honour; they do good, yet are punished as evil-doers. When punished, they rejoice as if quickened into life; they are assailed by the Jews as foreigners, and

23

are persecuted by the Greeks; yet those who hate them are unable to assign any reason for their hatred.

CHAPTER VI
THE RELATION OF CHRISTIANS
TO THE WORLD

To sum up all in one word - what the soul is in the body, that are Christians in the world. The soul is dispersed through all the members of the body, and Christians are scattered through all the cities of the world. The soul dwells in the body, yet is not of the body; and Christians dwell in the world, yet are not of the world. The invisible soul is guarded by the visible body, and Christians are known indeed to be in the world, but their godliness remains invisible. The flesh hates the soul, and wars against it, though itself suffering no injury, because it is prevented from enjoying pleasures; the world also hates the Christians, though in nowise injured, because they abjure pleasures. The soul loves the flesh that hates it, and [loves also] the members; Christians likewise love those that hate them. The soul is imprisoned in the body, yet preserves that very body; and Christians are confined in the world as in a prison, and yet they are the preservers of the world. The immortal soul dwells in a mortal tabernacle; and Christians dwell as sojourners in corruptible [bodies], looking for an incorruptible dwelling in the heavens. The soul, when but ill-provided with food and drink, becomes better; in like manner, the Christians, though subjected day by day to punishment, increase the more in number. God has assigned them this illustrious position, which it were unlawful for them to forsake.

CHAPTER VII
THE MANIFESTATION OF CHRIST

For, as I said, this was no mere earthly invention which

was delivered to them, nor is it a mere human system of opinion, which they judge it right to preserve so carefully, nor has a dispensation of mere human mysteries been committed to them, but truly God Himself, who is almighty, the Creator of all things, and invisible, has sent from heaven, and placed among men, [Him who is] the truth, and the holy and incomprehensible Word, and has firmly established Him in their hearts. He did not, as one might have imagined, send to men any servant, or angel, or ruler, or any one of those who bear sway over earthly things, or one of those to whom the government of things in the heavens has been entrusted, but the very Creator and Fashioner of all things - by whom He made the heavens - by whom he enclosed the sea within its proper bounds - whose ordinances all the stars faithfully observe - from whom the sun has received the measure of his daily course to be observed - whom the moon obeys, being commanded to shine in the night, and whom the stars also obey, following the moon in her course; by whom all things have been arranged, and placed within their proper limits, and to whom all are subject - the heavens and the things that are therein, the earth and the things that are therein, the sea and the things that are therein - fire, air, and the abyss - the things which are in the heights, the things which are in the depths, and the things which lie between. This [messenger] He sent to them. Was it then, as one might conceive, for the purpose of exercising tyranny, or of inspiring fear and terror? By no means, but under the influence of clemency and meekness. As a king sends his son, who is also a king, so sent He Him; as God He sent Him; as to men He sent Him; as a Saviour He sent Him, and as seeking to persuade, not to compel us; for violence has no place in the character of God. As calling us He sent Him, not as vengefully pursuing us; as loving us He sent Him, not as judging us. For He will yet send Him to judge us, and who shall endure His appearing? ... Do you not see

25

them exposed to wild beasts, that they may be persuaded to deny the Lord, and yet not overcome? Do you not see that the more of them are punished, the greater becomes the number of the rest? This does not seem to be the work of man: this is the power of God; these are the evidences of His manifestation.

CHAPTER VIII
THE MISERABLE STATE OF MEN BEFORE THE COMING OF THE WORD

For, who of men at all understood before His coming what God is? Do you accept of the vain and silly doctrines of those who are deemed trustworthy philosophers? Of whom some said that fire was God, calling that God to which they themselves were by and by to come; and some water; and others some other of the elements formed by God. But if any one of these theories be worthy of approbation, every one of the rest of created things might also be declared to be God. But such declarations are simply the startling and erroneous utterances of deceivers; and no man has either seen Him, or made Him known, but He has revealed Himself. And He has manifested Himself through faith, to which alone it is given to behold God. For God, the Lord and Fashioner of all things, who made all things, and assigned them their several positions, proved Himself not merely a friend of mankind, but also long-suffering [in His dealings with them.] Yea, He was always of such a character, and still is, and will ever be, kind and good, and free from wrath, and true, and the only one who is [absolutely] good; and He formed in His mind a great and unspeakable conception, which He communicated to His Son alone. As long, then, as He held and preserved His own wise counsel in concealment, He appeared to neglect us, and to have no care over us. But after He revealed and laid open, through His beloved Son, the things which had been prepared from the beginning, He conferred every blessing all at once upon us, so that we should both share in His benefits, and see and be active [in His service]. Who of us would ever have expected these things? He was aware, then, of all things in His own mind, along with His Son, according to the relation subsisting between them.

CHAPTER IX
WHY THE SON WAS SENT SO LATE

As long then as the former time endured, He permitted us to be borne along by unruly impulses, being drawn away by the desire of pleasure and various lusts. This was not that He at all delighted in our sins, but that He simply endured them; nor that He approved the time of working iniquity which then was, but that He sought to form a mind conscious of righteousness, so that being convinced in that time of our unworthiness of attaining life through our own works, it should now, through the kindness of God, be vouchsafed to us; and having made it manifest that in ourselves we were unable to enter into the kingdom of God, we might through the power of God be made able. But when our wickedness had reached its height, and it had been clearly shown that its reward, punishment and death, was impending over us; and when the time had come which God had before appointed for manifesting His own kindness and power, how the one love of God, through exceeding regard for men, did not regard us with hatred, nor thrust us away, nor remember our iniquity against us, but showed great long-suffering, and bore with us, He Himself took on Him the burden of our iniquities, He gave His own Son as a ransom for us, the holy One for transgressors, the blameless One for the wicked, the righteous One for the unrighteous, the incorruptible One for the corruptible, the immortal

One for them that are mortal. For what other thing was capable of covering our sins than His righteousness? By what other one was it possible that we, the wicked and ungodly, could be justified, than by the only Son of God? O sweet exchange! O unsearchable operation! O benefits surpassing all expectation! That the wickedness of many should be hid in a single righteous One, and that the righteousness of One should justify many transgressors! Having therefore convinced us in the former time that our nature was unable to attain to life, and having now revealed the Saviour who is able to save even those things which it was [formerly] impossible to save, by both these facts He desired to lead us to trust in His kindness, to esteem Him our Nourisher, Father, Teacher, Counsellor, Healer, our Wisdom, Light, Honour, Glory, Power, and Life, so that we should not be anxious concerning clothing and food.

CHAPTER X
THE BLESSINGS THAT WILL FLOW FROM FAITH

If you also desire [to possess] this faith, you likewise shall receive first of all the knowledge of the Father. For God has loved mankind, on whose account He made the world, to whom He rendered subject all the things that are in it, to whom He gave reason and understanding, to whom alone He imparted the privilege of looking upwards to Himself, whom He formed after His own image, to whom He sent His only-begotten Son, to whom He has promised a kingdom in heaven, and will give it to those who have loved Him. And when you have attained this knowledge, with what joy do you think you will be filled? Or, how will you love Him who has first so loved you? And if you love Him, you will be an imitator of His kindness. And do not wonder that a man may become an imitator of God. He can, if he is willing. For it is not by ruling over his neighbours, or by seeking to hold the supremacy over those that are weaker, or by being rich, and showing violence towards those that are inferior, that happiness is found; nor can anyone by these things become an imitator of God. But these things do not at all constitute His majesty. On the contrary he who takes upon himself the burden of his neighbour; he who, in whatsoever respect he may be superior, is ready to benefit another who is deficient; he who, whatsoever things he has received from God, by distributing these to the needy, becomes a god to those who receive [his benefits]: he is an imitator of God. Then thou shalt see, while still on earth, that God in the heavens rules over [the universe]; then thou shall begin to speak the mysteries of God; then shalt thou both love and admire those that suffer punishment because they will not deny God; then shall thou condemn the deceit and error of the world when thou shall know what it is to live truly in heaven, when thou shalt despise that which is here esteemed to be death, when thou shalt fear what is truly death, which is reserved for those who shall be condemned to the eternal fire, which shall afflict those even to the end that are committed to it. Then shalt thou admire those who for righteousness' sake endure the fire that is but for a moment, and shalt count them happy when thou shalt know [the nature of] that fire.

ENDNOTES

The epistle is taken from the *Anti-Nicene Fathers,* vol 1, 23.

[1] Everett Ferguson, ed., *Encyclopedia of Early Christianity* (1990) 266. David Noel Freedman, ed., *The Anchor Bible Dictionary,* vol. 2 (1992) 201.

APOSTASY—THE FALLING AWAY

> Let no man deceive you by any means: for that day shall not come, except there come a falling away first, and that man of sin be revealed, the son of perdition (2 Thessalonians 2:3).

Despite clear warnings of falling away, apostasy soon entered the church. Jude 1:3 reads: "Beloved, when I gave all diligence to write unto you of the common salvation, it was needful for me to write unto you, and exhort you that ye should earnestly contend for the faith which was once delivered unto the saints." The faith written about by Jude was to change, and keep changing, to the point where it would become unrecognizable to the Christian of the first century. Even when the Protestant Reformation came, it would result in going back to a more primitive, but still apostate time.

Paul warned in the Galatian letter:

> I marvel that ye are so soon removed from him that called you into the grace of Christ unto another gospel: Which is not another; but there be some that trouble you, and would pervert the gospel of Christ. But though we, or an angel from heaven, preach any other gospel unto you than that which we have preached unto you, let him be accursed. As we said before, so say I now again, if any man preach

any other gospel unto you than that ye have received, let him be accursed (Gal 1:6-9).

In the first two centuries the church was made up of autonomous congregations, overseen by elderships, guided by men Biblically qualified, a plurality of mature, spiritual men. Entrance into the church or congregation, for that is the meaning of the word church, was by baptism, by full immersion, for the remission of actual sins committed. Good Christian men would share with others without compulsion the wonderful news of Christ, making converts, for that is what the Great Commission is (Mat. 28:18-20, Mark 16:15,16 and Luke 24:47). In this early period infants were considered innocent, as scripture teaches. Later, the abomination of infant baptism and inherited total depravity (original sin) would destroy many congregations and is defended to this day.

Three accusations made by the Roman authorities against the early Christians were:

1. Atheism.

2. They murdered their own children.

3. They were cannibals.

1. The first accusation was made on the grounds that the Christians worshiped an invisible God outside of temples without an altar. To those enemies watching from afar, those early Christians were atheists. Today, many denominations worship in temples

31

(church buildings), often in Europe orientated towards the rising sun, having altars; in many respects a temple that would today be recognised as such by those pagan accusers of ancient Rome. The Jews worshiped in temples, the Temple at Jerusalem or synagogues. The Christians were distinctive, worshiping in their homes: "And to our beloved Apphia, and Archippus our fellowsoldier, and to the church in thy house"(Phm 1:2). "Salute the brethren which are in Laodicea, and Nymphas, and the church which is in his house" (Col 4:15). "The churches of Asia salute you. Aquila and Priscilla salute you much in the Lord, with the church that is in their house" (1Cor. 16:19). "Likewise greet the church that is in their house. Salute my well beloved Epaenetus, who is the first fruits of Achaia unto Christ" (Rom 16:5).

There is nothing wrong with using expediency to obtain a building in which to worship and meet, either by purchase or hire, but such are not temples. The Anglican Dr. William Cave in his *Primitive Christianity, or, the religion of the ancient Christians* says that in early times Christians had no temples (ornate buildings), priests (separate clergy), sacrifices to martyrs, because they are not gods (saint or ancestor worship).[1] Since the first century these innovations have been introduced, borrowed from pagan usage. Temple worship, now common in denominationalism, is incompatible with both the New Testament and first century practice and teaching as is Mary worship.

2. The second accusation provoked much discussion over the years. How could it be considered that early Christians murdered their own children? The answer, I believe, is plain. The pagan Romans like many societies, had a concept of original sin. Infants, the newborn, needed ritual cleansing known in ancient Rome as "lustration" by a priest ritually sprinkling holy water on the newborn to remove evil spirits and sin, whereby the child became a Roman citizen. William Williamson wrote of this "In Greece and Rome the newly-born children were sprinkled with holy water that the name was given, and the priest provided the parents with a document certifying to the regeneration of the infant, who was henceforth duly recognised as a legitimate member of the family and of society." Children that were not wanted did not go through the ceremony and could be "exposed," whereby they were literally thrown away, many taken away to become slaves. Severely disabled children not wanted by even the slave traders, would simply have been left to die, exposed to the weather. Once lustration had been carried out, the child was a Roman citizen with some rights, though the father could still treat a child as a slave.[2]

To the Romans, the refusal of lustration, today's equivalent of infant baptism, was considered murder. Similar accusations were still being made by parents into the 1700s in England against preachers in the churches of Christ. At times of high infant mortality, it is understandable that people ignorant of the innocence of children could believe such. Withholding a child from baptism and condemning it to hell would be considered murder. People having their children baptized today, especially in a "temple" setting, would not stand out from those pagans of ancient Rome.[3]

3. Cannibalism, the third accusation, is likely a reference to the Lord's Supper. Of course, those people who today believe the bread and wine are the literal body and blood of Christ (transubstantiation or consubstantiation) are sometimes accused of such, but it was not so in the early centuries when the Lord's Supper was a simple memorial meal held on the first day of the week. The Romans had made cannibalism illegal, though it was still common outside the empire.

Error crept in slowly, but, when measured throughout centuries was constant and enormous. Bit by bit the purity of the church established by the Lord was dismantled and replaced, at first by Jewish ritual and custom, and later by paganism. Then the Reformation came (to reform something, something had to previously exist). Many nonetheless hold to the view the Reformation restored the church to its original purity. It was never purposed to restore the church, but to reform the existing church. The Reformation took the Roman Catholic system back to an earlier, more primitive stage of apostasy.

The reformed denominations, the Lutherans, Baptists (when holding to reformed theology), Anglicans, Calvinists, Presbyterians, Protestants, however denominated, are a primitive version of the Roman Catholic system, sharing the same basic beliefs, such as inherited sin, either as in the Calvinist system of total depravity or the original sin of the Catholics and Anglicans; hence the need to retain infant baptism. All too often, the idea of a national church continued. These reformed churches like their Roman Catholic based original have temple-based worship and a clergy class. The altar too remains in some denominations. Reformation never brought restoration. Restored churches—churches of Christ—existed before, during and after the Reformation of the Catholic Protestors.

The church of the first and early second century was pure, separated from the world, but, after the second Jewish revolt (second Jewish-Roman war) of 132-135 AD, many Jews joined the church and influenced various congregations towards taking on Jewish custom and ritual. In time the church not only became part of the word, but under the Popes the church, now paganised, tried to rule entire kingdoms. The Church, "the called out from the world" as the word means in the Greek New Testament, now ruled the world by the tenth century, using the methods of the world. Of course, it was no longer the Church of Christ, but the church of men alienated from Christ. Such took time. Little by little the church changed from being the bride of Christ to the servant of the devil.

By the middle of the second century, the Passover, or Pasch, entered the church via Jewish Christians.[4] In time the Passover became the Easter of the northern European pagans. It is an example of how one addition mutates into another. Saturday, the Sabbath, also in time took on a special meaning for worship as a Christian day,[5] Whitesunday or Whitsunday, the seventh Sunday after Easter, and Pentecost came into usage in the church.[6]

Phillip Schaff, the Protestant Theologian, wrote concerning the office of elders and deacons in the early church. We will let him explain:

> We proceed to the officers of local congregations who were charged with carrying forward in particular places the work begun by the apostles and their delegates. These were of two kinds, Presbyters or Bishops, and Deacons or Helpers. They multiplied in proportion as Christianity extended, while the number of the apostles diminished by death, and could, in the nature of the case, not be filled up by witnesses of the life and resurrection of Christ. The extraordinary officers were necessary for the founding and being of the church, the ordinary officers for its preservation and well-being.

> The terms Presbyter (or Elder) and Bishop (or Overseer, Superintendent) denote in the New Testament one and the same office, with this difference only, that the first is borrowed from the Synagogue, the second from the Greek communities; and that the one signifies the dignity, the other the duty.

1. The identity of these officers is very evident from the following facts:

a. They appear always as a plurality or as a college in one and the same congregation, even in smaller cities) as in Philippi.

b. The same officers of the church of Ephesus are alternately called presbyters and bishops.

c. Paul sends greetings to the "bishops" and "deacons" of Philippi, but omits the presbyters because they were included in the first term; as also the plural indicates.

d. In the Pastoral Epistles, where Paul intends to give the qualifications for all church officers, he again mentions only two, bishops and deacons, but uses the term presbyter afterwards for bishop. Peter urges the "presbyters" to "tend the flock of God," and to "fulfil the office of bishops" with disinterested devotion and without "lording it over the charge allotted to them."

e. The interchange of terms continued in use to the close of the first century, as is evident from the Epistle of Clement of Rome (about 95), and the Didache, and still lingered towards the close of the second.

With the beginning of the second century, from Ignatius onward, the two terms are distinguished and designate two offices; the bishop being regarded first as the head of a congregation surrounded by a council of presbyters, and afterwards as the head of a diocese and successor of the apostles. The episcopate grew out of the presidency of the presbytery, or, as Bishop Lightfoot well expresses it: "The episcopate was formed, not out of the apostolic order by localization, but out of the presbyteral by elevation; and the title, which originally was common to all, came at length to be appropriated to the chief among them." Nevertheless, a recollection of the original identity was preserved by the best biblical scholars among the fathers, such as Jerome (who taught that the episcopate rose from the presbyterate as a safeguard against schism), Chrysostom, and Theodoret.

The reason why the title bishop (and not presbyter) was given afterwards to the superior officer, may be explained from the fact that it signified, according to monumental inscriptions recently discovered, financial officers of the temples, and that the had the charge of all the funds of the churches, which were largely charitable institutions for the support of widows and orphans, strangers and travelers, aged and infirm people in an age of extreme riches and extreme poverty.

2. The origin of the presbytero-episcopal office is not recorded in the New Testament, but when it is first mentioned in the congregation at Jerusalem, a.d. 44, it appears already as a settled institution. As every Jewish synagogue was ruled by elders, it was very natural that every Jewish Christian congregation should at once adopt this form of government; this may be the reason why the writer of the Acts finds it unnecessary to give an account of the origin; while he reports the origin of the deaconate which arose from a special emergency and had no precise analogy in the organization of the synagogue. The Gentile churches followed the example, choosing the already familiar term bishop. The first thing which Paul and Barnabas did after preaching the gospel in Asia Minor was to organize churches by the appointment of elders.

3. The office of the presbyter-bishops was to teach and to rule the particular congregation committed to their charge. They were the regular 'pastors and teachers.' To them belonged the direction of public worship, the administration of discipline, the care of souls, and the management of church property. They were usually chosen from the first converts, and appointed by the apostles or their delegates, with the approval of the congregation, or by the congregation itself, which supported them by voluntary contributions. They were solemnly introduced into their office by the apostles or by their fellow presbyters through prayers and the laying on of hands.

The presbyters always formed a college or corporation, a presbytery; as at Jerusalem, at Ephesus, at Philippi, and at the ordination of Timothy. They no doubt maintained a relation of fraternal equality. The New Testament gives us no information about the division of labor among them, or the nature and term of a presidency. It is quite probable that the members of the presbyteral college distributed the various duties of their office among themselves according to their respective talents, tastes, experience, and convenience. Possibly, too, the president, whether temporary or permanent, was styled distinctively the bishop; and from this the subsequent separation of the episcopate from the presbyterate may easily have arisen. But so long as the general government of the church was in the hands of the apostles and their delegates, the bishops were limited in their jurisdiction either to one congregation or to a small circle of congregations.

The distinction of "teaching presbyters" or ministers proper, and "ruling presbyters" or lay-elders, is a convenient arrangement of Reformed churches, but can hardly claim apostolic sanction, since the one passage on which it rests only speaks of two functions in the same office. Whatever may have been the distribution and rotation of duties, Paul expressly mentions ability to teach among the regular requisites for the episcopal or presbyteral office.

4. The Angels of the Seven Churches in Asia Minor must be regarded as identical with the presbyter-bishops or local pastors. They represent the presiding presbyters, or the corps of regular officers, as the responsible messengers of God to the congregation. At the death of Paul and Peter, under Nero, the congregations were ruled by a college of elders, and if the Apocalypse, as the majority of critical commentators now hold, was written before the year 70, there was too little time for a radical change of the organization from a republican to a monarchical form. Even if we regard the "angels" as single persons, they were evidently confined to a single church, and subject to St. John; hence, not successors of the apostles, as the latter diocesan bishops claim to be. The most that can be said is that the angels were congregational, as distinct from diocesan bishops, and mark one step from the primitive presbyters to the Ignatian bishops, who were likewise congregational officers, but in a monarchical sense as the heads of the presbytery, bearing a patriarchal relation to the congregation and being eminently responsible for its spiritual condition.

5. The nearest approach to the idea of the ancient catholic episcopate may be found in the unique position of James, the Brother of the Lord. Unlike the apostles, he confined his labors to the mother church of Jerusalem. In the Jewish Christian traditions of the second century he appears both as bishop and pope of the church universal. But in fact he was only *primus inter pares*. In his last visit to Jerusalem,

Paul was received by the body of the presbyters, and to them he gave an account of his missionary labors. Moreover, this authority of James, who was not an apostle, was exceptional and due chiefly to his close relationship with the Lord, and his personal sanctity, which won the respect even of the unconverted Jews.

The institution of episcopacy proper cannot be traced to the apostolic age, so far as documentary evidence goes, but is very apparent and well-nigh universal about the middle of the second century. Its origin and growth will claim our attention in the next period.

Deacons or helpers, appear first in the church of Jerusalem, seven in number. The author of the Acts 6 gives us an account of the origin of this office, which is mentioned before that of the presbyters. It had a precedent in the officers of the synagogue who had charge of the collection and distribution of alms. It was the first relief of the heavy burden that rested on the shoulders of the apostles, who wished to devote themselves exclusively to prayer and the ministry of the word. It was occasioned by a complaint of the Hellenistic Christians against the Hebrew or Palestinian brethren, that their widows were neglected in the daily distribution of food (and perhaps money). In the exercise of a truly fraternal spirit the congregation elected seven Hellenists instead of Hebrews, if we are to judge from their Greek names, although they were not uncommon among the Jews in that age. After the popular election they were ordained by the apostles.

The example of the mother church was followed in all other congregations, though without particular regard to the number. The Church of Rome, however, perpetuated even the number seven for several generations. In Philippi the deacons took their rank after the presbyters, and are addressed with them in Paul's Epistle.

The office of their deacons, according to the narrative in Acts, was to minister at the table in the daily love-feasts, and to attend to the wants of the poor and the sick. The primitive churches were charitable societies, taking care of the widows and orphans, dispensing hospitality to strangers, and relieving the needs of the poor. The presbyters were the custodians, the deacons the collectors and distributors, of the charitable funds. To this work a kind of pastoral care of souls very naturally attached itself, since poverty and sickness afford the best occasions and the most urgent demand for edifying instruction and consolation. Hence, living faith and exemplary conduct were necessary qualifications for the office of deacon.

In post-apostolic times, when the bishop was raised above the presbyter and the presbyter became priest, the deacon was regarded as Levite, and his primary function of care of the poor was lost in the function of assisting the priest in the subordinate parts of public worship and the administration of the sacraments. The diaconate became the first of the three orders of the ministry and a stepping-stone to the priesthood. At the same time the deacon, by his intimacy with the bishop as his agent and messenger, acquired an advantage over the priest.7

In time the presbyter became the priest, the bishop taking a position of rule over several congregations. At first this followed the pattern of the Jewish system, to be replaced later by the Papal system of Rome, which was an imitation of the pagan system with the rituals of those systems. In the New Testament Church all

Christians are priests, with Christ the High Priest in Heaven. In the denominational church, the office of priest, a member of the clergy, has an intermediary office between the laity and God. This denominational office is alien to the Christianity of the early church and opposed to the teachings of the inspired writers of the New Testament.[8]

Regarding infant baptism, the baptism of the early church was for believers, not infants. Dr. Gilbert Burnett (1643-1715), who was bishop of New Sarum (Salisbury, near Stonehenge, England), a very prestigious position within the Anglican Church, in his *Exposition of the 39 Articles*, Article 27 (page 392) wrote "By the first teaching or making disciples, that must go before baptism, is to be meant the Convincing the World, that Jesus is the Christ, the true Messiah, anointed of God." On page 401 Burnett writes: "There is no express precept, or rule, given in the New Testament for the baptism of infants." Here Burnett whilst defending infant baptism alludes to the biblical pattern of teaching believers prior to baptism. Regarding the mode, Burnett writes on page 351 that the mode is "dipped or washed," thus this leading Anglican divine confirms the mode as immersion. On page 353 he notes that "The doing all things to order and to Edifying, will authorise a church to all this; especially since the now universal practice of infant baptism makes this more necessary than it was in the first times, when chiefly the adults were baptised." Burnett, a respected Anglican, is a witness against his own church.

William Wall stated concerning practice in the Church of England:

> Calvin was, I think (as I said in my book vol 2, page 400) the first in the world that drew up a form of liturgy that prescribed pouring water on the infant, absolutely, without saying anything of dipping. It was (as Mr Walker has shewn) his admirers in England, who in Queen Elizabeth's time brought pouring into ordinary use, which before was used only to weak children. But the succeeding Presbyterians in England, about the year 1644, (when their reign began) went farther yet from the ancient way, and instead of pouring, brought into use in many places sprinkling: declaring at the same time against the use of all fonts, baptisteries, godfathers, or anything that looked the ancient way of baptising.[9]

Regarding the error of baptising at Easter, Wall wrote,

> The paschal season is known to have been the most solemn time, both with the Jews and Christians, for admitting proselytes or disciples by baptism. The Jews did then baptise all the proselytes that were ready, for this reason, that they might be admitted to partake of the Passover and sacrifices. The Christians observed the same for a like reason.[10]

John Charles Ryle, wrote in his *Principles for Churchmen*,

> So long as water is used in the name of the Trinity, or in the name of Christ, the precise mode of administering the ordinance is left an open question. This is the view adopted by the Church of England. The baptismal service

expressly sanctions "dipping" in the most plain term. To say, as many Baptists do, that the Church of England is opposed to baptism by immersion is a melancholy proof of the ignorance in which many dissenters live! Thousands, I am afraid, find fault with the Prayer-book without having ever examined its contents. If any one wishes to be baptized by "dipping" in the Church of England, let him understand that the parish clergyman is just as ready to dip him as the Baptist minister, and that "immersion" may be had in the Church as well as in Chapel.[11]

Ryle continued:

I begin by laying it down as a point almost undisputed, that all grown up converts at Missionary stations among the heathen ought to be baptised. As soon as they embrace the Gospel and make a creditable profession of repentance and faith in Christ, they ought at once to receive baptism. This is the doctrine and practice Episcopal, Presbyterian, Wesleyan and Independent Missionaries, just as it is the doctrine of Baptists. Let there be no mistake on the point. To talk as some Baptists do, of "believers' baptism," as if it was a kind of baptism peculiar to their own body, is simply nonsense. "Believers' baptism" is known and practiced in every successful Protestant Mission throughout the world.[12]

William Cave stated:

...the party to be baptized was wholly immerged or put under water, which was the almost constant and universal custom of those times, whereby they did most notably and significantly express the great ends and effects of baptism. For, as in immersion there are in a manner, three several acts, the putting the person into water, his abiding there for some time. And his rising up again, thereby

45

representing Christ's death, burial and resurrection. And in conformity thereto, out dying unto sin, the destruction of its power, and our resurrection to a new course of life. By the person's being put into water, was lively represented the putting off the body of sins of the flesh and being washed from the filth and pollution of them. By his abode under it, which was a kind of burial in the water, his entering into a state of death or mortification, like as Christ remained for some time under the state or power of death, therefore, as many as are baptized into Christ, are baptized into his death, and to be buried with him by baptism unto death, that the Old Man being crucified with him, the body of sin might be destroyed, that henceforth he might not serve sin, for that He that is dead is freed from sin, as the Apostle clearly explains the meaning of this rite: and then by his emersion, or rising up out of the water, is signified his entering upon the new course of life, that like as Christ was raised from the dead by the glory of the Father, so we should walk in newness of life.[13]

Waddington stated:

The sacraments of the primitive Church were two – those of Baptism and the Lord's Supper. The ceremony of immersion (the oldest form of baptism) was performed in the name of the three persons of the Trinity; it was believed to be attended by the remission of original sin, and the entire regeneration of the infant or convert, by the passage from the land of bondage into the kingdom of salvation. A great proportion of those baptised in the first ages were, of course, adults, and since the Church was then scrupulous to admit none among its members, excepting those whose sincere repentance gave promise of a holy life, the administration of that sacrament was in some sense accompanied by the remission of sin, not only of sin from Adam, but of all sin that had previously

committed by the proselyte – that is to say, such absolution
was given to the repentance necessary for admission into
Christ's Church.[14]

From the theologians quoted above we can establish the denominations knew and understood the practice of the church in the first century. As with other errors, apostasy crept in slowly, over centuries. The issues of baptism are not the mode, but whether sprinkling and pouring are allowed, in addition to immersion. Neither is believers' baptism doubted, but whether the baptism of infants is allowed. Proving believers' baptism by immersion has never been an issue; for the denominations, it has been the impossibility of proving the additions as apostolic. The answer when history and facts are revised is to neglect earlier statements and continue in a practice, teaching it as apostolic. Many denominations today deny salvation at the point of baptism, but in time past this was not so.

It is often demanded, in discussion of doctrine, that examples from the Old Testament to defend a particular practice be taken, as if it were still current and not old, having been replaced by the New Testament for the Christian dispensation. As Judaism entered the church, this led to the altar table, Passover, a priesthood clergy system, in time under paganism, which developed into Roman Catholicism under the papacy. For example, as already noted, in time the Passover became Easter. Judaism introduced ritual and a priesthood which the first century Church did not have and which is contrary to scripture.

Platonic philosophy entered the church soon after Judaism had influenced matters for the worse, which continues to have its ramifications not only in denominationalism, but in Western society in general. Through the Neo-Platonists, Plato influenced doctrine in an apostate church. When Platonic philosophy is talked about, what is really referred to is paganism, which allowed polytheism, original sin, infant baptism, exorcisms, various superstitions, rituals, mysteries and pagan holidays to enter an apostate church. These doctrines ultimately led to atheism, evolution and a rejection of an Almighty God. Church fathers influenced by Platonism include Justine Martyr (AD150) and later, Clement of Alexandria (150-215), Origen (176-254), Basil of Caesarea (330-379) Gregory of Nazianzus (329-390) and, lastly in this short list, Augustine of Hippo (354-430).

Augustine was born in the city of Thagaste, the present-day Souk Ahras, Algeria, to a Catholic mother named Monica. He was educated in North Africa and resisted his mother's pleas to become a Catholic. Living as a pagan intellectual, he took a concubine and became a Manichean. Later he converted to the Catholic Church, became a bishop, and opposed "heresies" such as freewill.

In the Roman Catholic Church and the Anglican Communion, he is a saint and pre-eminent Doctor of the Church, and the patron of the Augustinian religious order; Saint Augustine of Hippo's day is 28th August revered in both traditions. Many Protestants, especially Calvinists, consider him to be one of the theological fathers of Reformation teaching on salvation and divine grace. Through Augustine's doctrines, original sin, infant baptism and later, Calvinism were propagated. The origin of these lay in paganism. Was Augustine ever converted to the Christian faith? The result of his theology was to continue with pagan philosophy and belief under the guise of Christianity.

Many of the pagans were highly-educated, trained in rhetoric, skilled writers and debaters. While many people understand "Christian" holidays (holy days) are pagan in origin, such as Easter and Christmas, the problem is much deeper. The Christian calendar with its holy days is a continuation of the pagan days. The early church had no such special days. If we use the one example of Christmas, we can see how a pagan festival has become both a Christianised Holiday and secularised.

In origin Christmas is pagan, it is not found in the Scriptures; neither did the early pre-Catholic church celebrate it. The name itself is from the Old English "Mass of Christ" = Christmas. Pagan festivities, merrymaking, the giving of presents coupled with the worship of idols and pagan gods with horrific human sacrifice and cannibalism are lost in the myths of time. New Year was the time when pagans celebrated the return of the Sun God, and worshipped it. It was these festivals that continue today in the form of Christmas. The early church father, Tertullian (died 220?) wrote a treatise "De Idololatria" in which he chastises "Christians" for putting wreaths on their doors and other practices of idolatry practised at the new year. At that time many Christians were found and persecuted who did not decorate their homes with lamps, laurels and other decorations, at the New Year. Laurels were placed on doors to honour various door, home and hinge gods.

It is clear that the custom of giving presents and celebration was well established at this time (c200) from Tertullian's writing on Idolatry. The customs of giving presents at New Year can be traced back to Babel prior to the dispersion of mankind and was very widespread at this time. The Romans celebrated the great holiday Saturnalia from 17 to 21 December in remembrance of the great golden age. During this time slaves were given limited freedom and served by their masters. On the 22nd came Sigillaria, the feast of dolls when dolls were given to children amongst other toys. On 25th December came Brumalia, otherwise known as "Dies Natalis Invicti Solis," The Birthday of the Unconquered Sun. This was to celebrate the time of year when the days began to lengthen after the solstice. This date was quite recent being instituted by the Emperor Aurelian in honour of Mithras, the Persian Sun God (the same as

Jupiter, Osiris and Bacchus) of which he was a worshiper around 270-273.

The last date of the Roman holiday was Kalendae Januarri, New Year's Day when everybody gave gifts to everyone else. In Britain the New Year was celebrated in the feast of Yule and in Norway the feast or festival of the god Thor.

When Christianity was legalised in 316, the developing Romish Church incorporated these feasts into the one feast "Christmas." The pagan priests were excommunicated and their holidays (holy days) hijacked. Instead of ridding the church of idolatry they incorporated it into the church. From around 336 the church at Rome set the date of Christ's birth at 25th December, but this was not followed by other churches, the date finally being accepted in the fifth century. The Arminian church still celebrates Christmas on 6 January. Many dates were ascribed for the date of Christ's birth by the early church, 6 January, March 24 and 28, April 2, 19, May 20 and December 25, this last date being accepted by the church at Rome.

The ancients worshipped trees on all continents. Even today some pagans still worship trees. This practice was widespread in Europe before and after Christianity arrived. Pope Gregory I wrote a letter to Augustine of Canterbury (c600) to encourage the pagan use of decorating buildings with evergreens. Augustine had been concerned with paganism in what is now England, again the answer was to incorporate this into Catholicism. Many Druid temples were converted to "churches" sometimes even retaining the pagan priests. Hence started the concept of the church being the building/temple (the house of a god) as opposed to the church being the people of God.

Ivy was the badge of the wine god Bacchus and was banished to the outside of the house, Holly was allowed inside and hence we have the competition between "the Holly and the Ivy." In the West special days are called holy days – holidays, holly being named holy because of its special property of everlasting life (not dying in winter). Mistletoe is of Celtic origin and was known as "all-heal" and was believed to have certain miraculous powers. Mistletoe is found on the Oak tree which was highly venerated by the Oak Priests (Druids) of the many Celtic tribes across Europe and England. Because of its association with the Druids, many denominations have in times past refused its use in decorations in church buildings.

The northern tribes set fire to fir trees (hence their name) at the winter solstice, to encourage the return of the Sun god. Candles too in the heathen system is part of sun and fire worship, both being the worship of the Sun god. In ancient myth, the pagan god Woden rode in a sleigh pulled the reindeer through the air delivering presents, Saint Nicolas now has this and other attributes that formerly belonged to pagan deities and customs - particularly that of Santa Klaus.

Christmas hymns started in the Eastern Church from around 760. Carols, which are festive songs as opposed to devotional hymns, started around 1100 but were not in regular use until the 1300s. In the 1640s in England and what is now the USA, Christmas was dismissed as being pagan and outlawed. During the early nineteenth century, it was revived, largely by Albert the husband of Queen Victoria, who re-introduced the fir-tree into the celebrations. As Christianity came under attack from the atheists through the medium of evolution, Christianity turned to a more liberal pattern opposing the plain teaching of scripture.

"Thus saith the LORD; Learn not the way of the heathen" (Jer. 10:2), yet with the entry of paganism into the apostate church this is what has taken place. The world at this time of year worships Jesus as an infant, but He is Creator God. Matthew 7:21 tells us: "Not everyone who says to Me, 'LORD, LORD,' shall enter the kingdom of heaven, but he who does the will of My Father in heaven." Jesus is none other than Almighty God who created the heavens and the earth (Gen. 1:1, John 1:1, Heb. 1:1-3, Col. 1:12-18).

The wonderful prophecy of Isaiah 7:14 : "Therefore the LORD Himself will give you a sign: Behold, the virgin shall conceive and bear a Son, and shall call His name Immanuel" and repeated in Matthew 1:23, should convince all who have an open heart of who the infant Jesus really is— Almighty God. Nowhere do we

53

find in scripture or the early church the celebration of Christmas (or Easter), we do though find Christians remembering His death and resurrection every first day of the week (Acts 20:7). Early Christians met on the first day of the week, Sunday, to worship and remember the Lord through the Supper. [15]

Christians are to contend for the faith once given, not another pagan faith or will worship. A false faith that has been added to that one Godly faith found in scripture. Christians cannot contend for something that is false and hence sin. Pauls, in Colossians 2:20-23 says:

> Wherefore if ye be dead with Christ from the rudiments of the world, why, as though living in the world, are ye subject to ordinances, (Touch not; taste not; handle not; Which all are to perish with the using;) after the commandments and doctrines of men? Which things have indeed a shew of wisdom in will worship, and humility, and neglecting of the body; not in any honour to the satisfying of the flesh.

The doctrine of the church from the second century onwards first was infected by Judaism, and then paganism. The Jewish Passover became the Pasch and in time, the pagan Easter. The apostate church influenced by its now pagan beliefs became in outlook fatalistic, as in Calvinism. Dualism and concepts of good and evil led to original sin. These ideas were never founded on scripture, but pagan philosophy. All this took place over several centuries, by a continuous turning away from scriptural authority in small steps. What we then have in denominational church histories is not "church history" but the growth and history of apostasy.[16]

The result of the falling away is a system that found its way into the denominations, which system has continued with a pagan priesthood, worship and baptism. With the Reformation, four distinct denominations schemes came into being, though of course, there are a myriad of lesser schemes/denominations. They were: 1) Catholic, 2) Reformed, 3) Baptist, and 4) Congregational. The last two influenced to greater or lesser degrees by the churches of Christ who had some influence of varying degrees.

> And I say also unto thee, That thou art Peter, and upon this rock I will build my church; and the gates of hell shall not prevail against it (Mat. 16:18).

> Salute one another with an holy kiss. The churches of Christ salute you (Rom. 16:16).

ENDNOTES

[1]William Cave, *Primitive Christianity, or, the religion of the ancient Christians,* 4th ed. (1682) 104. Cave was an Anglican divine and at one time, chaplain to Charles II. He died in 1713.

[2]William Smith, LL.D, William Wayte, M.A. and G.E. Maradin, M.A., eds., *Dictionary of Greek and Roman Antiquities,* 3rd ed., vol. 2 (1891)101. John Potter D.D., *Antiquities of Greece,* 4th ed., vol. 2 (1732) 229. Alexander Adam, LL.D., *Adam's Roman Antiquities* (1834) 41. William Williamson, *The Great Law, A study of Religious Origins and of The Unity Underlying Them* (1899) 165. Williamson quotes from the Reverend Robert Taylor's Diegesis p.p. 233-4. Taylor had studied at St John's College, Cambridge for three years to qualify as a clergyman. At that time the University of Cambridge was under the established Church of England and most students were preparing for positions in the Anglican

Church. Taylor gave up Christianity and turned from evangelism to eccentric anti-clericalism. He set up a Christian Evidence Society and lectured in London pubs dressed in elaborate vestments, attacking the Anglican liturgy and the barbarities of the Establishment for what he called its "Pagan creed." At this time blasphemy was a criminal offence against the Anglican faith "by law established," and he was sentenced to a year in jail. In his cell he wrote *The Diegesis*, attacking Christianity on the basis of comparative mythology and attempting to expound it as a scheme of solar myths. Had Taylor studied the origins of Christianity, he would have had to conclude that the origin of the denomination system is routed in paganism, or his solar myths. Whilst much of his research was of a high standard, his conclusions were entirely wrong. Taylor would be remembered by Charles Darwin as a warning example of an nineteenth century outcast from society, who had dared to challenge Christianity and had been imprisoned for blasphemy, one of many warnings that gave him a fear of revealing his theory of evolution. Strangely, Taylor's research should have pointed Darwin in the direction of creation as a comparative study of pagan religion, as it reveals a common origin.

[3]Paganism entering the Christian system will be fully documented in The Devils' Door, the companion volume to Traces of the Kingdom.

[4]Ferguson, *Encyclopaedia of Early Christianity*, 695.

[5]William Cave, *Primitive Christianity, or, the religion of the ancient Christians*, (1682) 176. For the confusion of Easter in the early church please consult the fifth century church historian Socrates in *Nicene and post-Nicene Fathers, second series*, vol. 2, 130.

[6]Cave 191.

[7] Phillip Schaff, *History of the Christian Church*, vol. or 8 vol., (1910 reprint 1994) 491-498.

[8] Robert Robinson, *Ecclesiastical Researches* (1792) 124. Phillip Schaff, *History of the Christian Church*, vol. 2, (1910 reprint 1994) 428.

[9] William Wall, *A History of Infant Baptism,* 2nd ed., vol. 4 by "Rev." Henry Cotton (Oxford University Press, 1844)170. Dr Wall, an Anglican priest died in 1728. Wall had been in several discussions with the Baptists and his work was a refutation of believers' baptism.

[10]Wall, vol. 1, 36.

[11]John Charles Ryle, DD, *Principles for Churchmen* (1884) 223. Ryle (1816 - 1900) was educated at Eton and at Christ-Church, Oxford. In 1880, at age 64, he became the first Anglican bishop of Liverpool, at the recommendation of Prime Minister Benjamin Disraeli.

[12]Wall 229.

[13] William Cave, *Primitive Christianity, or, the religion of the ancient Christians* (1682) 320-1.

[14]"Rev." George Waddington, MA., *A history of the church from the earliest ages to the reformation* (1835) 27. Waddington (1793-1869) Fellow of Trinity College, Cambridge and Prebendary of Ferring, in the Cathedral Church of Chichester.

[15]The material on Christmas was taken from a track written by this author titled *Christmas is Pagan* (2009). The following are the sources used for this material: Tertullian *"On Idolatry" Ante Nicene Fathers*, vol. 3. TG Crippen, *Christmas and Christmas Lore"* (1923). Christian Hole, *English Custom and Usage* (1950). Clement A Miles, *Christmas* (1913). Everett Ferguson, ed., *Encyclopedia of Early Christianity* (1990). F.L. Cross and E.A. Livingstone, eds., *The Oxford Dictionary of the Christian Church* (1993). Venerable Bede (673-735) *Historia ecclesiastica gentis Anglorum (The Ecclesiastical History of the English People)* trans. J. A. Giles (1907). A. Hadrian Allcroft, *The Circle and the Cross* (1930). *Schaff-Herzog Encyclopaedia of Religious Knowledge* (1891). Sir James George Frazer, *The Golden Bough, A Study in Magic and Religion,* 13 vols. (1955). Alexander Hislop, T*he Two Babylons or The Papal Worship Proved to be the Worship of Nimrod and His Wife* (1932).

[16]Everett Ferguson, ed., *Encyclopedia of Early Christianity (*1990) 737. David Noel Freedman, ed., *The Anchor Bible Dictionary,* vol. 5 *(*1992) 378-381.

For more information on baptism in the early church and the falling away, please consult Mosheim, vol. 1, 117ff. Also Robinson on his chapter on Rome. Robert Robinson, *Ecclesiastical Researches* (1792). Robinson was for a time a minister of a church of Christ meeting in Hog Hill (now Downing Place), Cambridge. The author died in 1790; his book was published two years after his death.

4

THE EARLY BRITISH CHURCH: PELAGIUS AND "ST PATRICK"

First, I thank my God through Jesus Christ for you all, that your
faith is spoken of throughout the whole world (Romans 1:8).

In this chapter we will meet two Augustines, the first, Augustine
of Hippo, 354-430, who made the errors of Original Sin and Infant
Baptism popular and the second, Augustine of Canterbury, who died
in 604. This second Augustine introduced the doctrines of the first
Augustine, with other errors, into the British Church. We shall also
examine the evidence that Christianity when it arrived in Britain
was apostolic in nature and not Roman Catholic. Many histories
teach that Christianity came to Britain in 597 and, when it arrived,
was Roman Catholic in origin. This chapter will put to rest that
falsehood.

The gospel according to Matthew 28:18-20:

And Jesus came and spake unto them, saying, all power is given
unto me in heaven and in earth. Go ye therefore, and teach all
nations, baptizing them in the name of the Father, and of the
Son, and of the Holy Ghost: Teaching them to observe all things
whatsoever I have commanded you: and, lo, I am with you always,
even unto the end of the world. Amen.

Clearly the Great Commission was carried out, for Paul says in Romans 1:8, "First, I thank my God through Jesus Christ for you all, that your faith is spoken of throughout the whole world."

From Paul's inspired writing we understand that the Christian religion was professed through all parts of the Roman dominions; in this sense we should understand the words to mean, the whole world including the world outside the Roman Empire. The Great Commission had been carried out and the church established as Paul says "throughout the whole world." This included the British Isles. In the first century it is likely that many parts of the world were still uninhabited. Remote islands and continents such as Australia may have been unpopulated. Three thousand years earlier—depending on which timescale is used—the great dispersion from Babel had not even begun. At some point after the flood, the Ice Age had occurred and would during the apostolic age still been in retreat, as it still is today—which from a "young earth" perspective explains global warming. Many people wonder how the Great Commission was carried out in faraway places. In the first century, they may not have been populated!

In spite of the time that has passed, the information available on the introduction of Christianity into Britain is considerable; part is set out in this chapter. The setting for the introduction of Christianity into Britain is the background of animosity between the Celts and

Romans. For several centuries the Celts and Gauls, had been at enmity with the newly-emerging Roman state. In about 390 BC, the Gauls wreaked havoc throughout Italy, finally arriving at Rome. Several assaults on the city failed and both sides were starving. The Romans engaged with the Celtic leader (king), Brennus, for terms that would ensure that they depart. They agreed to leave Rome for the price of 1,000 lbs. of gold. The following passage from Livy, regarding these terms, gives us one of the most famous lines accredited to a Celtic chief in his dealings with Rome.

> Quintus Sulpicius conferred with the Gallic chieftain Brennus and together they agreed upon the price, one thousand pounds' weight of gold – the price of a nation soon to rule the world! Insult was added to what was already sufficiently disgraceful, for the weights which the Gauls brought for weighing the metal were heavier than standard, and when the Roman commander objected, the insolent barbarian flung his sword into the scale, saying "Vae Victis—Woe to the vanquished" – words intolerable to Roman ears.

The Romans refused to hand the gold over and in time the Celts were removed from Rome by force.[1]

Later in 279 BC, an army of Celts invaded Macedonia and northern Greece. The following year they crossed the Bosporus and settled in a part of Asia Minor that came to be called Galatia. It was to these settlers, some of whom had become Christians, that Paul wrote the Galatian letter.

As Rome grew in power, they sought the destruction of the

troublesome Celtic priests and leaders, the Druids. Druidism was the source of organised civil and religious law, with its colleges, physicians, lawyers, surgeons, teachers, poets, statesmen and legislators. Its powerbase was in Britain. The Druids taught the resurrection of the body, as did other pagan religions, and the need of atonement for sin. Edward Davies says that the favorite maxim of the Druids was, "To worship the gods, to do no evil and to exercise fortitude. According to Gaulish tradition, in the time of Caesar, Druidical discipline originated in Britain. The same account is confirmed by the institutional Triads of that British order."[2]

According to Julius Caesar, confirming the Celtic origin of the Gauls (sixth book of his Gallic Wars), the Gauls affirm they are all descended from a common father, Dis, and say this is the tradition of the Druids.[3] Druidism was the power behind the Celts, and the Romans sought the destruction of the Celtic powerbase. Normally the Romans were very tolerant of the various religious systems they came across, but in the case of Druidism, there would be no compromise. The Druids cleverly embodied all the evils of kingcraft and priestcraft, conferring all authority on the majority by the few.

As the Romans moved north towards Britain, some of the European Celts, including the Belgic tribe, fled into southern Britain. This large movement of people probably accounts for the final completion of Stonehenge and its unique structure. This stone circle seems to have the appearance of Greek influence in both the design and construction. According to Sir Thomas Kendrick, Stonehenge was in use when the Romans arrived and continued in use during the occupation.[4] This offers a sensible solution to the many controversies concerning the age of Stonehenge and the people responsible for completing it.

Below, Stonehenge and one of the burial mounds associated with it.

Prior to Christianity arriving in Britain, the Romans had forced the Druid priesthood north into Wales and eventually, Scotland, slaughtering many in the process. The Druids fled to Anglesey, an island off northwest Wales, which was a holy isle, much loved by the heathens. Some fled further north and found their way into what became Scotland, which never fell to Roman arms.

Britain was in a unique situation at the time. It was ripe for a new religion and that religion was Christianity. Unlike other countries, there was, it seems, little objection to the missionaries that arrived in Britain. Whilst the old pagan traditions and places of worship continued, there was no powerful influence from the Druids to oppose Christianity. The Jewish presence was established; they had been trading in tin in southern Britain, modern day Cornwall. It was not difficult for evangelists who had a Jewish background to find their way into the British Isles, already having contacts there. Roman communications, roads and shipping meant travel within the empire was quick and easy.

The earliest record of Christianity's arrival in Britain is the year 37, although other historians date it later at around the year 58/63. Eusebius the fourth century church historian wrote "and some have crossed the Ocean and reached the Isles of Britain."[5]

Early Christianity spread from Asia Minor to Europe and into Britain independent of Rome. The Christianity of Britain was of early Palestinian influence and not the later Roman. Testimony for the early planting of Christianity in Britain not only comes from British historians, but also the church fathers.[6]

Gildas, the most ancient British historian, who wrote about A.D. 564, in his De Vict. Aurelli Ambrossii, affirms, "that the Britons received the gospel under Tiberius (Tiberius Julius Caesar Augustus, born Tiberius Claudius Nero, 42 BC – 37 AD), the emperor under whom Christ suffered;" and that many evangelists were sent by the apostles into this nation, who were the first planters of the gospel, and who, he elsewhere says, "continued with them until the cruel persecution of Dioclesian the emperor," about AD 290. Gildas' British name may have been Badonicus and is thought to have been born in the year 520, the son of a wealthy bardic family (Druid priests). Gildas is believed to have studied in the college at Llantwit Major, a coastal town in Glamorganshire (South Wales). The college was renowned as a seat of learning and religion, attracting students from all over the world, and was reputed to have had seven halls, 400 houses and 2000 pupils. Gildas notes that Christianity "was propagated without impediment, and death threatened to those who interfered with its professors."[7] The pagan Druid priesthood under the Romans had been banished, their temples, circles and mounds lay without priests, though the old religion continued but without any powerbase. This allowed the free spread of Christianity with little opposition.[8]

Tertullian (160-225) writing of the spread of Christianity throughout the world stated, "and the haunts of the Britons—inaccessible to the Romans, but subjugated to Christ."[9] The church father, Theodoret (393-466), confirms the pre-Augustine (of Canterbury) mission to Britain stating the message of Christ had been preached and established,[10] prior to the Roman Catholic mission of Augustine of Canterbury in 597. The Roman Catholic Augustine is considered the "Apostle to the English" and a founder of the English Church, which is quite incorrect as Christianity was already established.

The historian Crosby says that Claudia Ruffina was an English convert to Christianity. Crosby and other historians have claimed she was wife to Pudens, a Roman Senator. Crosby says this is the Claudia mentioned by Paul in 2 Timothy 4:21. Tacitus says, that "Pomponia Greaecina, wife of Pautius, and Claudia Ruffina, a British lady, are supposed to be of the saints that were in Caesar's household, mentioned by Paul, Phil. 3:22." Pautius was in Britain in A.D. 45: it is probable that Claudia returned with him; and it has been thought, from this statement of Tacitus, that this lady was the first British Christian. Speed, a British author on ancient history, says, that "Claudia sent Paul's writings, which he calls spiritual manna, unto her friends in Britain; to feed their souls with the bread of life."[11]

Caratacus is named by Dio Cassius, the Roman historian, who died about 229, as a son of the Catuvellaunian king, Cunobelinus (Shakespeare's Cymbeline, died early 40s). One tradition credits him with introducing religion into Britain. Caratacus, of European Belgic descent, was king of Siluria, an ancient south-western British kingdom. Caratacus is also known as Caradoc. Cunobelinus, King of the Catuvellauni tribe, was acknowledged by Rome as early as AD 5 to be King of Britain.

Caratacus led much of the later British opposition to the Romans.

After several battles he was betrayed, captured and taken prisoner to Rome. Tacitus (Roman historian, died 117) records a version of his famous speech at his trial, to the Roman Senate, in which he says that his stubborn resistance made Rome's glory in defeating him all the greater:

> Had my government in Britain been directed solely with a view to the preservation of my hereditary domains, or the aggrandizement of my own family, I might long since have entered this city an ally, not a prisoner; nor would you have disdained for a friend a king descended from illustrious ancestors, and the dictator of many nations. My present condition, stripped of its former majesty, is as adverse to myself as it is a cause of triumph to you. What then? I was lord of men, horses, arms and wealth: what wonder if at your dictation I refused to resign them? Does it follow, that because the Romans aspire to universal dominion, every nation is to accept vassalage they would impose? I am now in your power, betrayed, not conquered. Had I, like others, yielded without resistance, where would have been the name of Caradoc? Where your glory? Oblivion would have buried both in the same tomb. Bid me live, I shall survive for ever in history one example at least of Roman clemency.[12]

He made such an impression that he was pardoned and allowed to live in peace in Rome. After his liberation, according to Dio Cassius, Caratacus was so impressed by the city of Rome that he said "And can you, then, who have got such possessions and so many of them, covet our poor tents."

In Geoffrey of Monmouth's *History of the kings of Britain*, there is, interestingly, no mention of Caratacus (Caradoc), but he mentions Arviragus who corresponds to Caratacus, naming him as the son of Kymbelinus (Cunobelinus). Tradition has it that while Caratacus was in Rome he was given 'libera custodia' seven years in free custody, from where he learned of the Christian faith, and was converted before his return to Britain. By the year 55 part of the British Silurian royal family was living in Rome, having obeyed according to legend, the gospel call. [13] The Lord had said to Paul in Acts 9:15 "But the Lord said unto him, Go thy way: for he is a chosen vessel unto me, to bear my name before the Gentiles, and kings, and the children of Israel." That the kings of Britain should hear the gospel should not be considered strange.

Below is the pool on the river Cam at Grantchester.

In the year 141, in the east of Britain, in what is now Cambridgeshire, in the village of Grauta (modern Grantchester), "many were baptized." Interestingly Cambridgeshire and the eastern fens have always been a problem for "heresy." Grantchester is a few minute's walk from Cambridge.[14]

In 167 (or there about), we learn from the Venerable Bede that "whilst Eleutherus (Eleutherius), a holy man, presided over the Roman church, Lucius, king of the Britons, sent a letter to him, entreating that by his command he might be made a Christian. He soon obtained his pious request, and the Britons preserved the faith, which they had received, uncorrupted and entire, in peace and tranquillity until the time of the Emperor Diocletian." Whether this king Lucius was related to the western British kings who he may have found, through pride, to turn to Rome for knowledge of the faith is open to conjecture.[15] A similar account is found in the *The Liber Pontificalis* (Latin for Book of the Popes), a book biography of popes from the apostle Peter until the 15th century.

We know from Geoffrey of Monmouth's *History of the Kings of Britain*, Lucius was the son of king Coilus of Gloucester. At this time Britain had several kings, or rather dukes and earls, tribal chiefs. Lucius could have turned to neighboring tribes, but chose Rome for his Christian faith who sent missionaries.[16] According to Tysilio (the Tysilio Chronicle of the Kings of Britain, died 640), the names of the missionaries were Dyvan and Fagan, he names Lucius as the son of King Cole, who may be the "good king Cole" of nursery rhyme fame.[17]

Roman influence in Britain was to decline when in 410 the last of the Roman soldiers and officials left Britain. The Emperor Honorious told the people of Britain that they no longer had a connection with Rome and that they should defend themselves. Relations with Rome had never been easy; in Boudicca's revolt of 61, several towns, including London, had been sacked and thousands died, before the Romans were able to muster their forces, who were in the west (Wales) seeking to destroy the Druid influence.

According to the eighth century British historian, Nennius:

> The Romans having obtained the dominion of the world, sent legates or deputies to the Britons to demand of them hostages and tribute, which they received from all other countries and islands; but they, fierce, disdainful, and haughty, treated the legation with contempt.

Nennius does not date this, but presumably it was before the invasion of A.D. 43. A previous invasion of 55 BC had failed.

Nennius wrote:

> Thus, agreeably to the account given by the Britons, the Romans governed them four hundred and nine year. After this, the Britons despised the authority of the Romans, equally refusing to pay them tribute or to receive their kings; nor durst the Romans any longer attempt the government of a country, the natives of which massacred their deputies.

This would be about A.D. 360 Nennius continues:

> Thrice were the Roman deputies put to death by the Britons,

and yet these, when harassed by the incursions of the barbarous nations, viz. the Scots and Picts, earnestly solicited the aid of the Romans. To give effect to their entreaties, ambassadors were sent, who made their entrance with impressions of deep sorrow, having their heads covered with dust, and carrying rich presents to expiate the murder of the deputies. They were favourably received by the consuls, and swore submission to the Roman yoke with whatever severity it might be imposed. The Romans, therefore, came with a powerful army to the assistance of the Britons; and having appointed over them a ruler, and settled the government, returned to Rome: and this took place alternately during the space of three hundred and forty-eight years. The Britons, however, from the oppression of the empire, again massacred the Roman deputies, and again petitioned for succour. Once more the Romans undertook the government of the Britons, and assisted them in repelling their neighbours, and, after having exhausted the country of its gold, silver, brass, honey, and costly vestments, and having besides received rich gifts, they returned in great triumph to Rome. After the above-said war between the Britons and Romans, the assassination of their rulers, and the victory of Maximus, who slew Gratian, and the termination of the Roman power in Britain, they were in alarm forty years. Vortigern then reigned in Britain. In his time, the natives had cause of dread, not only from the inroads of the Scots and Picts, but also from the Romans, and their apprehensions of Ambrosius.[18]

As can be seen, Britain was a country in considerable internal strife and civil war. Pagans were attacking the country from the north (Scotland); in answer Vortigern, the British king sought help from the German pagans. The breakdown of Roman law and civilisation was swift after the Roman military departed. To counter the raids from continental pirates, Vikings, Picts and Scots, towns would bring in mercenaries from northern Germany to defend them; these mercenaries were Angles and Saxons, who in time would become known as the English. Some of the British Celts moved into what is now Wales, but evidence of mass migration is lacking. The pagan religions returned to overthrow the Roman Catholic Church which had taken the pagan temples, converting them to temples, in Eastern Britain.

In the sixth century, the British historian Gildas wrote of the state of southern and western Britain, under what were apostate Christian leaders.

> Britain has kings. But they are tyrants; she has judges, but unrighteous ones; generally engaged to plunder and rapine, but always preying on the innocent; whenever they exert themselves to avenge or protect, it is sure to be in favour of robbers or criminals; they have an abundance of wives, yet are addicted to fornication and adultery; they are ready to take oaths, and as often perjure themselves; they make a vow and almost immediately act falsely; they make war, but their wars are against their countrymen, and are unjust ones; they rigorously prosecute thieves throughout their country, but those who sit at table with them are robbers, and they not only cherish but reward them; they give alms plentifully, but in contrast to this is a whole pile of crimes which they have committed; they sit on the seat of justice, but rarely seek for the rule of right judgement; they despise the innocent and the humble, but seize every occasion of exalting to the utmost the bloody-minded; the proud, murderers, the combined and adulterers, enemies of God, who ought to be utterly destroyed and their names forgotten. They have many prisoners in their gaols, loaded with chains, but this is done in treachery rather than in just punishment for crimes; and when they have stood before the altar, swearing by the name of God, they go away and think no more of the holy altar than if it were a mere heap of dirty stones.[19]

Britain was a lawless country with corrupt leaders, but had a Christian presence of educated men.

In the later part of the fourth century, the Christian world would be rocked by the doctrinal dispute over infant baptism, freewill and marriage in the clergy. The ramifications of this argument remain to this day. At the centre was a British Christian known as Pelagius. Pelagius, whose British name was Morgan (or Morgant) lived from about 354 to somewhere between 420 and 440. Pelagius lived through the early time of this strife. Pelagius, his name may be from the Greek, "over the sea," remains famous for his opposition to the doctrine of original sin, which was developed from paganism by Augustine of Hippo. Pelagius was declared a heretic by the Council of Carthage (418). His defense of freewill and good works became known as Pelagianism. Augustine referred to him as Brito.[20] Unfortunately we can only spend a few paragraphs on Pelagius, whereas to do justice he needs a volume, or more, just to himself.

Augustine of Hippo wrote in defence of the doctrine of original sin, called Pelagius a holy man, writing respectfully of him:

> The questions which you proposed that I should write to you about, in opposition to those persons who say that Adam would have died even if he had not sinned, and that nothing of his sin has passed to his posterity by natural transmission; and especially on the subject of the baptism of infants, which the universal Church, with most pious and maternal care, maintains in constant celebration; and whether in this life there are, or have been, or ever will be, children of men without any sin at all I have already

discussed in two lengthy books. And I venture to think that if in them I have not met all the points which perplex all men's minds on such matters (an achievement which, I apprehend, nay, which I have no doubt, lies beyond the power either of myself, or of any other person), I have at all events prepared something in the shape of a firm ground on which those who defend the faith delivered to us by our fathers, against the novel opinions of its opponents, may at any time take their stand, not unarmed for the contest. However, within the last few days I have read some writings by Pelagius, a holy man, as I am told, who has made no small progress in the Christian life, containing some very brief expository notes on the epistles of the Apostle Paul; and therein I found, on coming to the passage where the apostle says, "By one man sin entered into the world, and death by sin; and so it passed upon all men," an argument which is used by those who say that infants are not burdened with original sin. Now I confess that I have not refuted this argument in my lengthy treatise, because it did not indeed once occur to me that anybody was capable of thinking such sentiments. Being, however, unwilling to add to that work, which I had concluded, I have thought it right to insert in this epistle both the argument itself in the very words in which I read it, and the answer which it seems to me proper to give to it.[21]

Pelagius was well-educated, fluent in both Greek and Latin, and learned in the Bible, attesting to the British church of the fourth and fifth centuries. He most likely came from a wealthy family who could afford him a good education. He was, it seems, trained in law and used this to good effect. He lived a moral life, at a time when debauchery was entering the apostate church in Rome. He was a good orator and gained a reputation for persuasiveness. At first his reputation in Rome earned him praise, from such pillars of the

Church as Augustine. He was blind in one eye and unprepossessing in appearance; but his preaching was to win him fame. Most of his later life was spent defending the scriptures against theologians from the Roman Catholic Church. Where he died we do not know; it may have been in Egypt, or he may have returned to his native Britain. The Druid and hence the British belief was in freewill; hence the doctrine had not been a problem in Britain whereas heathen countries elsewhere denied freewill.[22]

Some accounts describe Pelagius as a monk from Bangor, where a British monastery existed; though there is no evidence that Britain had monasteries at this time. "British monasteries" is a term incorrectly used for the pre-Roman Catholic period. Such "monasteries," it seems, were colleges where both teachers and students were allowed to be married, lived in their own quarters and were allowed to leave after training. The collegiate system in Britain pre-existed the period of Roman occupation and continues, with changes, to the present time.

Pelagius defended freewill—taught believers' baptism (by immersion) for remission of actual sins (as opposed to the new erroneous doctrine of inherited sins). He also opposed infant baptism arguing that an infant un-baptised, who dies, does not go to Hell. Pelagius is good evidence for the soundness of the British church in the early fifth century. His defence of the scriptures rocked the

Roman Catholic Church and his teachings continue to do so to this day.

In order to refute the "Pelagian heresy" (by carefully reasoned argument), the Roman Catholic Church sent two bishops, Germanus and Lupus to preach against Pelagius, first in 425/6 and Germanus returned in 446. The British church was slowly coming under Roman Catholic influence. In later years the Roman Catholic Church would resort to terror to overcome its critics rather than reason.

During the fourth century the Celtic church had evangelised extensively into Europe and as the Roman Empire collapsed much evangelising from the Celtic church took place without hindrance from Rome. While the primitive Roman Catholic Church was trying to evangelise southern Britain, Celtic missionaries from Wales were evangelising Europe. The Christianity of Britain was of Palestinian (scriptural) influence and not the later Roman origin.

It is interesting that when the argument over freewill, good works, celibacy in the clergy (clergy itself being an error), infant baptism and original sin arose, it was a learned Christian from the British Church who debated with the erring Roman Catholic Church.

For many, Pelagius remains an enigma to this day, rejected and despised, maybe the problem is he was simply a Christian, knowledgeable in scripture and obedient to Christ.[23] After the mission to evangelise those who held to freewill, from the Roman

Catholic Church's two bishops, Germanus and Lupus, the pure British Church came under limited Roman, and hence pagan, influence. This influence and the power struggles endangered the church. Whilst the Druids never returned to the power they had before the Roman occupation of Southern Britain, they did change the British church by bringing in pagan doctrines. Easter and worship of the Goddess of spring, Easter, is one example, another is the priesthood. Their white gowns are still used today in the Anglican Church, which are Druid in origin.

The Arch-Druid became the Arch-Bishop. The Anglo-Saxon invasions, beginning in 450, all but destroyed the Celtic church and forcing the eastern side of southern Britain back to paganism. The apostate British Church, when it fell to Roman Catholicism never enjoyed an easy relationship, finally separating in the time of Henry the Eighth in the 1530s.

Paraphrasing Henry D'Anvers, who wrote of Augustine and the British Church, about the beginning of the seventh century, Austin (Augustine) endeavoured to reduce the Britains, as well as the Saxons, to a conformity with the Church of Rome. At that time, the old Britains were principally in Wales where Bangor on the north, and Cair Leon on the south, were the two principal seats, both for learning and religion. In Bangor was a college containing 2100 Christians, who dedicated themselves to the Lord to serve him in the ministry as they became capable (to whom was dedicated the name of the monks of Bangor). Yet they in no way accorded with the popish monks of those or the following age, for they were not reduced to any ecclesiastical order, but were for the most part laymen, who laboured with their hands, married and followed their callings. Some of them, whose spirits the Lord fitted and inclined to his more immediate service, devoted themselves to the study of the scriptures, and other holy matters, in preparation for the work of the ministry, and sent out many evangelists, many whom Austin got to a meeting (under subjection) in Worcestershire. There he propounded to them the embracing of the Romish rites, and to join with him in preaching and administering in their way; which they refused.

Then, as Robert Fabian informs us:

> He said to them, "Since you will not assent to my Hests generally, assent you to me specially in three things: The First in your keeping Easter-Day in the Form and Time as it is ordered. The Second, that you give Christendom to Children. And the Third, that you preach to the Saxons, as I have exhorted you. And the other Debate, I shall suffer amend and reform yourselves." But they would not thereof. To whom then Austin said, that if they would not take peace with their Brethren, they should receive war with their Enemies; And if they distained to preach with them the way of Life to the English Nation, they should suffer by their hands the revenge of Death; And which Austin accomplished accordingly, by bringing the Saxons upon them to their utter ruin. [24]

It appears obvious on the very face of Augustine's request to the British Christians, that he was urging them to adopt infant baptism.

He requested three things, the second of which was "that you give Christendom to Children." That demand would have made no sense had the British Christians been in the custom of baptising infants.

National churches, whether pre-reformation or protestant, require a number of shared features of pagan origin. These include infant baptism (pagan lustration, practised worldwide), the altar, clergy including a bishop (single, who has the roll of high priest) and a power status accepted by the authorities. Dedicated buildings (temples) and holy ground constitute another feature. As such national churches are no more than pagan enterprises given a Christian, but false, identity; they are not founded on scripture but pagan tradition, rites and ceremonies. There is no evidence from the writers of that period that the early Celtic Church was a national church, but when it moved north it came under Druid (heathen) influence which it has never lost.

To establish error and deny obedience to Christ the accusation made against Christians was that they espoused freewill, named *Pelagianism*. The accusation remains today and is particularly voiced by the Baptists, many whom have taken on Calvinism. Those Baptists who deny Calvin have still taken on the Protestant denial of baptism for salvation. Infant baptisers are no less guilty, forcing "salvation" onto children who are then led into error as they grow up.

The idea that one can choose how to get to heaven, through free choice or freewill, is an absurdity. Freewill is a poor and misleading term for individual responsibility to choose to obey God, rather than men:

> Then Peter and the other apostles answered and said, we ought to obey God rather than men (Acts 5:29).

> And if it seem evil unto you to serve the LORD, choose you this day whom ye will serve; whether the gods which your fathers served that were on the other side of the flood, or the gods of the Amorites, in whose land ye dwell: but as for me and my house, we will serve the LORD (Jos. 24:15)

Interestingly, those who oppose freewill have ended up worshiping the false gods mentioned by Joshua, who are made saints, or continuing their traditions, ceremonies and rites in the denominational or national church system. Those who make the false accusation of "freewill" have become partakers of the "will worship" mentioned by Paul in Colossians 2:23: "Which things have indeed a shew of wisdom in will worship, and humility, and neglecting of the body; not in any honour to the satisfying of the flesh." Those who make the accusation of freewill are engaged in will-worship. Are they not truly free-willers who chose their own system of salvation, or rather damnation, calling good evil, and evil good? Isaiah 5:20 states: "Woe unto them that call evil good, and good evil; that put darkness for light, and light for darkness; that put bitter for sweet, and sweet for bitter!"

The Pelagian system is not one of free choice of salvation and forcing man's plan of reconciliation on to God, but one of individual obedience to God having heard the Gospel and continued obedience. Hebrews 5:9 states: "And being made perfect, he became the author of eternal salvation unto all them that obey him." Pelagius remains to this day a major embarrassment to historians and theologians who deny it is the individual's responsibility to choose to know and obey God, "In flaming fire taking vengeance on them that know not God, and that obey not the gospel of our Lord Jesus Christ" (2 The. 1:8).

Iona, the holy island off northwestern Scotland, was originally a Druid centre. The island was taken over by the Culdee (Celtic) Church when Columba and his followers arrived in 563. One of Columba's followers, Oran, following the pagan practise, was sacrificed by being buried alive, to sanctify the church grounds. There is a chapel, the oldest building on the island, named after Oran – St. Oran's Chapel. Dedicating holy buildings on consecrated ground, naming them after the victim, was a heathen Druid practice. The Celtic Church was slowly becoming a national church with all the pagan error that it brings.[25]

Roman Catholics would be shocked to learn that "saint" Patrick, who lived in the fourth century (dates are uncertain), was never a Roman Catholic, and in fact, would be excommunicated for his anti Catholic beliefs today! He is credited with bringing Christianity into Ireland and banishing snakes from the island. The miracle of banishing snakes may have a simple explanation. Serpent, snake, fire and sun worship are all associated. If Patrick banished snakes from Ireland, it may be due to his having converted the Druids in the island from paganism.[26]

According to Gildas, Christianity had been planted in Ireland prior to the Queen Boudicca Iceni revolt of A.D. 61.[27] Patrick was not under the authority of the Pope but a member of the Celtic Church. He was the son of an elder and grandson of a deacon. His British name was Maelwyn. His father, Calpurnius, was a principal of a college in southern Wales and an official of the Roman authorities in Britain.[28]

As a young man Patrick was taken prisoner in a raid in 379 and taken captive to Ireland. He returned nearly fifty years later having spent some time in Gaul. The Venerable Bede fails to mention Patrick in his history, most likely because he was of the Celtic rather than Roman Church.[29] That Patrick today is a saint in the Roman Catholic Church owes nothing to his actual beliefs, works and history, which were opposed to Rome. Most of what we think we know of Patrick was written a long time after his death and reflects later Roman Catholic inventions, fabulous fables, miracles and myths, believed by an ignorant and superstitious people believing in salvation through good works and the Pope.

The Celtic Church that Patrick evangelised for, and who never called themselves the "Celtic Church," would be taken over and forced into submission to Rome over many decades. This is not reflected in the Roman Catholic Histories on Patrick and never mentioned is that Ireland did not become truly Roman Catholic until in the reign of Henry the Second, who was crowned King of England in 1154. Shortly after his coronation, Henry sent an embassy to the newly-elected Pope Adrian IV. Led by Bishop Arnold of Lisieux, the group of clerics requested authorisation for Henry to invade Ireland. After the invasion the Irish Church finally came under the control of the Pope, nearly seven hundred years after the death of "Saint" Patrick.

Interestingly, despite Catholicism's use of coercion, the "Pelagian (freewill) Heresy" was not dead. "Pope" Honorius wrote to the Irish requesting they "crush" the "Pelagian Heresy" which had "restarted." The letter is dated 643 and can be found in Bede. That Pelagianism was a problem in Ireland may be an important clue as to the type of Christianity Patrick evangelised, being definitely not of the Roman Catholic type.[30] Patrick founded numerous congregations in Britain and Ireland, baptised believers by immersion and established elderships in those churches, which was the Celtic, and of course, the scriptural pattern. He denied purgatory and taught the Lord's Supper was a memorial.[31]

Celtic Christianity was widespread, traces of which have been found as distant as America. Evidences and sources are presented in chapter four. The final death blow to the freedom of the Celtic Church came when Pope Gregory began to plan for the evangelization of England (land of the pagan Angles, Angle is the term from which England is derived). To lead this mission, Gregory chose Augustine, prior of St. Andrew's monastery in Rome.

In 596, with a party of Benedictine monks, Augustine set out from Rome. He carried letters of commendation to various Roman Catholic Gallic (French) bishops. Taking with them several Franks to act as interpreters, the party crossed safely over to the Isle of Thanet off the southeast English coast, in the domain of Ethelbert, King of Kent, whom they formally notified of their arrival and of their purpose in coming. Ethelbert's wife was a Catholic and he was converted to the Catholic faith.

Augustine's mission was simple; to convert the country to the Catholic faith. He did this by converting pagan temples to Roman Catholic Churches, retaining the pagan priesthood, holy days and customs. Pope Gregory sent more missionaries in 601, along with encouraging letters and gifts for the churches, although attempts to persuade the native Celtic bishops to submit to Augustine's and hence Roman Catholic authority failed.

In 601, "pope" Gregory sent to Abbot Mellitus, who was about to join the Augustine mission in Britain, the following letter, which can be found in Bede. The letter is important in that the pagan temples were to be converted for churches, hence from this pagan customs were to continue in the Roman Catholic Church.

To his most beloved son, the Abbot Mellitus; Gregory, the servant of the servants of God. We have been much concerned, since the departure of our congregation that is with you, because we have received no account of the success of your journey. When, therefore, Almighty God shall bring you to the most reverend Bishop Augustine, our brother, tell him what I have, upon mature deliberation on the affair of the English, determined upon, viz., that the temples of the idols in that nation ought not to be destroyed; but let the idols that are in them be destroyed; let holy water be made and sprinkled in the said temples, let altars be erected, and relics placed. For if those temples are well built, it is requisite that they be converted from the worship of devils to the service of the true God; that the nation, seeing that their temples are not destroyed, may remove error from their hearts, and knowing and adoring the true God, may the more familiarly resort to the places to which they have been accustomed. And because they have been used to slaughter many oxen in the sacrifices to devils, some solemnity must be exchanged for them on this account, as that on the day of the dedication, or the nativities of the holy martyrs, whose relics are there deposited, they may build themselves huts of the boughs of trees, about those churches which have been turned to that use from temples, and celebrate the solemnity with religious feasting, and no more offer beasts to the Devil, but kill cattle to the praise of God in their eating, and return thanks to the Giver of all things for their sustenance; to the end that, whilst some gratifications are outwardly permitted them, they may the more easily consent to the inward consolations of the grace of God. For there is no doubt that it is impossible to efface everything at once from their obdurate minds; because he who endeavours to ascend to the highest place, rises by degrees or steps, and not by leaps. Thus the Lord made Himself known to the people of Israel in Egypt; and yet He allowed them the use of the sacrifices which they were wont to offer to the Devil, in his own worship; so as to command them in his sacrifice to kill beasts, to the end that, changing their hearts, they might lay aside one part of the sacrifice, whilst they retained another; that whilst they offered the same beasts which they were wont to offer, they should offer them to God, and not to idols; and thus they would no longer be the same sacrifices. This it behoves your affection to communicate to our aforesaid brother, that he, being there present, may consider how he is to order all things. God preserve you in safety, most beloved son.

Given the 17th of June, in the nineteenth year of the reign of our lord, the most pious emperor, Mauritius Tiberius, the eighteenth year after the consulship of our said lord. The fourth indiction.[32]

The pagan (Druid?) sees of London and York continued as "Christian sees," the pagan Arch-Druid became the Arch-Bishop. The parish system (priestshire) of the pagans continued as the parish system that continues to this day.

The Celts did not enjoy good relations with the pagan Anglo-Saxons (English), which is not surprising since they were, in the eyes of the Celts, invaders. Augustine warned the Celts, at a meeting at Aust near Chepstow, that if they did not preach to the pagans, then the pagans would destroy them. He was critical of the failure of the Celts to administer baptism according to the Roman rite (infant triple immersion). Roman Catholics at this time used coercion in conversions; this meant many, if not most, brought their old customs, which they were allowed, into the new religion. The Celtic church evangelised by preaching and reason. When the Catholics evangelised, they converted kings and hence kingdoms, using of terror in forced conversions. The power secured through contacts with Roman Catholic Europe was a great incentive at a time of civil unrest and war for kings. In 613, a thousand Celtic Christians were massacred by the Anglo-Saxons at Bangor; their monastery (college) was burnt to the ground.

The Celtic Church disagreed with the Roman Catholics over baptism, which the Celts practised as single immersion for believers. Other areas of disagreement were over the organisation of the church, and religious festivals such as Easter. Lack of reliable information makes this period difficult to research, but we can be certain that under Roman Catholic influence paganism was being forced onto those who simply wished to stay with the scriptures.

The standing stones and monoliths of the pagans became the stone crosses and headstones in cemeteries. The stone circles became churches and the customs and ceremonies of the pagans continued in the state church. Eventually, possession of the Bible was banned on pain of death. The paganising of the church is explored in the companion volume—*The Devils' Door.*

Infant baptism would by law be forced onto the inhabitants of Britain. Baptising in Britain's church buildings did not begin until about the year 627 when king Edwin built a baptistery to be baptised (immersed) in. At the Royal Court in Yeavering, the pagan king Edwin allowed the Catholic bishop Paulinus to convert him to Christianity. The king then travelled to York for baptism in Paulinus' proto-Cathedral and persuaded all his nobles, as well as sub-Kings (such as King Eorpwald of East Anglia) to follow suit, thus ensuring unity within the country. It was a prestigious move, which brought letters and gifts from the Pope in Rome. Edwin also set about re-fortifying York. Though this city might be considered Edwin's capital, he held a number of important administrative centres and resided in them on a circuit basis similar to that used by later Saxon and Norman Kings.

In 689 King Inas, Ine or Iva of the West Saxons decreed that infants must be baptised (triune immersed) within thirty days of birth. He also made it an offence to break Sabbath laws and gave the right of sanctuary in church buildings (following pagan practice). The pagan celebration of Easter came into the Roman Catholic Church. Bede wrote: Eostur-month, which is now interpreted as the paschal month, was formerly named after the goddess Eostre, and has given its name to the festival, (see the Oxford English Dictionary on etymology of Easter).

Many historians incorrectly date the arrival of Christianity in Britain as 597 with the arrival of Augustine. This is not true, Augustine's mission overthrew biblical Christianity where it existed, either destroying it or forcing it underground. Augustine (of Canterbury) did not introduce Christianity but Roman Catholicism, which was forced onto the converts, often at the point of the sword.

In 1282, the death of King Llywelyn the Last led to the conquest of Wales by King Edward I of England. Since then the heir apparent to the English monarch has borne the title "Prince of Wales." The Welsh launched several revolts against English rule, the last significant one being that led by Owain Glyndwr in the early 15th century. Whilst the Roman Catholic Church was present in Wales from about 870, there is no evidence it was forced on the population. By the time Wales came under English and Roman Catholic law, the Churches of Christ (Lollards) in Britain were expanding. It is an interesting question whether any congregations survived the dark ages in Wales and Ireland, prior to Catholicism's being forced onto the population. Welsh Baptist historians, such as Jonathon Davis, make the claim, that Christianity survived in the Welsh mountains until the Reformation.[33]

In southern France, John Cassian established two monasteries at Marseilles, one for men and the other for women, in about 415. Around the year 428 opposition to the Augustinan views was being voiced by Cassian. The teachings of Cassian and his followers spread throughout the south of France. Regarded by some as sectarians, there is no evidence that they separated from the church of that time. What is interesting about Cassian and his followers is their opposition to the teachings of Augustine, and that this opposition continued for some time. Modern historians have accused them of being semi-pelagian in doctrine, but this is a recent invention and this was not a term used by their opponents.

They taught that salvation through Christ was available to all that ask and are obedient to Him, through free choice. Therefore, they have rejected teachings on original sin and predestination. Cassian in his writings refers to the early church fathers and Scriptures in defence of his position. The Roman Catholic (western) Church opposed these teachings, but they found favour with the Eastern Church. Doctrines of freewill continued in the western church until the sixth century, when they were condemned outright by the "Council of Orange, 529."[34] Justin Martyr, who lived about 100-165, wrote on freewill and responsibility:

> But lest some suppose, from what has been said by us, that we say that whatever happens, happens by a fatal necessity, because it is foretold as known beforehand, this too we explain. We have learned from the prophets, and we hold it to be true, that punishments, and chastisements, and good rewards, are rendered according to the merit of each man's actions. Since if it be not so, but all things happen by fate, neither is anything at all in our own power. For if it be fated that this man, e.g., be good, and this other evil, neither is the former meritorious nor the latter to be blamed. And again, unless the human race has the power of avoiding evil and choosing good by free choice, they are not accountable for their actions, of whatever kind they be. But that it is by free choice they both walk uprightly and stumble, we thus demonstrate. We

see the same man making a transition to opposite things. Now, if it had been fated that he were to be either good or bad, he could never have been capable of both the opposites, nor of so many transitions. But not even would some be good and others bad, since we thus make fate the cause of evil, and exhibit her as acting in opposition to herself; or that which has been already stated would seem to be true, that neither virtue nor vice is anything, but that things are only reckoned good or evil by opinion; which, as the true word shows, is the greatest impiety and wickedness. But this we assert is inevitable fate, that they who choose the good have worthy rewards, and they who choose the opposite have their merited awards. For not like other things, as trees and quadrupeds, which cannot act by choice, did God make man: for neither would he be worthy of reward or praise did he not of himself choose the good, but were created for this end; nor, if he were evil, would he be worthy of punishment, not being evil of himself, but being able to be nothing else than what he was made.[35]

Ignatius of Antioch, who died early second century, wrote "If anyone is truly religious, he is a man of God; but if he is irreligious, he is a man of the devil, made such, not by nature, but by his own choice."[36] Views that are not only Biblical, but Pelagian several centuries before Pelagius!

Interestingly, the actions of the Roman Catholic Churches in taking over pagan worship and temples, and converting them for their own use, resulted in the pagan Vikings and later Danes mounting attacks. Unlike the Celtic Church, the Catholic Church, which used the sword in conversion, often found itself under attack in Britain and, not infrequently, the new churches and monasteries (former pagan temples) were burned and the monks murdered, or taken away as slaves.

From the later 9th century the Danes turned from raiding to conquest. By 865 the Danes were invading England, which was then divided into three kingdoms. By 874 only the southernmost kingdom remained under their leader, King Alfred the Great. The English defeated the Danes in 878, the Danish king Guthrum making a treaty with the English. As a result, England was divided between them, the Danes taking the eastern part and Guthrum becoming converted to Roman Catholicism. England in the tenth century still had pagan worship; they immersed their children (infant lustration), which was a pagan practice worldwide as it was with the Druids in England. The pagans were ordered by the synod of Amesbury, in 997, to have all children baptised within nine days, which is the Roman rite and time for what was previously pagan lustration.[37] Such was not difficult for the pagans to obey, since the ceremonies are almost the same, and the Roman Catholic churches were built on, or converted from, former pagan temples. The names changed, but the former ceremonies and rites continued.

With these wars and unrest, there is no reason why Christianity could not survive in England and Britain in isolated places. Private gentry often owned the parish churches and paid for the ministers. This would have allowed Christianity to exist at a local level and one can guess, without interference. The problem with this time period is lack of records; much literature was lost when the Normans invaded. It is fair to say the Romish Church was not able to exert its authority as much as it would have liked, but in 1066 this was to change.

Duke William of Normandy had papal backing for the (Norman) Conquest in 1066, invading under the Papal Banner. The papacy after the invasion became much more powerful in England. Persecution of the church, as well as the remnants of paganism, would now be rigorous. The Cathedral Churches would be the property of the Roman Catholic Church, though local parish churches, or rather chapels, would remain owned by landlords.

The parish system goes back to Anglo Saxon pagan times, the word *parish* meaning "priestshire" (as previously mentioned). As such, the temples of the pagans were owned by the local population and this tradition continued with local "parish" church buildings. The Celtic Culdee church [38] continued into post Norman times though declared heretical by Rome in AD 705. One interesting point of this ancient church is that the sons of the ministers continued preaching, thus demonstrating they did not follow the Roman Catholic system of clerical celibacy. Unfortunately historians of the Culdee tradition are late nineteenth century and followers in infant baptism, though there is no evidence of which I am aware that stipulate what method of baptism was used by the Culdee Church. It is quite possible this ancient church or some in this ancient church in Britain, opposed by Rome, taught the truth. They clearly did not teach Roman theology! When eventually the Culdee churches were forced to cease, others heresies became prominent. Of those, the Waldensian and Lollard church, we know much more. Of the Culdee Church, we do not know enough to make an informed judgement. Some Celtic Churches mixed with the Druids and became an extension of paganism. Others could have continued with the truth. The Roman Catholic historians do not help as anything they considered heresy is too often lumped together under the same name. What we do know is that to call the church in England prior to the Norman invasion of 1066, Roman Catholic, is far too broad a claim. That there were churches in England up to and after this date that the Roman Catholic Church found objectionable is true.

A massive change would take place in England, felt for the next two hundred years. French would be the official language along with Latin for church, court, diplomacy and law. England previously had been aligned with the Scandinavian countries, which were to some degree pagan, having only had any form of Christianity for a hundred or so years. Paganism in England would remain until the late 1200s[39] when the Romish Church seems finally to have extinguished it, but by letting most of the ceremonies of paganism into the Church.

The pagans worshiped on high places, groves and in circles. "And say, Ye mountains of Israel, hear the word of the Lord GOD; Thus saith the Lord GOD to the mountains, and to the hills, to the rivers, and to the valleys; Behold, I, even I, will bring a sword upon you, and I will destroy your high places" (Eze. 6:3). The heathen gods Apollo and Jupiter became St. Michael. Their temples converted to Roman Catholic Churches. The next two examples are pictures of Brentor in Devon (England), where heathen gods were worshiped on the top of a volcano. The church is dedicated to St. Michael.

The following pictures are where a hermit

lived at Roche, Cornwall (England).

At the highest point of the volcanic rock is a church building.

Not only were the pagan places taken over, the rites and
ceremonies remained. The religion called Christianity in time bore
no resemblance to that which was introduced by the Lord Jesus

Christ. Paul wrote, "Wherefore, my dearly beloved, flee from idolatry" (1Cor. 10:14). Instead the pagans took over the apostate church, their priesthood remains as do their rites and ceremonies to this day in the denominational system. The pictures above are two of the more obvious examples, but most pre-reformation European church buildings show signs of having been built on former pagan worship or meeting places. This will be covered in more detail in volume two – *The Devils' Door.*

ENDNOTES

[1] Livy, *The Early History of Rome*, Penguin Classics, trans. Aubrey De Selincourt (1965) 379.

[2] Edward Davies, *Celtic Researches on the Origin, Traditions and Languages of the Ancient Britons* (1804) 168-182. Isabel Hill Elder, *Celt, Druid and Culdee* (1947) 46.

[3] Sir Thomas Kendrick, M.A., *The Druids, A Study in Keltic Prehistory* (1927) 77. Kendrick was a archaeologist, author and later the Director of the British Museum from 1950 to 1959.

[4] Kendrick 153-154.

[5] Eusebius Pamphili also known as Eusebius of Caesarea (260-340), *Proof of the Gospel*, vol. 1 (Bk III), trans. W J Ferrar (1920) 130.

[6] For the Palestinian origin of the church further information can be found in Diana Leatham's *Celtic Sunrise* (1951) 35-52. *The Times, Atlas of World History* pages 84, 92-93, 98-99, 100-101. Dean Spence, DD, *The Church History of England,* vol. 1 (1897) 2ff.

[7] Gildas Sapiens (Gildas the Wise 516-570) the early British historian, *Six Old English Chronicles*, trans. J. A. Giles (1906) 302.

[8] Gildas 300.

[9] An answer to the Jews, *Anti Nicene Fathers*, vol. 3, Chapter VII (A.D. 155–222) 158.

[10] Theodoret, *Nicene and Post Nicene Fathers, second series*, vol. 3, 109.

[11]Claudia quoted from Ivimey vol. 1. See also the preface to Crosby, vol. 1.

[12]The version of the speech quoted is taken from "Rev." R.W. Morgan, *St. Paul in Britain*, (1864)52.

[13] "Rev." R.W. Morgan, *St. Paul in Britain* (1864) 55. Andrew Gray, *The Origin & Early History of Christianity in Britain* (1897) 15ff.

[14] G H Orchard, *A History of the Baptists in England, from the earliest days of the Christian dispensation to the present time*, ed. J R Graves, vol. 2 (1855) 38. Orchard was a Baptist minister of a congregation in Stevington, Bedfordshire, England, a congregation that goes back to the 1600s when it was a church of Christ before becoming Particular Baptist.

[15]Bede (Venerable Bede 673-735), *Historia Ecclesiastica Gentis Anglorum (The Ecclesiastical History of the English People)* trans. J. A. Giles (1907).

[16]Geoffrey of Monmouth's (Galfridus Monemutensis, died 1155), *History of the Kings of Britain"(Historia Regum Britanniae)*, Penguin Books, trans. Lewis Thorpe, 22.

[17]Tysilio died 640, was a Welsh bishop, prince and scholar, son of the reigning King of Powys (a small country within modern Wales). The English translation was by Peter Roberts in 1811, page 90 taken from the 15th-century copy of a 12th-century original (now lost), it is known as the Jesus College MS LXI.

[18]Nennius quoted from *Six Old English Chronicles,* trans. J. A. Giles (1906).

[19]Gildas the Wise (516-570), quoted from *Six Old English Chronicles*, trans. J. A. Giles (1906) 314.

[20]*Nicene and Post-Nicene Fathers*, Augustine: Anti-Pelagian Writings. vol. 5, 3.

[21]*Nicene and Post-Nicene Fathers*, Augustine: Anti-Pelagian Writings, vol. 5, 69.

[22]Freewill—a British doctrine held by the Druids, British Church and British peoples. John Pryce, *The Ancient British Church, A Historical Essay* (1878)117. A. Hadrian Allcroft, *The Circle and the Cross*, vol. 2 (1930) 2.

[23]Further reading on Pelagius and sources used: British Monasteries – John Jamieson, *A Historical Account of the Ancient Culdees of Iona* (1890) 34. Pelagius – Everett Ferguson, *Encyclopaedia of Early Christianity* (1990)704-708. Louis Nedelec, *Cambria Sacra, or, The History of the Early Cambro-British Christians* (1879) 39-46. Theodore De Bruyn, *Pelagius' Commentary on St. Paul's Epistle to the Romans* (Oxford University Press, 2002). Robert F Evans, *Pelagius Inquiries and Reappraisals* (1968). Bede, trans. J. A. Giles (1907) 17. *Nicene and Post-Nicene Fathers*, Augustine: Anti-Pelagian Writings, vol. 5.

[24]Henry D'Anvers, *A Treatise of Baptism* (1674) 335ff. D'Anvers (a minister of a church of Christ, Staffordshire) quoted Fabian from his chronicle of 1507

for his source regarding Augustine. Danvers used materials prepared by John Tombes, another evangelist in the churches of Christ who was active in the 1650s.

[25]John Jamieson, *A Historical Account of the Ancient Culdees of Iona* (1890) 23-34.

[26] C. F. Oldham, *The Sun and the Serpent* (1905).

[27]Gildas quoted from Isabel Hill Elder, *Celt, Druid and Culdee* (1947) 106.

[28]Gildas 106.

[29]Gildas 107.

[30] Bede, *Honorius' letter* trans. J. A. Giles (1907) 104.

[31]"Nennius" from *Six Old English Chronicles*, trans. J. A. Giles (1906). G H Orchard, *History of the Baptists,* vol. 1 (1855) 178.

[32]Bede 55.

[33]Jonathon Davis, *A History of the Welsh Baptists* (1835).

[34]*Waddington's History of the Church* (1837) 180ff. *Oxford dictionary of the Christian Church*, 2nd ed., rev., 246 and 1258. Ferguson, *Encyclopaedia of Early Christianity*, 180-181. *Nicene and Post-Nicene Fathers, second series*, vol. 11, 160ff.

[35]Justin Martyr, *Ante-Nicene Fathers*, vol. 1, First Apology Chap. 43 (XL111) 177.

[36]*Ante-Nicene Fathers*, vol. 1, Epistle of Ignatius to the Magnesians, 61.

[37] G H Orchard, *A History of the Baptists in England, from the earliest days of the Christian dispensation to the present time*, ed. J R Graves, vol. 2 (1855) 94.

[38]Isabel Hill Elder, *Druid and Culdee* (1947).

[39] William Henry Summers, *The Lollards Of The Chiltern Hills: Glimpses Of English Dissent In The Middle Ages* (1906) 20.

5

AMERICA—ITS EARLY CHRISTIANITY
The Origin of the Original Inhabitants and
the "Flat Earth" Myth Refuted

Go ye therefore, and teach all nations, baptizing them in
the name of the Father, and of the Son, and of the Holy
Ghost (Matthew 28:19).

A curious tale is often told of the "Rev." Morgan Jones, who was
originally from Basaleg, Monmouthshire, Wales and an alumnus
of Jesus College, Oxford (University). Jones emigrated to North
America and told the following story. In 1669, he was travelling
in what is now called South Carolina amongst the Doegs of the
Tuscarora Nation on his way to Roanoke, when he was captured
by Indians. They were about to put him to death when he muttered
a few words in his native Welsh, and to his surprise the Indians
understood him though with some difficulty. They then befriended
him, Jones and his companions staying with them for four months.
The Tuscaroras were known as "the white Indians." Jones later in
1685 swore an affidavit confirming the event.[1]

Treated with incredulity, Jones' story has been dismissed as foolishness on his part. After all, how could members of an Indian tribe speak Welsh? Of course the Welsh language is pre-Roman Celtic and is considered a relative of the language of ancient Britain before the Romans arrived in AD43.

It could therefore be claimed that the language was an ancient Celtic dialect rather than Welsh. Celtic remains have been found in South Carolina that predate Roman times. Some versions of the story say the language was British, but as there is no such language as "British," we are still left with the Celtic tongue (the original British language).

Another popular story is of the Welsh prince Madoc, who legend has it, travelled to the Americas in 1170s. In 1625, George Abbot, the Archbishop of Canterbury, wrote in his world history that a Welsh prince had discovered America and that, "King Arthur knew of it." Incidentally, it was under Abbot that the King James Bible translation was undertaken. This means according to Abbot, Madoc's voyages could have been in the sixth rather than the twelfth century of legend, if the "prince" of Abbot's history is the same person as Madoc. There were two king Arthurs, both related. There would have been a third later had not prince Arthur, son of Henry VII died as a child. This Arthur was betrothed to Catherine of Aragon, Henry VIII's first wife. The Tudors were of Welsh stock, a line that goes back to the famous King Arthur of the Silurian Royal family.

King Arthur of the sixth century had a brother known as Madoc, who of course was a prince. Here we have a prince known as Madoc speaking the Celtic language (ancient British language). Such a date is consistent with the dating of coins found in North America and burial mounds which are of a Celtic design.

The English language that we speak today came from the Anglo-Saxon into the Old English. By the time of Chaucer, who died in 1400, we had the language we recognise today. Prior to that, the language of diplomacy and court was French. Latin was used in the established church, law and various Celtic dialects for the native British.

In 1398 the last Europeans (Norse-Celtic) travelled to North America, almost one hundred years prior to the accepted date of 1492 of the discovery of Americas by Columbus. The legend is that Prince Henry Sinclair, Earl of Orkney, led the last Norse Celtic Atlantic expedition, landing in what is now New England. In 1398, Sir John Gunn, a member of the expedition died at Westford, Massachusetts where a memorial cut in rock of his coat of arms may still be seen.[2] There is a notable similarity between the chamber tombs found on the Orkneys Islands (North of Scotland) and those found in north eastern America suggesting a Norse-Celtic link over many centuries.

Vinland was the name given to an area of North America by

102

the Norseman, Leif Eiríksson, about the year AD1000. In 1960 archaeological evidence of Norse settlement was found at L'Anse aux Meadows, on the northern part of the island of Newfoundland. Although this proved the Vikings' pre-Columbian discovery of North America, whether this exact site is the Vinland of the Norse accounts is still a subject of discussion.

According to Barry Fell, the magnetic compass had been available since 300 BC, using either a lodestone or needle.[3] Fell also claims that sophisticated analogue mechanical computers and aids were used from the same time period.[4] Such primitive mechanical navigational computers and compasses would allow early navigators to make sea journeys away from land. These mechanical devices were able to assist navigators, like their predecessors, using the sun and stars, to keep to a course when away from land. Since remains of Roman shipwrecks have been found off the eastern coast of the Americas, the idea that Roman sailors could not sail away from land is quite false.[5] What the Romans did have against them was that the use of slaves to provide rowers to power the galleys, in addition to sails, caused many problems on long journeys. Slaves required feeding which was impractical on long journeys away from land. Boats using sail power alone and designed for harsh weather overcame this problem; such were used by the Celts and Phoenicians.

Harvard professor Barry Fell, listed in his book *America BC* a number of sites both in North and South America where ancient artifacts from the Middle East and Europe have been found. A study of comparative pagan religions also reveals a common link. Roman and earlier navigators knew the earth to be round, not flat. The circumference of the Earth was measured two hundred years before the birth of Christ by Eratosthenes.

Eratosthenes of Cyrene (c.276 BC–194 BC) was a Greek mathematician, geographer and astronomer. He is remembered for devising a system of latitude and longitude, not known to the British navy until the time of Harrison (Eighteenth century), whose chronometer of course was accurate. Eratosthenes is also remembered for being the first known to have calculated the circumference of the Earth. He also created a map of the world based on the available geographical knowledge of the era. After the destruction of Athens and Alexandria, many ancient records were lost for all time, but, from what evidence remains, we know these ancient sea peoples had much more knowledge than is normally credited to them.

Eratosthenes studied in Alexandria and later, it is claimed, for some years in Athens. In 236 BC he was appointed by Ptolemy III as librarian of the Alexandrian library, succeeding the first librarian, Zenodotos. He made several contributions to mathematics and science, and was a friend of Archimedes. Around 255 BC he invented the armillary sphere, which was widely used until the invention of the orrery (a mechanical device that illustrates the relative positions and motions of the planets and moons in the solar system in heliocentric model) in the 18th century.

The Bible teaches that the Earth is a spherical. The British Celtic church taught that the Earth was round, a fact known to Celtic sailors. So where did the idea of a flat Earth come from? The first author to present a flat earth account in detail was Washington Irving. Irving, who died in 1859, wrote considerably on Christopher Columbus who late in the history of navigation is given the glory for discovering the Americas. Several editions of his work were produced, the first in 1828.

Pre-Columbian Native American legends tell of visitors from a strange land with strange powers. Could this be Christians with the power of miracles in the first century? Whilst speculation, Roman and earlier ships were capable of doing the voyage. Sailors knew the Earth is round, for when land disappears or another boat approaches, it is the highest point that is seen first and diappears last because the Earth's curvature hides the lower parts.

The legend of Columbus' sailors living in fear of falling off a flat Earth at the very edge of the sea grew from Irving's history. Church denominations, particularly the Anglican in England, with their high church liberal theology eagerly accepted such stories, along in 1859 with Darwin's published theory of evolution *The Origin of Species*.

Two English atheists in the 1800s (John Draper, d.1882, and Andrew D White, d.1918) promoted even further the story of Columbus and a flat Earth. The idea that the early pre-reformation church taught that the Earth was flat is a fabrication by anti-Christian Humanists living in the nineteenth century. The work of Irving has been countered by Samuel Eliot Morison, an expert on Columbus who has opposed the "flat Earth" story as "misleading and mischievous non-sense, ...one of the most popular Columbian myths." Morison's book, *Admiral of the Ocean Sea, a Life of Christopher Columbus*, came out in 1942. The Celts, and later British sailors had been reaching North America by way of Greenland and across to Newfoundland for centuries prior to Columbus reaching America in 1492. Vikings had been making the same perilous journey from about AD1000.[6]

In 982 the Norsemen who had settled in Iceland found America under Eric the Red. The Norsemen were at that time independent from Rome being pagan, though they started to come under Romish influence. By 1003 Thorvald was travelling to the Carolinas where settlements were established. Thorfinn, a Norse explorer, died in about 1014. His widow visited Rome for a pilgrimage where it is likely she made known the existence of the Americas. Its existence were published in 1067 by Adam of Bremen who wrote:

The king also made mention of another region discovered in the Northern Ocean, which had been visited by many people and was called Vineland, because grapes that produce a very good wine grew there spontaneously; corn also grows there, without sowing, in great abundance. We know this, not by fabulous hearsay, but from authentic accounts furnished by Danes.[7]

By 1347 Legates and Bishops from the Roman Catholic Church were discouraging further exploration and contact with America to prevent the discovery of a sea route to India and so damage the trade of the Levant (Orient). The Levant was originally the Mediterranean lands east of Italy, from the Middle French word Levant meaning "the Orient." Historically, the trade on the Levant between Western Europe and the Ottoman Empire was of great economic importance which the Romish Church sought to protect.[8]

In 1453 Constantinople fell to the Muslims, to which the Romish Church responded by expelling Muslims and Jews from Spain. The fall of the Roman Empire resulted in the loss of the lucrative Levant trade, which resulted in the Romish Church lifting its objections to westward exploration. The removal of this ban was followed by Columbus "discovering" America in 1492 and De Gama's opening of the sea-route to India.[9]

On instructions from Ferdinand and his queen, Isabella, Columbus would seek to find an alternative route to the Spice Islands to avoid Muslim pirates. Knowing the earth to be spherical, he attempted to establish a route that would avoid the pirates and create improved profits for the Portuguese. On at least three occasions before changing her mind, Isabella rejected Columbus's plan to reach the Indies by sailing west. It took her about two years to agree to his plan. His conditions (the position of Admiral; governorship for him and his descendants of lands to be discovered; and ten percent of the profits) were met.

Early sea travel was dangerous; death was common. If the small boats did not sink in a storm, they could be lost due to poor navigation and ignorance of longitude. Illness, particularly scurvy, was common after two to three weeks without fresh fruit and vegetables. Diet was salted pork, beef and biscuit when the fruit ran out. Later fruit and vegetables would be introduced as a necessity to prevent scurvy.

Columbus was a merchant-businessman. He wanted to find a short trading route from the East Indies. He knew of the British fishing fleets of Newfoundland and the impossibility of finding a passage there. He decided to go south, far more dangerous, but if he could find a passage for trading vessels, he would be rich. Columbus visited Ireland gathering information for his planned journey.

Saint Brendan of Clonfert or Bréanainn of Clonfert (c. 484–c. 578), also called "the Navigator," was an early Irish monk, famous for his semi-legendary journey to the Isle of the Blessed or America that may be the same legend as that of Bran. During his journey his log recorded huge sea monsters that went under his boat (whales?) and mountains of sea crystals (icebergs?). Several legends record Celtic adventurers from Ireland reaching America. That such legends may be based on truth is confirmed by American archeology.[10] In the eighth century an Irish monk named Vigile was accused by the pope (Zachary) of having taught heresies on the antipodes. The antipodes is that any place on Earth has its antipodal point; that is, the region on the Earth's surface which is diametrically opposite to it. Two points which are *antipodal* to one another are connected by a straight line through the centre of the Earth. The teaching of the antipodes also teaches the earth is spherical.[11]

Early Christians found their way to America and left their inscriptions cut in stone. Several inscriptions have been found in New England.[12] Celtic Christianity was not a perverted Roman gospel but at first was the pure Jerusalem gospel. One of the most famous fourth/fifth century Celtic Christians, who caused much controversy over freewill, was a man called Morgan, or better known as Pelagius (Chapter 4).[13] Celtic Christianity in later times came under the dominion of the Roman Catholic Church, but at first it was independent and practised full single immersion baptism, unlike the developing Roman Catholic Church.[14]

In the fifth century AD, Chinese and Japanese accounts tell us

109

they were trading with America, which they named Fusang, at a distance they set at about seven thousand miles.[15] The Chinese presence in America at this date is also confirmed by archeology.[16]

It is known that early American civilizations had temple pyramids and mounds. Whilst many modern historians deny the similarities between the old world and the American mounds and pyramids, it must be noted there is no such thing as a standard pyramid or mound. Stepped pyramids are found in Mesopotamia are known as ziggurats. Similar designs are found in South America.

We also know from archaeology that the Celts, Iberians, Egyptians Libyans and Phoenicians visited the Americas.[17] 1 Kings 10:22 reads, "For the king had merchant ships at sea with the fleet of Hiram. Once every three years the merchant ships came bringing gold, silver, ivory, apes, and monkeys." King Hiram was king of Phoenicia. The Phoenicians were not only capable of going to the Americas, but did so as confirmed by archeology.

According to the traditions of the people of Yucatan, the original inhabitants came in ships from the east. A similar tradition was communicated by Montezuma to the Spanish. The Abbe Brasseur de Bourbourg (1814-1874), speaking of the earliest civilization of the Mexicans and Central Americans says, "The native traditions generally attribute it to bearded white men, who came across the ocean from the east." Bourbourg claimed the Colhuas were the bearded white men who built Palenque and other cities, their lands including Guatemala, Chiapas, Yucatan and others. The Abbe also mentions the traditions amongst the natives of the Pacific coast who talked of people from distant lands coming to trade.[18]

There is in the Greek historian's, Diodorus Siculus' (c. 90 BC - c.27 BC) *Bibliotheca Historica* (Historical Library) book v., chapter ii, an important statement depicted as fact, rather than tradition, "Over against Africa lies a very great island in the vast ocean, many days sail from Libya westward. The soil is very fruitful. It is diversified with mountains and pleasant vales, and the towns are adorned with stately buildings."[19]

The mounds and burial chambers of North America are remarkably similar to mounds found in England and Scotland, both in orientation towards the Sun, and in layers of materials used. Their construction is the same in both continents. The implements found buried and sometimes the inscriptions are Celtic-Norse confirming the connection with the old world.[20]

The traditional view is that the first American settlers came via a land bridge over the Bering Sea from Asia, but this is now questioned. Dr Dennis Stanford, a leading American anthropologist, of the Smithsonian Institution in Washington, argued on evidence in 1999 that Stone-age Europeans were the first transatlantic sailors. Columbus and the Vikings were mere ocean-crossing latecomers, according to Stanford's theory outlined at an archaeology conference in Santa Fe, New Mexico, based on discoveries indicating that the ancient indigenous American people were culturally far more like the Neolithic tribes of France, Spain and Ireland than the Asian people whom scientists had previously thought to be the sole prehistoric settlers of North America.

Stanford also points out that although modern Native Americans have DNA similar to that of Asians, they also carry some variants that are found only in European people. This genetic input, he argued, could only be explained by accepting that Stone Age people were capable of sailing ocean-going boats.[21]

Early America was most likely populated from Europe as well as Asia. It was possible in the first century to make long sea journeys to the Americas. These are unlikely to have been undertaken by Roman naval transports, but privately owned trading ships. Roman ships were often huge, even by today's standards. The emperor Caligula in the first century AD had one luxury ship of 240 feet in length with a 60 foot beam; it had marbled mosaic heated floors. The Romans were clearly capable of building huge ships, as the grain carriers were reputed to be. Before the excavation of these barges from Lake Nemi, scholars had often ridiculed the idea that the Romans had that degree of sophistication needed to build a truly large ship. Below is shown the hull of one Roman ship recovered from Lake Nemi.

People in the foreground indicate its scale.

Another Roman cargo ship was the the Isis, a very large vessel that traded in the Mediterranean during the Roman Empire around AD150. The sophist Lucian described the Isis when he saw it in Athens's Piraeus. The Isis apparently was 180 feet long with a beam of 45 feet. Its hold was 44 feet deep.[22]

The SS Great Britain built in 1843 was the first ocean-going ship to have an iron hull and a screw propeller and, when launched, was the largest vessel afloat. She was 322 feet long, and 50 feet abeam, ten feet less than the big Roman boats and only eighty feet longer. HMS Victory, launched in 1765 was 186 feet long (gun deck) and just under 52 feet abeam, again, smaller than the big Roman boats.

To be saved without Christ (John 3:16-36; Mark 16:16) is impossible. All who have sinned are lost without putting on Christ (John 14:6). So the world is lost without Christ. This is of vital importance. Because of Adam's transgression, sin entered the world and through sin, death (Gen. 3:3, 19 Rom. 5:12-19 and 1 Cor. 15:45-49). In Romans 3:23 we learn that all have sinned. Because of the transgression of Adam and his wife, Eve, we need another "Adam," the man Jesus Christ who laid down His life as a sacrifice to redeem mankind, so that we may be saved (1Cor. 15:21-22, 45). The Bible describes all humans as sinners, since the beginning, and it follows that all people have descended from the first man, Adam (Gen. 3:20. Acts 17:26). We learn therefore that there is no salvation through Christ if Adam was not a real man. There is no room for long timescales or evolution here. There is no case not to believe, as Paul wrote under inspiration, that the Gospel was taught to the "Whole World" in the first century. That mankind has rejected that Gospel, the same Gospel we have today, is not the issue; people have been given the opportunity. The greatest obstacle in promoting the Gospel to a lost world is the rejection of the Gospel by a lost and dying world.

Objections made that people living in distant lands could not hear, then obey, the Gospel are not valid. "If ye continue in the faith grounded and settled, and be not moved away from the hope of the Gospel, which ye have heard, and which was preached to *every creature which is under heaven*; whereof I Paul am made a minister" (Col. 1:23).

In AD540 Europe was plunged into the Dark Ages. Some attributed this disaster to a comet causing destruction on a vast scale. Gildas, the sixth century British historian, wrote:

> The fire of righteous vengeance, kindled by the sins of the past, blazed from sea to sea. Once lit, it did not die down. When it had wasted town and country, it burned up the whole surface of the island until its red and savage tongue licked the western ocean. All the greater towns fell down. Horrible it was to see the foundations of towers and high walls thrown down bottom upwards in the squares, mixing with holy altars and fragments of human bodies.[23]

Europe in time went from the Dark Ages into the Middle Ages, but America did not undergo the same transition. When Columbus rediscovered America the natives had devolved into primitive barbarism from their former state. The archaeology of earlier civilisations remained, unexplained and ignored, from which the Native Americans were descended. Pope Julius the Second described in 1512 the new continent's inhabitants as "sinful Babylonians" who had escaped the flood![24]

Baron Alexander von Humboldt (1769-1859) was born into a wealthy family in Berlin. Charles Darwin said of him, "He was the greatest traveling scientist who ever lived. I have always admired him; now I worship him." Humboldt is widely respected as one of the founders of modern geography. Napoleon Bonaparte wrote, "You have been studying Botanics? Just like my wife!" Thomas Jefferson said "I consider him the most important scientist whom I have met."

Humboldt's travels, experiments, and knowledge transformed western science in the nineteenth century bringing a much greater understanding of geography to the world. Most of his explorations were in the Orinoco basin of Venezuela where he travelled in the company of the French botanist Aime Bonpland.

Humboldt's views of America remain of great interest, especially as he had little consideration for the abilities of the ancient sea travellers who previously visited the Americas. Humboldt is not only highly respected, he visited the native peoples who were still in touch with their past, and visited remains before being trampled underfoot by western visitors. His views are those of the modernists of his time who were developing the theory of evolution, though fortunately have now been proved wrong through archaeology, yet he was so close to discovering the truth in these matters concerning the origin of ancient civilisations and the dispersal from Babel. He is one of the major sources for the error in modern historians' adopting the theory that Columbus discovered the New World. Humboldt influenced the young Charles Darwin and later, the Cambridge anthropologist and Darwinist, Sir George Frazer. This will be looked in further detail in volume two, *The Devils' Door*.

Humboldt wrote in *The Description of the Monuments of America*:

> I have attempted to keep an equal tenor between the two methods followed by those learned men, who have investigated the monuments, the languages, and the traditions of nations. Some, allured by splendid hypotheses, built on very unstable foundations, have drawn general consequence from a small number of solitary facts: they have discovered Chinese and Egyptian colonies in America; recognized Celtic dialects and the Phoenician alphabet; and, while we are ignorant whether the Osci, the Goths, or the Celts are nations emigrated from Asia, have given a decisive opinion on the origin of all the hordes of the New Continent. Others have accumulated materials without generalizing an idea; which is a method, as sterile in tracing the history of a nation, as in delineating the different branches of natural philosophy. May I have been happy enough to avoid the errors, which I have now pointed out! A small number of nations, far distant from each other, the Etruscans, the Egyptians, the people of Tibet, and the Aztecs, exhibit striking analogies in their buildings, their religious institutions, and their division of time, their cycles of regeneration, and their mystic notions. It is the duty of the historian to point out these analogies, which are as difficult to explain as the relations that exist between Sanskrit, the Persian, the Greek, and the languages of German origin.[25]

Humboldt continued: "The works of the first inhabitants of Mexico hold an intermediary place between those of the Scythian tribes, and the ancient monuments of Hindustan."[26] He states:

A slight resemblance between the calantica of the heads of Isis, and the Mexican headdress; the pyramids with terraces, like those of Fayoum, and of Sakharah; the frequent use of hieroglyphical painting; the five complementary days added to the end of the Mexican year, similar to the epagomena of the Memphian (Egyptian) year; exhibit very remarkable points of comparison between the people of the Old and New Continent. [27]

Regarding the great pyramid of Cholula, Mexico, Humboldt wrote "It is impossible to read the descriptions, which Herodotus and Diodorus Siculus have left us of the temple of Jupiter Belus, without being struck with the resemblance of that Babylonian monument to the teocallis of Anahue."[28] Humboldt notes that the pyramids of Mexico and Egypt likewise are aligned on the cardinal points (north, south, east and west).[29] Humboldt noted that, "We cannot avoid being struck with the great resemblance, which we observe between the Mexican manuscripts preserved at Veletri, at Rome, at Bologna, at Vienna, and at Mexico; they seem at first sight to be copies of each other."[30]

Humboldt, writing of the origins of the Kingdom of Guatemala:

The inhabitants of Teochiapan had preserved traditions that went back to the epoch of a great deluge; after which their ancestors, led by a chief called Votan, had come from a country lying toward the north. In the village of Teopixa, there still existed in the sixteenth century descendants of the family of Votan, or Vodan; for these two names are the same, the Toltecks and the Aztecks not having the four consonants d,b,r,s, in their language. They

118

who have studied the history of the Scandinavian nations in the heroic times must be struck at finding in Mexico a name, which recalls that of Wodan or Odin, who reigned among the Scythians, and whose race, according to the very remarkable assertion of Bede, gave kings to a great number of nations.[30]

Humboldt notes that "As Odin and Boudha (Buddha), according to the learned researches of Sir William Jones, are probably the one and the same person, it is curious to see the names of Boudvar, Wodans-dag (Wednesday), and Votan, denote in India, in Scandinavia, and Mexico, a day of a small period." According to the ancient traditions, collected by the Bishop Francis Nunnez de la Vega; "The Wodan of the Chiapanese was grandson of that illustrious old man, who, at the time of the great deluge, in which the greater part of the human race perished, was saved on a raft with his family."[31]

Humboldt wrote regarding the Sun god Tonatiuh, "The Tonatiuh of the Mexicans appears also to be identical with the Krishna of the Hindus, recorded in the Bhagavatta Purana, and with the Mithras of the Persians."[32] Mithra in time became one of the Sun gods worshiped by the Romans and is remembered on the 22th December, the birth of the unconquered sun.

Regarding the languages of the ancient Americas Humboldt writes of Mr. Vater:

In general, out of eighty three American languages

119

examined by this respectable writer, and by Dr. Barton of Philadelphia, we have hitherto recognised but one hundred and thirty-seven roots, which were found in the languages of Asia and Europe; namely, in those of the Manchou Tartars, the Monguls, the Celts, the Biscayans, and the Esthonians.[33]

Like so many modernists of the nineteen and early twentieth centuries, Humboldt, whose belief was based on evolution, dismissed evidence that was in agreement with Genesis. Humboldt struggled with the facts laid before him; an explanation exists in Genesis chapters ten and eleven, the dispersal of mankind from Babel. It is strange how such highly educated people can be so mystified when a simple solution exists. That Darwin admired Humboldt's research and knew the above passages leaves no doubt that he (Darwin) too ignored evidence that was contrary to his theory.

There is no reason in light of ancient and modern research to dismiss the earliest settlers in the Americas from being part of the great dispersion from Babel found in Genesis chapters ten and eleven – The Table of Nations, and these ancient nations in America had opportunity to hear the gospel preached.

ENDNOTES

My main sources are listed below, others are too numerous to mention including standard reference materials such as encyclopedias.

[1]John Wells Foster, *Pre-Historic Races of the United States* (1873) 400. John D. Baldwin, *Pre-Historic Nations or Inquiries Concerning Some of the Great*

Peoples and Civilizations of Antiquity and Their Probable Relation to a Still Older Civilization of the Ethiopians or Cushites of Arabia (1869) 402-3. Catlin, *North American Indians,* 10th ed., vol. 1 (London, 1866) 206ff. Catlin considered that the Mandans Indians may have been descendents of Madoc's exhibition, noting the blue eyes and other features .

[2]Barry Fell, Harvard professor, *America BC (before Columbus)* (1976) v ff.

[3]Barry Fell, Harvard professor, *Saga America* (1980) 276-7.

[4]Fell , *America BC* 120-1.

[5]Fell, *America BC* 321.

[6]Baldwin 401.

[7]Alexander Del Mar, *The Worship of Augustus Caesar* (1899) 209-10.

[8]Del Mar 211.

[9]Del Mar 220.

[10]Fell, *America BC* 125.

[11]Baldwin 401.

[12]Fell, *Saga America* 172.

[13]Everett Ferguson, *Encyclopaedia of Early Christianity* (1990) 704-708.

[14]Keith Sisman, *Traces of the Kingdom* (2010) chapter 3.

[15]Baldwin 40.

[16]Fell, *Saga America* 323-4

[17]Fell, *America BC* v ff.

[18]Baldwin 394.

[19]Baldwin 399.

[20]Foster 202. Fell, *America BC* 164.

[21]Robin McKie, "Stone Age Sailors Beat Columbus to America," *The Observer,* 28 November 1999.

[22]Fell, *America BC* 16.

[23]Gildas Sapiens (Gildas the Wise 516-570) the early British historian, *Six Old English Chronicles,* trans. J. A. Giles (1906) 311.

[24]Alexander De Humboldt, *Vue des Cordillères et monuments des peuples indigènes de l'Amérique* (in French), 2 vols. folio (1810); English translation – *Researches concerning the Institutions and Monuments of the Ancient inhabitants of America with descriptions and views of some of the most striking scenes in the Cordilleras!* trans. (English) Helen Maria Williams (1814) introduction & 10-11.

[25]Humboldt 38.

[26]Humboldt 47.

[27]Humboldt 82.

[28]Humboldt 100, 107.

[29]Humboldt Ibid, pages 164, 165.

[30]Humboldt Ibid, pages 172,173, Humboldt refers to the early British historian, Bede, (c. 672-735) "Ecclesiastical History of the English people" c. 731.

[31]Humboldt 319-20.

[32]Humboldt 195.

[33]Humboldt 249.

Other sources referred to:

Charles Hapgood, *Maps of the Ancient Sea Kings, Evidence of Advanced Civilisation in the Ice Age* (1966) still in print and many editions.

D. Petersen, *Unlocking The Mysteries of Creation* (I do not agree with everything Petersen writes, but the book is worth consulting).

Graham Hancock, *Fingerprints of the Gods, A Quest for the Beginning and the End,* (First printed 1995) (some useful material from an agnostic).

Malcolm Bowden, *True Science Agrees With Bible.*

Samuel Eliot Morison, *Admiral of the Ocean Sea, A Life of Christopher Columbus* (1942).

Washington Irvine, *A History of the Life and Voyages of Christopher Columbus,* several editions from 1828.

6

THE EUROPEAN WALDENSIANS
AND LOLLARDS

Yet if any man suffer as a Christian, let him not be ashamed; but let him glorify God on this behalf (1 Peter 4:16).

Names such as *Waldensian* were given by the Roman Catholic Church, which used these accursed terms as derogatory statements of heresy. Anyone accused of a crime affecting state or church, closely intertwined in the middle ages, could so be accused by their enemies to force a charge of heresy.[1]

The Vaudois (Waldensians)[2], writes Muston, "have been represented as deriving their origin from Valdo (Waldo) of Lyons, and it is indisputable that the reformer had disciples to whom he left the name of Vaudois; but this is not sufficient to prove the Vaudois of the Alps derive their origin from him."[3] Faber states the name may have been used as early as 1054. Another name used interchangeably with the Waldensians is Lollard.[4]

Peter Valdes, often incorrectly spelt Waldo, is often given as the originator of the Waldensians. He died about 1205.[5] While the claim that his name is the origin of the various names given to these brethren may be questionable, there is no doubt the movement by whatever name pre-dated Valdes.

For our purposes, the terms *Lollard, Waldensian, Vaudios* (an alternative to Waldensian along with Vallenses) and *Albigenses* may be considered alternatives for the same people. That these names were also given to others whom the state or church disliked should be considered when further researching this topic. Some people given these names wanted only to reform the Roman Catholic Church to remove its excesses, and would have retained belief in infant baptism, for example. Those people do not concern us, though they may have been given, by their enemies, the same name. Churches that wear these names today are inevitably Calvinist, holding to reformed theology and infant baptism. The period that concerns us long predates Calvinism. Those faithful believers who concern us wore the name Christian and the church – the church of Christ.

In the third century, a separation took place at Rome over the prevailing corruption in the church. One sect earned the name *Novatians*, of one of their leaders, Novatus. They called themselves *Puritans*, or as the Greeks translated the word, *Cathari*. The names signified their disassociation from the lack of morals in the now developing Roman Catholic Church. From this time onwards, groups were separating, seeking to return to the pure apostolic church.[6]

At the top next page is a fourteenth century French picture of the Albigensian Crusade, *Albigensian* being a derogatory name used for Christians along with *Waldensian*. The house is being ransacked after soldiers expelled the inhabitants.

Robert Robinson traces the continuation of these people up to the Reformation and the rise of the Anabaptist movement. "Great numbers followed his (Novatian's) example," he says,

> [A]nd all over the Empire Puritan churches were constituted and flourished through the two hundred succeeding years. Afterwards, when penal laws obliged them to lurk in corners, and worship God in private, they were distinguished by a variety of names and a succession of them continued till the Reformation.[7]

Another group is the *Donatists*, who came into existence in the fourth century. Most, if not all, of what we know of them is written by their enemies and, accordingly, is derogatory. Henry D'Anvers, a seventeenth century church historian, wrote that Donatus was:

> [A] learned man in Africa, [who] taught that they should baptise

125

no children but only those that believed and desired it. That the followers of Donatus were all one with the Anabaptists, denying baptism to children, admitting the believers only thereto, who desired the same and that none ought to be forced to any belief. Augustine's third and fourth books against the Donatists do demonstrate that they denied Infant baptism, wherein he maintained the argument for Infant baptism against them with great zeal, enforcing it with several arguments.[8]

Alexis Muston, in his history of the Vaudois, states that "It is not they that have separated from Catholicism, but Catholicism which has separated from them by changing the primitive religion. Hence arises the impossibility of assigning any precise date for the commencement of their (Waldensian) history."[9]

Berengarius, who was born about 999 and died in 1088, was a scholastic theologian. He is also known as Berengar or Berengar of Tours. It seems Berengarius was able to oppose the developing doctrine of the Romish Church whilst holding high office in the Church, possibly the last continental European to do so without being executed. Sir Francis Walsingham (died 1590) says of John Wycliffe: "It was in the year 1381, that, that damnable heretic, John Wickliffe, reassumed the cursed opinions of Berengarius."

Today, Berengarius is mainly remembered for his objection to the teaching of transubstantiation—the false notion that the substance of the bread and fruit of the vine of the Lord's Supper changes into the body and blood of Christ. What is not taught is his objection to the many other doctrines of the Roman church, including that of infant baptism.

Berengarius was educated in the church as a pupil of Bishop Fulbert of Chartres (died 1028). By 1030, Berengarius was a Canon in the church of St. Martin's, Tours. Berengarius became famous as a lecturer and head of the school at Tours. By 1040, he was archdeacon and, by 1047, treasurer of Angers cathedral. In 1047 he wrote a treatise against the Eucharist, denying material change in the elements and for this was excommunicated by Pope Leo IX in 1050. Berengarius was not present and therefore unheard, his presence not being required and no doubt it was safer to stay away. In the years 1059 and 1079, Berengarius (under considerable pressure) yielded to Rome and subscribed to the doctrines he loathed.

It would seem that Berengarius was under the service and protection of Geoffrey Martel, Count of Anjou. Some time after 1060 Geoffrey the Bearded replaced Geoffrey Martel, and Berengarius slowly fell out of favour, especially with his constant battles with the pope. After 1080, Berengarius retired to the hermitage of St. Come, on an island three miles west of Tours. Berengarius died of natural causes in 1088. Whether he died excommunicated at the time of his death is presently unknown, as is his relationship with the Roman Catholic Church. Berengarius was one of the last opponents inside the Romish church of what would become the new Roman Catholic teaching on transubstantiation.

In the previous century, Rabanus Maurus and Ratramnus condemned the teaching of "realism" in the Eucharist, taught by Paschasius Radbertus in the year 818 (his abbot, they were both at the same abbey). Radbertus advanced the doctrine of transubstantiation, in his book *On the Body and Blood of the Lord,* in which he pushed to extremes (the real presence) the teaching of John of Damascus (c.710). In John of Damascus' book *De Fide Orthodoxa,* a step was taken towards the teaching of the real presence of the blood and flesh of Christ in the Eucharist, as opposed to the symbolic. Although started beforehand the doctrine of transubstantiation was slowly developing over three centuries from the eighth.

During the tenth century, theological arguments over the Eucharist did not become heated, but during the next century the pro-transubstantiation party became quite dogmatic and won the day. Lanfranc (an Italian), later to be Archbishop of Canterbury, wrote against Berengarius during 1087 whilst Lanfranc was in Normandy. The term *transubstantiation* was established by the Roman Catholic Church by 1080 and proclaimed formally as church doctrine by Pope Innocent III in 1215.

Berengarius preached the Gospel. His followers spread throughout Europe and became known as *Berengarians*. That Berengarius was opposed to the baptism of infants was learned from two witnesses. The first, Deodwinus, Bishop of Liege, wrote to Henry I, King of France in 1035 complaining about Berengarius who was at that time, deacon of Angers. The second Bruno, was the bishop of Angers. Berengarius was said to have attempted a reformation of the doctrines of Rome, including the rejection of infant baptism and using the Bible as their only authority, and rejecting other Romish traditions.

The same complaints were repeated by Guitmund von Aversa (or Guitmond), a Roman Catholic writer in the 1080s, who says that these "doctrines" had spread throughout France, Germany, Italy and England, in town, village and city, with the nobility and gentry "infected."

It has been suggested over the years by the Romish church that Berengarius was a heretic, and various accusations were made against him, but without the evidence. Evidence does suggest though that Berengarius did make an attempt to restore first century Biblical teaching which would be felt for centuries to come.[10]

It was stated by Lanfranc that Berengarius had said the following:

The Gospel was originally preached to all nations. Then the world believed, and then church was founded. For a season, it increased and fructified: but, through the un-skilfulness of men whose intelligence was evil, it afterward erred and perished. Such was the fate of the great body of the Church: and henceforth in us alone and in those who follow us, the Holy Church of Christ has remained on earth.[11]

Berengarius was followed later by Pierre de Bruis and Arnold of Brescia both of whom were opposed to many Catholic teachings including infant baptism, the Mass, church buildings and altars (because any place is suitable for prayer and meeting), prayers for the dead, veneration of the cross, celibacy, good works and transubstantiation. Pierre De Bruis died about 1140. He was regarded as a medieval heretic. He is also known as Peter of Bruys, Petrus, Bruis, or Von Bruys.

Bruis believed the "clergy" should marry, and is famous for his rejection of infant baptism which is not disputed by any historian. Pierre de Bruis was a Roman Catholic priest who was removed from office and began to preach in Dauphine and Provence, southern France. He seems to have been active from around 1100. His followers were known as *Petrobusians*. They appealed for a return to the authority of the Scriptures and believers' baptism, quoting "Go out into all the world, and preach the gospel to every creature: he that believeth, and is baptised, shall be saved; but he that believeth not shall be damned" (Mark 16:16). He is quoted as saying:

> But we await a time suitable to faith, and baptise a man, after he is ready to recognise God and to believe in Him: we do not, as you charge us, rebaptise him, because the man who has not been washed with the baptism by which sins are washed away ought never to be called baptised.

Peter de Bruis was able to preach for a while under the protection of Earl Hildephonus. A Papal Bull, a formal papal pronouncement, was made against preachers who taught doctrines contrary to the Roman Catholic church by Pope Urban II in 1096 and the "second Lateran Council of 1139." As a result he was burnt alive at St. Giles, near Nimes, southern France about 50 miles from Marseille by the local people infuriated by his teaching. There was no formal process of law, which no doubt suited the Romish church as no defence or debate of the issues took place.

Pierre de Bruis is considered by Catholic and later Protestant historians to be a heretic, and it has been suggested by these historians that he rejected a large proportion of Scripture, against all evidence. His associate "Arnold of Bresia," who tried to reform the Romish church, was executed (by burning) under the authority of the prefect of Rome in 1152/5 and his ashes were thrown into the Tiber.

The persecution that took place from the eleventh century resulted in the burning of many "heretics" across France and other parts of Europe. During this period, many evangelists came to support the churches that were being forced out of existence, particularly from Bulgaria, so that the term *Bulgare* became the equivalent of *Heretic*. Corruption of the word *Bougre* is still used as an insult (sodomite) and found its way into Middle English and continues today as the word *Bugger*.[12]

In 1147, Bernard, a Cistercian monk and Abbot of Clairvaux, wrote a letter to the Earl of St. Giles complaining that he was harbouring "Henry of Toulouse," a "heretick" who practised believers' baptism and denied Catholic teachings. He was also opposed to the clergy. Bernard said in his letter:

> The churches are without people, the people without priests, the priests without honour, and Christians without Christ. The churches are no longer conceived holy, nor the sacraments sacred, nor are the festivals any more celebrated. Men die in their sins, souls are hurried away to the terrible tribunal, without penitence or communion and baptism is refused to infants, who thus are precluded from salvation.

Thomas Crosby (1740) says that Henry was a follower of Pierre de Bruis. It should be noted that, as these preachers had decided to use the Bible as their sole authority, they would naturally reach the same conclusion. Henry managed to avoid capture, but was later arrested, and sent in chains to the bishop of Ostia, under whose authority he died, after a trial.

Everinus wrote to Bernard in 1146 complaining of a "sect" that had rejected infant baptism in favour of believers' baptism. Bernard was involved in oppression against "hereticks" throughout Europe. Many died under his instructions. Today he is revered as a saint in the Catholic Church.[13]

The Dominican monk, Reinerus, in about 1230, complained, writing of the method of evangelising used by this "vile and rustic race," as he called them,

> The heretics cunningly devise, how they may insinuate themselves

into the familiarity of the noble and the great. And this they do in manner following. They exhibit for sale, to the lords and the ladies, rings and robes and other wares which are likely to be acceptable. When they have sold them, if asked whether they have any more goods for sale, one of travelling pedlars will answer: I have jewels far more precious than these, which I will readily give you, if you will secure me against being betrayed by priests. The security being pledged, the heretic then proceeds to say: I process a brilliant gem from God himself; for, through it, man comes to the knowledge of God: and I have another, which casts out so ruddy a heat, that it forthwith kindles the love of God in the heart of the owner. In like manner proceeds to speak of all his other metaphorical gems. Then he recites a chapter from scripture or from some part of our Lord's discourses. When he finds his auditor to be pleased, he will proceed to rehearse the twenty third chapter of Matthew and the parallel passages in the twelfth chapter of Mark: wherein the scribes and Pharisees are described, as sitting in the seat of Moses; and wherein a woe in denounced against those who shut up the kingdom of heaven against men; neither entering themselves, nor suffering the persons who wish to enter. After this, the heretic draws a comparison between the state of the Roman Church and the state of the ancient Pharisees: applying, to the former, all that is said by Christ of the latter. Among the priests, he will remark, you can scarcely find a single doctor who is able to repeat by heart three chapters of the New Testament: but, among us, you can scarcely find either a man or a woman who knows not how to recite the whole text in the vulgar tongue. Yet, because we process the true faith of Christ, and because we inculcate upon all our people holiness of life and soundness of doctrine: therefore do these modern Scribes and Pharisees gratuitously persecute us to death, even as their Jewish predecessors persecuted Christ. Besides: they say and do not: but we practise all that we teach. Moreover: they enforce the traditions of men, rather than the commandments of God: but we persuade persons only to observe the doctrine of Christ and the Apostles. They impose on their penitents heavy punishments, which they will not alleviate with so much as a single finger: but we, after the example of Christ, say to a sinner; Go, and sin no more. Furthermore: we transmit souls by death to heaven: but they send almost all souls to the infernal region of Hell (purgatory). These matters being thus propounded, the heretic puts the question: Judge ye, what state and what faith is the more perfect; that of our community, or that of the Church of Rome? And, when you have honestly judged, choose that which is the best. Thus through their errors, is a person subverted from the Catholic faith: and thus, believing and harbouring and favouring and defending and for many months hiding a vagabond of this description, he learns, in his own house, the several particulars respecting their sect.[14]

Dr. William Wall, an Anglican priest and vicar of Shoreham, Kent, being a staunch supporter of infant baptism, wrote of Peter Bruis and Henry of Toulouse, "to be the first antipaedobaptist (opposed to infant baptism) preachers that ever set up a church or society holding that opinion against infant-baptism, and re-baptising such as had been baptised in infancy."[15] Dr. Wall clearly states that by the 1150s (the time of Bruis), independent of the Roman Catholic Church, a "society" was meeting that denied infant baptism, who baptised believers for remission of sins.[16] Wall coined the term *antipaedobaptist* for those who rejected infant baptism. If we accept Wall's statement, that prior to the 1150s no such congregations met, his statement still confirms that, 380 years before the Reformation, and 680 years before the Restoration Movements in the USA and Great Britain, such churches existed in the Middle Ages.[17]

Two Waldensians, Hans Koch and Leonhard Meyster, who were

descended from the Bohemian and Moravian Waldensians, were executed in Augsburg in 1524. They were executed as Anabaptists, the old charges against the Waldensians no longer being applicable in regard to the Mass and Romish ceremonies.[18] From this time forward, in England and Europe, Waldensians and Lollards would be known by a new name, *Anabaptist*, of course derogatory.[19] In time the old Waldensians and Lollards would be claimed as pre-reformation reformers, who naturally held to infant baptism, so a lie was invented. The Reformers needed an ancient heritage, otherwise they would be a new church. They of course had that heritage; it was the Roman Catholic Church now reformed into Protestant sects. The term *Anabaptist* referred to their re-baptising those who had been baptised as infants, which is contrary to the reformed churches.[20]

Objectors to the above will argue the Waldensians, Albigensians and other heretics were Arian, Gnostic, Manichean or engaged in some other heretical belief system, which would include witchcraft and the ability to fly through the air on a broomstick. That some groups were apostate to Scripture is not the issue here. Sufficient sayings have been handed down for us to see that indeed some within these groups held to first century Christian views. Hence, there are traces of the kingdom to be found. If we accept the Roman Catholic view that all dissenting groups were heretics, why did the Roman Catholic Church reject the scriptures in confronting such supposed heresy? In order to destroy these groups, the Bible was banned; the Roman Catholics refused debate and false charges were brought.

ENDNOTES

[1] John Lawrence Mosheim (Chancellor of the University of Gottingen), *An Ecclesiastical History, Ancient and Modern*, vol. 3, trans. Archibald Maclaine, (1803) 109.

[2] F.L. Cross and E.A. Livingstone, ed., *The Oxford Dictionary of the Christian Church* (1993) 1454.

[3] Alexis Muston, *Israel of the Alps, A Complete History of the Vaudois of Piedmont and Their Colonies*, trans. "Rev." John Montgomery (1857) 18.

[4] George Stanley Faber, *The History And Theology Of The Ancient Vallenses And Albigenses* (1838)595. Also from Mosheim, vol. 3, 354.

[5] Cross 1454.

[6] Robert Robinson, *Ecclesiastical Researches*, (1792)125.

[7] Robinson 126.

[8] Henry D'Anvers (a minister of a church of Christ, Staffordshire), *A Treatise of Baptism* (1674) 223.

[9] Muston 17.

[10] Crosby, vol. 1 page xlii ff. Joseph Ivimey, *A History of English Baptists*, vol. 1(1830) 22 ff. Henry C. Sheldon, *History of the Christian Church* (1894) 93. Lyon, *History of Christianity* 265 and 282. *Dictionary of the Christian Church*160. Walsingham's comments see Ivimey, vol. 1, 72. John of Damascus (c. 675-c.749) see *Dictionary of the Christian Church* 748, *Documents of the Christian Church* 147, and for the De Fide Orthodoxa (Exposition of the Orthodox Faith) see *Nicene and Post-Nicene Fathers*, 2nd series vol. 9, 1 second part. For John the Scot (Ernesti c. 810-c.877) see *Dictionary of the Christian Church* 468. *The History of Christian Doctrine* 252-53. Fisher, *History of Christian Doctrine* 209-10.

[11] Faber 161. Faber quoted from Lanfranc, Epist. Iii, ad Alex, II. Apud Baron, A.D. 1072.

[12] *Waddington's History of the Church* (1837) 348ff. *Oxford Dictionary of the Christian Church,"* 2nd ed., revised, 1071 and 92. Ivimey, vol.1, 20-21 and 24-25. See also, Sheldon, *History,* vol. 2, 234. Johannes Warns, *Baptism* (1957) 125ff. *Christian Baptism,* ed. A. Gilmore, (1959/60) 224. Dr. Hans Grimm, *Tradition and History of the Early churches of Christ in Central Europe* 27-28. *Collins English Dictionary* (1994) 210. Muston, who is an advocate of infant baptism states Bruys denied baptism to infants and taught monks should marry in, *Israel*

of the Alps, 3. Dr. Hans Grimm, *Tradition and History of the Early Churches of Christ In Central Europe* (undated, post 1963) 27.

[13]Waddington's *History of the Church* (1837) 350ff. *Oxford Dictionary of the Christian Church,* 2nd ed., revised, 636. Ivimey, vol.1, 20-21 and 24-25. See also, Sheldon, *History,* vol. 2, 234. Johannes Warns, *Baptism* (1957)125ff. *Christian Baptism*, ed. A. Gilmore (1959/60) 224. Dr. Hans Grimm, *Tradition and History of the Early churches of Christ in Central Europe*, 27-28. *Collins English Dictionary* (1994) 27.

[14]Faber 73.

[15]Dr.William Wall, *A History of Infant Baptism,* 2nd ed., vol. 2 by "Rev." Henry Cotton (Oxford University Press, 1844) 273. Dr Wall, an Anglican priest died in 1728. Wall had been in several discussions with the Baptists and his work being a refutation of believers' baptism.

[16]Wall 258.

[17]Thieleman J. Van Braght, *The Bloody Theater or Martyrs Mirror of the Defenseless Christians Who Baptized Only Upon Confession of Faith, and Who Suffered and Died for the Testimony of Jesus, Their Saviour, from the Time of Christ to the Year A.D. 1660,* 5th ed. (1950) 270.

[18]Thieleman J. Van Braght, *A Martyrology of The Churches of Christ, Commonly Called, Baptists*, vol 1, trans. Edward Bean Underhill (1850)1. Earlier versions were known as the *Martyrs Mirror*. There have been many editions of many titles—the collection of records beginning around 1540.

[19]Dr. Daniel Featley, *The Dippers Dipt or the Anabaptists Dunckt and Plunged Over Head and Ears"* 4th ed., (Nicholas Bourn and Richard Royston, 1646) 124. Featley confirms the name *Anabaptist* was a "nickname." Featley also confirms they called themselves church of Christ. The 1646 Confession of Faith produced by eight churches of Christ in London (one French and seven English) states that they are "falsely called Anabaptists" on the front cover.

[20]Van Braght, *The Bloody* 277, 363-4.

7

WALDENSIANS AND LOLLARDS IN ENGLAND

Bless them which persecute you: bless, and curse not
(Romans 12:14).

The term Lollard was applied to followers of John Wycliffe, who died in 1384. That they are so named Lollards is convenient for those wishing to tie up loose ends of history, but Lollardy in England and Europe pre-dated Wycliffe. The term probably derived from Walter Lollhardus, a Waldensian who was evangelising in England in about 1315.

The English King, William I, The Conqueror (Duke William of Normandy), had papal backing for the conquest of England, which he accomplished in 1066. He had invaded under the Papal Banner and, after the invasion, the papacy became much more powerful in England. Under previous kings, England had been much more tolerant, characterised by a mixture of pagan and Roman Catholic belief. We do not know if the true church, based on biblical precepts alone, existed in England immediately prior to the invasion. However, by the 1000s, some sixty-six years before the Norman conquest, complaints of the Waldensian heresy were being voiced in Europe, and this heresy had reached England.[1] After the invasion, complaints from the Roman Catholic authorities on this "heresy" in England were not only being voiced, but acted on.

The teachings of Gundulphus (also known as Gundulf) were examined by the Bishop of Cambray (Cambrai) and Arras, northern France, in the year 1025. Gundulphus was opposed to the doctrines of the Catholic church and taught against infant baptism, "Because to an infant, that neither wills nor runs, that knows nothing of faith, is ignorant of its own salvation and welfare." Gundulphus it seems was an itinerant travelling evangelist who established and strengthened congregations of the Lord's people throughout northern France, Belgium and England.[2]

Trying to date the origin of the churches of Christ in England is fascinating, as this chapter will show. The claim that England has had churches of Christ for a thousand years may not be far off the mark, and those churches were associated with congregations in Europe that were even older. Lack of records (evidence) means we cannot go back earlier in England.

Between the years 1157 and 1166, first thirty and then eighty men and women came to settle in Oxford and Worcester, about sixty miles apart. The "heretics" were French, or European, religious exiles fleeing the persecution in Europe. They were weavers by trade. As England at this time was under French control, it made travel much easier. They were arrested and brought before Henry the Second at Oxford (where parliament was meeting). They used this opportunity to proclaim and defend the Gospel to king and parliament.

At this time in England, parliaments met in different locations, including Oxford. They met on, or beside, what is known as a Gorsedd mound, manmade, a high place of religious and legal importance where laws were passed and religion practised. Our English word *law* comes from "hlaew" meaning a high place where laws are made. The mound was in French known as a Mott, from which we get the word *moot* (as in moot hall – old equivalent of town hall or county hall) and *meet* as in meeting. The Oxford Gorsedd mound still exists, in the centre of Oxford located in the County Council grounds.

The "heretics" rejected the Roman Catholic Church and its teachings. They said "that infants are not to be baptised, till they come to an age of understanding." They believed in the Trinity. When asked who they were, they replied that they were "Christians" and their only teaching came from the Bible, being "orthodox believers." They were called *Publicani* or *German hereticks*. The expression *Publicani* was also used in France during this period to refer to such Christians. It has been suggested that the term is a mistaken form of the Macedonian designation *Paulikanoi* (followers of the apostle Paul), which French crusaders had brought back with them.

Another account from a manuscript of Radulph, the monk:

> [S]hews that the hereticks, called Publicans, affirm that we must not pray for the dead; that the suffrage of the saints were not to be asked; that they believe not in purgatory; with many other things; and particularly, *asserunt isti Parvulos von baptisandos donec ad intelliigibilem perveniant Aetatem.* They assert that infants are not to be baptized, till they come to the age of understanding.

They denied the need for holy places, church buildings on dedicated ground, proclaiming any place was suitable for worship. Their leaders or elders were Dulcinus Nauarensis and Gerhardus. Nauarensis, and his wife Margaret, were both executed by the Catholic Church in Europe, having been forced to leave England after torture.

Their crime was teaching the "doctrines" of Bruys and Henry.

The English Roman Catholic Church demanded execution for these unfortunate people, but as no law was yet available for this, they were let out of prison, but as outlaws, having been branded in the forehead. They could have been castrated and blinded, but this was not carried out. Several returned to Europe where they suffered death on the orders of the Pope. Some starved to death as outlaws but others remained in England, survived and continued with their successors to spread the gospel into the time of Edward the Third, Walter Lollhardus and Wycliffe. In the time of Richard the First and King John, there seems to be no opposition to their teachings but in the time of Henry the Third, about the year 1235, the "Friars Minorites" were sent to England by the Roman Catholic Church to suppress this "heresy," which implies they were causing the authorities considerable concern.

We learn from Fox (*Fox's Book of Martyrs*), on the authority of Robert Gulsborne, that in the time of Henry II, about the year 1158, two eminent Waldensian preachers, Gerhardus and Dulcinus, came into England to propagate the gospel. According to Thomas Walden, Archbishop Usher, said that "several Waldenses that came out of France were apprehended, and by the king's command were marked in the forehead with a key or hot iron." "Which sect, (says William of Newbury, in his History of England,) were called the Publicani, whose origin was from Gascoyne; and who, being as numerous as the sand of the sea, did sorely infest both France, Italy, Spain, and England."

According to William of Newbury (also spelt Newburgh, depending on the source), they were stripped to the waist, scourged whilst being forced to walk through the city of Oxford, (a standard practice with "heretics") and then afterwards branded in the face. During this suffering they sang "blessed shall ye be when men hate you." Afterwards, some returned to Europe but others stayed in England. If Newbury's account is correct, this is of importance as we shall see.

Paul de Rapin (also known as Thoyras de Rapin), died 1725, in relating the transactions of the councils of Henry II, gives the following account of these people:

> Henry ordered a council to meet at Oxford in 1166, to examine the tenets of certain heretics, called Publicani. Very probably they were disciples of the Waldenses, who began then to appear. When they were asked in the council, who they were; they answered, they were Christians and followers of the apostles. Questioned upon the creed, their replies were thoroughly orthodox as to the trinity and incarnation. But, (adds Rapin,) if the historian is to be depended on, they rejected baptism, the eucharist, marriage and the communion of saints. They shewed great modesty and meekness in their entire behaviour. When they were threatened with death, in order to oblige them to renounce their tenets, they said only, "blessed are they that suffer for righteousness sake."

There is no difficulty in understanding their sentiments

on these heretical points. When a monk says they reject the eucharist, it is to be understood that they rejected the absurd doctrine of transubstantiation; when he says that they rejected marriage, he means that they denied it to be a sacrament and maintained it to be a civil institution; when he says that they rejected the communion of saints, nothing more is to be understood than that they refused to hold communion with the corrupt church of Rome; and when he says that they rejected baptism, what are we to understand but that they rejected the baptism of infants? These were the errors for which they were branded on their foreheads, by those who had "the mark of the beast, both in their foreheads and in their hands."[3]

Waldensians are reported to have been present in Rochester, Kent in 1181, and again recorded in 1197. This location is important, for in the next few centuries the churches of Christ would be active in areas where the Waldensian heresy was being recorded. Where we find Waldensians, we later find Lollards, and even later, the Anabaptists, who called themselves the church of Christ (It must be remembered that Waldensian and Lollards names were derogatory. These people called themselves Christians and the church, the church of Christ). They also settled in Henley-on-the-Thames, west of London, where the Waldensians, it appears, owned their own chapel prior to the 1300s and which presumably was confiscated. These Henley Waldensians were in fellowship with the Oxford brethren. Henley is about twenty-four miles distance from Oxford (and can also be undertaken by boat via the river Thames). Henley was to be a stronghold of Lollardy.[4]

King Henry the Second (of England), whose reign began in 1154, was friendly towards the "Waldensians" and allowed them to settle peacefully. One such group lived in the Manor of Derenth,[5] Kent, southeast of London. Henry clashed with the Roman Catholic Church, most seriously in 1164, when he reasserted his ancestral rights over the church. Archbishop of Canterbury, Thomas Becket, refused to comply. An attempted reconciliation failed and Becket punished priests who had co-operated with Henry. On hearing this, Henry reportedly exclaimed, "Will no one rid me of this turbulent priest?" Four knights took his words literally and murdered Becket in Canterbury Cathedral in December 1170. Almost overnight Becket became revered as a saint. Becket was canonised in 1173. The Roman church during this time was becoming arrogant and lawless. Its priests refused to submit to secular authority, placing themselves under canon (ecclesiastical) law, which caused conflict of jurisdiction. This problem would continue until the time of Henry the Eighth and the Reformation. Certainly this time of turbulence between the state church and the king allowed "heretics" to grow, evangelize and establish themselves. The descendants of one of the knights (William, de Tracy, Baron) responsible for the murder of Thomas Becket, were Lollards and, as we shall see later, members of the church of Christ.

In 1263, King Henry III wrote to the Sheriff of Oxford requiring him to suppress "certain vagabond persons", who were carrying on "meetings, conventicles (illegal church meetings separate from the state church), and unlawful contracts, against the honesty of the church and of all good manners."[6]

The following is taken from Ivimey.

> Roger de Hovedon, in his *Annals*, that in the year 1182, "Henry II was very favourable to the Waldensian sect in England; for whereas they burnt them in many places of Flanders, Italy, and France, in great numbers, he would not suffer any such thing here; and being in his own and his queen's right possessed of Aquitain, Poictou, Guien, Gascoyne, Normandy, etc. the principal places inhabited by the Waldenses and Albigenses, and they being his subjects, they had free egress into his territories here."
>
> During the reigns of kings Richard I and John, which were times of great trouble, we read of no opposition made to them. Richard was long absent in the holy war. John had great contests with the pope, who laid his kingdom under an interdict, and forbad for six years all public worship, only admitting of private baptism to infants. This, with the opposition made to him by the barons, found him so much employment, that these Christians had no molestation, but had great opportunities for disseminating their principles; while the king by his arms defended the Waldenses and Albigenses in Aquitain and Gascoyne, who were so much oppressed by the crusading army of the pope.
>
> In the reign of Henry III, archbishop Usher says, from Matthew Paris, "the orders of the Friars Minorites came into England to suppress this Waldensian heresy." And in the reign of Edward III, about the year 1315, Fuller informs

us in his ecclesiastical history that Walter Lollhardus, that German preacher came into England, a man in great renown among them; and who was so eminent in England that, as in France they were called Berengarians from Berengarius, and Petrobrusians from Peter Bruis, and in Italy and Flanders, Arnoldists, from the famous Arnold of Brescia; so did the Waldensian Christians for many generations after bear the name of this worthy man, being called Lollards.[7]

Lollhardus returned to Germany and was burnt at Cologne in 1322.

In the time of Walter Lollhardus being in England, about 1315, it is said that his followers (they are classed as heretics) increased, so that according to Knighton, the English chronicler (died 1396), "More than one half of the people in England, in a few years, became Lollards."[8] That such large conversions were taking place, even allowing for exaggeration, would suggest that the origins of the Lollards predated Walter Lollhardus, after whom they were named. Mosheim believes his surname is taken from the Lollards rather than the Lollards being named after him. Hallam says in his History of the Middle Ages: "An inundation of heresy broke in the twelfth century over the church, which no persecution was able to repress, till it finally overspread half the surface of Europe." The date, a hundred and fifty years earlier than Walter Lollhardus, places the heresy into the Waldensian period. The clergy were so alarmed that they dispatched the Archbishop of York and the Bishop of London to the King (then in Ireland), to entreat him immediately

147

to return to England to protect the church which was in danger of destruction. A contemporary historian wrote, "as soon as the king heard the representation of the commissioners, being inspired by the divine spirit, he hastened into England, thinking it more necessary to defend the church that to conquer kingdoms."[9]

It has been long debated whether the Lollards practiced believers' baptism and denied infant baptism. Fox says one of their articles of faith was "that faith ought to precede baptism." Such a statement indicates that the Lollards practised adult baptism most likely by immersion, as the mode of baptism in England in that time period was immersion.[10]

The Lollards, who had preceded Wycliffe whose beliefs were widespread, repudiated infant baptism (Neal, History of the Puritans, II. 354, later editions). The testimony of Neal is interesting. He says "the denial of the right of infants to baptism was a principle generally maintained among Lollards, is abundantly confirmed by the historians of those times" (Neal, History of the Puritans, II. 354).[11] The Lollard movement became in time Anabaptist, and this unity with the Anabaptists was hastened by the fact that their political principles were identical.[12] The Anabaptists called themselves Church of Christ and we shall learn more of this later.

In the 1100s, the locations of Worcester, Oxford, Henley and Rochester suggest a pattern for those evangelists travelling from one location to the next. On a map it is almost possible to draw a straight line between them, starting from Rochester and ending with Worcester. One can guess that there were other towns on the route we know nothing about in the twelfth century, where congregations existed unnoticed. In the thirteenth, fourteenth and fifteenth centuries we find records of more congregations on this (imaginary) and now broadening route. Evangelists travelling on foot or riding would have stopped frequently on return journeys. It would be unlikely they did not make more converts in those locations for which no records are known to exist.

In the sixteenth and seventeenth centuries, we find where these congregations existed, the Anabaptists continuing in the same locations on the same but now broadened and extended route. In some cases the family names of the inhabitants are the same. Of course, the Waldensians and Lollards referred to themselves as the church of Christ. By the 1500s, we have the records of the brethren themselves, rather than mere reports from their enemies, which by nature are derogatory. The evidence suggesting a continuation of the church from the 1150s to the late 1600s, when Calvinism took the church into apostasy, cannot be easily overlooked and dismissed. If anything, it requires further research. Along other such "lines" and locations in England where Lollards lived and settled, the churches of Christ continued in the fifteenth, sixteenth and later centuries.

The majority of church historians have the Lollards ceasing prior to, or just at, the start of the Reformation, and then simply disappearing. Part of the reason as noted is that the Lollards did not use that identity. Another reason is the failure to recognise their beliefs, such as denial of infant baptism whilst preaching believers' baptism. Congregational autonomy, plurality of elders, lay preaching, the universal priesthood of Christians continued with the Churches of Christ, not with the reformers. Shared with the reformers was a denial of worship of images, transubstantiation, pilgrimages, confession to priests, prayers to saints. Simply saying the Lollards were early reformers is not accurate; they sought freedom of worship separate from the State, not reformation. In order to have a reformation there is a need for something that preexist, something to reform. That something was the Roman Catholic Church. The Lollards were seeking restoration of the Biblical church, which it seems they had accomplished. Seeking liberty of conscience and freedom of worship placed such people on the radical left of the reformation when it came. Persecution would continue; there would be little respite from the Protestants. These people were the founders of liberty and freedom of worship, as we shall see later. This must not be confused with humanism and liberalism which has its background in the Renaissance and Reformation. It is noteworthy that those Christians who lived five hundred years ago and earlier, who were then on the radical left, espoused such beliefs that today are classed as fundamentally right wing. Society has changed from one extreme to the other, yet Christians with the same Biblical doctrine remain equally despised.

It was the churches of Christ, before, during and after the reformation that brought liberty and freedom of worship, not the Protestant Reformation, as we shall see later. It was also the churches of Christ who kept the Bible alive during the dark ages and early reformation period. In England, the Bible of the reformers and the later King James Version was based on the Tyndale and earlier Wycliffe Bible, which the churches of Christ had a considerable responsibility in producing, as we shall see.

The question of whether the Waldensians are the same people as the Lollards and later Anabaptists (all derogatory terms) in England is fascinating. If they are, then we have churches of Christ in England that can be shown to have existed from the twelfth century until the time of the Restoration Movement in the 1800s. They did not use the derogatory terms ascribed to them, rather, where we have their literature, they used the identity church of Christ. Groups that use those identities, ie., Waldensian and Anabaptist, today are quite different from their antecedents. Waldensian churches today use infant baptism and are Calvinist in doctrine, but this was not so in the period we are looking into.

As objections are several, I shall list the obvious four. Firstly, Lollards and Waldensians practised infant baptism. The answer is simple, both names are derogatory, being heretics in disagreement with the Roman Catholic Church. Whilst some accused of heresy retained infant baptism, this is not an area we are concerned with. That some primitive Catholics were labelled as heretics (Waldensian and Lollard), we know. Likewise, their denial of transubstantiation (the denial is correct), doess not make (the person) a Christian. Secondly, there is a lack of evidence that these groups continued from one to the next. Geographically, where we find one group, we then later find the next, witness also the family names being the same.[13]

The most obviously required evidence is of doctrine. Producing a list of doctrines is problematic. Historian, Professor Arthur Geoffrey Dickens, Fellow and Tutor, Keble College (Oxford), University Lecturer in Sixteenth Century English History (Oxford), who died 2001, gave his reasons that the Lollard and Anabaptists espoused similar but not identical doctrine. Anglican High Church theologian and historian, Canon H. Maynard Smith stated, however, that Anabaptists were "indistinguishable from Lollards except in name."[14] The dispute over doctrine is over infant baptism. Sufficient evidence exists that Lollards did practice believers' baptism.

William Henry Summers, author of *Our Lollard Ancestors*, 1904 and *The Lollards Of The Chiltern Hills*, 1906, reasoned that the Lollards and early Anabaptists (General Baptists) were of the same lineage, dating back to the Waldensians. Summers' research remains highly valued amongst academics and is often quoted; he cannot be dismissed any more than can Canon H. Maynard Smith. Summers researched the early pre-reformation "free-church" movement, which he identified with the Lollards, although his research is still highly valued amongst academics, his conclusions can be disagreed with as he does not deal with baptism. His research into the pre-reformation congregations meeting in the Chilterns and elsewhere remains valuable, as the locations show a continuing pattern of "heresy."

Michael Watts stated, "But while concrete literary evidence may be lacking, there is a good deal of circumstantial evidence to suggest a link between Lollardy, Anabaptism and the General Baptists of the Seventeenth Century."[15] When we examine Watt's statement, we need to remember the "General Baptists" of the early seventeenth century had not so denominated themselves, but identified themselves "Church of Christ," as did the Anabaptists and Lollards. The "General Baptists" use of a denominational title was gradual from the 1660s onwards, along with reformed theology, which came much later. As to "literary evidence," we should be looking at their written beliefs to see if their view of scripture is in agreement amongst themselves. Such indeed seems to be the case.

So, who is right? A resolution to this problem requires, in part, a listing of doctrines be taken from the scriptures and practises of the first century and then comparing the beliefs of our groups with this list. The list should include believers' baptism, congregational autonomy, no clergy class, denial of original sin and hence, no infant baptism, no worship at the altar and no dedicated buildings (i.e., holy places) and the use of biblical terms such as Christian and church of Christ. With such a list we find that the Waldensians, Lollards and the Anabaptists held mutual beliefs. When these groups are located in the same locality, when the family names are found to be the same, we can recognise a direct link through the centuries.

Even when we extend our list, there are still shared mutual beliefs. Our extended list will start with believers' baptism, i.e., for the remission of sins by immersion, which entails a denial of infant baptism and original sin. Secondly, that there is one church, the church of Christ based on the teachings of Christ and His apostles contained in scripture. Thirdly, that salvation lies in this church and entry into the church is through baptism. Fourthly, a denial of a clergy class, all Christians being priests. Fifthly, elders, bishops and presbyters being the same office with a plurality overseeing each autonomous congregation (provided men are qualified). Sixthly, a denial of individual predestination requires active evangelism.

Seventhly, the Lord's Supper is a memorial, the bread is bread and remains bread, as is the fruit of the vine. Eighthly, saint and Mary worship is error along with adoration or worship of images. Ninthly, the church is the people of God, not a building on dedicated ground. Tenthly, preachers can marry, denying Roman Catholic celibacy. We can add more, but such a list is sufficient for our purpose, especially when records of those we are looking into are lacking for various reasons (including length of time causing a loss of information, etc.). Since this list is based on Biblical precepts rather than man's doctrines (when applied to various groups), we can ascertain with a high degree of certainty that churches of Christ in Europe existed for many centuries prior to the Restoration Movement, which started almost simultaneously in Britain and North America but independently. These churches of Christ influenced considerably liberty of conscience in religion, believers' baptism with the later Baptists and congregational autonomy, which laid the foundations for the Restoration Movement in the nineteenth century.

Issues that we have today, such as ecumenism and denominationalism, marriage and divorce, and the instrument, were not issues in bygone times. The idea of denominationalism was anathema to all parties. The issue was, which is the true church, not that all churches have some truth. Families were much more united, lifespans were not as long as today, nor was divorce an issue for ordinary people. The instrument was not in regular use in the Roman Catholic Church. The use of the instrument in worship outside the Catholic/Anglican faith is a recent issue.

Another objection puts me at risk of being accused of teaching successionism, as many Baptist historians teach. We cannot trace the Lord's church all the way back to the apostolic church. Evidence is unavailable, therefore, I cannot teach successionism. What we can see is evidence, not of successionism, but that the biblical church has existed through the ages and did so prior to, during and after the protestant reformation. That people, in different times, from different cultures, can understand the scriptures alike is a proposition entirely different from successionism, and one that I affirm. We can say with certainty the churches of Christ are not Protestant, Anglican or Catholic, but in doctrine and foundation, biblical.

People, when using the scriptures alone, can find the church and obey the Lord (Mat. 13). This has been demonstrated since the first century. We can claim this with certainty before the Restoration Movement that was the case, and before the Protestant Reformation. Baptists suffer in their histories as to the requirement for baptism and predestination, taking on the Protestant denial of baptism for remission of sins. This is not a problem for us. Most Protestants say that one is saved at the point of belief and that baptism is for sins already forgiven. In the case of infant baptism, they say a depraved child cannot receive faith until baptised, or some other nonsense. This is the error of justification by faith alone (or faith only) as interpreted through the fifth century theology of Augustine. It is a continuation of Catholic doctrine, which in turn is pagan in origin. The sad truth is, those who claim faith only actually deny their own proposition. Their faith only belief is the imputation of faith through magic, where supernatural powers act on their hearts which previously was so depraved they could do nothing for their own salvation. Paul wrote, "So then faith cometh by hearing, and hearing by the word of God" (Rom. 10:17). It is no wonder the reformers detested some scripture, such as the books of James and Jude, whilst taking the Pauline epistles out of context (the requirement of obedience). Scripture used properly can be used to interpret scripture. Biblical faith, one that produces good works, requires a contrite heart to hear and obey. Obedience requires liberty of conscience to decide what is right. Sixteenth-century Europe, where the populace were vassals, property of kings, princes and aristocracy, demanded absolute submission. In this context where freedom of expression and liberty were on the radical left, the idea that people could study scripture and decide for themselves was absolutely contrary to both the established state churches and secular leaders.

The theology that has come from Luther and Calvin, whose error was founded on Augustinian predestination and depravity of infants, remains. On the other hand, the much heralded reformation principle of *Sola scriptura* (by scripture alone) i.e., that the Bible, Holy Scripture, is the only infallible or true authority for faith, that it contains all knowledge necessary for salvation, was held by those churches of Christ prior to the reformation and must not be confused with *faith only*. Those who claimed *Sola Scriptura* inevitably resorted to their own (Augustinian) doctrines apart from and contradicting scripture. With the reformation, we must never fail to understand, you cannot reform what did not previously exist.

The reformation produced a more primitive, reformed, but still apostate Roman Catholic faith, minus the pope and later errors, not the church of the first century. The reformation continued with national churches, that retained infant baptism and other pagan doctrines (e.g., the altar, clergy, priesthood and temples). National protestant churches were founded on paganism through Catholicism, ideals which have been grossly misrepresented by the reformers. The retention of the national church was never an option for discussion for the reformers. They knew of the arguments against such but had no intention of venturing in that direction. The Anabaptists were dismissed as heretics, to be hunted down and exterminated. Calvin's wife was a widow of an Anabaptist, but even this did not influence him in considering the case for believers' baptism and congregational autonomy. Luther at first engaged with the Anabaptists, who in turn smuggled his books into various parts of Europe including England.

While many see Calvin, Luther and their disciples as great theologians, their theology was based on worldly matters, the needs of princes and submission of peasants. In sixteenth-century Europe, the Pope, prior to the reformation, had considerable control of secular matters. Politics and religion were inseparable; an aftermath of this is still seen in the United Kingdom where Bishops from the Anglican Church have the right to sit in Parliament, viz., the House of Lords. The solution for Henry VIII was for him to become the Head of the Church of England. The Pope thereby lost his secular power during the reformation throughout Europe. Maybe we should see Calvin and Luther as the leading politicians of their time, with their own political agendas. Both had blood on their hands and dabbled in secular matters. Rather than seeing them as great theologians, they were not original thinkers following in the footsteps of Augustine, who lived a thousand years before. In their time the church ruled society but the church needed changing. Both achieved this objective by allowing for independent countries to have their own established religions. Each prince could worship as he pleased. The Reformation was as much political as religious. Jesus said, "My kingdom is not of this world: if my kingdom were of this world, then would my servants fight" (John 18:36). The reformation brought war and bloodshed for many decades.

Those accused of Lollardy went from the extremes of a fifteenth-century butcher, Standon in Herefordshire. He denied the need of baptism, which is at first consideration a Lollard belief (opposition to infant baptism), but he also claimed there was no god, except the sun and moon, which suggests he was pagan rather than a Christian.[16] The other extreme with the accusation of Lollardy is the many revolts that took place in England which the participants were accused of being Lollards.[17] The term *Lollard* seemed an easy label to place on anyone causing dissention, whether religious or political. It was a label the authorities would take notice of and prosecute with maximum effectiveness and little mercy, executing those who refused to recant.

Sir John Oldcastle, Knight, Lord of Cobham, was one of the most powerful Englishmen of early fifteenth century. He was a Christian, who died by being roasted alive by the State, after being found guilty of charges brought by the Roman Catholic Church.

In ancient times, the title of Knight was conferred normally only on military persons. Only someone of the same office could confer it, therefore excluding nobility including the monarchy. Therefore in grandeur it was superior to nobility, but less in rank. Oldcastle through his marriage to Joan, heiress of the Cobham estate, in Kent (1408), took on the title of Lord, in addition to his Knighthood.

As a young man, Sir John Oldcastle had sufficiently wealthy

parents to afford him an education. He became a professional soldier, and a good one. He fought well against France and earned his knighthood for his services there. In 1406, he was awarded a pension of forty pounds a year, a considerable sum in those days. Later, from his family home in the Olchon valley in Wales, he learned of the true faith and was by tradition baptized in the brook that runs through the valley.

In the Black Mountains of Wales, small groups of Christians were able to hold to their faith with little interference from the outside. In the Olchon valley, they had their own building, hidden on the side of a mountain, half cut into the rock. It was here John Oldcastle was to learn of the true faith. Sometime later he married into the nobility now holding both the title of Lord and Sir, hence the title Sir John Oldcastle (Knight), Lord Cobham.

As a Baron, Sir John Oldcastle now had the right to sit in Parliament. In 1410 he helped secure a law that heretics while under arrest had to be imprisoned by the State, rather than the Catholic Church. This was a blow to the Catholics who were now very concerned with Oldcastle.

Sir John Oldcastle was responsible for the training and keeping of many travelling preachers, (as a now wealthy man, he could afford this) becoming an enemy of the Catholic Church. While King Henry IV lived, Oldcastle was safe, for they were good friends.

When Henry died (1413), the crown passed to his son, Henry V. The Church took the opportunity to act and in 1414 Oldcastle was falsely charged with being part of an uprising, a false charge. He was imprisoned in the Tower of London by the constable Sir Robert Morley, but escaped, returning to his family home in Wales. He was outlawed and hence now a traitor. Warrants were issued for his arrest, one which still exists.

He was seized three years later, taken to London and handed over to Morley in the Tower. On December 15, 1417 he was publicly burnt alive in the fields near to Lincoln's Inn (now part of modern day London). After a trial he was found guilty. There would be no mercy. Stripped of his rank he was bound as a traitor, he knelt and prayed publicly for his enemies and proclaimed to those watching the need to obey the scriptures and them only. He was hung between two gallows by metal chains (for being a traitor) and then slowly burnt to death (for heresy). Throughout this appalling ordeal, he prayed constantly, staying steadfast to the end.

While the secular authorities carried out the execution, the Catholic Church had originally bought the charges (encouraging the prosecution). Without the intervention of the Catholic Church, it is unlikely that Sir John Oldcastle would have been found guilty. The Catholic Church washed their hands of the execution, like many others to follow, but, like Pilate, was no less responsible for what happened. With one of the leading men of the kingdom now dead for his religious beliefs, the Catholic Church knew they now held the upper hand. Regardless of their position in society, those seeking separation from the Catholic Church would die horribly in public.

The burning of Oldcastle

Christians were discovered by their absence from Catholic worship and service; often the village constable would visit the absentees. If there was good reason for their missing services, such as illness, they were excused. If they were found to have left the Romish Church, then punishment would come quickly.

In many histories Lord Cobham (Oldcastle) is presented as having organized several revolts, yet it must be stated, no historian of the time ever recorded any rape, pillage or murder caused by his "revolts," whereas his followers were often butchered or executed after trial. The prime example of this is the "uprising" of 1414. Fox, the martyologist, takes the view these were religious gatherings, not uprisings. Two locations where Lollardy had been previously active, and from where it would continue, were Rochester and Hereford. In both locations, where Oldcastle had property, the Lollards were protected.[18]

Richard Wyche was a preacher who was charged and found guilty of being a "Lollard," who was executed for his beliefs by being burned alive. The date of his execution was August 2nd, 1439 at Tower Hill, (Tower of London). The evidence presented below comes from a number of sources. What is presented is directly relevant and cannot be ignored when investigating pre-reformation churches of Christ and their later influence in the sixteenth century.

Originally, Wyche was a Roman Catholic priest from Hereford, having contact with Sir John Oldcastle. He had been caught dissenting from the Catholic Church, prior to 1402, from which he recanted at Bishop's Auckland, North East England, and then moved to Deptford. Deptford is on the south bank of the River Thames, where there was a ford on the main road from London to Kent. Then, Deptford was in North Kent, a county where pre-reformation churches of Christ were active. Deptford is now part of south-east London, not far from where the sixteenth century Bow Lane and Coleman Street London congregations met.[19]

On September 8th, 1410, Wyche wrote from Deptford to John Huss, in Bohemia, "a brother beloved in Christ, though unknown to me by face." Wyche rejoiced that Huss was now "walking in the light" and exhorted him to endurance. He saluted "all believers and faithful disciples in the truth." This letter Huss publicly read in a sermon before a congregation reckoned at ten thousand people. Huss said:

> Lo, our dearest brother and fellow soldier Richard, the companion of Wycliffe in the toils of the gospel, has written you a letter of such power that for my part, if I possessed no other writing, I would truly lay down my life for the gospel of Christ. Of a truth, with the Lord's help, I will do so yet.

Wyche writing anonymously signed the letter "Ricus Wychewits," a desperate act in a time when the Roman Catholic and

165

secular authorities were hunting down "heretics" and exterminating them. Huss replied:

> Dear brother, the people will hear nothing but the Scriptures, especially the gospels and epistles. And wherever, in town, village, house or castle, a preacher of the sacred truth appears, there the people flock together in crowds. Lo, I have but touched the tail of the Antichrist, and it has opened its mouth, that it may swallow me up with my brothers. Our lord the King and his whole court, queen, barons, and common people, are for the word of Jesus Christ. The Church of Christ in Bohemia salutes the Church of Christ in England.

The messenger, Woksa of Waldstein, a councillor of Prague, also exchanged letters with Sir John Oldcastle.[20] John Huss was excommunicated in 1411 and burned alive at the stake in Constance, on July 6, 1415, having been condemned by the Council of Constance on charges of heresy.

Huss's De Ecclesia played an important part in Luther's break with the papacy. At one point Luther confessed "We are all Hussites now." Johannes Slechta Costelecius wrote to Desiderius Erasmus Roterodamus from Bohemia in a letter dated October 10, 1519. Costelecius referred to some followers of Wycliffe in Bohemia, who were known as Hussites. This letter refers to the time of Huss and Wyche and says of his followers (Hussites) that they called themselves brother or sister; that they had no other authority than the Scriptures, opposed infant baptism, teaching believers' baptism by "dipping" and elected officers from the "laity."[21] All this is consistent with what is known of the "Lollards" and confirms that the congregation preached to by Wyche had separated from the Roman Catholic Church. They were following the scriptural pattern using the identity "Church of Christ" and believers' baptism by immersion.

Scultetus, writing against the Bohemian Brethren in 1528, accuses them of baptising adults. The Hussites were also known as Phygards or Pickards. Wyche was well known in England. He had been arrested and was brought to Westminster (London) to be questioned about Sir John Oldcastle, in October 1417. But no charges were brought.[22]

From an earlier trial we know Wyche opposed the worship of images, confession to priests and pilgrimages. He said that laymen ought to know the scriptures, and afterwards to preach it. He was opposed to both infant baptism and the doctrine of original sin. He stated that "every place is just as good as another for prayer," presumably opposing dedicated buildings; that the Cross should not be worshiped; that burning men is unlawful and, having a sense of humour, "They are fools who say Richard Wiche erred in anything!"[23]

Wyche had been tried for heresy in Durham, North England, at about the turn of the century. He was found not guilty and released. He continued in his associations, which suggests that there was an active group of Christians meeting in the Durham and Newcastle area. He was imprisoned for his beliefs in about 1420 (it seems without trial) and soon afterwards was preaching in Kent and Essex. Wyche again was arrested, this time the authorities were not going to let him slip away. He was charged and at his trial found guilty. When Wyche was executed, there was considerable disorder in England and especially London, mentioned in several sources. It was said of his death, he died "A gode Cristen man."

The chamber in the Lollards Tower, Lambeth, London
where the Roman Catholic Church held its prisoners

His servant/assistant Roger Norman was burned alive with him. The Vicar of All Hallows, Barking (East London), mixed the ashes with sweet smelling spices, to give the impression of some sort of miracle. These were sold to Londoners who had flocked to the scene of execution. In this period, the Roman Catholic Church produced "miracles" regularly for the superstitious. The vicar was arrested and confessed in prison. Presumably miracles were fine as long as it was good Catholics producing them, rather than dead heretics. The site of the execution was guarded for about six weeks before feelings died down.[24]

Prior to the Wycliffe (Lollard) Bible of the 1380s, there had been translations of the scriptures in England, but little is known of them.[25] The Old Latin Bible, The Italic, may have been circulated in England prior to the Vulgate of Jerome.[26]

The problem for ordinary people getting hold of the scriptures became increasingly difficult when the scriptures were used to debate with the Roman Catholic Church. One way to avoid all debates was to ban the Bible, to make it illegal. Pope Gregory VII (Hildebrand) wrote to Duke Wrateslaw of Bohemia in 1080 saying the word of God could remain in some locations in Latin, to the effect as long as Latin was unknown. From that time onwards various councils would make owning and reading the Bible in the vernacular nearly impossible.[27] The Roman Catholic Church in the year 1229, banned the Bible to the laity. It was proscribed on the list of forbidden books by the Council of Toulouse! Wycliffe and the Lollards produced an answer. Scriptoriums produced their own Bibles. Banning books, we can guess, made them popular and would have got people asking questions!

Whether Wycliffe had any great part in producing or translating the Bible into English is dubious. It seems the translation from the Latin was made by John Purvey and Nicholas Hereford.[28] The Purvey edition is dated 1388.[29] This would be the Bible of the English people until the Tyndale translation of the sixteenth century. What is so fascinating about the Lollard Bible is that those involved in distributing it would be Christians. In fact the brethren enthusiastically produced Bibles and tracts, and this before the invention of printing. In 1416, Archbishop Chichely issued a mandate directing that three people in each parish should be examined twice a year, upon oath, to inform of any persons who were meeting in private conventicles (meetings separated from the Roman Church), whose conversation or manners betrayed them, and, who might havie any suspected proscribed books.[30]

The language and spelling of this period, the early 1400s has changed from that of today. Mark's Gospel, 16:15,16 taken from the Purvey version of 1388 reads as follows "And he seide to hem, Go ye in to al the world, and preche the gospel to eche creature.

Who that bileueth, and is baptisid, schal be saaf; but he that bileueth not, schal be damned."[31] Today spelling is standardised, as has taken place with the invention of printing from the sixteenth century.

John Wycliffe (there are many alternative spellings) was born in the mid 1320s and died 31 December 1384. He was an English theologian, lay preacher and translator. Wycliffe was an early dissident in the Roman Catholic Church (during the 14th century) and his followers were known as Lollards, though the name was already in use in England and Europe as mentioned previously. He was a strong advocate of evangelism, and in reformed circles is considered a precursor of the Reformation. He is often called "The Morning Star of the Reformation."

Wycliffe was Master of Balliol College, Oxford in 1360 and 1361. Between 1366 and 1372, he became a Doctor of Divinity. In 1374, he received the crown living of Lutterworth in Leicestershire, which he retained until his death. He was so hated by the Romish Church that, although Rome was restrained in his lifetime from harming him, the church could not let his bones rest in peace. On October 8, 1427, on order of the Council of Constance (the same Council that sent John Hus to the stake), Wycliffe's body was exhumed, his body burned and his ashes strewn on the River Swift. A later chronicler described this event:

> [T]hey burnt his bones to ashes and cast them into the Swift, a neighboring brook running hard by. Thus the

brook conveyed his ashes into the Avon, the Avon into the Severn, the Severn into the narrow seas and they into the main ocean. And so the ashes of Wycliffe are symbolic of his doctrine, which is now spread throughout the world.

A typical burning of a "heretic," during this period.

Wycliffe stated that "the elect are in the church" and from this some consider him a Calvinist before Calvin was born, though the question must be asked, where else are the elect to be found?

He at one time denied infant baptism, regarding children who die unbaptized as safe. A strong advocate of evangelism and clearly rejecting original sin and infant baptism, he can also be regarded as holding to general atonement rather than individual predestination, a term he used in regard to the church.[32]

The Baptist historian, John Cramp quoted from Dr. Vaughan (John Wycliffe, a monograph) the following:

> On baptism his expressions are at times obscure; but, according to his general language, the value of a sacrament must depend wholly on the mind of the recipient, not at all on the external act performed by the priest; and, contrary to the received doctrine, he would not allow that infant salvation was dependent on infant baptism.

Cramp continues:

> Connect with this the charge brought against him by the Council of London, in 1391, as contained in one of the "articles" extracted from his "Trialogus," and which was to this effect, that those who held that infants dying without baptism could not be saved, were "presumptuous and foolish." Now, if Wycliffe believed that the ordinances of Christianity require faith in those who observe them, he would necessarily see the futility of infant-baptism, and the expression of even a doubt respecting the connection between infant baptism and salvation, would be regarded in that age as equivalent to a denial of the Divine authority of the rite. That great man, however, lived and died a priest of the Roman Catholic Church.[33]

Wycliffe like so many before and after him was in the position of knowing the truth but was unable due to reasons known to himself to act according to what is required to have salvation. The affairs of this world pressed him to confirm rather than follow the doctrine of Christ.

In the west of England, twenty-two miles from Tewkesbury, in the late 1300s, the Bishop of Worcester had banned five Lollards from preaching. Worcester is associated with the Waldensians and Lollards, and Tewkesbury we will visit later in the book.[34]

ENDNOTES

[1] G H Orchard, *A History of the Baptists in England, from the earliest days of the Christian dispensation to the present time,* ed. J R Graves, vol. 2 (1855) 103.

[2] Gundulphus quoted from Ivimey, vol. 1, 22, 62-63, 1811.

[3] Sources used and consulted for the Oxford brethren: Joseph Ivimey, *A History of the English Baptists* (1811), Chapter 2. "Rev." Henry Southwell, *Southwell's Book of Martrys-The New Book of Martyrs or Complete Christian Martyrology* (1790) 240. John Foxe (1517-1587), *Acts and Monuments of the Christian Church* better known as *Foxes book of Martyrs,* 9th ed., vol. 1 (1684) 228. *Waddington's History of the Church* (1837). Paul De Rapin Thoyras, *The History of England,* vol. 3 (1727). John T Christian, *History of the Baptists,* vol. 1 (1855) 182. John Gill, T*he divine Right of Infant-Baptism examined and disproved* (1749) Chapter 3. W H Summers, T*he Lollards of the Chiltern Hills* (1906) 24.

[4] William Henry Summers, *The Lollards Of The Chiltern Hills: Glimpses Of English Dissent In The Middle Ages* (1906) 26.

[5] "Rev." J Jackson Goadby, *Bye-Paths in Baptist History* (1871) 12.

[6] William Henry Summers, *The Lollards Of The Chiltern Hills: Glimpses Of English Dissent In The Middle Ages* (1906). Summers quotes Fox, but not the edition he used.

[7] Joseph Ivimey, *A History of the English Baptists* (1811) Chapter 2. A direct quote from Ivimey.

[8] Ivimey 184.

[9] Ivimey 184. John Christian quotes Walsingham, *Historia Anglica,* vol. 3, 213. Walter Lollhardus is usually known as Walter Lollard. Mosheim believes his surname is taken the from the Lollards rather than the Lollards being named after him. Mosheim, *Institutes of Ecclesiastical History,* III. 378.

[10]Ivimey187.

[11]Ivimey 187. (later editions of Neal's work)

[12]Hook, *Lives of the Archbishops of Canterbury*, VI, 123.

[13]*The Lollards Of The Chiltern Hills*, chapter 3, page 19f, 161. Michael R Watts, *The Dissenters* (Oxford University Press, 1985). Watts was a reader in modern history at University of Nottingham. Watt's remarks that the Baptist historian held at one time the view that the Baptists originated in the Lollards, though later, dropped the view (page 14). Watts noted the strongest evidence for linking the Lollards to the Anabaptists is geographical (page 13). Also see his comments advocating Lollardy and the Anabaptists being linked on page 7. Watts was familiar with the work of W H Summers (page 469), from whom he quotes. Modern academic research, independent from the Baptists, does confirm a link between the Lollards and Anabaptists, both who never used those names. It also disproves the much claimed modernist Baptist claim that John Smith founded the Baptists, an error too often followed by secular historians. For an example of this error, please see the *Oxford Dictionary of the Christian Church*, ed. F L Cross and E A Livingstone, 2nd ed. (1987). This standard reference work, under "Baptists" stated, quite incorrectly, that the first Baptist church in England was in 1612, under Thomas Helwys.

[14]Arthur Geoffrey Dickens, *Lollards and Protestants in the Diocese of York, 1509-58* (Oxford University Press, 1959)11.

[15]Watts, *The Dissenters* 8.

[16]John A. F. Thomson, *The Later Lollards, 1414-1520* (Oxford University Press, 1965) 241.

[17]Thomson 5f.

[18]James Gairdner, *Lollardy and Reformation in England, An Historical Survey*, vol. 1 (1908) 73. John A. F. Thomson, *The Later Lollards 1414-1520* (Oxford University Press, 1965) 4. William Henry Summers, *The Lollards Of The Chiltern Hills: Glimpses Of English Dissent In The Middle Ages* (1906) 50. Gilbert Burnet, late Lord Bishop of Sarum, *The History of the Reformation of the Church of England,* vol. 1 (Oxford University Press, 1860) 53.

[19]FD Matthew, *The Trial of Richard Wyche* (1890). Herbert B. Workman, MA, D.Lit, DD., "The age of Wycliffe," *The Dawn of the Reformation*, vol. 1(1933) 309-310. 1933.

[20]Herbert B . Workman, MA, D.Lit, DD., "The age of Hus," *The Dawn of the Reformation*, vol. 2 (1933) 147-9.

[21]Thomas Crosby, *The History of the English Baptists*, vol. 1, (1738)14-15.

[22]John A. F. Thomson, *The Later Lollards 1414-1520* (Oxford University Press, 1965) 15.

[23] James Gairdner, *Lollardy and the Reformation in England*, vol. 1 (1908) 181.

[24] John A. F. Thomson, *The Later Lollards 1414-1520* (Oxford University Press. 1965) 148-150.

[25] F.F. Bruce, *The English Bible, A History of Translations* (1961) 135. Edward Turner, *History of the Anglo-Saxons,* vol. 3 (1851) 431. James Gairdner, *Lollardy and the Reformation in England*, vol. 1 (1908) 104.

[26] G. W. H. Lampe, ed., *The Cambridge History of the Bible, The West From The Fathers To The Reformation,* vol. 2 (Cambridge University Press, 1969) 112.

[27] *Schaff-Herzog Encyclopedia of Religious Knowledge.* vol. 1 (1891) 258.

[28] F.F. Bruce, *The English Bible, A History of Translations* (1961) 138.

[29] *The New Testament in English according to the version by John Wycliffe,* about 1380, revised by John Purvey about 1388. (Clarendon Press: Oxford, 1879).

[30] George Stokes, *The Lollards* (1838) 31.

[31] *The New Testament in English according to the version by John Wycliffe*, about 1380, revised by John Purvey about 1388 (Clarendon Press: Oxford, 1879).

[32] G H Orchard, *A History of the Baptists in England, from the earliest days of the Christian dispensation to the present time,* vol. 2 (1855) 127. George Stokes, *The Lollards* (1838) 3. William Henry Summers, *The Lollards Of The Chiltern Hills: Glimpses Of English Dissent In The Middle Ages* (1906) 28.

[33] John Mocket Cramp, D.D., *Baptist History: From The Foundation Of The Christian Church To The Close Of The Eighteenth Century* (1871) 117. Cramp was highly regarded, particularly by Charles Spurgeon. His history still remains published.

[34] G. W. H. Lampe, ed., *The Cambridge History of the Bible, The West From The Fathers To The Reformation*, vol. 2, (Cambridge University Press, 1969) 400.

8

CHURCHES OF CHRIST IN THE
1400 AND EARLY 1500s

Salute one another with an holy kiss, the churches of Christ salute you (Romans 16:16).

Lollards and baptism, Old Lollard - New Anabaptist!

Arguments continue as to whether the Lollards denied infant baptism.[1] Fox, the martyrologist, being a Presbyterian and hence a believer in infant baptism, has denied Lollard beliefs on believers' baptism. The famous Lollard, Simon Fish, for example, who wrote a rarely mentioned book on believers' baptism, *The Summe*, remains largely unknown even to those who have researched this subject. Others of Fish's circle of close friends and brethren included William Tyndale, James Bainham and John Frith. All held to believers' baptism and wrote on the subject, but Foxe fails to mention this although he must have known, especially as he interviewed the widow of Fish and Bainham. Simon Fish, John Frith, James Bainham and William Tyndale will be discussed in a later chapter.

Lollards being executed by burning.

In the 1500s, the idea of proof of church succession from the apostolic Church was of great importance to the reformers. The church in the wilderness, the Lollards and Waldensians, would suit this purpose. Any clear statements that they denied infant baptism would be denied, but, as with any fraud, traces remain that they did deny original sin and, hence, did not baptise infants but practised believers' baptism. Infant baptism is pagan lustration. Both the Lollards and Waldensians objected to Romish ceremonies and doctrines; naturally these would have included original sin and infant baptism. Practise of infant baptism would have required their using Holy Water, which only the Romish Church had. Whilst some malcontents within the Romish fellowship may have been accused of Lollardy or Waldensian beliefs, these people do not concern us.

Prior to the rise of the Anabaptists, in the same locations in Europe where the Waldensian heresies were propagated, up to 200,000 were condemned to death in witchcraft trials, in areas where the Waldensians and later Anabaptists were most numerous. There can be no question that one of the accusations against Christians in the Middle Ages was that of witchcraft (demonology) for which the penalty was death. The subject of the churches of Christ known as the Waldensians, Lollards and later Anabaptists, who were falsely accused of witchcraft, merits a volume on this subject. A holocaust took place in Europe over several centuries and the victims were mainly Christians or their families. Luther himself in his persecution of Christians made accusations of demonic indwelling. According to the Romish doctors, those most at risk were un-baptised children, and cures against witchcraft included the Cross and Holy Water. When the witchhunts began in earnest in the twelfth century, Europe was still coming out of paganism and was still very superstitious.

The Romish Church was not infrequently frustrated in debates with the "heretics"; the heretics had an infuriating habit of winning. Witchcraft accusations and condemnations resulted in the immediate burning without proper trials of those whom the Roman Catholics and later Protestants accused. This had an advantage; if no case was presented, there could be no challenge and defence, and, consequently, no debates were lost. There was an advantage in forgoing the formality of holding a trial and the resulting debate where scripture could be used to determine Biblical authority.

The following pages are excerpted from Phillip Schaff's *History of the Christian Church*. We will let him inform us of this sad affair.

> At no point does the belief and experience of our own age differ so widely from the Middle Ages as in the activity of the devil and the realm of evil spirits. The subject has already been touched upon under monasticism and the future state, but no history of the period would be complete which did not give it separate treatment. For the belief that the satanic kingdom is let loose upon mankind was more influential than the spirit of monasticism, or than the spirit which carried on the Crusades. The credulity of monk and people and the theology of the Schoolmen

peopled the earth and air with evil spirits. The writings of popular authors teem with tales of their personal appearance and malignant agency, and the scholastic definitions are nowhere more precise and careful than in the department of satanology. After centuries of Christian culture, a panic seized upon Europe in the first half of the thirteenth century about the agency of such spirits, a panic which continued powerfully to influence opinion far beyond the time of the Reformation. The persecution to which it led, was one of the most merciless forms of cruelty ever practised. The pursuit and execution of witches constitute a special chapter in the history, but it is not fully opened till the fifteenth century. Here belong the popular and scholastic conceptions of the devil and his agency before the witch-craze set in.

The sources from which the Middle Ages derived their ideas of the demonic world were the systems of classical antiquity, the Norse mythology, and the Bible as interpreted by Augustine and Gregory the Great. In its wildest fancies on the subject, the mediaeval theology was only following these two greater authorities.

The general term for the dark arts, that is, the arts which were supposed to be under the control of satanic agency, was *maleficium* (Latin term) meaning mischief, or harmful magic, a term inherited from the Romans. The special names were magic, sorcery, necromancy, divination, and witchcraft. Astrology, after some hesitation, was included in the same list.

The popular belief is set forth by such writers as Peter Damiani, Peter the Venerable, Caesar of Heisterbach, Jacob of Voragine, Thomas of Chantimpré, Etienne de Bourbon, and the French writers of poetry. Even the

English writers, Walter Map and John of Salisbury, both travelled men and, as we would say, men of the world (from whom we might have expected other things), accepted, with slight modification, the popular views. Map treats Ceres, Bacchus, Pan, the satyr, the dryads, and the fauns as demons, and John discusses in six chapters the pestiferous familiarity of demons and men—*pestifera familiaritas daemonum et hominum.*

The wildest popular conceptions of the agency of evil spirits are confirmed by the theological definitions of Peter the Lombard, Albertus Magnus, Bonaventura, Thomas Aquinas, and other Schoolmen. According to the mediaeval theology, the devil is at the head of a realm of demons who are divided into prelacies and hierarchies like the good angels.

The region into which the devil and his angels were cast down was the tenebrous air. There, in the pits of darkness, he and his followers are preserved until the day of final judgment. Their full degree of torment will not be meted out to them till then. In the meantime, they are permitted to trouble and torment men. For this view such passages as Matt. 8:29 and Luke 8:31 are quoted.

In defining the mental power and the influence of evil spirits, Thomas Aquinas and the other Schoolmen follow Augustine closely, although in elaboration they go beyond him. The demons did not lose their intellectual keenness by their fall. This keenness and long experience give them power to foretell the future. If astronomers, said Albertus Magnus, foresee future events by the natal constellations, much more may demons through their shrewdness in observation and watching the stars. Their predictions, however, differ from the predictions of the prophets by being the product of the light of nature. The prophets received a divine revelation.

The mind of Europe did not become seriously exercised on the subject of demonic possession until after heresy made its appearance and the measures to blot it out were in an advanced stage. The Fourth Lateran did not mention the dark arts, and its failure to do so can only be explained on the ground that the mind of Christendom was not yet aroused. It was not long, however, before violent incursions of the powers of darkness, as they were supposed to be, rudely awakened the Church, and from the time of Gregory IX. The agency of evil spirits and heresy were closely associated. In one of his deliverances against the Stedinger (Frieslanders who were poor people, who rejected the Romish Church), this pope vouched for the belief that heretics consulted witches, held communion with demons, and indulged in orgies with them and the devil who, as he said, met with them in the forms of a great toad and black cat. Were the stars in heaven and the elements to combine for the destruction of such people without reference to their age or sex, it would be an inadequate punishment.

After 1250 the persecution of heretics for doctrinal error diminishes and the trials for sorcery, witchcraft, and other demonic iniquity become frequent. In the bull, *ad exstirpanda*, 1252, Innocent IV called upon princes to treat heretics as though they were sorcerers, and in 1258 Alexander IV, spoke of sorcerers as savoring of heresy. Before this, magic and sorcery had come exclusively under the jurisdiction of the state.

At this juncture came the endorsement of Thomas Aquinas and his great theological contemporaries. There was nothing left for the ecclesiastical and civil authorities to do but to ferret out sorcerers, witches, and all who had habitual secret dealings with the devil. A craze seized upon the Church to clear the Christian world of imaginary armies of evil spirits, demonizing men and especially women. Pope after pope issued orders not to spare those who were in league with the devil, but to put them to torture and cast them into the flames. The earliest trials for sorcery by the Inquisition were held in Southern France about 1250, and the oldest Interrogatories of the Inquisition on the subject date twenty-five years later. These prosecutions reached their height in the fifteenth century, and the papal fulminations found their ultimate expression in the bull of Innocent VIII, against witches, 1484.

Men like Albertus Magnus and Roger Bacon were popularly charged with being wizards. Bacon, enlightened beyond his age, pronounced some of the popular beliefs delusions, but, far from denying the reality of sorcery and magic, he tried to explain the efficacy of spells and charms by their being made at seasons when the heavens were propitious. Perhaps no chapter in human history is more revolting than the chapter which records the wild belief in witchcraft and the merciless punishments meted out for it in Western Europe in the century just preceding the Protestant Reformation and the succeeding century.

In the second half of that century, the Church and society were thrown into a panic over witchcraft, and Christendom seemed to be suddenly infested with a great company of bewitched people, who yielded themselves to the irresistible discipline of Satan. The mania spread from Rome and Spain to Bremen and Scotland. Popes, lawyers, physicians and ecclesiastics of every grade yielded their assent, and the only voices lifted up in protest which have come down to us from the Middle Ages were the voices of victims who were subjected to torture and perished in the flames. No Reformer uttered a word against it. On the contrary, Luther was a stout believer in the reality of demonic agency, and pronounced its adepts deserving of the flames. Calvin allowed the laws of Geneva against it to stand. Bishop Jewel's sermon before Queen Elizabeth in 1562 was perhaps the immediate occasion of a new law on the subject. Richard Baxter proved the reality of witchcraft in his *Certainty of the World of Spirits* (1691). On the shores of New England the delusion had its victims, at Salem, 1692, and a century later, 1768, John Wesley, referring to occurrences in his own time, declared that "giving up witchcraft was, in effect, giving up the Bible."

But it is not till the 15th century that the era of witchcraft properly begins. From about 1430 it was treated as a distinct cult, carefully defined and made the subject of many treatises. The punishments to be meted out for it were carefully laid down, as also the methods by which witches should be detected and tried. The cases were no longer sporadic and exceptional; they were regarded as being a guild or sect marshaled by Satan to destroy faith from the earth.

It is probable that the responsibility for the spread of the wild witch mania rests chiefly with the popes. Pope after pope countenanced and encouraged the belief. Not a single utterance emanated from a pope to discourage it. Side by side with the papal utterances went the authoritative statements of the Schoolmen. Leaning upon Augustine, Thomas Aquinas (d. 1274), accepted as real the cohabitation of human beings with demons, and declared that old women had the power by the glance of their eye of injecting into young people a certain evil essence. If the horrible beliefs of the Middle Ages on the subject of witchcraft are to be set aside, then the bulls of Leo XIII. and Pius X, pronouncing Thomas the authoritative guide of Catholic theology must be modified. The definitions of the Schoolmen justified the demand which papal deliverances made, that the Church tribunal has at least equal jurisdiction with the tribunal of the state in ferreting out and prosecuting the adepts of the dark arts. Manuals of procedure in cases of sorcery used by the Inquisition date back at least to 1270. The famous Interrogatory of Bernard Guy of 1320 contains formulas on the subject. The canonists, however, had difficulty in defining the point at which *maleficium* became a capital crime. Oldradus, professor of canon law in turn at Bologna, Padua and Avignon, sought, about 1325, to draw a precise distinction between the two, and gave the opinion that, only when sorcery savors strongly of heresy, should it be dealt with as heresy was dealt with, the position assumed before by Alexander IV, 1258–1260. The final step was taken when Eymericus, in his Inquisitorial Directory and special tracts, 1370–1380, affirmed the close affinity between *maleficium* and heresy, and threw the door wide open for the most rigorous measures against malefics.

The burning of witches was thus declared the definite policy of the papal see and the inquisitors proceeded to carry out its instructions with untiring and merciless severity. The *Witches Hammer*, published in 1486, proceeded from the hands of the Dominican Inquisitors, Heinrich Institoris, whose German name was Kraemer, and Jacob Sprenger. The plea cannot be made that they were uneducated men. They occupied high positions in their order and at the University of Cologne. Their book is divided into three parts: the first proves the existence of witchcraft; the second sets forth the forms in which it manifested itself; the third describes the rules for its detection and prosecution. In the last quarter of the 15th century the world, so it states, was more given over to the devil than in any preceding age. It was flooded with all kinds of wickedness. In affirming the antics of witches and other malefics, appeal is made to the Scriptures and to the teachings of the Church and especially to Augustine and Thomas Aquinas. Witches and sorcerers, whose father is the devil, are at last bound together in an organized body or sect. They meet at the weekly sabbats and do the devil homage by kissing his posterior parts. He appears among them as a tom-cat, goat, dog, bull or black man, as whim and convenience suggest. Demons of both sexes swarm at the meetings. Baptism and the eucharist are subjected to ridicule, the cross trampled upon. After an abundant repast the lights are extinguished and, at the devil's command 'Mix, mix,' there follow scenes of unutterable lewdness. The devil, however, is a strict disciplinarian and applies the whip to refractory members.

The human members of the fraternity are instructed in all sorts of arts. They are transported through the air. They kill unbaptized children, keeping them in this way out of heaven. At the sabbats such children are eaten. Of the carnal intercourse, implied in the words *succubus* and *incubus*, the authors say, there can be no doubt. To quote them, "it is common to all sorcerers and witches to practice carnal lust with demons."

Among the precautions which the book prescribed against being bewitched, are the Lord's Prayer, the cross, holy water and salt and the Church formulas of exorcism. It also adds that inner grace is a preservative. Other devilish performances dwelt upon, were the murder of children before baptism, the eating of their flesh after it had been consecrated to the devil and the trampling upon the host. One woman, in 1457, confessed she had been guilty of the last practice 30 years.

The popularity of the witch-delusion as a subject of literary treatment is shown by the extracts Hansen gives from 70 writings, without exhausting the list. Most of the writers were Dominicans. The *Witches Hammer* was printed in many editions, issued 13 times before 1520 and, from 1574–1669, 16 times.

The prosecution of witches assumed large proportions first in Switzerland and Northern Italy and then in France and Germany. In Rome, the first reported burning was in 1424. In the diocese of Como, Northern Italy, 41 were burnt the year after the promulgation of Innocent VIII's bull. Between 1500–1525 the yearly number of women tried in that district was 1,000 and the executions averaged 100. In 1521, Prierias declared that the Apennine regions were so full of witches that they were expected soon to outnumber the faithful.

In France, one of the chief victims, the Carmelite William Adeline, was professor in Paris and had taken part in the Council of Basel. Arraigned by the Inquisition, 1453, he confessed to being a Waldensian, and having habitually attended their synagogues and done homage to the devil. In spite of his abjurations, he was kept in prison where he died. In Briançon, 1428–1447, 110 women and 57 men were executed for witchcraft in the flames or by drowning.

In Germany, Heidelberg, Pforzheim, Nürnberg, Würzburg, Bamberg, Vienna, Cologne, Metz and other cities were centres of the craze and witnessed many executions. It was during the five years preceding 1486 that Heinrich

Institoris and Sprenger sent 48 to the stake. The Heidelberg court-preacher, Matthias Widman, of Kemnat, pronounced the "Cathari or heretical witches" the most damnable of the sects, one which should be subjected to "abundance of fire and without mercy." He reports that witches rode on broomsticks, spoons, cats, goats and other objects, and that he had seen many of them burnt in Heidelberg. In 1540, six years before Luther's death, four witches and sorcerers were burnt in Protestant Wittenberg. And in 1545, 34 women were burnt or quartered in Geneva. In England the law for the burning of heretics, 1401, was applied to these unfortunate people, not a few of whom were committed to the flames. But the persecution in the mediaeval period never took on the proportions on English soil it reached on the Continent; and there, it was not the Church but the state that dealt with the crime of sorcery.

According to the estimate of Louis of Paramo, himself a distinguished inquisitor of Sicily who had condemned many to the flames, there had been during the 150 years before 1597, the date of his treatise on the *Origin and Progress of the Inquisition*, 30,000 executions for witchcraft. The judgments passed upon witches were whipping, banishment and death by fire, or, as in Cologne, Strassburg and other places, by drowning. The most common forms of torture were the thumb-screw and the strappado. In the latter the prisoner's hands were bound behind his back with a rope which was drawn through a pulley in the ceiling. The body was slowly lifted up, and at times left hanging or allowed to suddenly drop to the floor. In our modern sense, there was no protection of law for the accused. The suspicion of an ecclesiastical or civil court was sufficient to create an almost insurmountable presumption of guilt. Made frantic by the torture, the victims were willing to confess to anything, however untrue and repulsive it might be. Death at times must have seemed, even with the Church's ban, preferable to protracted agonies, for the pains of death at best lasted a few hours and might be reduced to a few minutes. As Lecky has said, these unfortunate people did not have before them the prospect of a martyr's crown and the glory of the heavenly estate. They were not buoyed up by the sympathies and prayers of the Church. Un-pitied and un-prayed for, they yielded to the cold scrutiny of the inquisitor and were consumed in the flames.

Persons who took the part of the supposed witch, or ventured to lift up their voices against the trials for witchcraft, did so at the risk of their lives. In 1598, the Dutch priest, Cornelius Loos Callidus, was imprisoned at Treves for declaring that women, making confession under torture to witch devices, confessed to what was not true. And four years before, 1589, Dr. Dietrich Flade, a councillor of Treves, was burnt for attacking the prosecution of witchcraft.

One of the victims wrote from his prison-cell, the burgomaster of Bamberg, Bavaria, Germany, which was Protestant. Though he suffered a century after the Middle Ages had closed, 1628. After being confronted by false witnesses he confessed, under torture, to having indulged in the practices ascribed to the bewitched and he thus wrote to his daughter:

> Many hundred good nights, dearly beloved daughter, Veronica. Innocent have I come into prison, innocent must I die. For whoever comes into a witch-prison must become a witch or be tortured till he invents something out of his head and—God pity him—bethinks himself

of something. I will tell you how it has gone with me. Then came the executioner and put the thumbscrews on me, both hands bound together, so that the blood ran out at the nails and everywhere, so that for four weeks I could not use my hands, as you can see from the writing. Then they stripped me, bound my hands behind my back and drew me up. I thought heaven and earth were at an end. Eight times did they do this and let me drop again so that I suffered terrible agony (Here follows a rehearsal of the confessions he was induced to make). Now, dear child, you have all my confessions for which I must die. They are sheer lies made up. All this I was forced to say through fear of the rack, for they never leave off the torture till one confesses something. Dear child, keep this letter secret so that people may not find it or else I shall be tortured most piteously and the jailers be beheaded. I have taken several days to write this for my hands are both lame. Good night, for your father Johannes Junius will never see you more.

To give an insight into the thinking of secular and religious prosecutors, in the 1400s one charge made against the wives of men who were evangelising was the accusation of witchcraft. When the women were seen and reported by witnesses flying on their broomsticks, they were burned alive after the most basic of trials, where they were not allowed, because of their witchcraft, to produce a defence. Thus women, wives of gospel preachers, died for something clearly they could not do. Witchcraft trials of the Middle

Ages were most numerous where the gospel was being preached and converts made. As recently as 1926, the Catholic theologian, Montague Summers (1880-1948) defended the above by stating that there is a "close correlation between witchcraft and heresy." He states that the Bogomiles, Cathari, Paulicians, Vaudois, Waldenses and Albigenenses are not only charged with being Gnostics and Manichees, saturated with sorcery, witchcraft and revolutionary aims, but that "heresy, sorcery and anarchy were almost interchangeable terms."

In 1453, Guillaume Edelin confessed to being a witch (under torture) and claimed to have rode around on a broomstick. This became (under torture) a popular confession especially when witnesses could be produced. The more witches that were discovered, under torture, the more witches that were revealed. The task for the witch hunters was never ending; the harder they worked, the more they found. The more people that confessed under torture, the more that were arrested, and so it never ended. Children as young as four were put to torture. Nicholas Remy (1530-1612), Procurator General for Loraine, was responsible for the deaths of nine hundred witches. He even had one sixteen year old boy crucified for stealing, after the lad had been previously warned and whipped.

Henri Boguet, an eminent judge of Saint-Claude in the Jura Mountains (1550–1619), presided at witchcraft trials. He was famous for his cruelty, especially toward children. He had no doubt that Satan gifted witches with the ability to change shape into a variety of animal forms, especially the wolf, so that they might devour humans, and the cat, so they might better prowl by night. In his book *Discours des Sorciers* (1610), Boguet recounted his official investigation of a family of werewolves and his observation of them while they were in prison in 1584. According to his testimony, the members of the Gandillon family walked on all fours and howled like wolves. Their eyes turned red and gleaming; their hair sprouted; their teeth became long and sharp; their fingernails turned horny and clawlike. In another case recounted in his book, Boguet told of eight-year-old Louise Maillat, who in the summer of 1598 was possessed by five demons, who identified themselves as Wolf, Cat, Dog, Jolly, and Griffon. In addition, the little girl was accused of shapeshifting into the form of a wolf.

The Lutheran Judge, Benedict Carpzov (1595-1666), in 1635 published his *Practica Rerum Criminalum* to support systematic prosecution of witches. On his order, 20,000 death warrants for the arrest, torture and execution of German witches were issued. Even Carpzov, a man of "reason," argued that under the most excruciating torture, witches were likely to give a false account, but it should still be employed. This reformed Lutheran read the Bible, cover to cover over fifty-three times and took the Lutheran Mass each week.

The Reformers and Catholics missed no tricks in hunting down witches. They were masters of the art of torture and were exemplary in carrying out their trade at every opportunity. The witchfinder's power was almost unlimited. These diligent hunters would whip young children in front of their parents who were being burned to death. In Wurzburg, Germany, three hundred children, some as young as three confessed to engaging in sexual intercourse with demons. Many considered the minimum age of seven for execution unduly lenient.

When a decree was passed protecting girls under twelve from execution, the authorities knew how to be patient. Anne Hauldecoeur, who was aged seven, from Bouchain (northern France) confessed to being a witch (under torture). She was placed in prison on 1 September 1614; she was twelve on 11 July 1619, the day of her execution.

The number executed over 300 years in Europe has been estimated at 200,000. This served another purpose. Disasters in general, plague, crop and livestock failure in a fearful and superstitious society could be blamed on witchcraft. So, two advantages were gained, ridding "heresy" from Europe and increasing the need for the Roman Catholic Church to rid the witches. It was an instrument of terror. Eighty percent of those who died were women. And the areas in which they died were where the church of Christ could be found.

This disproportion is because women were more easily dispatched, without lengthy legal proceedings, as witches, while their men-folk were prosecuted and burned for heresy, more of a lengthy process.

The church is too often charged with barbaric acts, the persecutions and witch burnings in the Middle Ages in Europe. Yes, these acts were barbaric, amounting to genocide, but the perpetrators were not Christians. Their victims often were. Witches and witchcraft are in origin pagan; the cure too was pagan. There was nothing Christian in the persecution and punishment, but like the Roman Catholic system, the whole witchcraft system was based on paganism.[2]

At first John Calvin (*Jean Cauvin*; 1509–1564) had some sympathy for the church. His wife, Idelette von Buhren, was the widow of a member of the church of Christ.[3] From his early association with church of Christ he learned much, including church discipline. But he was an ardent believer in the "national church," so believers' baptism and congregational autonomy had no place in his scheme. He would attack the church of Christ ruthlessly.[4]

One charge against the witches was that they refused to baptise their children. Baptist historian, John Cramp, says of the Lollards:

> Some of them, perhaps the majority, opposed infant baptism.
> Indeed, it is expressly affirmed by several historians, that
> they refused to baptise their new-born children and that

they were charged before the ecclesiastical authorities with maintaining that infants who died unbaptised would be saved. This was an unpardonable sin in the eyes of the Romish Church, and the Lollards suffered grievously for it, often as witches in continental Europe.[5]

Lollards, under interrogation and torture, would be asked if they baptised infants. The issue of baptism repeats itself time and again. Our immediate witness for the Lollards prior to Simon Fish and his brethren in the 1530s is, unfortunately, their enemy, the Roman Catholic Church. It does not help that accounts are second and third-hand. Church historians too often have an agenda; in the case of Reformed historians, they needed a line of church succession back to the apostle Peter. As they could not use the Romish Church, for obvious reasons, they looked to Lollards and the Waldensians as the faithful church in the dark ages. But they needed a church that baptised infants and held to human depravity (original sin or predestination). This certainly helps to explain why those names of derision disappear suddenly with the reformation and the invention of a new derisory name—Anabaptist—springs up, where previously the Lollards and Waldensians were active. Amongst twentieth century historians of church history, John Thomson notes the indication of heretical traditions in Tenderden, Kent, the Chilterns and Bristol of the same beliefs over different periods of time rather than isolated outbreaks of unorthodoxy. Irvin Horst wrote that "it is striking to discover how generally Anabaptist supplanted Lollard as the name for English nonconformity from about 1530 until the end of Mary's reign (1558).[6] Reformed historians dispute whether Lollards and Waldensians withheld their children from baptism. Yet the witchcraft hunts over three centuries sought out people withholding their children from baptism in the places the Lollards and Waldensians were the most active.

Fox's and other historians' garbled account of Lollard beliefs regarding baptism is worth looking at. The Baptist historian, G. H. Orchard, in 1885/7 writes (the account is found elsewhere, but Orchard serves our purpose):

> Their enemies assert, continues Fox, that the Lollards here held that the sacrament of baptism used in the church is of slight importance; they also spoke against the christenings which the midwives used in private houses; against the opinions of such who think children to be damned who depart before they come to their baptism; that Christian people be baptised sufficiently in the blood of Christ and have no need of water for salvation.

The date of this account is 1428.[7] Let us look at this account of their beliefs, most likely gained under torture nearly six hundred years ago.

The Lollards disagree about the baptism of the Romish Church, but it is not mentioned with what they disagree. It has to be infant baptism; as all parties did not object to believers' baptism, the fault cannot be there. Then christenings by midwives were also rejected. In an era of high infant mortality, midwives were allowed to baptise children who were in peril of dying when a priest might well arrive too late, or was unavailable. For Lollards to have objected to this, they must have denied original sin (and infant baptism). The most interesting comment is that "Christian people be baptised sufficiently in the blood of Christ and have no need of water for salvation." This at first glance sounds plausible if you deny salvation in baptism, holding to reformed theology, but is this what they meant?

In the time period concerned, Roman Catholic baptism removed inherited original sin by the power of the Holy Water. Call it magic or superstition, the power was in the water, which was owned by the Romish Church. It is the pagan system that the Romish Church held to, and still holds to this day. If we agree the account is garbled, the only way it makes sense is that the water being denied is the Holy Water of the Romish Church. Holy Water removes sin from any object and was used to baptise new boats, church bells and other items as well as infants. Sprinkle it at anything and everything and the demons flee! With regard to "blood washing" as it was later called, notice that reference is not to the blood of dead martyrs, but the blood of Christ.

Simon Fish, William Tyndale and John Frith wrote that baptism for believers works through the blood of Christ, not Holy Water, that any water would suffice, quoting Revelation 1:5 as the proof text for this: "And from Jesus Christ, who is the faithful witness, and the first begotten of the dead, and the prince of the kings of the earth. Unto him that loved us, and washed us from our sins in his own blood." This washing took place in baptism for those who believed, having faith in Jesus and repentance. The power of water to remit sin was not in the water, but in the blood of Christ, which we contact in the watery grave of baptism after repenting of sin (Acts 2:38, Rom. 6).

The term "blood washing" continued in use into the 1640s when Henry Denne, in an argument with Daniel Featley, accused him of calling baptism for the remission of sins "Bloud washing," Denne quoting both Revelation 1:5 and Revelation 7:14.[8]

The Anabaptists, both in England and Europe denied the saving power of water. For them, water was just water. This too dismayed Martin Luther.[9] John Oyer stated the Anabaptists rejected infant baptism on the scriptural sequence of faith preceding baptism quoting Mark 16:16.[10] Like the later Lollards of England, this became a standard text in defence of believers' baptism. Not only does this verse deny infant baptism, it affirms believers' baptism and the preaching of the word, the gospel agency in conversion. Luther understood this perfectly well and denied it.

In 1443, Thomas Bikemore, who lived in the Lollard area of Oxford and Windsor, was examined by the authorities and found to hold the views that the Pope was Antichrist, the Romish Church the beast of the Apocalypse with the religious orders its tail. He denied the sacraments of baptism and confirmation, arguing that children have grace. He stated the church was the congregation of the saved. Confession should be to God. He denied marriage as needing solemnising in church. He denied Extreme Unction, denied that the bread is the actual body of Christ, pilgrimages, fasting at Lent, celibacy of the clergy, said that tithes and offerings were unlawful. He also stated the glosses on scriptures by Augustine, Ambrose, Gregory and Jerome and other doctors of the Romish Church should not be held in repute. He was also pacifist in his beliefs. He was a preacher and, as noted, was active in the Lollard areas and would have had contact with the nearby Lollard communities of the Chilterns.[11] His beliefs do not seem to differ from those of the Waldensian, Lollard and Anabaptist congregations which met in the same areas, from the 1100s to the 1700s, before becoming (incorrectly) termed General Baptist.

The excitement caused by the early reformation resulted in discussions with Luther, and for a while he was popular with the churches of Christ, his books being distributed and disseminated widely. This has certainly led to some members of the churches of Christ, named Lollards, being identified as Lutherans. As Luther developed his theology to include infant baptism and the national church, the two parties drifted apart. Churches of Christ did for a time take part in the early reformation, which continued until the reformers refused to restore the church staying with the traditions of the early Roman Catholic Church. Dogmatism, i.e., a rejection of the New Testament pattern established by Biblical authority, returned and was again forced by coercion onto Christians by use of the old methods of terror.

Initially the involvement of Luther with Andreas Carlstadt may have given the impression that the reformation was going to be far more radical than it was. Andreas Bodenstein (usually known as Carlstadt) by 1534 had joined the faculty at the University of Basel. Once professor of Biblical studies at Wittenberg, Carlstadt became involved in radical changes (congregational autonomy, believers' baptism, etc.) which brought him into conflict with Luther. In May 1523, Carlstadt had been invited by the church of Orlamunde to be its minister, which office he accepted. Here he instituted his radical reforms. Church music and art was set aside, clerical matrimony was preached, and infant baptism as well as transubstantiation rejected. For Luther, this was far too radical.[12] Carlstadt was set on restoration of the first century church using Biblical authority for practise, not reformation of the Romish Church where earlier rites and traditions were retained.

When a national church elects power to interpret scripture,

this will result in the doctors and theologians of that church interpreting through their own schemes. They will go no further back than Augustine and fourth century theology. Those doctors and theologians are far from honest, being part of the secular power of whatever country they live in. They will work hand in glove with the authorities to the extent that the secular power decides and enforces doctrine in the church. In other words, rather than Christ being the Head of the Church, the called-out, the world rules the church where every man is added by infant baptism. For evidence ne need look no further than the Anglican and Episcopalian Churches, where the Monarch of the United Kingdom sits as Governor, where women are being considered for the role of bishop, homosexuality and fornication promoted and other faiths that deny Christ as the Son of God fellowshipped. Such comes about through a lack of establishing Biblical authority in spiritual matters.

All the reformers stood firm on infant baptism. Christians, on the other hand taught that an active belief, faith and repentance preceded baptism. It was here the identifying mark for tracking down heretics was shared. Thousands died at the hands of the Protestant reformers across Europe for practising Christianity as described in the scriptures. The reformers were united in stipulating, despite their claim of *sola scriptura*, that the church should interpret scripture, just as was claimed by the Roman Catholic Church. Rather than allowing scripture to interpret scripture, the various denominations would determine through their own creeds and tradition, what scripture teaches, contradicting their own reformation ideal of *sola scriptura*. The ideal that the reformation could in time reproduce the church of the first century never developed, it was opposed. The need to look beyond reformation for restoration was apparent in that period as it was before. To have fellowship with Christ it is necessary to obey Christ.

> He that hath my commandments, and keepeth them, he it is that loveth me: and he that loveth me shall be loved of my Father, and I will love him, and will manifest myself to him. Judas saith unto him, not Iscariot, Lord, how is it that thou wilt manifest thyself unto us, and not unto the world? Jesus answered and said unto him, If a man love me, he will keep my words: and my Father will love him, and we will come unto him, and make our abode with him. He that loveth me not keepeth not my sayings: and the word which ye hear is not mine, but the Father's which sent me (John 14:21-24).

Dover, in Kent (England) is just a little over twenty miles across the English channel from Calais, France. To the north is London, making it ideal for communication with the continent and the capital. It was in Kent that Lord Cobham had his school to prepare men to preach the Gospel in the 1400s. Lollardy had long been associated with Kent. Movement was easy both ways to and from the continent between Amsterdam in Holland, Colchester, London and the Kent churches. These Christians, to avoid persecution, would flee to, and return from, any of the above.

On 29th April, 1511, six years before the Reformation, Luther nailing his "Ninety-five Theses of Religion" to the church door at Wittenberg, William Carder of Tenterden, Kent was indicted of heresy on a number of counts, listed below, including that "it was enough to pray to almighty God alone, and therefore we needed not to pray to saints for any mediation."

On May 2, 1511, six men and four women from Tenterden stood trial before William Warham, Archbishop of Canterbury. The hearing was held at the Archbishop's Mansion at Knoll (modern spelling Knole), where today Knole Hall stands, near Sevenoaks (where seven oak trees once stood), Kent.

The indictments were (modern spelling):

1 - That in the sacrament of the altar is not the body of Christ, but material bread.

2 - That the sacrament of baptism and confirmation are not necessary, or profitable for men's souls.

3 - That confession of sins ought not to be made to a priest.

4 - That there is no more power given by God to a priest than to a layman.

5 - That the solemnization of matrimony (by a priest) is not profitable or necessary for the well-being of a man's soul.

6 - That the sacrament of extreme unction is not profitable or necessary to a man's soul.

7 - That pilgrimages to holy and devout places are neither profitable, nor meritorious for man's soul.

8 - That images of saints are not to be worshipped.

9 - That a man should pray to no saint, but only to God.

10 -That holy water, and holy bread, are not the better after the benediction made by the priest, than before.

Indictment two - "That the sacrament of baptism and confirmation are not necessary, or profitable for men's souls," is ample evidence that these people had rejected the Roman Catholic rite of infant baptism.

The other indictments confirm that they had rejected the Roman Catholic Church and its errors. All were found guilty, sentenced, and abjured their opinions, under condition that they would inform on any others that held the same views. Alice Grevill, who had been a member of the church at Tenterden for twenty-eight years, was condemned to death after refusing to abjure. Her husband and two sons had appeared as witnesses against her. Her confession of her membership of the Tenterden church dates the church back to 1483.

Matters progressed quickly. On the 15th of May four men and a woman abjured at Lambeth (London) and on the 19th four more men abjured. On 3rd June, a man and women abjured and on the 26th another woman, on the 29th July two women, on 2nd August a man and on the 3rd, a woman likewise abjured. More followed, more names were given under duress or torture. More charges of heresy were added, "That images of the crucifix of our lady and other saints, ought not to be worshiped because they are made with men's hands," and, "money and labours spent in pilgrimages were all in vain." In Kent, congregations were started in Tenderden, Feversham, Maidstone, Canterbury and Eythorne. Eythorne and Canterbury continuing to this day as Baptist churches.

Joan Bocher on conviction of heresy was executed by burning on 2nd May 1550 at Smithfield, London. She was a member at one time of the church at Eythorne and was well known in the congregations in Kent. She was also known as Joan Boucher or Butcher, or as Joan Knell or Joan of Kent.

Joan's friendship with Anne Askew became well known; also their involvement in smuggling William Tyndale's New Testament into Kent from the London Bow Lane congregation. Anne Askew had even taken the Tyndale's New Testament into the Royal Court, under her skirts. The Bible being banned it was a brave move to distribute the scriptures in such a high profile environment where enemies and spies were plentiful.

If not earlier, by the 1520s the Churches of Christ in Kent and London were in fellowship, despite persecutions, burnings and imprisonments for the next one hundred and fifty years.[13] Anne Askew was from a well-known Lincolnshire family. Her father,

Sir William, forced her to marry a Roman Catholic at fifteen. Her marriage did not work and she left to go "gospelling." Her husband, a Roman Catholic was opposed to evangelical Christianity. She was charged with heresy, found guilty, carried to execution at Smithfield, London, on 16 July, 1546, in a chair as she could not walk after her torture on the rack. She was fixed by a chain to the stake, as was normal (ropes would burn through leaving the victim able to escape the fire, though badly burned). Burned with her was Nicholas Belenian, a former priest from Shropshire, John Adams, a tailor and John Lacels, a gentleman of the court of King Henry. During the execution gunpowder placed below the fagots would blow up, mercifully increasing the speed of the burning more and shortening the suffering.[14]

From Thomas Crosby (1738), who quotes from the "Dutch Martyrology," we know of Sir Lucius (Lewis) Clifford, who was arraigned as a Lollard, confessed and recanted over believers' baptism, thereby acknowledging that they opposed infant for that of believers' baptism. Unfortunately, Crosby in his account does not mention from which edition of the "Dutch Martyrology" he quoted.[15] By the 1550s, the church was well established. Burnett says "At this time there were many Anabaptists in several parts of England.... Who held that infant baptism is no baptism."[16]

Hatred of Anabaptists was further shown by excluding them

from general Acts of pardon. Such Acts were promulgated in 1538, 1540, and 1550; but those who held that "infants ought not to be baptised" were excluded from the benefit. Thieves and vagabonds shared the King's favor, but Christians who practiced believers' baptism were not to be tolerated.

Protestantism nominally flourished in the reign of Edward VI, but there were many who continued in the Romish faith keeping alive old traditions. The use of the reformed liturgy was enforced by the pains and penalties of law. Nicholas Ridley, Bishop of Rochester and later Bishop of London, himself a martyr in the next reign, was joined in commission with Bishop Stephen Gardiner, Lord Chancellor, afterwards notorious as a persecutor of Protestants, to root out Anabaptists. Among the "Articles of Visitation" issued by Ridley in his own diocese, in 1550, was the following: "Whether any of the Anabaptists' sect or other use notoriously any unlawful or private conventicles, wherein they do use doctrines or administration of sacraments, separating themselves from the rest of the parish?" It may be fairly gathered from this article that there were churches of Christ in England at that time separated from the State Church of England.

A Royal Commission was issued by Edward VI, empowering thirty-one persons therein named, Thomas Cranmer, Archbishop of Canterbury at the head and Hugh Latimer, Bishop, as one of its members, to proceed against "heretics and contemners of the Book of Common Prayer." The "wicked opinions" of the Anabaptists are specifically mentioned, and the Commissioners (or rather inquisitors, for such they were) were directed, in case the persons accused should not renounce their errors, to deliver them up to the secular power, that is, to death. Joan Boucher, or "Joan of Kent," as previously mentioned, was the first victim. She was a Christian lady, well known at Court, and very zealous in her endeavors there to introduce Christian truth. Strype the historian says:

> She was at first a great disperser of Tindal's New Testaments, translated by him into English, and printed at Colen (Cologne), and was a great reader of Scripture herself; which books she also dispersed in the Court, and so became known to certain women of quality, and was more particularly acquainted with Mrs. Anne Ascue (Anne Askew), cruelly tortured, and afterwards burned alive, in the year 1546.

Joan Boucher was burnt at Smithfield. Bishop Story preached on the occasion, and, as Strype says, "tried to convert her;" but his misrepresentations and calumnies were so gross that she told him he "lied like a rogue," and bade him "go and read the Scriptures." It was doubtless needful advice.

John Rogers, who was the first Protestant martyr in Mary's reign, approved this execution. When some unknown person remonstrated with him on the subject, and particularly urged the cruelty of the method, he replied that "burning alive was no cruel death, but easy enough." Protestant Archdeacon Philpot, in his sixth examination before the Queen's Commissioners, Nov. 6, 1555, six weeks before his own martyrdom, said, "As for Joan of Kent, she was a vain woman (I knew her well), and a heretic indeed, well worthy to be burnt."[17]

William Sawtre (or Sawtrey, Santree), was burnt alive in March 1401. He was the first Lollard martyr, his condemnation was highly controversial due to the speed and punishment. The King, Henry IV, (died in 1413) and Archbishop Arundel were at one in their opinion of the heretics. Henry upheld the church in its persecution of the Lollards, and aided the bishops to suppress them by force. The Parliament of 1401, at the special request of Arundel, the persecuting archbishop of Canterbury, passed a statute authorizing the burning of heretics, the Statute De Hoeretico Comburendo, which was the first law passed in England for the suppression of religious opinions. According to this statute, the sheriffs, mayors, and bailiffs were to carry out the sentence of the ecclesiastical court in the case of a person refusing to abjure, or who, having once abjured, had relapsed. They were to cause such persons to be burnt "in a high place that such punishment might strike fear into the minds of others." Even while this bill was before parliament, William Sawtre, vicar at Lynn, was burnt alive by command of the king. Norfolk was one of the places in England where preaching against infant baptism took place and baptizing believers was practised.

Sawtre was born in Bishop's Lynn (now Kings Lynn), Norfolk, and was rector of St Margaret's in the town. Like many others at the time, he was receptive to the message of the Lollards, opposing with others the Romish Church and its practices, which they saw as obscuring the message of Christianity. He said, "Instead of adoring the cross on which Christ suffered, I adore Christ who suffered on it." He also said that, "every priest is bound to preach", preaching in that time being a rare event and services held in Latin.

In 1399, the Bishop of Norwich questioned Sawtre on his beliefs and subsequently had him arrested and imprisoned on charges of heresy. After a time he recanted his beliefs and was released, though he felt he had betrayed Christ. Later he moved to London and preached at St. Osyth's, eventually attracting the attention of church authorities.

Thomas Arundel, Archbishop of Canterbury, summoned Sawtre to appear at St. Paul's Cathedral in London on 12 February 1401 to be questioned once again on his beliefs. His views on a number of issues (including transubstantiation and adoration of the cross) were found to be contrary to the position of the church, and he was indicted on eight counts of heresy. Arundel tried to persuade him to change his views, but Sawtre defended his position with scripture and refused to be swayed.

On 26th February 1401, Sawtre was condemned as a relapsed heretic, the punishment for which was death by burning. He was degraded (stripped of his priesthood) and given over for execution. He appealed to the King and Parliament, but both appeals were denied. In March he was burnt at the stake before a crowd at Smithfield, London, an illegal execution as the act of Hoeretico Comburendo had yet to be passed by Parliament.[18]

It may be argued that Sawtre was seeking reformation of Roman Catholic excesses and doctrines such as that of transubstantiation. Norfolk, where he was based, presented a problem for the authorities with Lollards who denied infant baptism. It was not unusual for priests in that period and later to teach against error. By the mid 1500s, some parish churches had stained glass removed, altars replaced with kitchen tables to serve the Supper, instruments removed and clergy who denied clerical office and dress. It may well have been that Sawtre was preaching the Bible and nothing else. There was no effort of a concerted reform movement at that time, but there is evidence that the Lollards were seeking to establish plain Bible teaching. After the 1660s, it would become impossible to preach the truth in Anglican Churches due to the Acts of Uniformity of 1549, 1552, 1559, 1662. Slowly the instrument, stained glass and altars would return from those dates.

*The river Cam at Chesterton today, a few
minutes walk from Cambridge.*

*Downing Place, Cambridge ,formerly Hog Hill, where
a church of Christ met in the 1600 and 1700s.*

At Chestertown (modern Chesterton), a small congregation met just a few minutes walk from Cambridge city centre. This congregation met separately from the Catholic Church in their members' homes. It consisted of six people, primarily two families. They had no separate clergy, but did have men who preached. Gray, Lord Bishop of Ely, complained in 1457 of the existence of this congregation when it came to the notice of the authorities.

A Christian being punished in the stocks, to force their penance as a "heretic."

The six of them were accused of heresy, tried, found guilty, condemned to abjure, and do penance half naked, with a faggot at their backs, and a taper in their hands, in the public marketplaces of Ely and Cambridge, and in the churchyard of Great Swaffham. The charges against them were in substance that they denied infant baptism and rejected extreme unction, and said that the pope was antichrist and his priests were devils incarnate. In the 1400s, a ferry operated for those crossing from Cambridge to Chesterton. In the mid 1700s, the manager of the ferry was Robert Robinson, the preacher of the church of Christ that met in Hog Hill, later Downing Street, Cambridge. To reach the footbridge today, a walk down Ferry Lane is needed, a remembrance of the time a ferry operated the short distance—a ferry which in the 1450s was operated by members of the Lord's Church and three hundred years later was managed by a preacher for the Lord's Church.

Another group of "Lollards" were arrested at nearby Ely on April 3, (Easter Sunday) 1575, a hundred years after the Chesterton congregation. Religious festival days such as Easter and Christmas were a favourite time at which to arrest "heretics" due to their lack of participation in such services (Easter, Christmas and the Lord's Day was always a good time to arrest Christians, as they were missing from services).

In 1428, Abraham, a monk from the abbey at Colchester

215

with Milburn White and John Wade, both Catholic priests were apprehended on a charge of heresy. These three men were found guilty by trial of rejecting transubstantiation, claiming that the elements used in the Lord's Supper remained unchanged. The Catholics claimed that the wine became the blood of Christ and that the bread became the flesh of Christ. These men objected to this, claiming that Christ sacrificed but once, and not at each mass. They asserted that the Lord's Supper is a memorial, not a sacrifice as it had become under Catholicism. They had rejected their positions within the Catholic Church teaching that all Christians are priests, upholding the universal priesthood of believers. For authority for this they quoted from the book of Revelation 5:10, "He hath made us kings and priests unto our God."

They taught that:

> No man is bound to keep Lent and other Popish holy days. That the Pope is the antichrist. That "priests" may marry, that pilgrimages are not found in the Scriptures, that images and relics are not to be worshipped, that prayer in all places is acceptable to God, that saints are not to be prayed to. That the ringing of bells only served to fill the purses of the priests charging for protection.

In this time the Catholic Church claimed the ringing of bells frightened away "devils that lurked beside the beds of those who were dying." They renounced the Catholic Church; teaching that the true church of Christ is the congregation, the faithful of Christ, those that had been added by the Lord through baptism into His one church. It would seem that Milburn White first shared these beliefs with the other two, who had then adopted them. They were found preaching the Gospel and arrested. Milburn White had resigned from the Catholic Church and married a lady called Joan. White was burned alive by the Bishop of Norwich. When he tried to preach at the stake to those watching a servant of the Bishop injured him sufficiently to prevent his talking further, hitting him in the mouth. He had refused to recant and died for his "heresy."

Soon after this Abraham too suffered the same fate at Colchester, along with John Waddon. John Wade was taken to London where he too died at the stake. There are many other stories of persecution, far too many to list but a few brief accounts are given. Many other folk from the Colchester and Norwich areas were arrested, tried, and found guilty of heresy. Most stood fast in the faith, suffering the flames of Popish oppression.

At the same time, thirty-six people were found guilty of the same "crimes." They were taken to St. Giles' fields, London (where Lord Cobham had been burnt alive). They were hung on gibbets and slowly strangled, whilst fires were lit below their feet. Catholic priests looked on, gladly triumphant. Of those who suffered, only one name has come down to us, Sir Roger Archer. He was dealt with differently in that he was stripped naked first, and then executed in the same manner. In 1431, Thomas Bagley, a priest who was based in Malden, Essex was caught preaching the gospel. He was brought to Smithfield's, London and was burnt alive. Again in 1439 another priest was caught preaching the gospel. Richard Wick was burnt alive on Tower Hill. In 1499, a gentleman called Brabram was caught preaching the gospel in Norwich. He too died in the flames of Popish arrogance, remaining steadfast to the end.

Under such persecution, the Lord's Church survived. Congregations, being autonomous, were able to meet in secret. But Catholic Priests knew their parishes well. Those not attending mass were sought out. After arrest, torture would follow to encourage the unfortunate victim of the Pope to abjure. When this failed, they would be offered to the flames. Sometimes death was quick, though doubtless for the victim not fast enough. Sometimes a kind executioner would knock the brains out of a suffering victim. Other times if the wood burnt slowly and the wind blew in the wrong direction, death could take many hours.

An example of the cruelty meted out is that to Mr. Collins in 1538. Collins was a Catholic and mentally subnormal. He was known as an idiot lacking common sense, in the terms of the day, a madman. During mass at a church in London, when the priest lifted up the host, Collins lifted up his dog. He was arrested, along with his dog and taken immediately to Smithfield's. Both were burnt.

People recognised that if he was wrong, he should have been tied to a cart and whipped, or sent to the madhouse. People felt that there was no excuse for the cruelty that took place.

Questions were asked that the Catholic Church has never answered. For the dog to be burnt under Church law, it had to be excommunicated first, but before you can excommunicate a dog, it would have to have been baptised! Equally the same applied to poor Collins, whilst he was baptised into the Catholic Church, he was not excommunicated before burning. His burning was murder by the law of the time. Yet the church was so evil and so powerful it could murder in this way without trial and laugh at the questioning of this illegal act. Objections were raised then, and the same questions still remain unanswered. By Canon and English law at that time, Collins was murdered by the Catholic Church, which to this day has remained unrepentant.

Within a year or so, the Church of England became Anglican under the Act of Supremacy (1534), but the same punishment of burning alive was still meted out to those in disagreement with it, including those who sought to baptise believers. It was normal practice for the Roman Catholic Church to force the spouse or children of the victim to light the fagots, and then watch their relatives suffering close up. There is no evidence that the Catholic priests and church hierarchy was anything other than thoroughly gratified by the suffering of their victims.

This was their greatest mistake, because right-thinking people who saw the suffering of the Pope's victims learnt the importance of the gospel through the shear cruelty shown. Far from the Lord's church being extinguished by the flames of persecution, it won fervent appeal throughout Britain. It is shameful that today Catholic historians tend to dismiss this savage and cruel time and to continue to defend the actions of their church, arguing heresy, rather than admitting from their own evidence that many of these people were doing nothing other than following scripture.[19]

In about 1587, Dr. Some in *A Godly Treatise, Wherein Are Examined and Confuted Many Execrable Fancies* not only tells of "the Anabaptistical conventicles in London, and other places," but he likewise affirms that many of the Anabaptists were educated at the universities.[20] Robert Cooke was a celebrated Anabaptist who lived during the reigns of Henry VIII, Edward VI, Mary and Elizabeth, He was connected with the court for more that forty years where he had friends. He was ardent in his opinions, full of debate, eloquent and well-educated. He was probably the person against whom John Knox wrote his celebrated book on the Anabaptists. Dr. William Turner also wrote a book against him (A Preservative, or triacle, against the poyson of Pelagius, lately renewed and styrred up in the furious sect of Anabaptists).

Turner was described as a "noted and forward theologist and physician of his time." On coming to court, he and Cooke would debate in private. At length, he preached a sermon against the Anabaptists which was reported to Cooke and he answered it. Turner had already written against the Anabaptists. A book had appeared in 1548 called *The Sum Of Divinity* by Robert Hutton. The introduction was by Turner. In the chapter on baptism are found these words;

> Repentance and remission of sins, or, as Saint Paul sayeth a regeneration or new birth for the dipping into water signifieth that the man to be mortified with sin, the coming up again or deliverance out of the water signifieth the new man to be washed and cleansed and reconciled to God, the Father, the Son, and the Holy Ghost.

These persons mentioned as dipped into the water were adults. A striking contrast is drawn by Dr. Turner. Cooke and his church dipped believers only; Turner and his church dipped infants. Both practised the same form of baptism, dipping, but they differed in regard to the subjects.[21]

About thirty miles from Tenterden, previously mentioned, where in the early 1500s Christians meeting apart from the Romish Church, in the village of Eythorne, a similar congregation was growing. In 1868, it was reported that the Eythorne Baptist Church had been in existence for three hundred years, giving a date of 1586. The congregation was involved with that at Canterbury.[22]

Similar congregations were discovered at Bocking, in Essex, at

Faversham, in Kent, and other places. Their number must have been considerable, as four preachers were arrested when the discovery was made. They were Humphrey Middleton, Henry Hart, George Brodebridge, and Cole. At the time of their apprehension, they were assembled at Bocking. Besides the preachers, about sixty members of the congregation were apprehended. Their Christian organization appears to have been correct and complete with elders. They met regularly for worship and instruction; the ordinances of the Gospel were attended to; contributions were made for the support of the cause; and so great was their zeal that those who lived in Kent were known to go occasionally into Essex to meet the brethren there, a journey of eighty miles, which, in the sixteenth century, was no small undertaking. When they were brought into the ecclesiastical court, they were examined on forty-six articles, and indicted with Pelagianism (freewill).[23]

As early as 1522, complaints were being made against "Anabaptists" being in Kent, and presumably, were the cause of considerable concern.[24] At first the Eythorne brethren held their meetings in private homes, in both Eythorne and neighboring villages.[25] From 1600 to 1780, four John Knotts were pastors, or elders of the congregation and would have seen it go from freewill (Pelagianism) sentiments to Baptist beliefs, as by 1776 the congregation held to Calvinism.[26]

There was another congregation close by at Dover. Their meeting house was locked up by the authorities to prevent its use, but the brethren removed the locks and continued worship. This was in 1670. At about the same time another congregation started meeting in a house in Deal. The captain of Deal castle, Samuel Tavener, informed of their illegal meetings, observed them by hiding behind a hedge and listening; hearing and believing, he was baptized. He later built a chapel in 1682 where they could meet.[27] The Eythorne Church today has gone from Calvinism at one extreme to the other extreme, a universal belief that anyone who believes in Jesus without obedience is saved.

In England, and it is the same in Europe, those called Waldensian were later termed Lollard. After the reformation the new charge was anabaptism (the re-baptising of those baptised as infants).

The following maps detail how these pre-reformation churches of Christ spread out. The maps are produced from reports of heresy. It is possible they evangelised further without being reported and prosecuted. Despite the maps being a rough estimation, they serve their purpose.

The map above is an approximation of where the Waldensian heresy was being reported by the late 1100s.

By the late 1300s the heresy was being reported was Lollardy, as the map shows, it is an extension of where Waldensian heresy had previously been reported, the map being identical except for further locations.

The map shows the post reformation mid 1500s, the heresies
was being reported was Lollard, Pelagian and Anabaptism,
as the map shows, it is an extension of the Waldensian
and Lollard areas of heresy, of the previous centuries.

The final map is the mid 1650s where the churches of Christ met prior to becoming
Baptist over the next two hundred years. As the map shows, it is an extension
of the Waldensian, Lollard and Anabaptism areas of heresy of the previous
centuries. The people termed by their enemies Waldensian, Lollard, Pelagian and
Anabaptist on the maps called themselves the church of Christ, and as individuals,
Christians. They baptised by immersion for the remission of sins. They rejected
Augustinian theology of inherited depravity (original sin) teaching freewill.

In Zurich, Switzerland, two conferences were held in 1525 to discuss the problems of believers' as opposed to infant baptism. The first was held on the 17th of January, at the Council House. The other was held on the 20th of March. What could not be proved by scriptural authority by the reformers was proved by secular authority. The reformers won and violence would be used against those who refused to have their children baptised and preached against infant baptism.[28]

Johannes Warns wrote that "since Luther forthwith brought over into the so-called 'Christian' States, the Old Testament theocratic appointments of the Jewish State; naturally he was able to find in the Old Testament examples enough of these 'magisterial' duties." He cites David, who banished "false teachers and heretics, Jehoshaphat, Josiah, Hezekiah, Nebuchadnezzar, Darius and Cyrus, who are highly praised by the Holy Spirit that they rightly ordered Divine service and took a strong line against idolatry."

In April 1532, Luther wrote to Duke Albrecht of Prussia that "no authority should be permitted to tolerate Sacramentarians or Anabaptists in their country." He declared it to be the duty of the Christian conscience of every subject to denounce to the magistrate for punishment every "interloping preacher." He considered them "stiff-necked villains whose devilish sect has the spirit of hell for its origin."[29] Luther is accusing the Anabaptists of witchcraft and demonic indwelling.[30] Infant baptism in that period was as much an exorcism as it was to remit original sin, and, of course, any actual sins a baby only a few days old had managed to commit. It is not difficult for the Reformers to believe in that period that the Anabaptists who had not been baptised by the Romish baptism were demon infected as (infant) baptism was required to allow faith in the infant having removed both demons and original sin.

Dr. Ludwick Keller (1849-1915) quoted two Catholic authors, witnesses of the persecutions against the Anabaptists, Leopold Dickius, an Imperial Councillor and Procurator of the Supreme Court, who wrote in 1533:

> Neither age nor sex is spared, and while men are killed the women and children perish in misery and hunger. Those kept in horrible, perpetual imprisonment, languish in filth and privation. No friendly service, no kind action, no obligation is known toward these people. Each is regarded as if he were guilty of the worse, most pestilent of crimes.

The other witness is the chronicler Kilian Leib:

> In Salzburg and Munich they were most severally punished by sword, fire, and water, and all these forms of death have the obdurate, unfortunate men, women and maidens not only patiently endured, but at times have borne with joy, while the devil makes the poor people his playthings and show pieces.[31]

The burnings of "heretics."

In a letter to Menuis and Myconius of 1530, Luther stated Anabaptists should be executed.[32] Bocholt is a city in the northwest of Westphalia, Germany. In the 1530s, it was a centre for Anabaptist activities. The Bocholt conference took place in August 1536. Those who attended the conference came from Holland, Germany and England, about 25 representatives from various congregations. It seems the purpose of the conference, an initiative of the English brethren, was to seek unity amongst the various groups of the churches of Christ. According to Irvin Horst, it was the English brethren who financed the conference (It is interesting to note, that an international conference was instigated and financed by the English Churches of Christ in 1536). That they were sufficiently well organised and financed says something for the state of the English church at that time; they were very much in the lead, rather than as many historians tell, the poor relation against the disorganised churches in Europe.[33]

The problem of looking for evidence of congregations meeting by historians too often lacks understanding of what a congregation is. They will look for signs of an established clergy and a church building. Jesus said (Mat. 18:20) "For where two or three are gathered together in my name, there am I in the midst of them." For a church to exist, there is only the need for two or more brethren meeting together. Using this scripture as our standard, when looking for the existence of congregations, it is clear that congregations meeting the Biblical definition of a church (congregation) of as little as two or three people, meeting in their homes, did exist in the 1500s and earlier.

Lollards called themselves "known men" referring to their knowledge of scripture. This angered their opponents as the Lollards argued that those who know and obey the scriptures have salvation and those who do not are erring and shall perish. It is safe to assume the Roman Catholics were not too happy with such pronouncements, however true.[34] The Lollards took the expression "known men" from first Corinthians.

Today, it is rarely if ever mentioned how barbaric pre-Christian times were. The depravity and barbarity of ancient times are now entirely forgotten. We think of the classical Greek and Roman period and the influence this had on the renaissance. The truth is quite simple, the ancient world was cruel beyond imagination. Prisoners had no rights, the mechanism was enslavement and torture of prisoners or the helpless, all done for pleasure. Worse of all, cannibalism was commonly practiced for religious reasons, as well as a necessity in times a famine. Christianity was the great redeemer of a deprived and barbaric world. No single person has had more influence against depravity than that of Jesus Christ; the testimony is how the world changed from the first century onwards. As the

Romish Church evangelised, this barbarity was retained.

To help understand the persecution that Christians suffered, I quote William Edward Hartpole Lecky (1838-1903). Lecky was an Anglo-Irish historian and essayist. He was perhaps the greatest historical scholar Ireland has ever produced. In his last years of his life he entered into Parliament, where as a Liberal Unionist he opposed the separatism of the Irish home rule movement. In 1897 he was made a privy councilor and in 1902 a member of the exclusive Order of Merit. Lecky died in London on Oct. 22, 1903. In 1865 he wrote *A History of the Rise and Influence of Rationalism in Europe* (2 vols). Lecky remains influential to this day as to the development of secularism and rationalism.

Lecky wrote:

> In 1208, Innocent III established the Inquisition. In 1209, De Montfort began the massacre of the Albigenses. In 1215, the Fourth Council of the Lateran enjoined all rulers, "as they desired to be esteemed faithful, to swear a public oath that they would labour earnestly, and to the full extent of their power, to exterminate from their dominions all those who were branded as heretics by the Church."

> It is in itself evident, and it is abundantly proved by history, that the virulence theologians will display towards those who differ from them, will depend chiefly on the degree in which the dogmatic side of their system is developed. "See how these Christians love one another," was the just and striking exclamation of the heathen in the first century. "There are no wild beasts so ferocious as Christians who

differ concerning their faith," was the equally striking and probably equally just exclamation of the heathen in the fourth century. And the reason of this difference is manifest. In the first century there was, properly speaking, scarcely any theology, no system of elaborate dogmas authoritatively imposed upon the conscience. Neither the character of the union of two natures in Christ, nor the doctrine of the atonement, nor the extent of the authority of the Church, had been determined with precision, and the whole stress of religious sentiment was directed towards the worship of a moral ideal, and the cultivation of moral qualities. But in the fourth century men were mainly occupied with innumerable subtle and minute questions of theology, to which they attributed a transcendent importance, and which in a great measure diverted their minds from moral considerations. However strongly the Homoousians and Homooisians were opposed to each other on other points, they were at least perfectly agreed that the adherents of the wrong vowel could not possibly get to heaven, and that the highest conceivable virtues were futile when associated with error. In the twelfth century, when persecution recommenced, the dogmatic or ecclesiastical element had been still further aggrandised by the immense development of ecclesiastical ceremonies, and the violence with which it was defended was proportionally unscrupulous. The reluctance to shed blood which had so honourably distinguished the Fathers completely passed away, or, if we find any trace of it, it is only in the quibble by which the Church referred the execution of her mandates to the civil magistrate, who, as we have seen, was not permitted to delay that execution for more than six days, under pain of excommunication. Almost all Europe, for many centuries, was inundated with blood, which was shed at the direct instigation or with the full approval of the ecclesiastical authorities, and under the pressure of a public opinion that was directed by the Catholic clergy, and was the exact measure of their influence.

That the Church of Rome has shed more innocent blood than any other institution that has ever existed among mankind, will be questioned by no Protestant who has a competent knowledge of history. The memorials, indeed, of many of her persecutions are now so scanty, that it is impossible to form a complete conception of the multitude of her victims, and it is quite certain that no powers of imagination can adequately realise their sufferings. Llorente, who had free access to the archives of the Spanish Inquisition, assures us that by that tribunal alone more than 31,000 persons were burnt, and more than 290,000 condemned to punishments less severe than death. The number of those who were put to death for their religion in the Netherlands alone, in the reign of Charles V, has been estimated by a very high authority at 50,000, and at least half as many perished under his son. And when to these memorable instances we add the innumerable less conspicuous executions that took place, from the victims of Charlemagne to the free-thinkers of the seventeenth century, when we recollect that after the mission of Dominic the area of the persecution comprised nearly the whole of Christendom, and that its triumph was in some districts so complete as to destroy every memorial of the contest, the most callous nature must recoil with horror from the spectacle. For these atrocities were not perpetrated in the brief paroxysms of a reign of terror, or by the hands of obscure sectaries, but were inflicted by a triumphant Church, with every circumstance of solemnity and deliberation. Nor did the victims perish by a rapid and painless death, but by one which was carefully selected as among the most poignant that man can suffer. They were usually burnt alive. They were burnt alive not unfrequently by a slow fire. They were burnt alive after their constancy had been tried by the most excruciating agonies that minds fertile in torture could devise. This was the physical torment inflicted on those who dared to exercise their reason in the pursuit of truth; but what language can describe, and what imagination can conceive, the mental suffering that accompanied it? For in those days the family was divided against itself. The ray of conviction often fell upon a single member, leaving all others untouched. The victims who died for heresy were not, like those who died for witchcraft, solitary and doting women, but were usually men in the midst of active life, and often in the first flush of youthful enthusiasm, and those who loved them best were firmly convinced that their agonies upon earth were but the prelude of eternal agonies hereafter. This was especially the case with weak women, who feel most acutely the sufferings of others, and around whose minds the clergy had most successfully wound their toils. It is horrible, it is appalling to reflect what the mother, the wife, the sister, the daughter of the heretic must have suffered from this teaching. She saw the body of him who was dearer to her than life, dislocated and writhing and quivering with pain; she watched the slow fire creeping from limb to limb till it had swathed him in a sheet of agony; and when at last the scream of anguish had died away, and the tortured body was at rest, she was told that all this was acceptable to the God she served, and was but a faint image of the sufferings He would inflict through eternity upon the dead. Nothing was wanting to give emphasis to the doctrine. It rang from every pulpit. It was painted over every altar. The Spanish heretic was led to the flames in a dress covered with representations of devils and of frightful tortures, to remind the spectators to the very last of the doom that awaited him.

All this is very horrible, but it is only a small part of the misery which the persecuting spirit of Rome has

236

produced. For, judging by the ordinary measure of human courage, for every man who dared to avow his principles at the stake, there must have been many who believed that by such an avowal alone they could save their souls, but who were nevertheless scared either by the prospect of their own sufferings or of the destitution of their children, who passed their lives in one long series of hypocritical observances and studied falsehoods, and at last, with minds degraded by habitual deception, sank hopeless and terror-stricken into the grave. And besides all these things, we have to remember that the spirit which was manifested in acts of detailed persecution had often swept over a far wider sphere, and produced sufferings not perhaps so excruciating, but far more extensive. We have to recollect those frightful massacres, perhaps the most fearful the world has ever seen: the massacre of the Albigenses which a pope had instigated, or the massacre of St. Bartholomew for which a pope returned solemn thanks to Heaven. We have to recollect those religious wars which reproduced themselves century after century with scarcely diminished fury, which turned Syria into an Aceldama, which inundated with blood the fairest lands of Europe, which blasted the prosperity and paralysed the intellect of many a noble nation, and which planted animosities in Europe that two hundred years have been unable altogether to destroy. Nor should we forget the hardening effects that must have been produced on the minds of the spectators who at every royal marriage in Spain were regaled by the public execution of heretics, or who were summoned to the great square of Toulouse to contemplate the struggles of four hundred witches in the flames. When we add together all these various forms of suffering, and estimate all their aggravations, when we think that the victims of these persecutions were usually men who were not only entirely guiltless, but who proved themselves by their very deaths to be endowed with most transcendent and heroic virtues, and when we still further consider that all this was but part of one vast conspiracy to check the development of the human mind, and to destroy that spirit of impartial and unrestricted enquiry which all modern researches prove to be the very first condition of progress as of truth; when we consider all these things, it can surely be no exaggeration to say that the Church of Rome has inflicted a greater amount of unmerited suffering than any other religion that has ever existed among mankind. To complete the picture, it is only necessary to add that these things were done in the name of the Teacher who said: "By this shall all men know that ye are my disciples, that ye love one another."

But while the preeminent atrocity of the persecutions of the Church of Rome is fully admitted, nothing can be more grossly disingenuous or untrue than to represent persecution as her peculiar taint. She persecuted to the full extent of the power of her clergy, and that power was very great. The persecution of which every Protestant Church was guilty was measured by the same rule, but clerical influence in Protestant countries was comparatively weak. The Protestant persecutions were never so sanguinary as those of the Catholics, but the principle was affirmed quite as strongly, was acted on quite as constantly, and was defended quite as pertinaciously by the clergy. In Germany, at the time of the protestation of Spires, when the name of Protestant was assumed, the Lutheran princes absolutely prohibited the celebration of mass within their dominions. In England a similar measure was passed as early as Edward VI. On the accession of Elizabeth, and before the Catholics had given any signs of discontent, a law was made prohibiting any religious service other than the Prayer Book; the penalty for the third offence being imprisonment for life; while another law imposed a fine on any one who abstained from the Anglican service. The

Presbyterians through a long succession of reigns were imprisoned, branded, mutilated, scourged, and exposed in the pillory. Many Catholics under false pretences were tortured and hung. Anabaptists and Arians were burnt alive. In Ireland, the religion of the immense majority of the people was banned and proscribed; and when in 1626 the Government manifested some slight wish to grant it partial relief, nearly all the Irish Protestant bishops, under the presidency of Usher, assembled to protest in a solemn resolution against the indulgence. "The religion of Papists," they said, "is superstitious, their faith and doctrine erroneous and heretical; their Church in respect of both apostatical. To give them therefore a toleration, or to consent that they may freely exercise their religion, and profess their faith and doctrine, is a grievous sin." In Scotland, during almost the whole period that the Stuarts were on the throne of England, a persecution rivalling in atrocity almost any on record was directed by the English Government, at the instigation of the Scotch bishops, and with the approbation of the English Church, against all who repudiated episcopacy. If a conventicle was held in a house, the preacher was liable to be put to death. If it was held in the open air, both minister and people incurred the same fate. The Presbyterians were hunted like criminals over the mountains. Their ears were torn from the roots. They were branded with hot irons. Their fingers were wrenched asunder by the thumbkins. The bones of their legs were shattered in the boots. Women were scourged publicly through the streets. Multitudes were transported to Barbados, infuriated soldiers were let loose upon them, and encouraged to exercise all their ingenuity in torturing them. Nor was it only the British Government, or the zealous advocates of episcopacy, who manifested this spirit. When the Reformation triumphed in Scotland, one of its first fruits was a law prohibiting any priest from celebrating, or any worshipper from hearing mass, under pain of the confiscation of his goods for the first offence, of exile for the second, and of death for the third. That the Queen of Scotland should be permitted to hear mass in her own private chapel, was publicly denounced as an intolerable evil. "One mass," exclaimed Knox, "is more fearful to me than if 10,000 armed enemies were landed in any part of the realm." In France, when the government of certain towns was conceded to the Protestants, they immediately employed their power to suppress absolutely the Catholic worship, to prohibit any Protestant from attending a marriage or a funeral that was celebrated by a priest, to put down all mixed marriages, and to persecute to the full extent of their power those who had abandoned their creed, In Sweden, all who dissented from any article of the Confession of Augsburg were at once banished. In Protestant Switzerland numerous Anabaptists perished by drowning; the freethinker Gentilis by the axe; Servetus, and a convert to Judaism, by the flames. In America, the colonists who were driven from their own land by persecution, not only proscribed the Catholics, but also persecuted the Quakers—the most inoffensive of all sects—with atrocious severity. If Holland was somewhat more tolerant, it was early remarked, that while the liberty allowed there was unusually great, the power accorded to the clergy was unusually small. As late as 1690 a synod was held at Amsterdam, consisting partly of Dutch and partly of French and English ministers who were driven to Holland by persecution, and in that synod the doctrine that the magistrate has no right to crush heresy and idolatry by the civil power, was unanimously pronounced to be "false, scandalous, and pernicious." When Descartes went to Holland, the reformed clergy directed against him all the force of their animosity, and the accusation by which they endeavoured to stir up the civil power against the author of the most sublime of all modern proofs of the existence of the Deity, was atheism.

The right of the civil magistrate to punish heresy was maintained by the Helvetic, Scottish, Belgic, and Saxon Confessions. Luther, in reply to Philip of Hesse, distinctly asserted it; Calvin, Beza, and Jurieu, all wrote books on the lawfulness of persecution. Knox, appealing to the Old Testament, declared that those who were guilty of idolatry might justly be put to death. Cranmer and Ridley, as well as four other bishops, formed the commission in the reign of Edward VI for trying Anabaptists. The only two exceptions to this spirit among the leaders of the Reformation, seem to have been Zuinglius and Socinus. The first was always averse to persecution. The second was so distinctively the apostle of toleration, that this was long regarded as one of the peculiar doctrines of his sect. With these exceptions, all the leading Reformers seem to have advocated persecution, and in nearly every country where their boasted Reformation triumphed, the result is to be mainly attributed to coercion. When Calvin burnt Servetus for his opinions on the Trinity, this, which, in the words of a great modern historian, "had perhaps as many circumstances of aggravation as any execution for heresy that ever took place," was almost unanimously applauded by all sections of Protestants. Melanchthon, Bullinger, and Farel wrote to express their warm approbation of the crime. Beza defended it in an elaborate treatise. Only one man of eminence ventured openly to oppose it, and that man, who may be regarded as the first avowed champion of complete religious liberty, was also one of the most eminent of the precursors of rationalism. He wrote under the name of Martin Bellius, but his real name was Chatillon, or, as it was generally latinised, Castellio.

Castellio was a Frenchman, a scholar of remarkable acquirements, and a critic of still more remarkable boldness. He had been at one time a friend of Calvin, and had filled a professorship at Geneva, but the daring spirit which he carried into every sphere soon scandalised the leaders of the Reformation. Having devoted himself early to Biblical criticism, he had translated the Bible into Latin, and in the course of his labours he came to the conclusion that the Song of Solomon was simply a Jewish love song, and that the allegory that was supposed to underlie it was purely imaginary. A still graver offence in the eyes of the Geneva theologians was his emphatic repudiation of the Calvinistic doctrine of predestination. He assailed it not so much by any train of arguments, or by an appeal to authority, as on the broad grounds of its repugnance to our sense of right, and he developed its moral atrocity in a manner that elicited from Beza a torrent of almost frantic invective. Driven from Geneva, he at last obtained a professorship at Basle, where he denounced the murder of Servetus, and preached for the first time in Christendom the duty of absolute toleration, based upon the rationalistic doctrine of the innocence of error. The object of doctrines, he said, is to make men better, and those which do not contribute to this end are absolutely unimportant. The history of dogmas should be looked upon as a series of developments, contributing to the moral perfection of mankind. First of all, polytheism was supreme. Christ came and effected the ascendency of monotheism, in which Jews, Turks, and Christians all agree. Christianity again introduced a specific type of character, of which universal charity and beneficence were the leading features. Questions concerning the Trinity, or predestination, or the sacraments, are involved in great and perhaps impenetrable obscurity, and have no moral influence, and ought in consequence not to be resisted upon. "To discuss the difference between the Law and the Gospel, gratuitous remission of sins or imputed righteousness, is as if a man were to discuss whether a prince was to come on horseback, or in a chariot, or dressed in white or in red." To persecute for such questions is absurd, and not only absurd but atrocious. For if the end of Christianity be the diffusion of a spirit of beneficence, persecution must be its extreme antithesis; and if persecution be an essential element of a religion, that religion must be a curse to mankind.

Such new and startling sentiments as these, coming from a writer of considerable eminence, attracted much attention, and aroused great indignation. Both Calvin and Beza replied in a strain of the fiercest invective. Calvin especially, from the time when Castellio left Geneva, pursued him with untiring hatred, laboured hard to procure his expulsion from Basle, denounced him in the preface to an edition of the New Testament as "one who had been chosen by Satan to deceive the thoughtless and indifferent," and attempted to blast his character by the grossest calumnies. In the friendship of Socinus, Castellio found some compensation for the general hatred of which he was the object, and he appears to have inclined greatly to the doctrines of his friend. Separated alike from the Protestants and the Catholics, his prospects in life were blighted, he sank into a condition of absolute destitution, and is said to have been almost reduced to literal starvation, when death relieved him of his sufferings. A few kindly sentences of Montaigne, who pronounced his closing scene to have been a disgrace to mankind, have in some degree rescued this first apostle of toleration from oblivion.

Some years after the murder of Servetus, Beza, in relating its circumstances, declared that Castellio and Socinus were the only men who had opposed it, and although this statement is not strictly true, it but very little exaggerates the unanimity that was displayed. When we recollect the great notoriety of this execution, and also its aggravated character, so general an approbation seems to show clearly not only that the spirit of early Protestantism was as undoubtedly intolerant as the spirit of Catholicism, which is an unquestionable fact, but also that it flinched as little from the extreme consequences to which intolerance leads. It seems to show that the comparative mildness of Protestant persecutions results much more from the circumstances under which they took place, than from any sense of the atrocity of burning the heretic. And, indeed, while the Romish persecutions were undoubtedly unrivalled in magnitude, it must be admitted that there are some aspects under which they contrast not unfavourably with the Protestant ones. Catholicism was an ancient Church. She had gained a great part of her influence by vast services to mankind. She rested avowedly upon the principle of authority. She was defending herself against aggression and innovation. That a Church so circumstanced should endeavour to stifle in blood every aspiration towards a purer system, was indeed a fearful crime, but it was a crime which was not altogether unnatural. She might point to the priceless blessings she had bestowed upon humanity, to the slavery she had destroyed, to the civilisation she had founded, to the many generations she had led with honour to the grave. She might show how completely her doctrines were interwoven with the whole social system, how fearful would be the convulsion if they were destroyed, and how absolutely incompatible they were with the acknowledgment of private judgment. These considerations would not make her blameless, but they would at least palliate her guilt. But what shall we say of a Church that was but a thing of yesterday, a Church that had as yet no services to show, no claims upon the gratitude of mankind, a Church that was by profession the creature of private judgment, and was in reality generated by the intrigues of a corrupt court, which, nevertheless, suppressed by force a worship that multitudes deemed necessary to their salvation, and by all her organs, and with all her energies, persecuted those who clung to the religion of their fathers? What shall we say of a religion which comprised at most but a fourth part of the Christian world, and which the first explosion of private judgment had shivered into countless sects, which was, nevertheless, so pervaded by the spirit of dogmatism that each of these sects asserted its distinctive doctrines with the same confidence, and persecuted with the same unhesitating virulence, as a Church that was venerable with the homage of more than twelve centuries? What shall we say of men who, in the name of religious liberty, deluged their land with blood, trampled on the very first principles of patriotism, calling in strangers to their assistance, and openly rejoicing in the disasters of their country, and who, when they at last attained their object, immediately established a religious tyranny as absolute as that which they had subverted? These were the attitudes which for more than a century Protestantism uniformly presented; and so strong and so general was its intolerance that for some time it may, I believe, be truly said that there were more instances of partial toleration being advocated by Roman Catholics than by orthodox Protestants. Although nothing can be more egregiously absurd than to represent the Inquisition as something unconnected with the Church, although it was created by a pope, and introduced into the chief countries of Europe by the sovereigns who were most devoted to the Church, and composed of ecclesiastics, and directed to the punishment of ecclesiastical offences, and developed in each country according to the intensity of Catholic feeling, and long regarded as the chief bulwark of Catholicity—although all the atrocities it perpetrated do undoubtedly fall upon the blood-stained Church that created it—it is nevertheless true that one or two popes endeavoured to moderate its severities, and reproved the excesses of Torquemada in language that is not without something of evangelical mildness. Erasmus, too, at all times endeavoured to

245

assuage the persecution, and Erasmus lived and died in communion with the Church. Sir Thomas More, though he was himself a persecutor, at least admitted the abstract excellence of toleration, and extolled it in his *Utopia*. Hôpital, and Lord Baltimore, the Catholic founder of Maryland, were the two first legislators who uniformly upheld religious liberty when in power; and Maryland continued the solitary refuge for the oppressed of every Christian sect, till the Protestant party, who were in the ascendant in its legislature, basely enacted the whole penal code against the coreligionists of the founder of the colony. But among the Protestants it may, I believe, be safely affirmed, that there was no example of the consistent advocacy or practice of toleration in the sixteenth century that was not virulently and generally denounced by all sections of the clergy, and scarcely any till the middle of the seventeenth century. Indeed, even at the close of the seventeenth century, Bossuet was able to maintain that the right of the civil magistrate to punish religious error was one of the points on which both churches agreed; and he added that he only knew two bodies of Christians who denied it. They were the Socinians and the Anabaptists.[35]

I have quoted Lecky as an independent and respected historian of past events. Had I written the above, I would risk accusations of poor research and bias resulting in discrimination. Today, Christianity is often derided for its cruelty and corruptions in times past. Those opposed to Christianity will use the persecutions quoted to prosecute their case. Yet much of the cruelty quoted was against those who held to the Scriptures alone. In others words, the persecutions were by the Roman Catholics, Protestants and Anglicans in a holocaust lasting several centuries, meted out a cruelty considerably more evil than anything that Hitler implemented. Why is it necessary to bring this up several centuries after events now largely forgotten? Today, Christianity has been both relegated to a myth and secularised because of its past behaviour, although, Christians did not commit these atrocities. This fact must be exposed along with what Christianity is, which is not what the denominations teach and practice. Christians are more than believers in Christ; they are doers, followers of Christ. Such cannot be said of the denominations. The awful truth is that denominationalism, however presented today, was founded on blood—the blood of Christians who never used violence themselves but willingly went to the torture and fires, professing their faith in Christ—"Yea, and all that would live godly in Christ Jesus shall suffer persecution" (2 Tim. 3:12). Christianity, on the other hand, is founded on the Blood of Christ giving himself for mankind.

The persecution of the European Church was such that a few moved to England, others moved eastwards into Bosnia and other bordering countries. The Roman Catholic Church objected under Pope Innocent III (died 1216) and, with the help of the King of Hungary pressured the leaders of Bosnia. Civil war followed and the rulers were replaced by leaders friendly towards the Christians of those parts. The Romish response was with the inquisition and crusades against Christians in Europe. Meanwhile Islam was becoming an increasing danger for Europe. Rather than Europe uniting to overthrow Islam, Islam with little opposition was able to move into Eastern Europe. The Battle of Kosovo (1389) extended Muslim rule over Serbia. The Bosnians driven to desperation with the Romish persecution turned to the Turks. Under Islam Christians over many decades became Muslims. The issues in Eastern Europe and the consequences of Romish oppression remain felt to this day in Bosnia and Serbia.[36]

The burning of "heretics"

Today, when religious persecution (now surprisingly in the West is from the left rather than previously, which was from the right) is largely tempered by our legal systems, it is surprising that morally-minded people still cleave to the Roman Catholic and later Reformed Churches. A clear headed look at European history alone should convince most people that such religions are not apostolic in origin, but evil. Over the centuries devout men and women have sought to maintain the purity of the scriptures, and accordingly, enraged the religious tyrants of the time.

ENDNOTES

[1]John A. F. Thomson, *The Later Lollards 1414-1520* (Oxford University Press, 1965) 245.

[2]Johannes Warns, *Baptism, Studies in the Original Christian Baptism, Its History and Conflicts, Its relationship to a State or National Church and Its Significance for the Present Time*, trans. G. H. Lang (from German) (1957) 133. Phillip Schaff, History of the Christian Church 8 vols., (1910 reprint 1994). Vol. 5, Chap 16., *Demonology and the Dark Arts*, 878; Vol 6, Chap. 7, *Witchcraft and its Punishment*, 514. Sir James George Frazer, *The Golden Bough, A Study in Magic and Religion* (1955). Richard Marshall, *Witchcraft, the History and Mythology* (1995). Augustus Montague Summers, *The History of Witchcraft and Demonology* (1926).

[3]Warns 195.

[4]Roger Williams, *The Bloudy Tenent of Persecution, for the Cause of Conscience, Discussed in a Conference Between Truth and Peace* (1644) 29.

[5]John Mocket Cramp, D.D., *Baptist History: From The Foundation of the Christian Church to the Close of the Eighteenth Century* (1871) 118.

[6]Thomson 3. Michael Watts, Reader in Modern History (1978) at the University of Nottingham, notes the link between the Anabaptists and Lollards in *The Dissenters* (Oxford University Press, 1985) 7. Irvin Buckwalter Horst, *The Radical Brethren* (1972) 56.

[7]G. H. Orchard, *A History of the Baptists in England, From the Earliest Days of the Christian Dispensation to the Present Time*, ed. J. R. Graves, vol.

2 (1855) 158. Orchard was a Baptist minister of a congregation in Stevington, Bedfordshire, England, a congregation that goes back to the 1600s, when it was a church of Christ before becoming Particular Baptist. Thomas Crosby, *History of the English Baptists*, vol. 1 of 4 vols. (London,1738) Crosby quoted Foxe, 24. All four completed by 1740.

[8]Henry Denne, *Antichrist Unmasked In Two Treatises - The Arguments For Children's Baptism Opened and Answered* (1645) 19.

[9]John S. Oyer, *Lutheran Reformers Against Anabaptists* (1964)124.

[10]Oyer 81.

[11]Thomson 66.

[12]Oyer chap. 1.

[13]Crosby 25. Gilbert Burnet, late Lord Bishop of Sarum (died 1715), *The History of the Reformation of the Church of England,* vol. 1 (Oxford University Press, 1860) 54. Edward Bean Underhill, *Tracts on Liberty of Conscience and Persecution* (1846) Cii.

[14]John Foxe (1517-1587), *Acts and Monuments of the Christian Church* better known as *Foxes Book of Martyrs,* 9th ed., vol. (1684) 289.

[15]Crosby 24. T.C. O'Connor, *Poems and Ballads on Protestantism* (1888) 34.

[16]Burnet, vol. 3, 227.

[17]Cramp 208-10. Cramp was highly regarded, particularly by Charles Spurgeon, and his history remains published. Regarding the 1538 Proclamation against the Anabaptists, consult Thieleman J. Van Braght, *A Martyrology of The Churches of Christ, Commonly Called, Baptists,* trans. Edward Bean Underhill (from Dutch) vol. 1 (1850) 185. Earlier versions were known as the *Martyrs Mirror*. There have been many editions of many tittles, the collection of records beginning around 1540.

[18]Crosby 20-23, 41. George Stokes, *The Lollards* (1838) 11. Orchard 147.

[19]Crosby 23. Orchard 160. Stokes 34.

[20]John T. Christian, *History of the Baptists,* vol. 1 (1855) 201.

[21]Christian 201.

[22]W. Phillip Clark, *Eythorne, Our Baptist Heritage* (1981) 9.

[23]Cramp 215. Underhill cix.

[24]Clark 9.

[25]Clark12.

[26]Clark 15-16.

[27]Clark 23.

[28]Van Braght 7.

[29]Warns 181-2.

[30]Oyer 133-135.

[31]Warns 202.

[32]Oyer 124.

[33]Horst 78.

[34]Reginald Pecock, *The Repressor of Over Much Blaming of the Clergy*, 1455, ed. Churchill Babington, vol. 2 of 2 (1861) 53 ff.

[35]William Edward Hartpole Lecky, *History of The Rise and Influence of the Spirit of Rationalism in Europe* vol. 2 of 2 vols. (New Impression 1904) 30ff.

[36]Edmund Hamer Broadbent, *The Pilgrim Church* (1931) 60ff. Dr Hans Grimm, *Tradition and History of the Early Churches of Christ In Central Europe* (undated, post 1963) 24ff.

9

JOHN FRITH

And the servant of the Lord must not strive; but be gentle
unto all men, apt to teach, patient (2 Timothy 2:24).

John Frith (or Fryth), date of birth unknown, was executed
in July 1533 for heresy. He was born to an innkeeper, Richard,
in Sevenoaks at Westerham, Kent. The inn is now known as The
Grasshopper on the Green. Even then the inn was already several
centuries old. Henry VIII was a frequent visitor to these parts when
courting Anne Boleyn, who lived at nearby Hever Castle. Anne was
sympathetic to members of the church and forwarded their views to
the establishment. It is difficult to conclude, in view of the number
of congregations meeting in Kent, that Anne Boleyn and the Frith
family would have been ignorant of the church and its opposition
to the national Roman Catholic Church (England being Roman
Catholic in this period).

The Grasshopper Inn, where Frith was born.

Frith went to Sevenoaks Grammar School where his tutor was Stephen Gardiner, who would later, as Bishop of Winchester, take part in condemning him to death. After leaving school, Frith was educated at Eton College and admitted as a scholar to Queens' College, Cambridge, though he received his B.A. from King's College, Cambridge.

While Frith was at Cambridge, he met Thomas Bilney, a graduate student of Trinity Hall and began to have meetings concerning the reformation at the Whitehorse Tavern in King's Lane. Bilney was later executed by burning on 19 August, 1531. In many areas Bilney, though a reformer, held to many Roman Catholic views. It may have been at one of these popular meetings that Frith met William Tyndale; the two developed a close friendship.

After graduating in 1525, Frith became a junior canon at Wolsey's College, Oxford, now Christ Church College. While in Oxford, Frith was imprisoned (along with nine others) in a cellar where fish was stored, because of his possession of what the University's officials considered "heretical" books. Frith was released and fled England, staying with Tyndale in Antwerp, where he assisted him in translating the Bible.

The following is taken from *The History of the Reformation In The Time Of Calvin*, by J.H. Merle d'Aubigne. Frith had been in a discussion with a brother in the Bow Lane congregation, where Frith had been preaching, about the Lord's Supper. Then a spy got hold of the information Frith had put in writing:

> One of those who listened was in great doubt relative to the doctrine of the Lord's Supper; and one day, after Frith had been setting Christ before them as the food of the Christian soul through faith, this person followed him and said: "Our prelates think differently; they believe that the bread transformed by consecration becomes the flesh, blood, and bones of Christ; that even the wicked eat this flesh with their teeth, and that we must adore the host. What you have just said refutes their errors, but I fear that I cannot remember it. Pray commit it to writing." Frith, who did not like discussions, was alarmed at the request, and answered; "I do not care to touch that terrible tragedy;" for so he called the dispute about the Eucharist. The man having repeated his request, and promised that

he would not communicate the paper to anybody, Frith wrote an explanation of the doctrine of the Sacrament and gave it to that London Christian, saying: "We must eat and drink the body and blood of Christ, not with the teeth, but with the hearing and through faith." The brother took the treatise, and, hurrying home with it, read it carefully.

In a short time everyone at the Bow Lane spoke about this writing. One man, a false brother, named William Holt, listened attentively to what was said, and thought he had found an opportunity of destroying Frith. Assuming a hypocritical look, he spoke in a pious strain to the individual who had the manuscript, as if he had desired to enlighten his faith, and finally asked him for it. Having obtained it, he hastened to make a copy, which he carried to Sir Thomas More, who was still chancellor.

Frith soon perceived that he had tried in vain to remain unknown; he called with so much power those who thirsted for righteousness to come to Christ for the waters of life, that friends and enemies were struck with his eloquence. Observing that his name began to be talked of in various places, he quitted the capital and traveled unnoticed through several counties, where he found some little Christian congregations whom he tried to strengthen in the faith.

Tyndale, who remained on the continent, having heard of Frith's labours, began to feel great anxiety about him. He knew but too well the cruel disposition of the bishops and of More.'"I will make the serpent come out of his dark den." Sir Thomas had said, speaking of Tyndale, "as Hercules forced Cerberus, the watch-dog of hell, to come out to the light of day… I will not leave Tyndale the darkest corner in which to hide his head." In Tyndale's eyes Frith was the great hope of the Church in England;

he trembled lest the redoubtable Hercules should seize him. "Dearly beloved brother Jacob," he wrote, — calling him Jacob to mislead his enemies, — "be cold, sober, wise, and circumspect, and keep you low by the ground, avoiding high questions that pass the common capacity. But expound the law truly, and open the veil of Moses to condemn all flesh and prove all men sinners. Then set abroach the mercy of our Lord Jesus, and let the wounded consciences drink of him… All doctrine that casteth a mist on these two to shadow and hide them, resist with all your power… Beloved in my heart, there liveth not one in whom I have so great hope and trust, and in whom my heart rejoiceth, not so much for your learning and what other gifts else you may have, as because you walk in those things that the conscience may feel, and not in the imagination of the brain. Cleave fast to the rock of the help of God; and if ought be required of you contrary to the glory of God and his Christ, then stand fast and commit yourself to God. He is our God, and our redemption is nigh."

Tyndale's fears were but too well founded. Sir Thomas More held Frith's new treatise in his hand: he read it and, gave way by turns to anger and sarcasm. "Whetting his wits, calling his spirits together, and sharpening his pen," to use the words of the chronicler, he answered Frith, and described his doctrine under the image of a cancer. This did not satisfy, him. Although he had returned the seals to the king in May [More had since resigned as Lord Chancellor to the king], he continued to hold office until the end of the year. He ordered search to be made for Frith, and set all his bloodhounds on the track. If the reformer was discovered he was lost; when Sir Thomas More had once caught his man, nothing could save him — nothing but a merry jest, perhaps. For instance, one day when he was examining a gospeller named Silver: "You know," he said, with a smile, "that silver must be tried in the fire." "Yes," retorted the accused instantly, "but not quicksilver." More delighted with the repartee, set the poor wretch at liberty. But Frith was no jester: he could not hope, therefore, to find favor with the ex-chancellor of England.

Sir Thomas hunted the reformer by sea and by land, promising a great reward to anyone who should deliver him up. There was no county or town or village where More did not look for him, no sheriff or justice of the peace to whom he did not apply, no harbor where he did not post some officer to catch him. But the answer from every quarter was: "He is not here." Indeed, Frith, having been informed of the great exertions of his enemy, was fleeing from place to place, often changing his dress, and finding safety nowhere.

Determining to leave England and return to Tyndale, he went to Milton Shore in Essex with the intention of embarking. A ship was ready to sail, and quitting his hiding-place he went down to the shore with all precaution. He had been betrayed. More's agents, who were on the watch, seized him as he was stepping on board, and carried him to the Tower. *This occurred in October 1532.*

Frith was executed by burning alive, 4 July, 1533, aged between 24 and 30, depending on source, his parents claiming he was 30. His trial and sentence of heresy was for his denying purgatory and transubstantiation (the material presence of the Lord in the bread and wine used in communion). He was not sentenced for his "Anabaptist" beliefs, which was in this time period not being prosecuted strongly, but would be after the reformation where both purgatory and transubstantiation were denied by the English reformers.

For this reason Frith has by historians been made a protestant reformer, whereas due to his associations and beliefs on baptism and the church, he should be identified as a restorer, an Anabaptist, not a protestant reformer.

Like Tyndale and other restorers, Frith's character was gentle, a peaceable person, unlike the reformers who were prepared to and did use violence to force their views. He opposed a national church and hence, infant baptism, the altar and clergy. Whether we agree with all his statements or not, Frith must not be counted as a reformer, but a restorer who sought to return to the Biblical church. He had contacts with the Lord's Church, and, it seems, may have had at one time the support of (queen) Anne Boleyn, who was instrumental in getting books and tracts into the court of Henry VIII.

Much of the language used by Frith copies that of Simon Fish and William Tyndale, showing a familiarity with their beliefs. Like others, he believes in original sin, but follows the thinking that it is the consequence of Adam's sin we inherit, rather than damnation for infants inherited directly from Adam. Therefore, he denied the need for infant baptism.

The following is taken from *The History of the Reformation in the Time of Calvin*, by J.H. Merle d'Aubigne.

A young mechanic of twenty-four, Andrew Hewet by name, was placed in his cell. Frith asked him for what crime he was sent to prison. "The bishops," he replied, 'asked me what I thought of the sacrament, and I answered, I think as Frith does. Then one of them smiled, and the Bishop of London said: Why Frith is a heretic, and already condemned to be burnt, and if you do not retract your opinion you shall be burnt with him. Very well, I answered, I am content. So they sent me here to be burnt along with you.

On the 4th of July they were both taken to Smithfield; the executioners fastened them to the post, back to back; the torch was applied, the flame rose in the air, and Frith, stretching out his hands, embraced it as if it were a dear friend whom he would welcome. The spectators were touched, and showed marks of lively sympathy. "Of a truth," said an evangelical Christian in after days, "he was one of those prophets whom God, having pity on this realm of England, raised up to call us to repentance." His enemies were there also. Poke, a fanatic priest, observing some persons praying, called out: "Do not pray for such folks, any more than you would for a dog." At this moment a sweet light shone on Frith's face, and he was heard beseeching the Lord to pardon his enemies. Hewet died first, and Frith thanked God that the sufferings of his young brother were over. Committing his soul into the Lord's hands, he expired.[1]

Frith's comments on baptism, and hence, the church are reprinted in part below, being excerpted from his *Sacrament Of Baptism Described*, 1533. In 1533, verse numbers had not been invented; hence, he quotes only the sixteenth chapter of Mark. The Reformation in England started in 1526. Frith's book below is dated nine years later. We may not agree with all Frith wrote, but we can state his thinking is what was then called an "Anabaptist," that he is teaching baptism by immersion, which remits sin through faith, through the blood of Christ.

Many historians deny that any English Anabaptists existed as early as the 1530s, many preferring a date of 1612, with the Helwys congregation. The Helwys congregation is incorrectly said to be the first Baptist church on English soil, which at such a late date excludes a link with the pre-reformation Lollards. It is also claimed, incorrectly, that the Helwys congregation poured rather than immersing. Frith is counted as being a Lollard, or Lutheran reformer, with no links to the "Anabaptists." Such is incorrect. He held to believer's baptism, as did his brethren. The following is evidence that in England in the 1530s, baptism by immersion for believers, for the remission of sins, was being taught in congregations separated from the Roman Catholic and Church of England.

Frith follows the expressions of Tyndale and Fish on baptism. All three were closely acquainted and used the identity—church of Christ.

A MIRROR, OR LOOKING GLASS,

WHEREIN YOU MAY BEHOLD

THE SACRAMENT OF BAPTISM DESCRIBED.

ANNO M.D.XXXIII.

BY ME,

JOHN FRITH.

He that will believe and be baptized, shall be saved: but he that will not believe shall be condemned. Mark xvi.

CONSIDERING the manifold and lamentable errors wherewith not the ignorant people only, but also the learned, (as they seem,) have been seduced long, as touching the blessed sacrament of baptism, I thought it expedient therein to write my mind, trusting, by that means, to bring again the blind hearts of many unto the right way; and I doubt not but that the elect and chosen of God, that know their Shepherd's voice, and have the spirit to judge all things, shall easily perceive whether this be conformable to their master's voice, and shall hereby be admonished to leave their wandering in the dark and loathsome ways which lead unto death, and to walk without stumbling in the comfortable light which bringeth their conscience to rest, and such peace that passeth all understanding.

One error is this: They put so great confidence in the outward sign, that without discretion they condemn the infants, which die or they be baptized, unto everlasting pain. Another is this: They cleave so strongly unto the weak ceremonies, that they think if a drunken priest leave out a word, as *Volo* say ye, or *Credo* say ye, or forget to put spittle or salt in the child's mouth, that child is not christened; yea so much give they thereunto the beggarly salt, that they will say, Spill not the salt, for it is our Christendom; and use also to swear by it; saying, By this salt, that it is my Christendom. Alas! what blindness is this. These two errors are the principal that I do intend at this time to confute; for when they are fallen, the other that are grounded on these must needs decay. First, we must mark three things in every sacrament to be considered, the sign, the signification, and the faith which is given unto the words of God. The sign in baptism, is the plunging down in the material water, and lifting up again, by the which, as by an outward badge, we are known to be of the number of them which profess Christ to be their Redeemer and Saviour.

This outward sign doth neither give us the Spirit of God; neither yet grace, that is the favour of God. For if through the washing in the water, the Spirit or grace were given, then should it follow that whosoever were baptized in water should receive this precious gift; but that is not so, wherefore I must needs conclude that this outward sign, by any power or influence that it hath, bringeth not the Spirit or favour of God. That every man receiveth not this treasure in baptism, it is evident; for put the case, that a Jew or an infidel should say that he did believe, and believed not indeed, and upon his words were baptized indeed, (for no man can judge what his heart is, but we must receive him unto baptism if he confess our faith with his mouth, albeit his heart be far from thence,) this miscreant, now thus baptized, hath received this outward sign and sacrament, as well the most faithful man believing. Howbeit, he neither receiveth the Spirit of God, neither yet any grace, but rather condemnation. Wherefore, it is evident that the exterior sign giveth not this gift: which is also as certain in all other sacraments, yea, in the sacrament of the altar, which may be called a double sacrament...

...And for this cause, when we baptise one that is come unto age of discretion, we ask of him whether he believe? If he answer yea, and desire baptism, then he is baptised: so that we require faith in him before he is baptised...

Now will I proceed with the second point of this

sacrament, which is the signification. The signification of baptism is described of Paul in the sixth of the Romans: that, as we are plunged bodily into the water, even so we are dead and buried with Christ from sin: and as we are lifted again out of the water, even so are we risen with Christ from our sins, that we might hereafter walk in a new conversation of life. So that these two things, that is, to be plunged in the water, and lift up again, do signify and represent the whole pith and effect of baptism, that is, the mortification of our old Adam, and the rising up of our new man. What is the old Adam? Verily, even that by natural inheritance is planted through Adam's fall in us, as to be unfaithful, angry, envious, covetous, slothful, proud, and ungodly: these, and such other uses, wherewith our nature is venomed, ought we with all diligence to cut off and mortify, that we may daily be more patient, liberal, and merciful, according to that our baptism doth signify; insomuch that a Christian man's life is nothing else save a continual baptism, which is begun when we are dipped in the water, and is put in continual use and exercise as long as the infection of sin remaineth in our bodies, which is never utterly vanquished until the hour of death; and there is the great Goliath slain with his own sword, that is, death, which is the power of sin, and the gate of everlasting life opened unto us. And thus is Paul to be understood (Gal. iii.) where he saith, All ye that are baptized into Christ, have put Christ on you; that is, you have promised to die with Christ as touching your sins and worldly desires past, and to become new men, or creatures, or members of Christ. This have we all promised unto the congregation, and it is represented in our baptism. But alas! There are but few which indeed fulfil that they promise, or rather that the sacrament promiseth for them. And for this cause it is called of Paul the fountain of the new birth and regeneration, (Tit. iii.) because it signifieth that we will indeed renounce and utterly forsake our old life, and purge our members from the works of iniquity through the virtue of the Holy Ghost, which, as the water or fire doth cleanse the body, even so doth it purify the heart from all uncleanness: yea, it is a common phrase in Scripture to call the Holy Ghost water and fire, because these two elements express so lively his purging operation...

Now have we expounded the signification of baptism, which signification we may obtain only by faith; for if thou be baptized a thousand times with water, and have no faith, it availeth thee no more towards God, than it doth a goose when she ducketh herself under the water. Therefore, if thou wilt obtain the profit of baptism, thou must have faith, that is, thou must be surely persuaded that thou art newly born again, not by water only, but by water and the Holy Ghost, (John iii.) and thou art become the child of God, and that thy sins are not imputed to thee, but forgiven through the blood and passion of Christ, according unto the promise of God. This faith have neither the devils, neither yet the wicked; for the wicked cannot believe the remission of their sins, but fall into utter desperation, and make God a liar as much as in them is; for promises they believe not the testimony which he gave [of] his Son, and this is that testimony, that all which believe on him have everlasting life. (John v.) And the devils cannot believe it, for they have no promise made unto them. Thus, through Christ's blood, whereof our baptism hath his full strength and vigour, are we regenerate and made at one with the Father; for by our first natural birth we are the children of wrath, (Ephes. ii) and the enemies of God. (Rom. v.)

Finally, baptism is an ordinance institute of God, and no practice of man's imagination, put in use in Christ's time, and after his resurrection commanded to be ministered unto all that believe, whether they were Jews or Gentiles; for Christ saith to his apostles, Go ye and teach all nations, baptizing them in the name of the Father, and of the Son, and of the Holy Ghost : wherefore, although it seem never so exterior thing, yet ought it to be had in great price and much reverence, because it was commanded of God to be done...[2]

The burning of Andrew Hewet and John Frith.

ENDNOTES

[1]J.H. Merle d'Aubigne, *The History of the Reformation in the Time of Calvin*, vol 4.

[2]The Works of the English Reformers: William Tyndale and John Frith. *A Mirror, Or Looking Glass, Wherein You May Behold The Sacrament Of Baptism Described,* ed. Thomas Russell, vol. 3. *(*1831) 281ff.

10

WILLIAM TYNDALE

And the things that thou hast heard of me among many
witnesses, the same commit thou to faithful men, who
shall be able to teach others also (2 Timothy 2:2).

Tyndale is famous for his translation from the Greek of Erasmus
into English of the New Testament, which was printed in several
editions. At that time the Bible was produced by scriptoria, each
copy being produced by hand, copied from another source. As
language changed, the Bible of the Lollards became antiquated and
in time, marred with minor mistakes and was scarce. The Bible
of Tyndale would remedy all three short comings; it would be up
to date; printing would reduce mistakes made by copyists; and it
would be common and affordable. The work though, translating
and distribution would be illegal, punishable by burning. Several
translations were produced, the most notable in 1526 and 1534.

Standard reference books such as *William Tindale*, a biography
by Robert Demaus, 1904 and James Mozley's 1937 book *William
Tyndale* are written from a reformed infant baptism position. It would
have helped if, in his two comprehensive volumes, Christopher
Anderson's *Annals of the English Bible* (1845), a most extensive

publication on Tyndale, would have established Tyndale's position in regard to church fellowship and doctrines. Although Anderson was a respected theological writer and Baptist preacher he failed to mention Tyndale's belief in, and association with those who held to believers' baptism. Modern books on Tyndale are no different. Anyone consulting a book on Tyndale, recent or old, will be disappointed in searching for his beliefs and affiliations regarding where he stood on baptism and his associations.

Older Baptist historians such as Thomas Crosby, who in 1738 produced four massive volumes, and nearly a century later, Joseph Ivimey, who produced another four-volume history on the English Baptists, do allude to Tyndale's holding to believers' baptism and being a member of or affiliating with Anabaptist congregations. Other Baptist historians (Crosby followed by others), have claimed that Tyndale came from a Lollard family or background, but no evidence is provided other than geographical. Crosby, of course, could have been working from witness accounts that were not documented, but he does not specify. From there the claim passed into myth. Older historians may have had access to documents and witnesses no longer available. Equally, they may be mistaken; such is the frustrations of historical research when seeking evidence.

These historians are remarkably accurate. Tyndale did come from a Lollard background, was associated with the then Churches of Christ, who not only distributed his books, but whose members helped finance his Bible translations. William Tyndale and John Frith are the only sixteenth-century Christians of whom there is any evidence of financial support to undertake full time work, either in book production, or Bible translating.

The Baptists who claim Tyndale as Baptist, using the original sense of the word, are correct. But, of course, those whom he associated with rejected Luther's justification by faith alone, and Calvinism. This is reflected in Tyndale and Frith's later writings. At first, both men did for a time reflect Luther's theology, which is most unhelpful for us today as they can be misquoted, but neither at any point held to infant baptism despite often being (mis) quoted as doing so.

To do Tyndale justice, not only is an entire volume required, but several. What follows is merely a very brief introduction to the man, much of which is missing from other histories.[1] There was no standard spelling for his name, variously given as Tindale, Tindall, Tyndale or Tindalus when Latinised. (His first name was often spelt Wyllyam). The name he used at University and elsewhere was Sir William Hychyns (Hitchins) (Sir was a common prefix in that time, as was master. We still use "sir" when addressing strangers. So do students address their male teachers). Tyndale was not knighted and hence the use of "sir" must not be thought of as a knighthood or rank.[2]

Tyndale was a complex man, born about 1495 at Slymbridge, near the Welsh border (Western England), an area where Lollardy was prevalent. He studied at Oxford University where humanism and Catholicism was taught along with Augustinian theology. He was later to come under Lutheran influence and even later to be closely involved with the Churches of Christ in England, though from evidence his association dates from his childhood. After a trial, conviction and imprisonment, he was executed in 1536.

There are no church records of his birth, as one would expect if his parents denied infant baptism. He grew up in the lovely Gloucestershire countryside, where his father farmed land belonging to the Lords of Berkeley who resided in Berkeley Castle. Once a year all of the farmers on the estate had to visit the Castle to pay their rents and this day was made a holiday. At the Castle oxen and pigs were roasted and games played. The tenants also went to the Castle Chapel for services. Some years before Tyndale was born one of the Lords of Berkeley, Thomas, the fifth baron, had been a Lollard. Baron Thomas had appointed as his chaplain a man called John Trevisa who had painted on the ceiling of the Chapel verses of Scripture selected from the Revelation. As William Tyndale attended these yearly functions with his parents, he would have seen these texts on the Chapel ceiling, and they were his introduction to the Holy Scriptures.[3]

His parents were able to afford to send him to Oxford where he received his degrees from Magdalene College, his B.A. in 1512, and his M.A. in 1515. Later he studied at Cambridge where the great Greek scholar Erasmus had been teaching. He was ordained to the Roman Catholic Priesthood in 1521.[4]

Site of the White Horse Inn

Known as 'Little Germany' where Cambridge scholars debated the works of Martin Luther in the early sixteenth century

A birthplace of the Reformation in England

At Cambridge, Tyndale studied and became identified with the "new learning." Cambridge University was much more sympathetic to reform of the Church than Oxford. Some students began meeting in a room at The White Horse Inn for Bible study where Frith and others participated. He eventually left the University and became Tutor and Chaplain to the Walsh family residing at Little Sodbury. The White Horse Inn was located on the site of King's Lane, to the west of King's Parade. When the King's College screen was extended in 1870, the tavern was demolished, but a Blue Plaque on the college's Chetwynd Court commemorates it, as seen in the picture on the previous page.

Below is the location where the White Horse Inn stood.

The following are views of Kings College;
views familiar to Frith and Tyndale.

Whilst in the service of the Walsh family, Tyndale began translating Greek texts into English. His eventual aim was to translate the Bible into English. Foxe, the martyrologist, records a conversation between Tyndale and a "certain learned man," who said "We were better be without God's laws than the Pope's." Tyndale replied "I defy the Pope and all his laws if God spare my life, ere many years I will cause a boy that driveth the plough shall knowest more of the Scripture than thou doest."[5] Erasmus (Desiderius Erasmus Roterodamus, 1466-1536) had said "I totally dissent from those who are unwilling that the sacred scriptures, translated into the vulgar tongue, should be read by private individuals, as if Christ had taught such subtle doctrines that they can with difficulty be understood by a very few theologians, or as if the strength of the Christian religion lay in men's ignorance of it. The mysteries of kings it were perhaps better to conceal, but Christ wishes His mysteries to be published as widely as possible. I would wish even all women to read the Gospel and the Epistles of Paul. And they were translated into all languages of all people, that they might be read and known, not merely by the Scotch and the Irish, but even by the Turks and the Saracens. I wish that the husbandman may sign parts of them at his plough, that the weaver may warble them as his shuttle, that the traveler may with their narratives beguile the weariness of the way."[6] We can see from Erasmus where Tyndale might have received his thoughts on this.

In the Anglican Church Tyndale is remembered on October 6th, having his own saint's day. It is ironic that the Anglicans sought his death and Tyndale opposed the idea of saints and their days. Today, many churches of various beliefs make Tyndale their own, when Tyndale opposed their beliefs and they denied him.

According to Copeland the teaching of William Tyndale on baptism was that:

> The washinge preacheth unto us that we ar clensed wyth Christe's bloud shedynge which was an offering and a satisfaction for the synne of al that repent and beleve consentynge and submyttyne themselves unto the wyl of God. The plungynge into the water sygnyfyeth that we die and are buried with Chryst as coserning ye old life of synne which is Ada (Adam). And the pulling out again sygnyfyeth that we ryse again with Christe in a new

lyfeful of the holye gooste which shal teach us, and gyde us, and work the wyll of God in us; as thou seest Rom.[7]

In modern English it reads, with the preceding paragraph, I have consulted David Daniell's updated English for this:

> The washing without the word helpeth not: but through the word it purifieth and cleanseth us: as thou readest, Ephesians 5, how Christ cleanseth the congregation in the fountain of water through the word. The word is the promise that God hath made. Now as a preacher, in preaching the word of God, sayeth the hearers that believe; so doth the washing, in that it preacheth and representeth unto us the promise that God hath made unto us in Christ. The washing preacheth unto us, that we are cleansed with Christ's blood-shedding; which was an offering, and a satisfaction, for the sin of all that repent and believe, consenting and submitting themselves unto the will of God. The plunging into the water signifieth that we die, and are buried with Christ, as concerning the old life of sin, which is Adam. And the pulling out again signifieth that we rise again with Christ in a new life, full of the Holy Ghost, which shall teach us and guide us, and work the will of God in us, as thou seest, Romans 6.[8]

Tyndale also wrote:

> Repentance goeth before faith, and prepareth the way to Christ, and to the promises. For Christ cometh not but unto them that see their sins in the law, and repent. Repentance, that is to say, this mourning and sorrow of the heart, lasteth all our lives long: for we find ourselves, all our lives long, too weak for God's law, and therefore sorrow and mourn, longing for strength. Repentance is no sacrament: as faith, hope, love, and knowledge of a man's sins, are not to be called sacraments. For they are spiritual

and invisible. Now must a sacrament be an outward sign that may be seen, to signify, to represent, and to put a man in remembrance of some spiritual promise, which cannot be seen but by faith only. Repentance, and all the good deeds which accompany repentance, to slay the lusts of the flesh, are signified by baptism. For Paul saith, Romans 6, as it is above rehearsed: "Remember ye not (saith he), that all we which are baptized in the name of Christ Jesus are baptized to die with him? We are buried with him in baptism for to die;" that is, to kill the lusts and the rebellion which remaineth in the flesh. And after that he saith, "Ye are dead, as concerning sin, but live unto God through Christ Jesus our Lord." If thou look on the profession of our hearts, and on the Spirit and forgiveness which we have received through Christ's merits, we are full dead: but if thou look on the rebellion of the flesh, we do but begin to die, and to be baptized, that is, to drown and quench the lusts, and are full baptized at the last minute of death. And as concerning the working of the Spirit, we begin to live, and grow every day more and more, both in knowledge and also in godly living, according as the lusts abate: as a child receiveth the full soul at the first day, yet groweth daily in the operations and works thereof.[9]

Tyndale's teaching on baptism follows the same reasoning as that of Simon Fish in his "Summe." Baptism is for believers, by immersion, whereby the blood of Christ takes away sin for those who "repent and believe, consenting and submitting themselves unto the will of God."

Commenting on Tyndale, faith-only proponents lift Tyndale totally out of context and claim opposite Tyndale's reasoning on salvation. Tyndale wrote with the fires of the stake very near, yet he taught plainly and succinctly, as was his manner, against infant baptism and dead rites of man's religion which attempt, as counterfeits, to supplant faithful obedience to that living Book of books so long held captive. He did not throw out baptism as unnecessary, but instead showed forth true baptism by contrasting the false baptism of priestcraft. "As a child receiveth the full soul at the first day." In this we see Tyndale well understood the time at which the Christian is born again a new child of God, "and whosoever doth acknowledge his sins, receiveth forgiveness," as saith John, in the first of his first epistle (1 John 1:9).

> If we knowledge our sins, he is faithful and just to forgive us our sins, and to cleanse us from all unrighteousness; that is, because he hath promised, he must for his truth's sake do it. This confession is necessary all our lives long, as is repentance. And as thou understandest of repentance, so understand of this confession; for it is likewise included in the sacrament of baptism. For we always repent, and always knowledge or confess our sins unto God, and yet despair not; but remember that we are washed in Christ's blood: which thing our baptism doth represent and signify unto us.

Many Protestants claim Tyndale as either some kind of proto-Calvinist or Lutheran. That he was influenced by Luther cannot be denied. Luther, at first, was seen by Christians of the time as a man who directly withstood the papacy. Little did they know Luther only sought to reform the excesses of the Roman church, not to restore the Biblical Church of Jesus Christ.

Tyndale had tenacious independence from man-made creeds and signs and symbols, and preached of the gospel patiently, with a deep understanding of the Word. Tyndale was a Christian and possibly from a Christian family, he was ordained as a priest in the Roman Catholic Church (the only way at that time a man could legally preach the Gospel in England). He taught that only those who believe may be baptised into Christ for the remission of sins and, thereupon, they could partake of the Lord's Supper. It seems that Tyndale's religious background was influenced by the Welsh Lollards. Tyndale's brother, John, was a faithful member of the Lord's church (Bow Lane congregation) and his brother's children continued in the faith after the death of William.

Tyndale was acquainted with William Tracy, who died in 1531. The Tracy family lived in Western England, in the same area where Tyndale, as a younger man, lived, worked and studied. Tracy's ancestor, Sir William de Tracy, Knt., (died c1189), was Lord of the Manor of Toddington, Gloucestershire, feudal Baron of Bradinch, near Exeter, and Lord of Moretonhampstead, Devon. He remains notorious as one of the four knights who murdered the Archbishop of Canterbury, Thomas Becket, in December 1170. Henry failed to arrest the knights, apparently having great sympathy for their crime, especially after his question to his knights – "Who will rid me of this meddlesome priest?" Tracy was one of the men who provided the answer! Becket, whilst a saint today, had defended immoral priests and was firmly set on increasing the power of the Roman Catholic Church in secular matters. Tracy himself was present during the murder, but did not hold the sword that half decapitated the unfortunate Becket.

Were the Tracys an old Lollard family? Sir William, who had been knighted by Henry VIII in 1513, wrote his will which was widely circulated in England amongst the churches of Christ and the greater public. His will was refused probate because of the anti-Catholic preamble and was condemned in convocation. Because of the controversial publicity it caused anti Romish sentiment, his body was exhumed and posthumously burned in 1532. He was condemned by the Bishop of London's court, resulting in an order being sent to Parker Chancellor to raise his body (1532). The Chancellor officiously burned the corpse, although the recorder only authorized him to raise the body according to the law of the church. In consequence, the recorder fined the chancellor £400 and turned him out of the chancellorship.

His will, dated 1530, reads as follows:

> In the Name of God, Amen. I, William Tracy, of Toddington, in the County of Gloucester, make my testament and last will as hereafter followeth: "First and before all things I commit myself to God, and to his mercy, believing, without doubt or mistrust, that by his

grace and the merits of Jesus Christ, and by the virtues of his passion, and the Resurrection, I have and shall have, remission of all my sins, and resurrection of body and soul, according as it is written: I believe that my redeemer liveth, and that at the last day I shall rise out of the earth, and in my flesh shall see my Saviour. "This my hope is laid up in my bosom. And touching the wealth of my soul, the faith that I have taken and rehearsed, is sufficient, as I suppose, without any other Man's Works or Merits. My Ground and belief that there is but one God and one Mediator between God and Man, which is Jesus Christ; so that I accept none other in Heaven or in Earth to be Mediator between me and God, but only Jesus Christ; all others to be but as Petitioners in receiving of Grace, but none able to give influence of Grace; and therefore will I bestow no part of my goods for that intent, that any man shall say or do to help my soul, for therein I trust only to the promise of Christ. He that believeth and is baptized shall be saved, and he that believeth not shall be damned.

As touching the burying of my body, it availeth me not whatsoever be done thereto; for St. Augustine saith, De Cura Agenda Pro Mortuis. As the funeral Pomps are rather the Solace of them that live, than the Wealth and comfort of them that are dead, therefore I remit it only to the discretion of my Executors. And touching the distribution of my temporal Goods, my purpose is, by the Grace of God, to bestow them to be accepted as the Fruits of Faith; so that I do not suppose that my Merit shall be by the Good bestowing of them, but my Merit is the Faith of Jesus Christ only, by whom such works are good; according to the words of our Lord: "I was hungry and Thou gavest me meat", etc. And it followeth, That which ye have done to the least of my brethren, ye have done it to me. And ever we should consider the true saying That a good work maketh not a good man, but a good man maketh a good work; for faith maketh a man both good and righteous, for a righteous man liveth by Faith, and whatsoever springeth not of Faith is sin. For my temporal goods, etc.[10]

Tracy's use of Mark 16:16, "He that believeth and is baptized shall be saved; but he that believeth not shall be damned" is not only evidence of his familiarity of the Bible at a time when owning the Bible was a crime, but his use of a text familiar to those who taught believers' baptism could not have gone unnoticed by the authorities. That the will was made public, printed and used as a tract, was quite deliberate. This is a text used by the Lollards (churches of Christ) and would have been out of place for Tracy, who had Lollard connections, if we follow conventional thinking. Anabaptism at this time was not, according to established historians, practised by the English, especially so far from Kent and London where the foreign Anabaptists were based (we are told). The other explanation is that the Lollards were Anabaptists as previously stated, but this will be unacceptable to many who deny the Anabaptists (churches of Christ) being both pre-reformation and active in England at such an early date. Of course, these Anabaptists were Christians whose doctrine was based on Biblical authority. Another local Gloucester family was the Bainhams. Sir Alexander Bainham, who was sheriff of Gloucestershire in 1497, 1501, and 1516; was a nephew of William Tracy. His son, James, who was educated in Greek and Hebrew, was a lawyer by profession and a preacher at the Church of Christ meeting in Bow Lane, London.

William Tracy's third son, Richard, took his MA at Oxford. He too was involved in the Bow Lane congregation before settling down in Gloucestershire, where from 1559 he held the position of Sheriff, having also been a Member of Parliament, Justice of the Peace and Royal Commissioner. He owned the lands of the Abbey of Tewkesbury, which came into the family by grant of land from the crown.

As owner of the former land of the Abbey of Tewkesbury, Richard Tracy is interesting to us. Maybe it is more than just a coincidence that immediately opposite the Abbey was a meeting place, converted from several houses, owned by a church of Christ originating from an unknown date. The congregation is known to have been well established by 1623, and only much later did the congregation convert to Calvinism (becoming part of the Baptist denomination). Some of the descendants of William Shakespeare were members of this congregation. The old Baptist Chapel (as it is now known) remains, having been restored by the local council. Did Tracy provide the houses, owned formerly by the Abbey, for the congregation to build a meeting place? Such a location required powerful men who could defend the church from persecution. The Bainhams and Tracys were such people. It is an interesting question but unfortunately one we cannot answer.[11]

The old meeting house in Tewkesbury, dating from the 1400s.

Tyndale was part of the circle of brethren meeting at Bow Lane, that included John Frith, Simon Fish, James Bainham, Richard Tracy and his brother John Tyndale, in the 1530s. Tyndale was a close friend of some of the brethren named. Tyndale's religious affiliations are difficult to find in established histories, yet it is easily established he was involved with the churches of Christ in England, particularly those meeting at Bow Lane. Simon Fish was involved in importing early editions of Tyndale's New Testament. He had died by the time later editions appeared.[12] Not only did Simon Fish involve himself with the distribution of Tyndale's New Testament, so did the church of Christ at Canterbury.

Tyndale's brother John, a London merchant, had been prosecuted in 1530 at the Star Chamber for distributing Tyndale's translation.[13] In London at this time was the "Society of Christian Brethren" which seems to have been an organised society with its own accounts and auditors. It subsidised people such as William Tyndale, and it underwrote the dangerous, but not unprofitable ,godly trade of smuggling into England, Scotland and Wales, his and others books. This society also seems to have held Bible studies in which materials were handed out. This organization had contacts throughout the country operating clandestinely and successfully.[14] Henry Monmouth, wealthy wool merchant (London Alderman, Sheriff 1534-7), was a leading member of the society. He had allowed Tyndale to reside in his home for six months in 1523. In 1528 he was arrested by Sir Thomas More, Lord Chancellor, and put into the Tower for assisting Tyndale. He was released soon after. Monmouth was a leading supporter of Tyndale and helped to fund his translation of the New Testament. Historians have labeled Monmouth as the first London Alderman to become protestant, the circle of religious friends who Monmouth associated were not protestant, but members of the church of Christ being labeled as protestant against evidence to the contrary.

Knowing that Tyndale's Bibles were distributed and smuggled in by members of the churches of Christ, it seems entirely feasible that some brethren had set up this organisation to finance this project, separate from the Lord's Church. There is also some evidence this "Society of Christian Brethren," which was run by merchants who were brethren, had existed for many years, being pre-reformation. At first, it distributed Lollard hand-written materials. The Lollard Bibles were extensively copied and circulated around the country despite the church systematically burning thousands of them. More Lollard (Wycliffe) Bibles have survived than any other medieval manuscript (two hundred and thirty exist) in spite of the constant burnings of the Bible and punishment of the owners. The closest in number are manuscripts by Chaucer, which number sixty. There is no evidence the "Society of Christian Brethren" was a missionary society; it existed simply as a project to finance the writing, printing and distribution of materials. Churches and individual Christians gave away the books for free. Other booksellers sold the books for profit. The arrangement seemed to work well. The distribution network seems to have been in place prior to the reformation, a continuation of the old Lollard network known to us as the "Society of Christian Brethren."

Despite attempts to make Tyndale a Lutheran, Reformer or Anglican, there is no evidence he was any of these. He plagiarised some of Luther's writings to which he added, but was no friend of Luther or any of the reformers. Tyndale was a restorationist, not a reformer.

William Tyndale and the title page of his New Testament.

Tyndale's N.T. which first appeared during 1526, was translated directly from the Greek third edition of Erasmus, and was far superior to Wycliffe's old Vulgate orientated Bible, which was now out of date and difficult to find. Tyndale's New Testament was mass printed. Because of it, many of the Catholic doctrines could be seen to be totally without any Bible authority. The established church was furious with his translation which they (Thomas More) claimed was inaccurate, which certainly led to his execution.

Tyndale at work with his assistant.

Tyndale's translation of five Greek words enormously angered his enemies. In each case his translation was absolutely accurate to the Greek. He translated the Greek word *presbuteros* as "elder," whereas the church had always translated it as "priest"; he translated *agape* as "love," where the church had always had it as "charity"; he translated *ekklesia* as "congregation," whereas the church had had it as "church"; and he translated *exomologeo* as "acknowledge," where the church used "confess." In that era people's idea of Church was the all-powerful Roman Catholic system, not the idea of the people of God, the congregation.

Mark 16:16 – "*and preach the glad tidings to all creatures: he that believeth, and is baptised, shall be saved. But he that believeth not, shall be damned*".

Acts 2:28 – "*Brethren, what shall we do? And Peter said unto them: repent, and be baptised every one of you in the name of Jesus Christ, for the remission of sins.*"

Romans 6:4 – "*We are buried with Him by baptism, for to die, that likewise as Christ was raised up from death by the glory of the Father: even so we also should walk in a new life.*"

Looking at the above translations of the Scriptures and the background of the church of that time it is difficult to imagine how Tyndale could have believed in infant baptism and not in believers' immersion.

Tyndale was tried on a charge of heresy in 1536 at Antwerp and condemned to the stake, despite Thomas Cromwell's intercession on his behalf. On 6 October 1536, Tyndale was first strangled, then burned, dying for translating the Bible into English. His final words reportedly were, "Oh Lord, open the King of England's eyes." Later Henry VIII would allow Bibles into church buildings.[15] Tyndale as noted, has often been accused of being a Lutheran. It must be noted at the time of Tyndale's translating the New Testament Luther did not offer him patronage, whereby he could work in safety.

On April 5, 1533 there appeared from the press of "Nicolas Twonson" of Nuremberg a treatise entitled "The Supper of the Lord." It was anonymous, but some consider it to be Tyndale's work.[16]

> ...then distribute to the ministers, which, taking the bread with great reverence, will divide it to the congregation, every man breaking and reaching it forth to his next neighbour and member of the mystic body of Christ, other ministers following with the cups, pouring forth and dealing with the wine, all together thus being now partakers of one bread and one cup...

In 1526 in Colchester, Tyndale's New Testament was selling for four shillings.[17]

Tyndale's thoughts on the working of the Word can be found in this statement.

> The Spirit of God accompanieth faith, and bringeth with her (i.e. with faith) light, wherewith a man beholdeth himself in the law of God, and seeth his miserable bondage and captivity, and humbleth himself, and abhorreth himself: she (faith) bringeth God's promises of all good things in Christ. God worketh with His Word, and in His Word: and when His word is preached, faith rooteth herself in the hearts of the elect; and as faith entereth, and the Word of God is believed, the power of God looseth the heart from

the captivity and bondage under sin.[18]

Tyndale certainly held to the view that faith works through the Word. In regard to the books of Hebrews and James, Tyndale concludes, in direct opposition to Luther, that the books are "no more to be refused for holy, godly, and Catholic than the other authentic Scriptures, but ought of right to be taken for Holy Scripture."[19]

Tyndale wrote that the office of elder and presbyter were the same as that of bishop.[20] Regarding repentance preceding baptism, Tyndale states this in his *Obedience of a Christian Man*.[21] In his translation of the Bible, Tyndale used the word *congregation* instead of *church*. During this period of the early reformation, the Roman Catholic Church was in the language of the day, the clergy, who were the church. Tyndale realised the need to convey the fact that where "church" is used in scripture, it refers to the people of God. The remedy was to use the word *congregation* to enforce the point. Elsewhere Tyndale was happy to use the word *church*.[22] Tyndale retained the word *baptism*, which in the sixteenth century meant immersion, so was not an issue. It was not until the 1640s that Calvinists in the Church of England would adopt "pouring and sprinkling."[23] For Tyndale it was at baptism when a person became a member of the "church of Christ."[24] Duffield notes that Tyndale in his translations may have been influenced by Lollard phraseology, possibly due to his early days in the west county where Lollard influence was strong.[25]

The changing English of the time, along with improvements in translation skills can be seen here by comparing renderings of scripture from three versions of the Bible. First is the King James Version of 1769, in common use today, it is normally referred to as being (incorrectly) the 1611.

Acts 20:7 – "And upon the first day of the week, when the disciples came together to break bread, Paul preached unto them, ready to depart on the morrow; and continued his speech until midnight."

Now we read two of the Wycliffe, or Purvey versions of the 1300s, the first in modern English – "And in the first day of the week, when we came to break bread, Paul disputed with them, and should go forth in the morrow; and he drew along the sermon into midnight."[26]

Purvey's 1388 revision reads – "And in the first dai of the woke, whanne we camen to breke breed, Poul disputide with hem, and schulde go forth in the morew; and he drow along the sermoun til in to mydnygt."[27] Another translation reads – "And in the first days of the woke, whanne we camen to breke breed, Poule disputid with hem, and schulde go forth in the morrowe; and he drows along the sermoun til in to mydnygt."[28]

Tyndale's 1526 translation reads – "On a saboth daye the disciples cam togedger for to breake breed, and Paul preached unto them (redy to departe on the morrow) and continued his preachynge unto mydnyght."[29] His 1534 translation reads – "And on the morrowe after the saboth days, the disciples came to geder for to breake breed and Paul preached vnto them (redy to departe on the morrowe) and continued the preachynge vnto mydnyght."[30]

The versions above in their time period were good renderings. But language changed, the need for Bible versions to reflect changes in language and dialect were required. Printing allowed greater accuracy as mistakes were less likely than handwritten Bibles. The effect that Tyndale's translation had on the English language must not be underestimated. The endurance of Tyndale's version is attested by the survival of so much of it through the intermediate versions into the Authorised Version of 1611.[31]

Sir Frederic Kenyon wrote:

> The genius of Tyndale shows itself in the fact that he was able to couch his translations in a language perfectly understood of the people and yet still full of beauty and dignity. If the language of the Authorised Version has deeply affected our English prose, it is to Tyndale that the praise is originally due. He formed the mould, which subsequent revisers did but modify him.[32]

Professor Bruce quoted from H. Wheeler Robinson of Oxford University, "When we talk of Tyndale's version of the New Testament as being basic to the successive revisions which have appeared between his day and ours, more particularly the Authorised Version, the Revised Version and the Revised Standard Version, it is his 1534 edition that is meant." "Tindale's honesty, sincerity, and scrupulous integrity," says Professor J. Isaacs:

> His simple directness, his magical simplicity of phrase, his modest music, have given authority to his wording that has imposed itself on all later versions. With all the tinkering to which the New Testament has been subject, Tindale's version is still the basis in phrasing, rendering, vocabulary, rhythm, and often music as well. Nine-tenths of the Authorised New Testament is still Tindale, and the best is still his. More than that, in a number of places where the Authorised Version of 1611 departs from Tyndale's wording, the Revisers of 1881 return to it.[33]

The work of Tyndale in translating the scriptures into English and that of the brethren who ensured it was financed and distributed was not a work of the denominations, but brethren who were proud to wear the name of Christ as Christians and who were members of His Church, the church of Christ.

Objections to my placing Tyndale with the churches of Christ, practising believers' baptism by immersion for remission of sins, rather than a Lutheran will be made. Tyndale stated he had never been "confederated with Luther," a statement with which his arch-enemy, Thomas More was satisfied.[34] Unlike Luther, Tyndale defended the canonicity of the books of James, Jude and 2 Peter.[35]

The main objection cited is Tyndale's prologue to the Romans and his (claimed) comments over election and predestination. Firstly, only one copy to my knowledge exists of the prologue, which according to Henry Golde in February 1527 was ascribed to Tyndale and Roye. This must date the prologue to 1526 or earlier. The prologue is clearly based on Luther, but there are disagreements.[36] If the prologue is Tyndale's, then he changed his views on election and predestination since, by 1534, in his exposition of the Tracy will, he talks of God's plan being predestined for the church rather than the individual. If Tyndale was a Lutheran, with the fires of persecution waiting, surely the safest and most sensible course he could have ever taken would have been to work under the patronage of Luther. But if he was at enmity with Luther, with the fires of persecution at hand, we can understand and allow his making mistakes in his enthusiasm to share the scriptures.

If Tyndale held to predestination, why bother to evangelise? He had a great desire to reach out with the Scriptures. We have noted he previously said, "I will cause a boy that driveth the plough shall knowest more of the Scripture than thou doest." He sought to make the scriptures known, why bother if salvation is out of the hands of the individual? His final prayer was "Oh Lord, open the King of England's eyes" to having the scriptures made available for all people. Why die for a belief that says man cannot through the scriptures find salvation as predestination teaches?

We must read Tyndale in the context of the society in which he lived. In the Romish Church, salvation was by works, ritual and soul-cleansing in purgatory. For Tyndale, the church was a spiritual place, separate from the world where Godly men were in fellowship with God. This is reflected in his writings where he makes considerable mention of the Spirit. For the working of the Spirit, Tyndale said "God worketh with His Word, and in His Word: and when His word is preached." (Quotations taken from above.)

Tyndale translated the Greek word *metanoeo* as "repent." *Metanoeo* is a classical and New Testament Greek word meaning "a change in the mind." It means that sort of complete change in ones thinking and the direction of their lives. The Latin Church had always translated it as *paenitentiam agite*, meaning "do penance." In the Catholic system, to do penance meant paying money, building (funding) a new monastery, taking a pilgrimage or providing a church building. They did not want the New Testament to be saying "repent." Far from "repenting," as long as the wealthy were paying into the coffers, they could continue blissfully to sin. In the Catholic view Tyndale had wilfully mistranslated their words "do penance" and were absolutely horrified!

The system of salvation in the Romish Church was by penance, through good works consisting of giving, pilgrimages and shrine worship, etc. This was on the path to heaven. Once dead, the deceased would then work their way through the purifying fires of purgatory, helped by those left behind by paying the church for intercession through prayers to grant indulgences. This salvation was only possible in the Romish Church through good works. In 1440, Loenzo Valla (d. 1457) proved by linguistic analysis that the "Donation of Constantine," a document which the Roman Catholic Church relied upon for its "temporal authority," was a forgery from the ninth century. Valla in 1444 made a critical comparison with the N.T. Vulgate and the Greek N.T. pointed out that the Greek word *metanoia,* which in the Vulgate is translated "do penance," actually means "repentance." Erasmus incorporated this change in his 1516 edition of the Greek New Testament; in turn Luther found this new reading the basis of his famous assault on the practises of indulgences (1517) Tyndale in his translation used "Repentance." The Bibles used by the Lollards, which predate the time of Valla, sometimes used two middle English words where "do penance" is used in the Latin Vulgate, viz., "forthink" and "forthenkith." Both have the same meaning as repent and repentance.[37]

The Bibles used by the Lollards were surprisingly good. Whilst based on the Latin Vulgate, they carried over readings such as Acts 8:37, the longer ending of Mark (including Mark 16:15-16) and 1 John 5:7. All three are found in the Lollard and later Bibles. Modern versions based on the Westcott and Hort theory dumb down the deity of Christ and question verses mentioned above. Prior to the Lollard Bibles, the Waldensians were producing Bibles in the common language of the day.[38] After the Conquest of 1066, the language of England would be French, a language used by the Waldensians.

Far from Roman Catholic versions keeping the Word of God safe, in this and other cases it has been the vernacular Bibles used by Christians which has remained faithful, a tradition kept by Tyndale and continued in the King James and New King James versions. Going back before the time of the Lollards, in the Anglo-Saxon Gospel, repentance was *dæd bòt* to make amends.[39] The Anglo-Saxon Gospel is dated to about AD 597 [40] being translated from the Old Latin, which itself dates back to the Italic which is prior to AD 157.[41]

The preaching that salvation could be found outside the Romish Church through repentance rather than good works was intolerable, and the Roman Catholic Church used every means possible in barbaric times to oppose the truth, but failed. The idea that there were not good Bibles before the age of printing is not correct. The Waldensians and Lollards had perfectly good translations of the scriptures. The problem for the Romish Church was over "penance." Sir Thomas More (1478-1535), who was Chancellor of England, objected strongly to Tyndale's use of "repentance." Again More finds fault with Tyndale for using "acknowledge" rather than "confess." The false Romish doctrines were being refuted as they had for centuries.[42]

Since Bible Criticism, whether higher or lower, has come into fashion, the effort has been over the Greek text. Little work by comparison has been undertaken in the field of the scriptures used in the vernacular. Miss A. C. Paues of Cambridge University partly corrected this anomaly in her work, *A Fourteenth Century English Biblical Version,* produced in 1902. She makes some interesting comments concerning the scriptures in the English language. In the preface, she notes that a proper study of Bibles prior to Wycliffe (d. 1384) "had never been treated, and that for many years past the subject scarcely been touched."[43] Certainly little has changed since Paues wrote this, and she claims some manuscripts are both misdated and consequently attributed to the wrong author. Miss Paues makes the case that English Bibles prior to Wycliffe are not only very good, but in one case a Bible produced in French was actually translated from the Anglo-Saxon.[44]

Margaret Deanesly considered the Lollard Bible to be "a very good English translation of the Vulgate."[45] For the Lollards the scriptures of the New Testament were "Christis law,"[46] a serious blow for the Romish Church who sought to make the Church the final authority, not the Bible.

The problem for the Romish Church was that for the first time, with printing, Bibles could be produced relatively cheaply and easily. The Lollard Bibles were produced by hand, being laboriously copied and often, only produced in books, e.g., Matthew, James, Hebrews, etc. Burning these Bibles (or part of the Bible) when found kept the number in circulation limited. But with printed Bibles, the price dropped whilst the quantity and quality increased.

It is interesting to note, and a point that seems missed by the higher critics of the Bible, is that the vernacular Bibles were not only very good but, from the second century onward they have kept a consistency of text that remains to this day in the KJV and NKJV. This is tradition retained by Tyndale in his translation, continued in part with some Lollard, and hence, earlier readings, from which has passed into modern versions where the Westcott and Hort text and its daughters are lacking.

When Tyndale's New Testament first appeared, Tunstall, Bishop of London, employed Augustine Packington (the son of Sir John and Lady Ann Packington) to purchase all he could find for the purpose of having the translation burned. Meanwhile, in Antwerp, Tyndale was greatly distressed. He had printed many copies of his New Testament and was aware of serious mistakes in translation and sought to make a better version, but his money had been spent on the first edition. For Tyndale the problem was irresolvable, then into this dilemma Packington arrives. He explained his purpose, to purchase

Tyndale's translation for the purpose of burning. Both are happy, Tyndale having now the required financing for a second printing, and Packington having purchased the Bibles demanded by the Lord Bishop of London, Tunstall. All three were delighted, the Bishop of London had the Bibles for burning, Packington had the thanks from both, and Tyndale had the money, his cash-flow problems solved. Duly the Bibles were burned by the clergy in a big show for Londoners in Cheapside, which is only a few minutes walk from the church of Christ that met in Bow Lane.

After this, Tyndale corrected the New Testament and within months they were coming into England. The Bishop learning this sent for Packington, and said to him: "How comes it that there be so many New Testaments abroad? You promised me that you had bought all." Replied Packington, "Surely, I bought all there was to be had, but I perceive they have printed more since. I see it will never be better so long as they have letters and presses. Wherefore you were best to buy the presses too, and so you shall be sure" at which the Bishop smiled, and so the matter for Packington ended.

Soon after, George Constantine was apprehended by Sir Thomas More, who was then Chancellor of England. Constantine was a member, it seems, of the church. Before interrogation, More had Constantine shown and demonstrated various torture and interrogation techniques, as was the practise of the time. More then asks:

> Constantine, I would have thee plain with me in one thing
> that I will ask, and I promise thee I will shew thee favour
> in all other things whereof thou are accused. There is
> beyond the sea, Tyndale, Joye, and a great many more of
> you. I know they cannot live without help. There are some
> that help and succour them with money, and thou being
> one of them hadst thy part thereof and therefore knowest
> from whence it came. I pray thee tell me, who be they that
> help them thus?

"My lord," said Constantine, "I will tell you truly. It is the Bishop of London that hath holpen us, for he hath bestowed among us a great deal of money upon the Testaments to burn them. And that hath been, and yet is, our only succour and comfort." "Now by my troth," quoth More, "I think even the same, for so much I told the Bishop before he went about it." It is recorded by Burnet that at Constantine's answer, all in the room laughed.

Constantine walked free, Packington had kept to his contract and Tyndale was producing Bibles, having been financed generously by his enemy, the Lord Bishop of London. One way to make any work popular is to proclaim against it in public, and have it burned, which Tunstall had done. An aside to this story is Robert, another son of Sir John and Lady Ann Packington, who was the first man to be murdered with a gun in London. On the 13th November 1536, Robert was shot. The plot was organised by Doctor Vincent, Dean of Saint Paul's, who hired a stranger for sixty crowns to do the deed. Was this a revenge killing on Augustine, Robert being shot by mistake, we do not know but intrigue is a fascinating subject.[47]

Tyndale's execution, he was strangled first before his body was burned. The date given by Fox is October 1536, others have argued a month earlier in September. It is recorded Tyndale's final prayer was "Lord, open the King of England's eyes." Tyndale's prayer was not unanswered. Within a year Miles Coverdale's and Matthew's Bibles were granted licences, both translations relying on the work of Tyndale.[48]

Large numbers of Luther's books were widely distributed in England in the early part of the Reformation, due in no small part to the brotherhood mistakenly thinking initially that a restoration of the church looked possible. Later the Reformation as it developed in England looked to Calvin, not Luther. The brotherhood did not make the same mistake twice; Calvin they left alone. It was not until the 1640s that Calvinism entered the church of Christ, and that was over a hundred years later when the events of the early reformation were forgotten in the churches of Christ.

What Tyndale achieved was to leave us the Bible printed in modern English. The English language started as a mixture of Roman and Celtic. It used originally the Runic alphabet rather than Latin. It was the language spoken and written in parts of what are now England and south-eastern Scotland between at least the mid-5th century to the mid-12th century. Old English is a West Germanic language and is closely related to Old Frisian. It also experienced heavy influence from Old Norse, a member of the related North Germanic group of languages.

After the Conquest of 1066, the language evolved from Old to Middle English, which died out by about 1470. This was followed by the Chancery Standard, a form of London-based English, which began to become widespread, a process aided by the introduction of the printing press into England by William Caxton in the late 1470s. This was encouraged by the government, which realised a standard form of English was required. What followed in the 1530s is called Modern English, which interestingly is due not to Caxton or Chaucer, Shakespeare or the 1611 King James Bible. It is due to printing the Bible in English, a work funded by the London Church of Christ who financed Tyndale's translation of the Bible. Tyndale's English is classified as very early Modern English, an improvement over Chancery Standard. By the 1650s, Modern English had come into use. The English of the King James Bible, whilst modern, is influenced by Tyndale and Elizabethan English, being in some respects an English of its own. Nonetheless, it is technically Modern English.

For examples of English through the ages, I've set forth the Lord's Model Prayer (often erroneously referred to as the "Lord's Prayer"—the true Lord's Prayer being found in John 17) as recorded in Matthew 6:9-13, beginning with the Old English and ending with the Modern English of the 1769 King James Bible.

The Old English version as given in the West Saxon Gospels which is about AD 990:

> Fæder ure þu þe eart on heofonum, Si þin nama gehalgod.
> to becume þin rice, gewurþe ðin willa, on eorðan swa swa
> on heofonum. urne gedæghwamlican hlaf syle us todæg,
> and forgyf us ure gyltas, swa swa we forgyfað urum
> gyltendum. and ne gelæd þu us on costnunge, ac alys us
> of yfele. soþlice.

The Middle English version given in the Wycliffe Bible which is about AD 1380:

> Oure fadir that art in heuenes, halewid be thi name; thi
> kyngdoom come to; be thi wille don 'in erthe as in heuene;
> yyue to vs this dai oure breed ouer othir substaunce; and
> foryyue to vs oure dettis, as we foryyuen to oure dettouris;
> and lede vs not in to temptacioun, but delyuere vs fro
> yuel. Amen.

The very Early Modern English version as given in the Tyndale
Bible of AD 1534:

> O oure father which arte in heven, Halowed be thy name.
> Let thy kyngdome come. Thy wyll be fulfilled, as well in
> erth, as it ys in heven. Geve ys this daye oure dayly
> breede. And forgeve yu oure treaspases, even as we
> forgeve oure trespacers. And lede yu not into
> temptacion: but delyver yu from evell. For thyne is the
> kyngedome and the power, and the glorye for ever. Amen.

The Early Modern English version as given in the King James
Bible of AD 1611:

> Our Father which art in heauen, hallowed be thy Name.
> Thy kingdome come, Thy will be done in earth, as it is
> in heauen. Give vs this day our dayly bread. And forgiue
> vs our debts, as we forgiue our debters. And leade vs not
> into temptation, but deliuer vs from euill: For thine is the
> kingdome, and the power, and the glory, for euer. Amen.

The Modern English version as given in the King James Bible
of AD 1769 (the version of the King James in common use today):

> Our Father which art in heaven, Hallowed be thy name.
> Thy kingdom come, Thy will be done in earth, as it is
> in heaven. Give us this day our daily bread. And forgive
> us our debts, as we forgive our debtors. And lead us not

into temptation, but deliver us from evil: For thine is the kingdom, and the power, and the glory, for ever. Amen.

ENDNOTES

[1] To know more of Tyndale consulted: Robert Demaus, *"William Tindale, A Biography; Being A Contribution to the Early History of the English Bible,"* ed. Richard Lovett (1904). James Frederic Mozley, *William Tyndale* (1937). Christopher Anderson, *Annals of the English Bible* (1845), 2 volumes, although the original is now getting rare and expensive, later editions are abridged. William Tyndale, *The Obedience of a Christian Man* (1528)—modern version David Daniell, (Penguin Books, 2000). G. E. Duffield, ed., *The Work of William Tyndale* (Cambridge: Lincoln College, Oxford and Trinity Hall, 1965). Thomas Russell, ed., *The Works of the English Reformers: William Tyndale and John Frith*, vol.3 (1831) 3.

[2] Demaus 39.

[3] Demaus 29.

[4] S. L. Greenslade, ed., *The Cambridge History of the Bible, The West From The Reformation To The Present Day*, vol. 3 (Cambridge University Press, 1963) 141.

[5] Demaus 86.

[6] Demaus 54-55.

[7] Wyllyam Copland (imprinted), *The Obedience of All Degrees Proved By Gods Worde"* (London, 1561)—copy at Cambridge University Library.

[8] Tyndale 109.

[9] Tyndale 115.

[10] Information on the Tracy family is from encyclopaedias, histories, and on-line resources including Foxe and Nicholas Tyacke, *Aspects of English Protestantism*, c. 1530-1700 (Manchester University Press, 2001) 44. Russell, (contains the Tracy will).

[11] *Old Baptist Chapel, Tewkesbury,* Tewkesbury Borough Council (n.d.). The congregation sometime took on the Midland Confession of 1655, which was not printed or signed. The date is unknown but it is 1655 or later. The confession is Calvinistic, the main advantage for them taking this step was unity and association with other brethren. It is sad because most midland congregations were not Calvinistic and why they took this move is unknown. William L. Lumpkin, *Baptist Confessions of Faith*, 6th print (1989) 198.

[12] Tyacke 45.

[13]Demaus 22-23.

[14]Society of Christian Brethren: J.H. Merle d'Aubigne, *The History of the Reformation in the Time of Calvin*" vol. 4, 6. Irvin Buckwalter Horst, *The Radical Brethren*" (1972) 49.

[15]Demaus 543.

[16]Demaus 419.

[17]Demaus 175.

[18]Demaus 213 (quoted the *Wicked Mammon*).

[19]Demaus 452.

[20]Duffield 15. Tyndale 86 and 111.

[21]Tyndale 66.

[22]Duffield xx.

[23] William Wall, *A History of Infant Baptism,* vol. 4 (Oxford University Press, 1844) 170. Second edition by the Rev. Henry Cotton.

[24]Duffield 190.

[25]Duffield xxiii. *The Cambridge History of the Bible*, 143.

[26]*Wycliife New Testament*, transcribed by W. R. Cooper into modern spelling (The British Library, 2002).

[27] John Purvey, (revised by about 1388), *The New Testament in English according to the version by John Wycliffe, about 1380,* (Forshall & Madden, Clarendon Press, Oxford, 1879).

[28]John Wycliffe taken from the Samual Bagster, *English Hexapla* (1841)

[29]*Tyndale 1526 New Testament* transcribed by W. R. Cooper retaining original spelling (The British Library, 2000).

[30]*Tyndale's 1534 New Testament* taken from Samual Bagster, *English Hexapla* (1841).

[3]Greenslade 144.

[32]Sir Frederic Kenyon, former Director of the British Museum, *Our Bible and the Ancient Manuscripts* (1939) 117.

[33]F.F. Bruce, *The English Bible, A History of Translations (*1961) 44. Bruce quoted from H. W. Robinson, *The Bible in its Ancient and English Versions* (1940) 160.

[34]H. Maynard Smith, D.D. Oxon, Canon of Gloucester, *Henry Vlll and the Reformation* (1948) 288.

[35]Smith 313.

[36]Duffield 117.

[37]Mozley 94. Purvey 525.

[38]Waldensians had their own versions of the scriptures: G. W. H. Lampe, ed., *The Cambridge History of the Bible, The West From The Fathers To The Reformation,* vol. 2, (Cambridge University Press, 1969) 391.

[39]Joseph Bosworth (Professor of Anglo-Saxon, Oxford) and George Waring (Trinity College, Cambridge and Magdalen Hall, Oxford), *The Gothic and Anglo-Saxon Gospels in Parallel Columns with the Versions of Wycliffe and Tyndale* (1865) introduction xvii

[40]Bosworth introduction x.

[41] Edward Miller (revised), *Scrivener's Introduction to the Criticism of the New Testament*, 4th ed. in 2 vols. (1894). For the date of the italic, see vol. 2, 43. For versions prior to the Wycliffe Bible see: Bruce 135. Lampe 112. Edward Turner, *History of the Anglo-Saxons*, vol. 3 (1851) 431. James Gairdner, *Lollardy and the Reformation in England*, vol. 1 (1908)104.

[42]Mozley 94.

[43]A.C. Paues, *A Fourteenth Century English Biblical Version* (Associate of Newham College, Cambridge: Cambridge University Press, 1902) First page of preface.

[44]Paues, introduction.

[45] Margaret Deanesly, *The Significance of the Lollard Bible* (University of London, 1951) 3. Deanesly was professor emeritus in the University of London. She is considered an authority of the pre-reformation English Church History. She died in 1944.

[46]Deanesly 11.

[47]The account of Packington and Tyndale: Mozley147 and Gilbert Burnet, late Lord Bishop of Sarum, *The History of the Reformation of the Church of England,* vol. 1 (Oxford University Press, 1860) 323 ff. For the shooting of Robert: John Foxe (1517-1587), *Acts and Monuments of the Christian Church*, better known as *Foxes Book of Martyrs*, 9th ed., vol. 2 (1684) 365-6.

[48]Mozley 341.

11

THE BOW LANE, LONDON, CHURCH OF CHRIST, MEETING IN THE 1530s.

He that believeth and is baptized shall be saved; but he
that believeth not shall be damned (Mark 16:16).

A question raised by this heading is whether members of this
congregation called themselves the Church of Christ. The answer
is yes, but, as their activities were illegal, they did not advertise
their identity as we do today. It has often been asserted there were
no congregations in England, made up of English people who were
separated from the Romish Church and practised believers' baptism
by immersion for the remission of sins in the 1530s or earlier. The
Bow Lane congregation had English gentry in its membership,
such as Richard Tracy and James Bainham, and had others from
the emerging middle class, including John Frith, Simon Fish, and
John Tyndale, and John's brother, William Tyndale, was involved.
These were all Englishmen, gentlemen or gentry, unlike the Dutch
or German Anabaptists present in London in the 1530s. All these
men's families, it seems, held to Lollard beliefs. The background

of the congregation is Lollard, and those congregations with which it fellowshipped are classed as Lollard by conventional historians.

Below, Bow Lane as it is today.

The brethren met separately from the Romish Church, in a warehouse in (London's) Bow Lane.[1] This congregation is of importance as establishing that autonomous Churches of Christ existed in this time period.

Below, St. Paul's Cathedral from Bow Lane, showing the short distance between the two locations.

Conventional historians of this period of the reformation have, wrongly in my opinion, divided the Waldensian, Lollard, Anabaptist and the "first General Baptist Church" of Thomas Helwys (1612). This division is quite wrong, and these names were never used by these groups. I shall now try to set this confusion in its correct order.

In the early 1500s, in continental Europe, England, Wales and Scotland, we have Christians meeting who are separated from the Roman Catholic Church, which at this pre-reformation time is dominant. In fact, they had been meeting for many centuries in this clandestine way.

These Christians shared beliefs; the various congregations were made up of Godly people. The Romish Church included ungodly and worldly people such as murderers, thieves, etc. This is the problem with "national" churches; everyone is a member.

They rejected infant baptism, on two reasoned arguments. The first argument was that original sin, although inherited, the consequences did not pass on to the child. They supported this with the following verses, Ephesian 2:3 "Among whom also we all had our conversation in times past in the lusts of our flesh, fulfilling the desires of the flesh and of the mind; and were by nature the children of wrath, even as others," and Romans 5:12, "Wherefore, as by one man sin entered into the world, and death by sin; and so death passed upon all men, for that all have sinned." Whilst affirming original sin, they denied that children dying unbaptised were unsaved. It was the consequence of Adam's sin that was inherited. They believed in freewill of the individual to obey the scriptures. Whilst they used the term original sin, it was not used in the Roman Catholic sense where an unbaptised child is worthy of damnation.

The second argument was made from Ezekiel 18. This is summarised in verse 20. "The soul that sinneth, it shall die. The son shall not bear the iniquity of the father, neither shall the father bear the iniquity of the son: the righteousness of the righteous shall be upon him, and the wickedness of the wicked shall be upon him." They also argued from Matthew 18:3 that children are innocent, "And said, Verily I say unto you, Except ye be converted, and become as little children, ye shall not enter into the kingdom of heaven."

In both cases, infants were considered innocent and denied baptism to them. Their proof text was Mark 16:16 since an infant cannot believe, "He that believeth and is baptized shall be saved; but he that believeth not shall be damned." They used this verse to demonstrate that teaching and faith precedes baptism. They taught that the blood of Christ, not the water of baptism, saves, that it is the blood of Christ, through believers' baptism, that saves the individual.

Each congregation was autonomous, overseen where possible by a plurality of elders, with all Christians being priests. They saw themselves as the only true church of Christ, and used that identity.

The Romish doctrines of the mass, transubstantiation, clergy, pilgrimages, worship of images, relics (bones of saints), dedicated (holy) ground along with holy water and confession to priests were rejected. The enemies of these Christians called them Waldensians and/or Lollards, amongst other names. In the 1520s, these groups disappeared from history in continental Europe, and the Lollards (from history) in England as late as the 1550s (due to the Catholic queen Mary retaining Romish doctrines).

In conventional histories in continental Europe, from the 1520s the Anabaptists appear, arriving in England from the 1530s to disappear later in the same century. In 1612, Thomas Helwys would establish the first General Baptist Church in London. Such, while convenient for some, is entirely wrong.

St. Mary-le-Bow church yard, where the church of Christ evangelised.

St. Mary-le-Bow church in the centre of old London.

Champlin Burrage authored *The Early English Dissenters In the Light of Recent Research (1550-1641)*. For many this is a standard reference work of this period. His work was published in 1912 by the Cambridge University Press. Now, out of copyright, it has been republished by several including the Baptist Standard Bearer.

In brief, the claim presented by Burrage and others is that believers' baptism by immersion was reintroduced in England in the 1640s by a group of Calvinists, separated from the Church of England in London. This group was later known as the Particular Baptists, the forerunners of the various (Calvinistic) Baptist denominations of today. Another group, the Helwys Church, meeting in London in 1612, opposed Calvinism and were the forerunners of the General Baptists. However, they baptised by pouring. Prior to these groups, except for some continental Anabaptists, few if any English practised believers' baptism. Thus the Baptists reintroduced believers' baptism in the seventeenth century. Some Baptists go through the Helwys congregation to the Waldensian churches, but of course that line of baptismal tradition denies reformation and Augustinian theology. The advantage with the Calvinists of the 1640s is that it places the reintroduction of believers' baptism nicely under reformed theology, thus denying that baptism saves.

Are they right? Firstly the continental Anabaptists (by name) appeared from about 1520 onwards, but soon earned a bad reputation from which they still suffer to this day. These Anabaptists soon found themselves in opposition to the reformation, which they saw as not going far enough to restore true Christianity. In reality these were continental Baptists of differing opinions, united in their opposition to both the Catholic and Protestant State churches, upholding the concept of autonomous congregations (elders and deacons) and in church discipline turning to the authority of the scriptures in all things. These people stood for the restoration of the apostolic church as opposed to reformation and died by the thousand in both Protestant and Catholic countries alike.

During 1533-5, a small group of Anabaptists tried by force to establish the Kingdom of God at Munster. This group also believed in and practised polygamy, as well as sharing all goods and property. It was from this the Anabaptists were to acquire a name quite unjustified. In England such groups would be persecuted to death.

Continental Anabaptists first arrived in England in the 1530s. At first some, but not all, Anabaptists baptised by pouring. The Anabaptists saw themselves as Christians and members of the church of Christ. Later, these continental Anabaptists in England would cease to meet.

It needs to be understood that the Catholic and later Reformed Churches have never denied believers' baptism. What they introduced was infant baptism and sprinkling/pouring as modes for baptism.

Arguments over baptism turned to infants and mode. In theory, the "Baptists" of the seventeenth century could not reintroduce what the Roman Catholics practised. Romish baptism is not valid, as the candidate is placed in the wrong church with the wrong baptismal ceremony for the wrong reasons.

In opposition to the Romish church were the Lollards and other groups. The Reformation did away with the Romish doctrines of the mass, transubstantiation, pilgrimages, worship of images, relics, confession to priests and other ceremonies. The two issues of contention that remained from the Waldensian and Lollard times (derogatory names) were those of infant baptism and congregational autonomy.

Irvin Horst, in his *The Radical Brethren*, 1972, states, "There is truth no doubt in the claim that 'Anabaptists were indistinguishable from Lollards' except in name; still, a name means something, and we must try to find out in this case why it was changed."[2] The issue was now believers' baptism, which was very highly offensive to the reformers, who claimed that those who were baptised again, having been baptised as infants, were re-baptized, or anabaptised. Thus new Anabaptist is old Lollard. Nothing in doctrine changed from the Lollards to the Anabaptists (both were derogatory names given by their enemies). The doctrines now emphasised of rebaptism and separation from state.

As early as the mid sixteen hundreds, brethren in the Churches of Christ were arguing that they were not a new church. Daniel Featley, a seventeenth century eyewitness, states that Anabaptist was a "nickname" and not used by them. His *Dippers Dipt* is quite clear; they called themselves the church of Christ.[3]

Hercules Collins, a church of Christ minister at Wapping, London, published a work in 1691, *Believers' baptism from heaven, and of divine institution: Infant baptism from earth, and of human invention.* Collins (correctly) denied that the English Baptists received their baptism from Mr. John Smyth (the Helwys church). Collins work is not as well researched as that published by Colonel Henry D'Anvers, a minister of a church of Christ in Staffordshire, who published *A Treatise of Baptism* in 1674, claiming that in England and Europe such congregations go back to apostolic times. He was not claiming successionalism; just that churches who admit believers upon profession and baptism existed prior to the reformation.

Even before 1674, brethren such as John Tombes and Henry Denne had made the same argument that believers' baptism by immersion was practised in England prior to Smyth.

John Lawrence Mosheim, Chancellor of the University of Gottingen, who was a learned Lutheran historian, wrote:

> The true origin of the sect which acquired the denomination of the Anabaptists, by their administering anew the rite

of baptism to those who came over to their communion, and derived that of Mennonites, from that famous man to whom they owe the greatest part of their present felicity, is hid in the remote depths of antiquity, and is, of consequence, extremely difficult to be ascertained... It may be observed, in the first place, that the Mennonites are not mistaken when they boast of their descent from the Waldenses, Petrobrusians, and other ancient sects, are usually considered as witnesses of the truth in the times of darkness and universal superstition. Before the rise of Luther and Calvin, they lay concealed in almost all the countries of Europe, particularly in Bohemia, Moravia, Switzerland and Germany, many persons, who adhered tenaciously to the following doctrine, which the Waldenses, Wyclifites, and the Husites had maintained, some more disguised, and others more open and public manner, vis *that the kingdom of Christ, or the visible church he had established upon earth, was an assembly of true and real saints, and ought therefore to be inaccessible to the wicked and unrighteous, and also exempt from all those institutions, which human prudence suggests, to oppose the progress of iniquity, or to correct and reform transgressors.* This maxim is the true source of all the peculiarities that are to be found in the religious doctrine and discipline of the Mennonites (Anabaptists), and it is most certain, that the greatest part of these peculiarities were approved of by many of those, who, before the reformation, entertained the notion already mentioned, relating to the visible church of Christ. [4]

This opinion of Mosheim, who was not an Anabaptist, expressed in 1755, of the ancient origin of the Anabaptists and of their connection with the Waldensians and of other witnesses of the truth, meets with the approval of historians in church history of our own times, as we shall see. Sir Isaac Newton (1642-1727), mathematician and physicist (one of the foremost scientific intellects of all time), declared it was "his conviction that the Baptists were the only Christians who had not symbolized with Rome" (*Memoirs of the Life and Writing of Mr. William Whiston*, M.A., written by him, 201). William Whiston, who records this statement, was the successor of Newton in the Chair at Cambridge University, and lectured on Mathematics and Natural Philosophy. He himself became a member of the church of Christ and wrote against infant baptism. "Baptist" and "Anabaptist" at this time referred to those who practised believers' baptism and was not used denominationally as it is today.

Alexander Campbell, in his debate with Mr. Macalla, says:

> I would engage to show that baptism as viewed and practiced by the Baptists, had its advocates in every century up to the Christian era and independent of whose existence (the German Anabaptists), clouds of witnesses attest the fact, that before the Reformation from Popery, and from the apostolic age to the present time, the sentiments of Baptists and the practice of baptism have had a continued chain of advocates, and public monuments of their existence in every century can be produced (Macalla and Campbell Debate on Baptism, 378, 379, Buffalo, 1824).

Again in his *Christian Baptism* (409, Bethany, 1851), Alexander Campbell says:

> There is nothing more congenial to civil liberty than to

enjoy an unrestrained, unembargoed liberty of exercising the conscience freely upon all subjects respecting religion. Hence it is that the Baptist denomination, in all ages and in all countries, has been, as a body, the constant asserters of the rights of man and of liberty of conscience. They have often been persecuted by Pedobaptists; but they never politically persecuted, though they have had it in their power." [5]

Such statements from Alexander Campbell suggest that the Church of Christ in Europe, prior to the Reformation and Restoration, laid the foundations of the Restoration Movement of the nineteenth century.

Church of England historian, Canon, H. Maynard Smith D.D. Oxon, stated in 1938, "more Anabaptists were burned under Henry VIII than Lollards in the XV century, Anabaptists being indistinguishable from Lollards except in name.[6] He also stated:

Lollards no doubt rejoiced when they heard of what Luther was doing in Germany... But I do not suppose they were interested in Lutheran theology, which was quite alien to their own, for they symbolised with Luther's enemies, the Anabaptists. It was the same class which provided most the victims in Queen Mary's reign. They were true descendants of the Lollards, They did not die for Lutherism or Calvinism. [7]

We have a statement from a respected twentieth century Anglican historian and theologian, that the Anabaptists were the same as the Lollards and that they were not Calvinists or Lutherans. In other words, they did not hold to reformed theology and their predecessors were pre-reformation, being Lollards.

Michael Watts, Reader in Modern History at the University of Nottingham (1978) in his *The Dissenters* states that "the anabaptists were fed from the fifteenth century Lollardy." He also states they were not Calvinists, but "re-emerged as the General Baptists of the sixteenth century" (a title they never wore, but which referred to their belief of general atonement as opposed to particular redemption of the Calvinists).[8]

The Rev. William Henry Summers, who was a Congregationalist, being associated with the Free-Churches in England, wrote in the early 1900s a number of works, including *The Lollards Of The Chiltern Hills: Glimpses Of English Dissent In The Middle Ages* (1906), and *Our Lollard Ancestors* (1904). Summers' research discovered where Lollardy was strong, the General Baptists were strong in the next century. Summers was the first to notice the geographical link with Lollardy and the General Baptists (who opposed Calvinism).[9]

The problem has always been of providing a link to make the case, whether old Lollards were new Anabaptists? Summers, a hundred years ago provided a case based on geographical location, but not on doctrine. Whilst he is widely quoted, no one to my knowledge has provided the needed link between the General Baptists of the 1600s and the Lollards of the 1520/30s. I shall now set forth the case for such a link existing between the General Baptists and Lollardy, being the Bow Lane congregation meeting in the 1530s.

We have no idea when they first started meeting, but by the 1530s they were well established, having their own meeting place, a warehouse, and were wealthy, quite capable of printing and distributing books, Bibles and tracts. It is this that makes this congregation so important; we can read their books, where these still exist. For the first time we can read their actual words, rather than secondhand reports, gained under duress.

The first name that comes to notice is that of Simon Fish. Prominent twentieth-century historians have him listed as a reformer (Lutheran), a Lollard (who opposed the Lutherans) and Roman Catholic (who opposed Lutherans and Lollards), all of whom were at enmity with each other. It also gives an idea of the problems in this area of early reformation sects. That historians cannot agree as to his beliefs may give us a clue. They have not mentioned believers' baptism – Anabaptism.

Simon Fish (of various spellings including Symon Fishe) is well known in the early period of the Reformation in England. What is virtually unknown is that, far from being a reformer he sought with others the restoration of the church, meaning a separation of church and state. Fish, and Oxford graduate, was a barrister of Gray's Inn, called to the bar in 1525. An educated and cultured gentleman, he was born in Bristol, a part of England long associated with those seeking obedience to the scriptures (Lollardy). We know Fish was married, and in the late 1520s had a daughter. It is from 1525 that Fish became noticed. [10]

Pre-reformation England was full of superstition and Catholic ritual. John Charles Ryle, DD, (1816 - 1900) educated at Eton and Oxford, makes an interesting comment about this time period. As Anglican bishop of Liverpool, he said, "It is no exaggeration to say that for three centuries before the Reformation, Christianity in England seems to have been buried under a mass of ignorance, superstition, priestcraft and immorality." [11] Ryle conveniently failed to mention that the Prayer Book of The Church of England was based on the religion he found fault with, but his comments of this time period are interesting to us in regard to the Lord's Church in the late pre-reformation middle ages and the state of society in general. The Bible was unknown, banned, and inaccessible except for small groups of Christians meeting outside the Catholic Church.

Heresbach, a friend of Erasmus, reported these words from Thomas Linacer, the respected Oxford professor and the personal physician to both King Henry the VII and VIII of England. On reading the New Testament for the first time (1524), Linacer said "Either this is not the gospel, or we are not Christians" having thrown the scriptures to one side. Even the school of Theology of Paris did not scruple to declare before the French parliament, "There is an end of religion if the study of Hebrew and Greek is permitted."[12]

Andreas Ammonius, (Latin secretary to Henry VIII) on November 8th 1531, wrote to Erasmus (Desiderius Erasmus Roterodamus, who produced the printed Greek New Testament) of the great numbers of Christians in England, who he calls "anabaptists." He wrote, "Is it not astonishing that wood is so dear and scarce the heretics cause so many holocausts, and yet their numbers grow." Erasmus replied that Ammonius "has reason to be angry with the heretics for increasing the price of fuel for the coming winter" This was horrible jesting concerning the burning alive of brave Christians and shows the true state of the thinking of the Roman Catholic Church in that period towards those who desired to turn the scriptures for authority.[13]

In the Middle Ages and to the reformation, the Catholic Church tried to gain superiority to secular authority. The Catholic Church presumed the power to excommunicate kings and have nations under the interdict of the Pope in defiance of Christ and His apostles, "Let every soul be subject unto the higher powers. For there is no power but of God: the powers that be are ordained of God (Rom 13:1)." Popes, cardinals, bishops, friars, priests had arrogated to themselves an exemption from the authority of the temporal sovereign and secular law.

The Church of England under the Popes had degenerated into

superstitious customs, rites and ceremonial observances with no Biblical teaching from the scriptures. The relics, pilgrimages, pictures and images, commemoration of the saints, burning of candles, the kissing of the shoe of St. Thomas and praying to the image of "Our Lady of Walsingham" was the life of religion. The great Universities of Cambridge and Oxford did not teach the scriptures but "Doctor Sanctus," the "Angel of the Schools," "divus Thomas de Aquino," the doctrine of the Holy Catholic Church. The Lord's Prayer was said in Latin, a language unknown to the uneducated majority. Few priests even knew the Lord's Prayer was found in the Bible, and then, it looked towards the Kingdom which was established on the first Pentecost after the Resurrection.

The clergy had sanctuaries where criminals could find refuge and evade the jurisdiction of secular courts. This was not to help criminals, but to find a way for the clergy to evade the secular courts which they despised. The rite of sanctuary was a carryover from pagan times which was abused by the clergy. Such was the abuse by the clergy of secular law; they could commit crime including rape and murder without sanction. It reached such notoriety that a term was coined, viz., "the neck verse." This refers to psalm 51, the first verse "Have mercy upon me, O God, according to thy loving kindness: according unto the multitude of thy tender mercies blot out my transgressions." The clergy spent little time studying scripture, but this one verse for those intent on abusing their privileges, when repeated to the secular authorities, could absolve from crime one who claimed to be under "holy Orders." This verse when repeated was used as proof of their rank, an exemption from law (hence the name of the verse, which more than once saved a criminal member of the clergy from the hangman's noose – "The Neck Verse").

The Neck Verse and the abuse by the clergy of lay people ran contrary to the law of Christ. The Lord addressed the "who is my neighbour?" in the parable of the Good Samaritan, which is found in the Gospel of Luke, chapter 10 verses 25-37. Other verses include the Golden Rule - "Therefore all things whatsoever ye would that men should do to you, do ye even so to them: for this is the law and the prophets" (Mat. 7:21), and "And the Lord make you to increase and abound in love one toward another, and toward all men, even as we do toward you" (1The. 3:12). Another verse, "As we have therefore opportunity, let us do good unto all men, especially unto them who are of the household of faith" (Gal. 6:10).

When and where Fish became a Christian we do not know, but at Christmas 1526 a certain "mister" Roye, who was also a barrister, organised a play or satire on the current political and religious situation in England, primarily against Cardinal Wolsey. Fish played the part of the Cardinal. Roye (various spellings, Row or Roo) ended up in the "Tower" and Fish fled to Antwerp, Belgium, where there were brethren, including William Tyndale, taking advantage of the security there to produce literature for distribution in England, through a network previously established. This was no later than 1527. Shortly afterwards, Fish is known to be back in England, at the Wight Friars, London, where with others, at great risk, he is distributing the Tyndale Bible (the first Bible printed in English). Roye later worked with Tyndale in translating the New Testament.

Either whilst in Belgium or in England, Fish wrote his first pamphlet, which has been reprinted many times since, including in the nineteenth century. It has also been reprinted in many editions of Fox's *Book of Martyrs*. The "Supplication of Beggars" (*A Supplycacion for the Beggers)* was an attack on Sir Thomas More, The Roman Catholic Church, and purgatory, the founding doctrines of Catholicism, salvation by works and salvation through the church. The *Supplication* was printed and distributed during 1529, followed by a second edition in 1531.

An attack on the Catholic system was an attack that would result in either banishment or death. Fish's pamphlet also reintroduced the scandal concerning Richard Hunne. In March 1511 Hunne's child died and according to law, had to be buried in the local cemetery. The law then stated that the un-baptised could not be buried in the cemetery (Sanctified Ground). The Catholic Church turned a blind eye and allowed the funeral. Not to be outdone by such an easy outcome, Hunne then sued the Catholic Church over some other matter to do with a title of a tenement, in November (St. Michael's, Cornhill, London).

Hunne was a wealthy merchant, well able to pay the fees for burial, but the church asked for the baptismal clothing, which Hunne did not have. The white baptismal cloth, known as a Chrisom, became, if the child died within a month, a shroud. If the child lived, the cloth was given to the priest, or money. If the child lived longer than a month, the cloth belonged to the priest.

Hunne was then sued by the rector, Thomas Dryffeld, of St. Mary Matfelon (Whitechapel) for the mortuary fee and baptismal charges (the baptism gown) for his child (who had not been baptised). Hunne appeared in the ecclesiastical Court of Audience in April 1512. The court found in judgement according to a point of law for the rector, as could be expected at this first hearing, before requesting appeal to a higher court under the Statute of Praemunire, 1353.

When on 27 December 1512, Hunne attended vespers at the same church (St. Mary Matfelon, Whitechapel), the priest refused to proceed with the service until Hunne left. According to the account, which is mentioned in John Fox's *Book of Martyrs,* the priest shouted "Hunne, thou art accursed and standest accursed!," referring to the excommunication of Hunne by the ecclesiastical court. Hunne did not worry about being excommunicated, we know he was not part of the Catholic Church being a Lollard.

Hunne then responded in January 1513 by suing the priest for slander claiming his character and business had been ruined by the priest's false accusation. In Catholic London in the early sixteenth century, many would not have been prepared to trade places with Hunne and risk being sought out by the authorities.

Hunne then with legal assistance counteracted with a praemunire charge against the church court in which he had been arraigned and argued that its authority derived from a Papal legate, and that it was therefore a foreign court, which could have no legitimate jurisdiction over the King of England's subjects. This law has even been used recently to challenge the jurisdiction of those who are pro-European.

The bishop of London, Richard Fitzjames, responded by again charging Hunne, this time with heresy. Hunne was then sent to the small prison at St. Paul's, the episcopal prison, London. This was after a raid on his house in October 1514, which had uncovered an "English Bible", with, we are told, a prologue sympathetic to Wycliffe's doctrines and other materials.

The Catholic Church now engaged in a major and public battle with Hunne, were relieved when he was found hanging in his cell on the 4th December 1514. His body was burned on 20th December, as befitting a "heretic." His accusers claimed that he had committed suicide, although they could not convince the coroner's jury, which in February 1515 found that Hunne had died an unlawful death, murdered by the bishop's chancellor, Dr. Horsey and two others.

Below, Hunne found murdered in his cell.

The citizens of London were furious with Bishop Fitzjames and his officials. Then, when his chancellor was arrested and charged with the murder, Fitzjames besought Cardinal Wolsey to help him, "For assured I am if my chancellor be tried by any twelve men in London, they be so maliciously set in favour of heretical pravity that they will cast and condemn my clerk though he were as innocent as Abel." And that the bishop did not say this in momentary anger appears from the fact that he repeated it some weeks later in the House of Lords, adding with gross exaggeration that if the obstinate jurymen went unpunished, "I dare not keep my house for heretics." It is clear from this that Hunne had won great sympathy and his murder did not go unnoticed. The four were duly charged with murder, tried and found guilty.

The Roman Catholic Church then appealed to Rome. The King, Henry VIII intervened with the words "By the permission and ordinance of God we are King of England: and Kings of England in past times never had any superior but God only. Therefore, know you well, that we will maintain the right of our crown, and of our temporal jurisdiction, as well in this as in all other points, in as ample a manner as any of our predecessors have done before our time." The bishop's chancellor, Dr. Horsey, and his two companions received a Royal Pardon from the king, but had to pay £1500 (a considerable sum in that day) to the victims family. In 1515, as a result of this affair and due to Hunne's powerful friends, Parliament debated whether to approve a Bill to restore to Hunne's children the property which had been forfeited to the crown when their father was found, posthumously, guilty of heresy.

The House of Commons petitioned Henry VIII to reform the law on mortuary fees and an attempt was made to extend laws against benefit of clergy. None of the proposed bills was passed, being rejected by the House of Lords and the King. John Fox's Book of Martyrs recounts Hunne's case as evidence of the unfairness and unaccountability of English ecclesiastical courts on the eve of the Reformation. It also presents Hunne as a martyr and one of the forerunners of the Protestantism that would soon enter England in the wake of the reformation.

The nation was shocked by these events, which in part led to the English Reformation, the people being firmly set against the power of the Church. When King Henry VIII, for personal reasons (his marriages), moved against Rome, he had the sympathy of many ordinary people.

Fish attacked the immorality and numbers of Catholic clergy, monks, priests and friars. His attack exposed the high cost to society of the Roman Church with its abbeys, large estates and churches. It was devastating. The Roman Catholic Church ran the largest business in England.

The most reliable date for the first printing of the Supplication of Beggars is between spring and summer of 1529. There was a ready Lollard network for its distribution. There has been some attempt to date it earlier by about two years, but there is no evidence for an earlier date.

In 1529 King Henry became engaged to Lady Anne Boleyn

(who later was to be Queen of England). After discussing the matter with her brother, she presented a copy of Fish's book to Henry. During this time, Anne had influence and had no small part to play in the early reformation in England and break with the Church of Rome. The existence of the book had been kept secret from Henry by Cardinal Wolsey. Henry studied it for several days, after which he asked about the author. This resulted in Anne's introducing Fish's wife to Henry. Henry promised protection for her husband, who appeared shortly at court, suggesting he was living close by and not at this time on the continent, despite being a hunted man. Henry and Fish discussed the excesses of the Roman Catholic Church over several days and hunted together. Fish was safe from attack from the Catholic Church, having the seal (signet) of Henry, but his wife was not. She too was granted protection after an attempt to bring her to trial for heresy.

A most remarkable, unknown and extremely rare book can be found in the Cambridge University Library. It is Fish's second work. Fish's first work, *The Supplication*, gained him a reputation and protection in high places, when Henry was seeking to leave the Roman Church. The second work, *The Summe*, published by Fish in 1529, argued for separation between church and state, freewill and believers' baptism (by immersion). All which were opposed by Henry and the reformers. Fish was now in serious trouble for the second work and had he not died in 1531 from the plague, would have no doubt died at the stake (by being burned). His wife nursed their sick daughter, but whether the child died of the plague like her father is unknown.

Fish's most important work, *The Summe,* is rarely mentioned, despite Fish's influence on the Reformation in England with his first work. Fish's first work dealt with the Roman Catholic Church, and fitted in with the needs of the reformers and state. His second work dealt with the nature of Christ's Church. This second work proves that Fish was no reformer of the Church of England and no Lutheran, as found in other histories. Fish was a member of the Church of Christ meeting in Bow Lane, London.

Where I have quoted Fish, I have updated the spelling but retained his words (English has changed during the last five hundred years, this will help explain the poor writing style of Fish). The original does not have page numbers which, for convenience, I have added. *The Sum of Holy Scripture* was first printed anonymously in Basle (Holland) in 1523; the original author still remains unknown. This was when John Calvin was just fourteen years old and thirteen years before he published his first edition of the Institutes. *The Sum* was printed only four years after Martin Luther's works and his letter, known as the 95 Theses, were to be widely distributed from 1517.

The second edition of *The Sum* published by Fish was printed in 1529, six years after the Dutch edition. Several editions were printed in Dutch, Latin and English. The edition quoted from below is Fish's English 1529 version. The Dutch edition of 1523 is held in the British Library C. 57. a. 20). I only know of two English copies, one is held at the British Library and the other at the Cambridge University Library. This second is cited below. John Day, the same printer who published the first edition of Fox's Martyrs in 1563, reprinted the *Sum* in 1548. To my knowledge no copies of this 1548 printing have survived.

Below is a picture taken from the first page of the Summe.

¶ The sum
me of the holye scripture /
and ordinarye of the Chriſten teachyng /
the true Chriſten faithe / by the which we
be all iuſtified. And of the vertue of bap-
teſme / after the teaching of the Goſ
pell and of the Apoſtles / with an informacyon howe
all eſtates ſhulde ly
be / accordynge
to the Goſ-
pell.
✠

Anno. M.CCCCC.XXIX.

The title page reads:

> The Summe of the Holye Scripture and the ordinary of the Christian teaching the true Christian faith by the which we be all justified. And of the virtue of baptism after the teaching of the Gospel and of the Apostles with an information how all estates should live according to the gospel.

On page 2-3 Fish notes that the "water of baptism" does not take away sin, he refutes by reason both the pagan and Catholic system of supernatural power with "holy" water. Fish wrote:

> The water of baptism taketh not away our sin for then it were a precious water. And then it behoved us daily to wash us there. Neither hath the water of the font any more virtue than the water that runneth in the river of Rhine. For we may as well baptise in Rhine as in the font. When saint Phillip baptised Eunuch the servant of Candace a queen of Ethiopia (as writeth saint Luke in the acts of the apostles) there was then no hallowed water, salt, candle, chrism, but he baptised him in the first water they came to upon the way. Whereby mayst thou perceive that the virtue of baptism lyeth not in hallowed water or in other outward things that we have in the font, but in faith only. That is to say when any person is baptised he must believe steadfastly that his sins to him are pardoned, that he is made the child of God and that God has become his father and is made certain that he shall be saved. And is made partaker of the passion of Christ whereof the baptism has this virtue. And when one is baptised he is born again and getteth another father and other brethren for God is made his father and he is made the brother of Jesus' Christians writeth Saint Paul unto the Romans where he calleth

Christ a sonne first begotten among other. And therefore is Christ called in the holy scripture the first child of his father and we all are begotten afterward when we be baptised. And therefore is the baptism called in the holy scripture the second nativity. As writeth Saint John in his gospel. Without one being born again (sayeth Christ unto Nicodemus) he may not enter into the kingdom of heaven. For we be thereby born again and they that was the children of the devil because of original sin are made children of God by baptism. As sayeth Saint Paul Christ hath healed us by the bath of regeneration and reconciliation of the Holy Ghost.

Fish and others (Tyndale/Frith) held to original sin, but not as did the Catholic Church and later denominations. For Fish and his brethren original sin was the sin of Adam and Eve, the consequences of which mankind inherited. He quotes Eph 2:3. For Fish, original sin did not condemn infants; it was actual sin committed that condemned and therefore children were innocent; but as they grew up, they would sin. They believed in choice to decide (freewill) and hence the gospel agency in conversion. There is corruption, but not guilt; depravity, but not sin. So whilst infants had original sin, they could be guilty of nothing and hence were not damned if they died before baptism. They inherited the consequences of Adam's sin, but not damnation because of his sin, having freewill later to decide on hearing the gospel. The argument for the innocence of children was defended through the use of Matthew 18:3. "And said, Verily I say unto you, Except ye be converted, and become as little children, ye shall not enter into the kingdom of heaven." The person being baptised is seen in page 5 as dying to Christ. Quoting Romans chapter 6 who is thus "plonged" under the water is seen as a burial and arising to a new life free of sins previously committed.

The mode of baptism we read (page 8) is plunging or immersion, "When we be plonged (plunged) under the water." This shows the false claim of many Baptist and mainstream historians that prior to the 1640s, immersion (dipping under) was not practised for believers' baptism.

On page 9 we read "What thing baptism betokeneth and how it is but a sign." For Fish the forgiveness of sins was not by the water, but by faith and believing in Christ. Therefore, baptism is to wash away sin, but through faith in the blood of Christ. An infant cannot, of course, have faith.

On page 11 Fish states concerning baptism "By his bloud he have bought us again from the devil. By the water we be purged and sanctified by our faith... being pure and clean before God". He is denying the ritualistic and superstitious nature of baptism in that time period. His argument is that of the Lollards regarding the power and necessity of the Blood of Christ to remit sin through believers' baptism. On page 15, Fish states "The faith that we have at the baptism taketh away our sins and the water is nothing but a sign or token". Again, Fish is denying the power of the "holy" water used in the Catholic Church. On page 16 Fish writes "Baptism of the water is also a sign of the grace of God, whereby God maketh us sure that we shall enjoy his grace and mercy and that he pardoneth us our sins and maketh us his children." Again, this is a denial of superstition prevalent in that period.

On page 20, Fish comments on Matthew 28:19 "Go ye therefore, and teach all nations, baptizing them in the name of the Father, and of the Son, and of the Holy Ghost." For Fish, the gospel (Bible) is not private to the priests and monks, but is to be shared with all mankind. When Fish so commented, the consequences of owning a Bible included being burned alive. On page 21, Fish then quotes the apostle Paul from the Corinthian and Roman letters, which were written to Christians and not to priests and monks only. He says that it is "necessary everyone learn his children as men were to do in afore time" referring to the Jews who educated their children in the scriptures. At a time when many people were ignorant in scripture, as were the priests, Fish recognises the need for people to read and advocates study of the scriptures.

On page 24 he continues to attack on clerical illiteracy saying:

> a great number of priests and monks unlettered and knowing nothing in the Christian church. For now there are many priests, monks and friars that for lack of literature are nothing of benefit for that office. For by the unlettered priests is this great error come into the world that is that in the stead of the pure scriptures which is the

lovely word of God which they know not, they preach narrations, fables, lies and traditions.

Fish on page 25 states that "the faith to believe is that the Father, the Son and the Holy Ghost is one only God". Thus we can see he believes in the triunity of the Godhead. He quotes from James 2:19 "Thou believest that there is one God; thou doest well: the devils also believe, and tremble." Fish comments that the Devil believes in life everlasting in either Hell or Heaven and in God, In Fish's words "the Devil is no better for it." Fish was no soul sleeper, the name given to those who were accused of believing there was no consciousness after physical death until the judgment. Fish, unlike Martin Luther, who regarded the book of James as "the Epistle of Straw," being frustrated by the emphasis on works in the book and questioning its canonicity, was like Tyndale, happy to quote from James as Scripture. There is no evidence that Fish was a Lutheran, as some historians claim. Luther rejected believers' baptism and continued to insist upon baptism of infants because he believed those who insisted upon believers' baptism placed too much emphasis on the will of man. Unlike Luther, the Lollards held the book of James in high regard.

Fish writes in page 27 that "Jesus is our patron and mediator, having paid for our sins." Again, he refutes the prevalent Catholic teaching of that period, especially that of Mary as mediator along with pilgrimages and purgatory. On page 30 Fish writes:

> So steadfast and so certain must we should unto the word of God be and all though it were so that all men, angels and devils would persuade us to the contrary we must believe surely that the word of God is true and that he will fulfil all that he has promised.

> What thing hath God promised us, he hath promised us everlasting life, saying, repent the Kingdom of Heaven is at hand. And in another place: he whosoever shall believe and be baptised shall be saved, he hath also promised unto us remission of all our sins as said saint Peter speaking of Christ to Cornelius the centurion.

> To him saith him giveth all the prophets witness that through His name shall receive remission of sins, all that believe in Him, that is to say that all they that with enter courage forsake their life and put all their trust in the grace and mercy of him shall have remission of all their sins. Moreover he hath promised us that we shall be children of God as saith St. John. We hath given to them power to be the children of God to them that believe in his name.

On page 35 Fish says Christians will continue to sin, but can pray to God asking for forgiveness in the name of the Lord when they have repentance. In page 41/2 Fish refutes the Catholic teaching of salvation through "good works." On page 66 Fish states that God wants our hearts and not works. For Fish, man's good works will come because of love and faith in God; see also pages 80, 87 & 89. In this time salvation was through good works, pilgrimages and giving generously to the church and monasteries. In defence of this Fish quotes James 2:26, "For as the body without the spirit is dead, so faith without works is dead also." On page 129 Fish blames parents who send their children to schools run by monks, who then teach the necessity of good works to the children who know nothing of the Christian faith, like the monks who taught them.

Regarding marriage, (pages 154 ff) Fish teaches a man should love and respect his wife; that she should obey him. The man should work to keep the house which his wife will tend. He teaches that the husband should love his wife as she is a sister in the faith. He teaches that Eve was taken from the side of Adam and not his feet and so that they were equals with separate roles.

With regard to children, Fish gives the excellent advice that parents need to teach their offspring the Christian faith and keep them from immorality. He states that young people should be taught an occupation and not beg, a problem in that period with the monks. He also teaches the advantages of owning a home. In business he teaches the need for honesty and morality in dealings.

On pages 178 and 179 Fish teaches the need to deal with personal matters with brethren quoting Matthew 18:15-17. On page 187, he warns the rich, quoting from James chapter five. Fish teaches in pages 197 and 198 the spiritual nature of the kingdom, "there are two sorts of people in the world, the first belong unto the kingdom of God the other to the kingdom of the world." From Romans chapter thirteen he teaches the need to obey the secular authorities. Again (on page 219) he teaches that we must obey the "temporal" authorities unless it is contrary to scripture, when the "temporal law must give place". Fish takes God's use of secular law back to Genesis 9:5 "And surely your blood of your lives will I require; at the hand of every beast will I require it, and at the hand of man; at the hand of every man's brother will I require the life of man." Fish continues through the Old and into the New Testament, separating secular power from the Kingdom of God. In page 205 (Fish wrote), "Jesus Christ hath not ordained in his spiritual kingdom, which is all true Christian people, any sword, for he himself is the king and governor, without sword, and without any outward law… Christian men among themselves have nought to do with the sword, nor with the law, for that is to them neither needful nor profitable; the secular sword belongeth not to Christ's kingdom, for in it is none but good, and just." Fish's teaching regarding the Holy Spirit taught that the Spirit works through the word.

Criticisms aimed at Fish and this work may include that he denied water in baptism, whereas he denied supernatural power of holy water. He taught that baptism takes place when a repentant believer is immersed in (any) water for the forgiveness of sins whereby he becomes a Christian. Another fault may be claimed, that Fish stated that the Paternoster should be said in English. The Paternoster is the so-called Lord's Prayer. Fish taught the church and kingdom are the same. In a time of great wrath from the Roman Catholic Church, stating the Lord's Prayer should be understood in English, is quite sensible. His wife, when undertaking Bible study with the friars in their home, demanded the friars use the gospels in English. There is nothing wrong with Bible study in one's own language which is opposed to those who wished to keep the masses ignorant of its teaching, keeping to themselves the power that comes with false religion.

We may conclude that Fish was neither Calvinist, Lutheran, Arminist nor Catholic, the main religious reformers of that period. He is a restorer, not reformer, teaching clearly the need for separation of the church and state. All the reformers had blood on their hands as they sought to impose their doctrines on others, whereas Fish taught the spiritual nature of Christ's kingdom. Millennialism was not taught, the Church of Christ being the Kingdom. The issue for Fish and the reformers was whether the church/kingdom was physical, where all were added to the church through infant baptism (reformers, who were reestablishing a primitive Catholicism), or a spiritual kingdom where men were added after hearing the gospel plan of salvation (restoration, going back to the first century). Prior to the reformation, the Pope was not only head of the Catholic

Church; he demanded submission from kings. The reformation still retained state religion, but removed the power of the Pope. In time, this led to the concept that each prince had the right to worship as he chooses, whilst forcing his religion onto his subjects. The seeds of denominationalism were thereby planted. The Peace of Augsburg of 1555 established that each prince (king) would have the right to determine the religion of his own state, the options being Catholicism, Lutheranism and Calvinism. This resulted in various wars between Catholic and protestant countries. On May 15th and October 24th, 1648, the Peace of Westphalia was signed at Osnabruck and Munster bringing the various wars to an end, but only for a while. It would not be until the Act of Toleration in 1689 that England would recognise the right to worship outside the state church.

Fish's work teaches the plan of salvation. The word of God must be first preached, it must be believed through faith, Christ confessed, the believer must repent and then be baptised by immersion for the remission of sins through which a person contacts the blood of Christ and is added to the church. This is not the teaching of Luther or any denomination; it is the pure gospel plan of salvation, preached nearly three hundred years before the Restoration Movement. The Reformation in England had not begun, continental Europe and England were highly superstitious and Roman Catholic; it was no better than pagan and fatalistic religions, with people praying to and petitioning saints. Natural disasters were blamed on God or the Devil; astrology was a science. In midst of this wretched depraved society, across England were gentle autonomous congregations preaching the pure Gospel, calling themselves Christians and members of the Church of Christ, teaching how men could become Christians and live peaceably. This was a hundred and thirty years before anyone was to wear the name Baptist, and over two hundred years before the Methodist Church. Yet we know similar congregations named Lollards had been doing the same for centuries before.

The Anabaptists (Christians) were made Lutherans by historians, which is ridiculous, as Luther was busy hunting down Anabaptists and exterminating them. The Protestants made the Anabaptists Catholics and Catholics made them Lutherans. Wherever they went, they were hunted down and exterminated, for no other reason than they rejected the authority of the established church in preference for scripture. The term Anabaptist in this time period was used as a derogatory name and did not refer to any particular group of people.

After Fish's death from the bubonic plague (which infected much of London) and his being denounced as a "damnable heretic", his widow was then remarried to James Bainham, becoming a widow twice-over in April 1532, when Bainham was burnt at the stake. James Bainham was the son of Sir Alexander Bainham (Syr

349

Alexander Baynham), a knight of Gloucestershire, where the church was, or had been strong. The family was known to William Tyndale, who was from a Lollard area. He received an education suitable to his family's rank and made considerable progress in the Latin and Greek languages. Then he was called to the bar, in which he set a good example to all of his profession, being liberal to his clients and willing to give advice to the needy, to widows, orphans, and all who were afflicted, without fee or reward. He was a man of virtuous disposition and godly conversation, constant in prayer, read in the scriptures and abounding in all good works. This conduct exposed Bainham to suspicion, especially when he married the widow of Simon Fish. It was no surprise we find Bainham at the Bow Lane congregation, which he would have known about through his family, and his fellow barrister and preacher, Simon Fish.

As to his character, Anglican Bishop Burnet wrote "that for true generosity, he was an example to the age in which he lived." This is truly remarkable testimony coming as it does from a bishop of the Church of England.[12] Bainham belonged to the same congregation in Bow Lane where Simon Fish and John Frith preached. Whilst Bainham preached there, he was a barrister by profession.

Next page,
James Bainham holding fagots at his adjuration
in St. Paul's Church (Cathedral).

Fish's wife, who was suspected of, but avoided charges of heresy, married Bainham, burnt for heresy in 1532. Bainham was arrested at the Middle Temple, London in 1531. Bainham was whipped at the "Tree of Truth" in the Lord Chancellor's (Thomas More) garden, and was then sent to the Tower to be racked, Sir Thomas More being present himself, till in a manner he had "tamed him." Bainham, under torture recanted, and later retracted his recantation, first before the brethren at the Bow Lane congregation where he asked forgiveness of God and all the world for what he had done. The following Sunday, at the church of St. Augustine, he rose in his seat with Tyndale's English New Testament in his hand, and declared openly, before all the people, with weeping tears, that he had "denied God," praying them all to forgive him, and beware of his weakness, "for if I should not return to the truth," he said, "this Word of God would damn me, body and soul, at the day of judgment." And then he prayed "everybody rather to die than to do as he did, for he would not feel such a hell again as he did feel for all the world's good." With such a public apology and repentance he would find no mercy, he was arrested.

After these proceedings, Sir Thomas More sent Bainham to Stokesly, then bishop of London, before whom he was brought on December 15th 1531 and examined upon several articles. Asked if he believed there was purgatory for souls departed this life, he answered quoting 1John 1:7-9:

> If we walk in the light, as he is in the light, we have fellowship one with another; and the blood of Jesus Christ his Son cleanseth us from all sin. If we say we have no sin, we deceive ourselves, and the truth is not in us. If we confess our sins, he is faithful and just to forgive us our sins, and to cleanse us from unrighteousness.

Being then asked what he thought of purgatory, he answered, that if any such thing as purgatory had been mentioned to St. Paul, he thought the apostle would have rejected it as heresy.

The second question was whether the saints departed hence are to be honored and prayed unto, entreating them to pray for us. He answered from 1Jo 2:1,2 "My little children, these things write I unto you, that ye sin not; and if any man sin, we have an advocate with the Father, Jesus Christ the righteous: and he is the propitiation for our sins, and not ours only, but also for the sins of the whole world."

And further, being asked what he meant when he used the words of the Popish liturgy, "all ye saints of God pray for us," he answered that he meant the saints that were alive, and not those who were dead, as St. Paul exhorteth the Corinthians: "pray for us," (2 Cor. 1:11). He said he prayed not to the dead, because he thought that those who are dead could not pray for him. And when the whole church was gathered together, they used to pray for one another, or desire one to pray for another, with one heart; and that the will of the Lord might be fulfilled, and not ours. And I pray, (said he,) as our Saviour Christ prayed. "Father take this cup from me, if it be possible, yet thy will be done."

Under examination he said that "the truth of the Holy Scriptures was never these eight hundred years past so plainly and expressly declared to the people as it had been within these six years." (In reference to the printed Bible of Tyndale, which the Bow-Lane congregation had helped to finance and distribute, with brethren from nearby Coleman Street.)

He also stated of baptism, "That as many as repent shall be saved. That is, as many as die concerning sin, shall live by faith with Christ. Therefore it is not we that live after that, but Christ in us. And so whether we live or die, we are God's by adoption, and not by water only but by water and faith. That is, by keeping the promise made. For ye are kept by Grace and Faith, saith saint Paul, and that not of yourselves, for it is the gift of God." Under torture he stated there are but two churches, "The Church of Christ militant and the Church of Antichrist, and this Church of Antichrist may and doth err, but the Church of Christ doth not."

He stated concerning the New Testament that it "doth preach and teach the word of God." We know dipping (immersion) for baptism was the practice in the English Churches of Christ in this period for the remission of sins. Anglican clergyman, Dr. Daniel Featly (one of the translators of the King James 1611 bible), wrote in 1645 of the Churches of Christ meeting in London and elsewhere, where he calls the rebaptizing of adults "a new leaven," and that their position "is soured with it." Featly dates these congregations back to 1525 when he quotes from them "That baptism ought to be received by none but such as can give a good account of their faith; and in case any have been baptized in their infancy, that they ought to he rebaptised after they come to years of discretion, before they are to be admitted to the Church of Christ."

After being racked over several weeks, James Bainham died a triumphant death at the stake on April 20th 1532, at Smithfield (London). Prior to being executed he spoke to the crowd, "I come hither, good people. Accused and condemned for a heretic; Sir Thomas More being my accuser and my judge. And these be the articles I die for, which be a very truth, and grounded on God's Word, and no heresy. They be these: first, I say it is lawful for every man and woman to have God's book in their mother tongue. The second article is that the Bishop of Rome is Antichrist, and that I know no other keys of heaven-gates but only the preaching of the Law and the Gospel; and that there is no other purgatory, but the purgation of Christ's blood; and the purgatory of the cross of Christ, which is all persecutions and afflictions; and no such purgatory as they feign of their own imagination: for our souls immediately go to heaven, and rest with Jesus Christ forever."

He was then chained to the stake (this prevented those being burned from walking away after the rope had burned through, keeping the victim upright and alive longer throughout the ordeal). After the fire had, on Fox's account, "half consumed his arms and legs," he spake these words: "O ye papists, behold, ye look for miracles, and here now you may see a miracle; for in this fire I feel no more pain than if I were in a bed of down, but it is to me a bed of roses."

Below, the burning of James Bainham.

Among the lay officials present at the stake, was "one Pavier," town clerk of London. Pavier was a Catholic fanatic who had as the flames were about to be kindled, burst out in violent and abusive language. The fire blazed up, and the dying suffered (as the red flickering tongues licked the flesh from off his bones), turned to him and said, "May God forgive thee, and shew more mercy than thou, angry reviler, shewest to me." The scene was soon over; the town clerk went home.

One morning a week later, when his wife had gone to mass, Pavier sent all his servants out of his house on one pretext or another, a single girl only being left, and he withdrew to a garret at the top of the house, which he used as an oratory. A large crucifix was on the wall, and the girl having some question to ask, went to the room, and found him standing before it "bitterly weeping." He told her to take his sword, which was rusty, and clean it. She went away, and left him; when she returned, a little time after, he was hanging from a beam, dead.[15]

Modern medical knowledge informs us that pain receptors in the skin, without which we are not able to feel pain, are destroyed in severe burning. This may explain the many accounts of Christians; at the stake, burned alive by their enemies, being able to converse coherently, despite the most horrific injuries including limbs dropping into the fire. The first stages of being burned before the pain receptors are destroyed are the most horrific. During this stage it was not uncommon for bystanders to kill the victim if allowed.

The victim was drawn on a hurdle to the place of execution. This mirrors the pagan custom, particularly of the ancient Egyptians who burned people alive for religious crimes, and were also drawn on a hurdle. The Catholics until recently viewed cremation as a pagan practice and a denial of the doctrine of the Resurrection.[16] The Roman Catholics were happy not only to practise cremation on those whom they disagreed with, but to do it whilst they were alive. The ancient Egyptians developed an intricate transmigration of soul theology, which prohibited cremation, except for their enemies who they burned alive for religious crimes.[17]

In 1415, 30 years after John Wycliffe's death, the Council of

Constance declared him a heretic, condemned him on 267 counts, ordered that his writings be burned and directed that his bones be exhumed from consecrated ground, burned and cast into the river. They also excommunicated him. It was not until 1428 that the orders were carried out, to prevent his being resurrected. They took Wycliffe's bones, burned them and scattered their dust in the nearby River Swift, which flows into the River Avon. The purpose of burning a victim was not only to make them suffer in this life, but to prevent their resurrection in the next. We may conclude the cruel and despotic burning of heretics was not Christian, but pagan in origin, born of ignorance of scripture, done in the name of Christianity when it was no such thing. The burnings not only were pagan in origin, but a relic of Fire (Sun) Worship.

Those convicted in the sixteenth and seventeenth centuries, caught for example clipping silver or gold coins, were boiled alive in oil. The executioner would hold their head down for a quick death (the purpose being to deter crime). Christians had a much more severe punishment along with traitors, who were executed by hanging, drawing and quartering, again a practice going back to pagan times. Burnings were for religious offences including witchcraft. For the state, the idea of liberty and free thought was the most serious crime there was. Christians, for promoting liberty, found themselves on the radical left in those times.

The Bow Lane congregation was responsible for the distribution of books and Bibles, which means they had to know of other congregations of similar belief. Fish's book on baptism was widely distributed and printed more than once in the sixteenth century (this means there was recipients who sought after it). One of the brethren associated with the Bow Lane congregation was John Hacker (also spelt Hakker and Hagar). He also had the nickname of "Old Father Hacker." He was a water-bearer who lived in nearby Coleman Street. Hacker was well known to the various Lollard communities throughout England, where he helped distribute books and preached. Hacker was arrested and under examination revealed the names of several congregations and members, across the south of England, who then faced torture and imprisonment (such were the times and hazards these brethren faced for the sake of the gospel).

In 1555, when England had returned to Catholicism under Queen Mary (died 1558), the congregation at Bow Lane was prosecuted under the Act for Lollard heresies. A brother, named Rose, who led in the Supper, and about thirty other brethren were jailed. What was the outcome is not certain, but it seems they were still meeting at the same location in 1555.[18] Of course, by taking the Supper, they would be deemed to deny the Catholic Mass, which was an offence to fail to attend. "Yet if any man suffer as a Christian, let him not be ashamed; but let him glorify God on this behalf" (1 Pet. 4:16).

The greatest objection that may be raised to my outline of Bow Lane, Tyndale, Fish and Frith will be one of election and predestination. As the Reformation developed, Luther's ideas were met with enthusiasm, but as Luther's resentment of the "Anabaptists" grew, along with his justification of faith only, the two parties distanced themselves, that is, if they were ever close. The churches associated with these brethren were known as free-will or Pelagian, holding that infants are born innocent, the gospel agency in conversion and baptism, by immersion for remission of sins.

According to Herbert Skeat, the first Presbyterian church met in Wandsworth (South West London) in 1572, which means the Bow Lane congregation is forty years too early to be Presbyterian.[19] Fox has the first independent congregation, says Skeat, meeting in London in 1555, again, twenty five years too late for our Bow Lane congregation.[20] Congregationalism cannot be dated much earlier than the 1580s, fifty years too late for Bow Lane to be classed as "congregational."[21] Congregationists held to infant baptism. In church organisation, the Bow Lane congregation was, of course, autonomous, but "congregational" is unfortunately a denominational term. Bow Lane was Biblically congregational. Established historians have suggested the Bow Lane congregation was reformed, but it did not hold to infant baptism and the "national church" ideal, thus, it was not reformed (Lutheran). It was not Calvinistic, John Calvin was twenty one years of age in 1530 and had not yet developed his "system." Other historians have claimed Bow Lane to be Lollard, which we can accept if we agree Lollard is a derogatory name for the churches of Christ in that and earlier times in England.

In 1593, in England, it was made a legal requirement for all people over eighteen to attend Church of England worship, and later, baptismal records were to be kept to check that parents were having their children baptised. Those parents that did not could be prosecuted, to the point of being punished with death by burning. Such was the state religion and their desire to wreak hatred and revenge on any that dare disagree, who today make much of their "wonderful traditions," by not mentioning such inconvenient facts.

We may not agree with everything taught in Bow Lane, their use of English today is quaint. They did not have the scholarship we enjoy; often their leaders were dead in their thirties, spent time in prison and died at the stake. The books they had for study they produced themselves. Nonetheless, in England in the 1530s, the Bow Lane Church of Christ held to the tenets that three hundred years later, in the 1830s, would be termed "Campbellism."

Investigation shows that both Campbellism and the Lollards of Bow Lane were nothing other than Christians committed to the scriptures for authority of religious practice, even adopting the same identity—church of Christ. The Christians meeting in Bow Lane have an ancient heritage that was not Reformation in origin, but Lollard, who predated the Reformers by several centuries. When Reformation of the Catholic Church came, Christians were engaged at the very beginning, encouraging Restoration.

> And I heard a voice from heaven saying unto me, Write, Blessed are the dead which die in the Lord from henceforth: Yea, saith the Spirit, that they may rest from their labours; and their works do follow them. (Rev. 14:13)

ENDNOTES

[1]J.H. Merle d'Aubigne, *The History of the Reformation in the time of Calvin*, vol. 4, 105.

[2] Irvin Buckwalter Horst, *The Radical Brethren* (1972) 31.

[3] Dr. Daniel Featley, *The Dippers dipt or the Anabaptists Dunckt and Plunged Over Head and Ears*, 4th ed. Nicholas Bourn and Richard Royston, 1646) 124.

[4]John Lawrence Mosheim, Chancellor of the University of Gottingen, *An Ecclesiastical History, Ancient and Modern*, vol. 4, trans. Archibald Maclaine, (1803) 439.

[5]Newton and Alexander Campbell quoted from John T. Christian, *A History of the Baptists,* vol. 1(1922) 84.

[6]H. Maynard Smith, Canon of Gloucester, *Pre-Reformation in England* (1938) 280.

[7]Smith,292.

[8] Michael R. Watts, *The Dissenters* (Oxford University Press, 1985) 7. Watts was Reader in Modern History at University of Nottingham.

[9] William Henry Summers, *The Lollards Of The Chiltern Hills: Glimpses Of English Dissent In The Middle Ages* (1906) 161.

[10]John Foxe, *Acts and Monuments of the Christian Church* better known as *Foxes Book of Martyrs*, 9th ed., vol. 2 (1684) 206 ff, 228 ff. George Stokes, *The Lollards* (1838) 91 ff.

[11]John Charles Ryle, *Principles for Churchmen* (1884) 223.

[12]Jean Henri Merle D'Aubigne, vol. 1 43.

[13]Burnet quoted from John T. Christian's *Baptist History,* vol. 1, chapter 15.

[14]For Egyptian practice see Manetho, 119 & 203 (Loeb Classical Library). Sir George Frazer, in *Balder The Beautiful,* vol. 2 (1955), (vol. 11 of the *Golden Bough*) on page 42 concludes the burning of humans alive by the Roman Catholic church. This dates back to Druid practice.

[15]Foxe 245 ff. Stokes 135 ff.

[16]Foxe 245 ff. Stokes 135 ff.

[17]Sir E.A. Budge Wallis, *Osiris and the Egyptian Resurrection,* 2 vols. (1911) particularly the preface in vol. 1.

[18] Gilbert Burnet, late Lord Bishop of Sarum (died 1715), *The History of the Reformation of the Church of England,* vol. 3 (Oxford University Press, 1860) 602. Foxe 95.

[19]Herbert S. Skeats, *A History of the Free Churches of England, From A.D. 1688 – A.D. 1851* (1868) 17.

[20]Skeats 18.

[21]Skeats 18 ff.

GENERAL SOURCES

Dr. Daniel Featley, *Dippers Dipt* (1646) 20. Featley's book remains an excellent firsthand source for the churches of Christ in the seventeenth century, before the growth of the Baptist denomination. Featley, an Anglican theologian, served on the King James Bible committee. He opposed the church, condemning it in his book.

John Foxe (1517-1587) *Acts and Monuments of the Christian Church* better known as *Foxes Book of Martyrs.* This massive work was first published by John Day in 1563. I have used the ninth edition of 1684, which many consider the best as it had been updated and expanded. The 1684 edition in English contained three massive volumes. Later editions are abridged and some contain only a little from the ninth edition. Foxe was a Presbyterian and opposed the Lord's Church, which he failed to mention when dealing with believers' baptism.

Simon Fish (1529), *A Supplication for the Beggars,* reprinted with notes in the English Scholar's Library of Old and Modern Works, ed., Edward Arber, FSA, Lecturer in English Literature, (London: University College, 1878).

The Summe of the Holye Scripture. The quotations are taken from the 1529 edition (copy held at Cambridge University Library), Shelf mark Syn. 8. 52. 37.

Edward Bean Underhill, *Tracts on Liberty of Conscience and Persecution 1614-1661* (1846).

Gilbert Burnett (1643-1715) Lord Bishop of Sarum (Salisbury), *Reformation of the Church of England,* 7 vols. (Oxford University Press, 1829) vol.1, 325-6, vol. 2, 389.

Primary source for the "Neck Verse" – Robert Demaus, *William Tindale, A*

Biography; Being a Contribution to the Early History of the English Bible, ed. Richard Lovett (1904) 230.

William Tyndale, *Obedience of a Christian Man* (first published 1528).

George Stokes, *The Lollards* (1838).

William Henry Summers, *The Lollards Of The Chiltern Hills: Glimpses Of English Dissent In The Middle Ages* (1906).

John A. F. Thomson, *The Later Lollards 1414-1520* (Oxford University Press, 1965).

Brewer, *Letters and Papers of Henry VIII,* vol. 1, 285-297.

12

EDWARD WIGHTMAN

But the other of love, knowing that I am set for the defence
of the gospel (Philippians 1:17).

From the 1400s, the opposition to Christian faith would increase. Rarely at first sight do we get a glimpse of the faith for which so many died. Their beliefs are hidden, both at the time and later by reformed historians who mistaked stating their true beliefs. In fact many of these heretics were Christians following the pattern established in the first century. They were loyal to the state, and meant no harm to anyone. It is without doubt that the true church of Christ flourished throughout England, during the time of Henry VIII and earlier, in spite of hundreds of Christians being killed by the cruelest of methods. During this time of the Reformation, Roman Catholic activists in England were normally beheaded, not burned.

Christians were burnt at Westminster, Tower Hill, Stratford-le-Bow, Smithfields (London), Ely, Cambridge, Wisbech, Coventry, Canterbury, Lewes, Colchester, Newbury, Exeter, Wymondham, Uxbridge, Brentford, Beccles, Ipswich, Rochester, Norwich, Edinburgh, Litchfield, Buckingham, Ashford, Malden, and Cardiff.

The legal process was based on terror, not justice. Warrants were issued on the filmiest evidence. If indeed any evidence existed, it would have been used as an excuse to examine, under torture, those accused or their associates. Most feared was the Star Chamber, an English court of law that sat at the royal Palace of Westminster until 1641. It was made up of Privy Counsellors, as well as common-law judges, and supplemented the activities of the common-law and equity courts in both civil and criminal matters. The court was set up to ensure enforcement of laws against prominent people, those so powerful that ordinary courts could never convict them of their crimes. Court sessions of the Star Camber were held in secret, the public barred. There was little if any legal redress, especially in matters of religious liberty and conscience.

This changed from 1670, after the case of the Quaker preacher William Penn (1644-1718). Pennsylvania is named after him. Penn was arrested with William Meade. Penn was accused of preaching before a gathering at Gracechurch Street (London) on 14 August, 1670. Penn had deliberately provoked the court case in order to test the validity of the new law against assembly. Penn pleaded for his right to see a copy of the charges laid against him and the laws he had supposedly broken, but the judge, Sir Samuel Starling, Lord Mayor of London, refused. Penn's right was guaranteed by the law. Furthermore, the judge directed the jury to come to a verdict without hearing the defense.

Despite heavy pressure from the Lord Mayor to convict Penn, the jury returned a verdict of "not guilty." When invited by the judge to reconsider their verdict and to select a new foreman, they refused and were sent to a cell over several nights to mull over their decision. The Lord Mayor then told the jury, "Gentlemen, You shall not be dismist till we have a Verdict, that the Court will accept; and you shall be lockt up, without meat, drink, fire, and tobacco; you shall not think thus to abuse the Court, we will have a Verdict, by the help of God, or you shall starve for it." Penn was sent to the loathsome Newgate Prison (on a charge of contempt of court) and the jury followed him! They were additionally fined the equivalent of a year's wages each.

The next day the jury returned and after clashes with the judge, who now being exasperated said he wished for an inquisition in England as there is in Spain, dismissed the jury with the words "Your Verdict is nothing, you play upon the Court; I say you all together, and bring in another Verdict, or you shall starve; and I will have you carted about the City, as in Edward the third's time." The members of the jury were forced by circumstances to fight their case from prison, in what became known as Bushel's Case, after Edward Bushel, the jury foreman. They won the right for English juries to be free from the control of judges. They used in their defence the Magna Carta (the Great Charter of Freedoms) issued in the year

1215. Slowly, liberty of conscience in religious matters could be defended at law with an expectation of justice. The influence of the Church of England in secular legal matters was in progress of being removed.[1]

Thus it developed a right in law for those arrested to be provided a fair trial in which a proper defence could be mounted to refute the charges. Thanks to William Penn, the old system of terror had run its course being replaced by one in which justice could be expected.

Below, a typical court setting of the period
with the bishop top centre.

The last burnings of believers (Wightman and Legate) took place during 1612. Edward Wightman (born c 1566) of Burton upon Trent was convicted of heresy, including preaching against infant baptism, on the 14th December 1611. This was before the bishop of Coventry and Litchfield (now spelt "Lichfield). He was burnt at Litchfield on the 11th April 1612, two hundred and eleven years after William Sawtre was burnt. Most histories state that Wightman and Legate (1575 - 18 March 1612) were anti-Trinitarian. The charge was that both rejected the Nicene and Athanasian Creeds. The Nicene and Athanasian Creeds are Catholic in origin and, whilst accepted by most denominations (Catholic, Anglican and Protestant), are an addition to the New Testament.

Bartholomew Legate was born in Essex and became a dealer in cloth. In the 1590s, Bartholomew and his two brothers, Walter and Thomas, began preaching around London. Their message rejected the Roman Catholic Church, the Church of England and their rituals. They taught that preaching and hearing precede baptism and were, accordingly, labeled Anabaptists and anti-Trinitarian.

The anti-Trinitarian charge is useful as all opposing parties, Calvinists, Anglican and Catholic, held to the Nicene and Athanasian Creeds. This is no evidence, other than the accusations of his enemies, that Edward Wightman rejected the three persons of the Godhead. In 1611, together with his brother Thomas, Bartholomew Legate was imprisoned on conviction for heresy. Thomas died in Newgate Prison (London). Refusing to recant, Bartholomew was burnt at the stake at Smithfield on 18 March 1612. Bartholomew Legate was the last person burned in London for his religious opinions.

The confession of faith used by some of the churches of Christ in 1611 was this "That there is one God, the best, the highest, and most glorious Creator and Preserver of all; who is Father, Son, and Holy Spirit." The 1646 confession reads:

> The Lord our God is but one God, whose subsistence is in Himself; whose essence cannot be comprehended by any but himself, who only hath immortality, dwelling in the light, which no man can approach unto; who is in Himself most holy, every way infinite, in greatness, wisdom, power, love, merciful and gracious, long-suffering, and abundant in goodness and truth; who giveth being, moving, and preservation to all creatures. In this divine and infinite Being there is the Father, the Word, and the Holy Spirit; each having the whole divine Essence, yet the Essence undivided; all infinite without any beginning, therefore but one God; who is not to be divided in nature, and being, but distinguished by several peculiar relative properties.

Confessions of faith are not creeds, but tracts used to defend or promote the stance of those using the confession.

Edward Wightman (1566 - April 11, 1612) was burned at Litchfield. He was the last to suffer in this way in England. Future "heretics" would be starved to death in prison, as were nine thousand under Charles II, who reigned from 1660-1685. This came about because of public opposition of the burnings of people who were no threat to society. The charges brought against Wightman included eleven counts of heresy. Part of the indictment was that he believed "that the baptizing of infants is an abominable custom; that the Lord's Supper and baptism are not to be celebrated as they now are in the Church of England; and that Christianity is not wholly professed and preached in the Church of England, but only in part." His contemporaries said that if Edward really held all the opinions of which he was accused, he would have been either an idiot or a madman, and, if so, he ought to have had the prayers of his persecutors rather than to have them put him to a cruel death. As in Legate's case, one charge was denying the Trinity, or more precisely, denying the Nicene Creed.

Edward Wightman was convicted of heresy, the executioner made an aborted attempt to carry out the sentence on March of 1612. When the flames started to burn Wightman, he shouted out something that seemed to imply that he had changed his mind and was ready to accept the faith of the Church of England. The spectacle which unfolded before the populace of Litchfield was so painful that Edward Wightman was rescued from the flames before it could burn him too badly, possibly fearing a breach of the peace. Wightman was not too badly injured; he recovered from his ordeal being allowed his freedom.

371

Wightman refused to make a formal retraction and continued to preach his "heresies"; a few weeks later, on April 11, 1612, tied to the stake, he was executed by burning. The following is a copy of the order issued by the King for the consent required for death of Edward Wightman.

> The King to the sheriff of our city of Litchfield, Greeting. Whereas, the reverend father in Christ, Richard, by divine providence, of Coventry and Litchfield, Bishop, hath signified unto us, that he judicially proceeding, according to the exigence of ecclesiastical canons and of the laws and customs of this kingdom of Burton-upon-Trent, in the diocese of Coventry and Litchfield, of and upon the wicked heresies of Ebion, Cirinthus, Valintian, Arrius, Macedonius, Simon, Magnus, of Manes, Manichees, Photinus, and of the Anabaptists, and other arch-heriticks; and moreover of other cursed opinions, belched by the instance of Satan, excogitated and here-to-for-unheard of; the aforesaid Edward Wightman appearing before the aforesaid reverend father, and other divines and learned in the law, assisting him in judgment, the aforesaid wicked crimes, heresies and other detestable blasphemies and errors, stubbornly and perniciously, knowingly and maliciously, and with a hardened heart, published, defended and dispersed, by definite sentence of the said divine father, with the consent of divines, learned in the law aforesaid, justly, lawfully and canonically, against the said Edward Wightman in that part brought, stands adjudged and pronounced a heretick, and therefore as a diseased sheep out of the flock of the Lord, lest our subjects he do infect by his contagion, he hath decreed to be cast out, and cut off. Whereas, the holy mother church hath not further in this part what it ought more to do and prosecute, the same reverend father hath left to our secular power the same Edward Wightman as a blasphemous and condemned heritick to be punished

with the condign punishment as by the letters patent of the aforesaid reverend father, the bishop of Coventry and Litchfield, in this behalf thereupon made, as certified unto us in our Chancery. We, therefore, as the zealot of justice and the defender of the Catholick faith, and willing the holy church, and the rights and liberties of the same, and the Catholick faith to maintain and defend, and such like heresies and errors everywhere, so convict and condemn to punish with consign punishment, holding that such a heritick in the aforesaid form convicted and condemned, according to the customs and laws of this our Kingdom of England in this part accustomed, out to be burned with fire. We command thee that thou cause the said Edward Wightman, being in thy custody, to be committed to fire in some publick and open place below the city aforesaid, for the cause aforesaid before people; and the same Edward Wightman in the same fire cause really to be burned in destation of said crime, and for the manifest example of other Christians, that they may not fall into the same crime. And this no ways omit, under the peril that shall follow thereon.

Below is the market place next to the church where the burning took place.

Below is the plaque that commemorates the
burning of Edward Wightman.

Wightman's wife Francis and their children left Burton upon
Trent to live in London, where they attended the church of Christ

meeting at White Alley, Newgate. From there, his family moved to Rhode Island, America where they continued in the faith.

The last time according to my research that the accusation of "anti-Trinitarian" was used, by getting members of the church to deny the Nicene Creed, was in the famous debate held on October 17th 1642 at Southwark (London). Dr Daniel Featley (spelling of his name varies - 1578 - 1645) was a member of the translation committee of the King James Bible and was an Anglican theologian of high repute. Featley participated in the disputation with four "anabaptists" at Southwark, which is commemorated in his *The Dippers Dipt or the Anabaplists Dunckt and Plunged Over Head and Ears* (1645). The accusation of being anti-Trinitarian was denied. By this time the charge of denying the Trinity was known to be based on denying the Nicene Creed. Refutation of the charge was made by confirming belief in the triunity of the Godhead. The following is an excerpt from the *Dippers Dipt* when Featley was arguing with a Scottish Christian.

Featley:

> I will propound a Question or two to you concerning the blessed Trinity, that I may know whether you are well instructed in the principles of Catechisme, who yet are so well conceited of your selves, that you take upon you to teach others.

Featley:

> Doe you beleeve that the holy Ghost proceeds from the

Father and the Sonne? If you doe so, how then doe you answer the words of our Saviour, John 15.26. The Spirit which proceeds from the Father? There is no mention at all of proceeding from the Sonne, but the Father onely. To the latter of these Queries nothing was answered, by either of them; to the former they both answered. First the Scotchman. Scotchman: We never intend to deny that every Person in Trinity is God, for the Text you alledge, it proves not what you bring it for. Here the Text being read, the Scotchman answered, Christ opposeth his Father, as the true God, to all false gods.

Featley also argued that baptism should be by triple dispensing, whereas the those practising believers' baptism used single immersion, but as they noted in their defence, in the name of the Trinity (Mat. 28:19). For Featley, the use of single immersion was a denial of the Trinity.

There is no evidence I am aware of in the period of King James of any Anabaptist group being anti-Trinitarian. Bartholomew Legate and Edward Wightman were, from the sum total of evidence no more or no less, than members of the church of Christ, preaching the Gospel who died opposing the thirty nine articles of the Church of England (Anglican party), which includes the Nicene Creed. As such, they were restorationists rather than reformers. They sought to restore the pure church of the apostolic period rather than turn to Rome and its creeds. There is to my knowledge no statement recorded where Wightman denies the Trinity. Wightman is recorded as saying "that Christianity is not wholly professed and preached in the Church of England, but only in part." A view he was entirely right to hold.

Throughout the prosecution and persecutions in Europe that were deeply religious and superstitious, three accusations would persist: 1) denial of the Trinity, 2) a denial of the State church, 3) rebaptism of those baptised as infants in the State church (Anabaptism). These three charges would cross boundaries and be acceptable to Lutherans, Calvinists, Catholics, and Protestants alike, as would the horrendous consequences for those brave Christians. It must be remembered in the majority of cases, those imprisoned or burned alive could have walked away upon abjuring their beliefs. They went to their deaths voluntarily confessing Christ, Lord, King and Prophet, preaching the plan of Salvation, baptism by immersion for the remission of sins, preaching the visible church of the saved is not a denomination but His one and only church—the church of Christ. They denied predestination, they denied original sin and taught salvation is available to all men who ask.

Much has been made of Wightman's background prior to his repentance and baptism, but there can be no justification in discussing the views he may have held at some point previous to his conversion. Neither is there any defence for inventing a religious group to which they are said to have belonged (Anti-Trinitarian Anabaptists) when no such group existed in that time in England.

In the mid 1500s, a strong anti-Trinitarian movement amongst some continental Anabaptists started in Italy, from whence they were driven eastwards into Poland and, eventually, came under the influence of Faustus Socinus (1539-1604). The movement was named "Socinianism." In 1638, it was driven out of Poland and arrived in England in about 1651, nearly 40 years too late for Wightman and Legate to be party. This was the start of the Unitarian movement which was in England from the 1650s.

Another earlier accusation was against those who rejected Mary as sinless. The accusation was that the belief that Mary was capable of sin would entail a rejection of her as "Mother of God" and, therefore, a rejection of the deity of Christ. Later this argument developed into the Trinitarian denial with the rejection of the thirty nine articles of the Church of England, when the Nicene Creed was rejected. Bishop Burnett made an interesting observation concerning the Lollards, about seventy years after Wightman was executed:

> It is generally observed, that the proceedings against Lollards, the clergy always mixed some capital errors, which all Christians rejected, with those for which they accused them; and some particulars being proved, they gave it out that they were guilty of them all, to represent them the more odious.

Both the Protestants and Roman Catholics in this period were engaged in converting the indigenous population of the Americas, and neither denied believers' baptism by immersion. Prosecuting Christians for doing what was being done elsewhere was going to cause problems with ordinary people, who were getting deeply concerned about the cruelty shown in punishing these Christians. The charge of anti-Trinitarianism was useful; it did not cause resentment in other Romish and Protestant countries, who were Trinitarian, an important factor when wars were often religious. The legal system was not only biased towards the prosecutors, it was run by them. After the burnings ceased, death would be by starvation in prison, which was far less public.

> If any man speak, let him speak as the oracles of God; if any man minister, let him do it as of the ability which God giveth: that God in all things may be glorified through Jesus Christ, to whom be praise and dominion forever and ever. Amen. Beloved, think it not strange concerning the fiery trial which is to try you, as though some strange thing happened unto you: But rejoice, inasmuch as ye are partakers of Christ's sufferings; that, when his glory shall be revealed, ye may be glad also with exceeding joy (1 Pet. 4:11-13).

ENDNOTES

[1] Hans Fantel, *William Penn: Apostle of Dissent* (New York:William Morrow & Co., 1974)117-124. *The Peoples Ancient and Juft Liberties Asserted in the Tryal of William Penn and William Mead* (1670) 27-30.

Crosby, *Baptist History*, vol 1. Thomas Armitage, *History of the Baptists* (1887). Herbert S. Skeats, *A History of the Free Churches of England, From A.D. 1688 – A.D. 1851,* vol. 1 (1868) 59. Gilbert Burnett (1643-1715) Lord Bishop of Sarum (Salisbury), *Reformation of the Church of England,* 7 vols. (Oxford University Press, 1848). Dr. Daniel Featley, *The Dippers Dipt or the Anabaptists Dunckt and Plunged Over Head and Ears"* 4th ed. (Nicholas Bourn and Richard Royston, 1646).

Below, a Christian forced to make public penance, by holding a lighted candle and whipped through the streets.

13

JOHN SMITH (IOHN SMYTH), THOMAS HELWYS AND JOHN MORTON

Remember the word that I said unto you, the servant is not greater than his lord. If they have persecuted me, they will also persecute you; if they have kept my saying, they will keep yours also (John 15:20).

John Smith (more properly, "Smyth," 1554-1612) is in many established histories and reference books the founder of the Baptists along with Thomas Helwys (1570-1616).

The Oxford Dictionary of the Christian Church (second edition) states Smyth was educated at Cambridge University and ordained in the Church of England. A Calvinist, he became a puritan preacher at Lincoln within the Church of England (1603-5). In 1606, on his leaving the Church of England, he became a nonconformist preacher at a separatist congregation at Gainsborough, which is about twenty miles north of Lincoln. In 1608, Smyth led his congregation to Amsterdam, where he baptised himself, hence the title "Se-Baptist." It is stated in the Oxford Dictionary of the Christian Church that he became in 1609, in Amsterdam, the founder of the first Baptist church. He styled the community "The Brethren of the Separation of the Second English Church at Amsterdam." Membership was for baptised believers. During this time Smyth came under Mennonite (Anabaptist) influence. He died in Amsterdam in 1612, having never returned to England. Whilst brief, that pretty much sums up what is generally taught concerning Smith.

Having previously established there were churches of Christ in England prior to Smyth, the history of Smyth merits closer consideration. Smyth had by 1605 abandoned the title "City Preacher of Lincoln," now calling himself "Minister and Preacher of the Word of God," a brave move in this time for a preacher of the Church of England. We know and shall not argue that Smyth was at first a puritan and Calvinist. When he left Lincoln for Gainsborough, he had rejected Calvinism, as indeed fits in with such independent congregations of the time. Whilst at Gainsborough, he learned of baptism by immersion for believers, contradicting that he learned of Biblical baptism from the Mennonites. We learn this from a manuscript which purports to be the minutes of the Baptist Church at Epworth and Crowle (Dr. John Clifford, *The General Baptist Magazine,* London, July, 1879, vol. 81). It records:

> 1606, March 24. This night at midnight elder John Morton baptised John Smyth, vicar of Gainsborough, in the River Don. It was so dark we were obliged to have torch lights. Elder Brewster prayed, Mister Smith made a good confession; walked to Epworth in his cold clothes, but received no harm. The distance was over two miles. All

of our friends were present. To the triune God be praise.

The Epworth and Crowle congregation, who baptised believers by immersion for the remission of sins, started in 1597. Whilst a Baptist church today, they were then associated with other congregations who denied modern Baptist doctrine calling themselves the church of Christ and meeting each Sunday for the Lord's Supper.

Another account of this event is recorded by John Christian concerning the congregation at Epworth and Crowle in the Isle of Axholme, Lincolnshire, England. The church Covenant, dated January 4, 1599, is recorded in these words:

> We, this church of Christ, meeting at Epworth, Crowle and West Butterwick, in the county of Lincolnshire, whose names are underwritten, give up ourselves to the Lord and one to another according to the will of God. We do promise and covenant in the presence of Christ, to walk together in the laws and ordinances of baptized believers according to the rules of the Gospel through Jesus Christ, so helping us. Signed by James Rayner, John Morton, Henry Helwise, William Brewster, William Bradford, elders of ye church.[1]

There are appended thirty-two names, some with a "x" only, made by those who could not write. It is further stated that William Bradford was "baptised in the old river Don below Epworth town at midnight, 1595." There is also a record that the church desired to leave for Holland, "where we hear there is freedom for all men."

It is further recorded that John Smith, vicar of Gainsborough enquired about baptism in February 4, 1604, was convinced of its truth May 7th and "at midnight on the 24th of March, 1606, he was baptised by elder John Morton in the river Don, and walked to Epworth, a distance of two miles, in his wet clothes." And the document also records that "John Smith, John Morton (who immersed him), Henry Helwise and others held a meeting in regard to removing the church to Holland." The document is dated 4th of April, 1609. Clearly Smith soon gave up his title of "vicar."

This account has caused great controversy amongst the Baptists. Whether the Gainsborough church practised believers' baptism we do not know, but Gainsborough is a short distance of about ten miles to Epworth. The church at Epworth would not in 1606 have used the name Baptist; such churches used the identity "church of Christ," of that there can be no dispute and neither was it Calvinist. We see a plurality of elders, and baptism by full immersion, otherwise a walk of over two miles, at night, in the cold would not be necessary. We should also note that confession was required prior to baptism and that in this period baptism was always for remission of sins. England was in this time, according to the Anglican Church, "infested" by those who practised believers' baptism. Therefore the account should not surprise us.

Gainsborough is about fifteen miles from Scrooby, where another such church met. Members, like Smyth and his friends, fled to Holland. The Scrooby and Gainsborough churches were in fellowship, but we know little about them, except that those who led these churches would become involved in two separate works; establishing another church of Christ in London, and establishing several churches of Christ in New England.

When the Mayflower landed in 1620, William Brewster and his family were on board. Brewster was a former elder at Scrooby, and former postmaster. He would later become instrumental in the new colony being perhaps the most famous of the "Pilgrim Fathers." Many of the Pilgrim Fathers, whilst holding to the baptism of infants, had when worshiping in London had a minister who practiced believers' baptism. Baptism would in the New World be a major point of contention for the settlers.

Interestingly, John Morton, one of the elders at the Epworth congregation, was involved in the London congregation started later by Thomas Helwys in 1611/12. It was possibly at this time at Epworth in 1606 that Thomas Helwys was baptised and, though this cannot be proven, it seems his father Henry was an elder in the congregation.

Due to disputes and persecutions from the Church of England, who sought prosecution, Smyth was now a hunted man. He left with others to Amsterdam (Holland). The journey was an easy, a short voyage by sea. The Dutch were far more tolerant of religion and many English people had sought refuge in Holland for decades. This would be a natural and safe move, and Holland being so close, would mean in future years the possibility of returning made easy when the authorities were not watching. Smyth had sailed to Amsterdam with Thomas Helwys, who is one of the popular and early pioneers of Baptist history. Smyth had met Helwys at Gainsborough.

Shortly after Smyth arrived in Holland he repudiated his former baptism. This was probably about the year 1609. He remained convinced of believers' baptism and preached successionism. He was then excluded by the church which he had organised, leaving Thomas Helwys who became leader. At a later date Smyth applied to the Mennonites for membership, but after much discussion and disturbance among them, his application was rejected. This was the occasion of a great debate and much acrimony among the Mennonites. Letters were written by several parties. Some of the Mennonite churches went as far as to condemn formally the union in severe terms. Two Mennonite preachers, Ris and Gerritz, wrote Confessions which were favourable to the Mennonites and had Smyth and others sign them. The Confessions only dissatisfied both parties and failed to bring union of the forty-two English who signed one of them. Eleven erased their names, and the gravest dissatisfaction arose over it among the Mennonites themselves. The result was that Smyth was not received by the Mennonites and the remnant of his company was only received after years of waiting, and then not without friction. Smyth died in 1612 without returning to London. It is clear Smyth had little influence on the churches of Christ in the England, and the later Baptist denomination. He had been disfellowshipped and died in Holland. What was Smyth's point of contention of baptism which earned him his disfellowship? It seems he held to successionalism in baptism. He believed that true baptism required a succession of ministers at baptism. This as we have noted required the first baptiser to baptise himself, which Smyth did.

Thomas Helwys married Joan Ashmore and together they had seven children. He was a wealthy land-owner but this he gave up for the cause of Christ. Smith and Helwys agreed on many points; church autonomy, plurality of elders, separation of church and state, baptism by full immersion for the remission of sins whereby one is added to the church of Christ.

There was a serious doctrinal difference between Helwys and Smyth over successionalism, for which Smyth had been disfellowshipped. Smyth having formerly been an ordained priest in the Church of England, which held to successionalism, qualified him to restart Biblical baptism may have been the issue, nonetheless, his belief for the requirement for successionalism was rejected, but they disagreed with the following:

1. That Christ took his flesh of Marie, having true earthlie, naturall bodie.

2. That a Sabbath or day of rest is to be kept holy everie first day of the weeke.

3. That there is no succession or privilege to persons in the holie things.

4. That magistracie, being an holy ordinance of God debarreth not any from being of the Church of Christ.

5. Smyth's self baptism at Amsterdam and the rejection of the baptism at Epworth is what is referred to in point 3.

The issue of Smyth's baptism has long been argued. Smyth stated "in the Old Testament every man that was unclean washed himself; every priest going to sacrifice washed himself. Every master of a family ministered the Passover to himself and all of his family." He adds: "A man cannot baptise others into the church, himself being out, of the church. Therefore it is lawful for a man to baptise himself together with others in communion, and this warrant is a periphery for the practise of that which is done by us."[1]

Helwys demanded the Lord's Supper be taken every first day of the week which was contrary to the Mennonites. He also rejected original sin, but it is claimed he changed his mind on this later, or someone changed at a later date one of his leaflets. It was usual to reprint tracts for generations in the 1600s and sometimes by people not in direct association with the original writer. Concepts of original sin for the churches of Christ had not been settled in regards to whether the expression should be used, or, it was the consequences that are inherited and, hence, it was acceptable to use the expression but on the condition no penalty was inherited, children being innocent.

Whilst Baptists claim Helwys started the first Baptist Church in London, we do know this:

1. He baptised by immersion for the remission of sins upon repentance and on confession of faith for believers, rejecting infant baptism. He called infant baptism "the mystery of iniquity".

2. Through baptism one is added to the Church of Christ.

3. Church and State are separate.

4. The Lord's Supper is to be taken every first day of the week.

5. Congregations are overseen by a plurality of elders.

6. Christ was born of Mary being incarnate.

7. He never used the term "Baptist Church" but "church of Christ."

8. He taught the church is the called out of God.

9. He taught the word only in establishing doctrine.

10. He taught Freewill.

11. Helwys rejected succession in baptism, teaching that the unbaptised can baptise, and from there the now baptised Christian can baptise his baptiser, so a church can grow through the word.

12. Helwys' church was established on Biblical principles

alone. He had rejected Augustine, Catholicism, Anglicanism and Calvinism. His congregation wore the identity "church of Christ," and had none of the marks of the Baptist denominations that would come into being thirty years later.

After establishing a congregation in London, Helwys boldly pleaded to King James for Religious Liberty. Preparing an autographed copy of his only theological treatise, the *Mistery of Iniquity*, Helwys challenged the King to grant religious freedom to all men. King James responded by throwing Helwys in London's notorious Newgate prison, where he died (1616). The House of Lords still has his plea for liberty in their library.

Crosby wrote in 1738:

> It may be proper to observe here that there have been two parties of the English Baptists ever since the beginning of the reformation; those that have followed the Calvinistical scheme or doctrines, and from the principal points therein, personal election, and have been termed Particular Baptists: And those that have professed the Arminian or remonstrant tenets; and have also from the chief of those doctrines, universal redemption, been called General Baptists."[3] Crosby said "There were likewise many Baptists in England who did not choose to assume either name, because they receive what they think to be truth, without regarding with what human schemes it agrees or disagrees.[4]

Crosby said of Enoch Clapham, who wrote against the church in 1608, one year before the Helwys church:

> The Anabaptists, according to his account held, that repentance and faith must precede baptism, that baptism of both the Church of England and the Puritans was invalid and that true baptism was amongst them. He says further that they complained against the term Anabaptist, as a name of reproach unjustly cast upon them."[4]

The term "Anabaptist" refers to rebaptism, the church of Christ holding to Biblical baptism denied their baptism was rebaptism but followed the Biblical practice. Puritan baptism was infant baptism which is taken from the Roman Catholics minus the exorcisms but in origin, it is pagan.

It has been assumed by some that Smyth was baptised by affusion, and started the Baptist church with affusion as the mode of baptism. Again, Crosby comments "If he (Smyth) were guilty of what they charge with him," says Crosby, "'tis no blemish on the English Baptists; who neither approved any such method, nor did they receive their baptism from him."[6] In the early and mid 1700s the term "Baptist" referred to those who baptised believers for the remission of sins by immersion. Later it would be used as a distinct identity. In the 1600s the term used was church of Christ and from other sources previously referred to, the mode was immersion.

We know from history that there were congregations (churches of Christ) in London and England, prior to Helwys bringing his congregation to London in 1611/12. By the 1650s there are three distinctive groups in England baptizing believers by immersion:

1. The churches of Christ, which pre-existed Smyth, Helwys and later Baptist denominations.

2. The General Baptists with their Arminian theology which would develop from the 1660s onwards.

3. The Particular Baptists and their Calvinist theology, the forerunners of the Baptist (Calvinistic) denominations.

Regarding the identity and associations of the "Baptist Church," Crosby wrote "In the year 1683, the Baptists, who had hitherto been intermixed among the Protestant Dissenters, without distinction, and so consequently shared with the Puritans in all the Persecutions of those times, began now to separate themselves, and form distinct societies of those of their own persuasion." [7] Crosby is quite wrong; those holding to freewill had been separating for several centuries before, during and after the reformation. Baptist historians in their books and web sites often replace the identity "church of Christ" with either "Baptist Church" or just "church," both are a falsification of history. J. M. Cramp in his *Baptist History* 1871, is a typical example, as is Crosby in his four volumes (1738-40). Original source documents use the term church of Christ such as the 1646 Confession.

According to Herbert Skeats, there were congregations separated from the Church of England baptising believers in England prior to Helwys. Skeats gives the earliest date of 1417, another date he cites is 1589, regarding several congregations.[8] According to Skeats, were there no "Baptists" in England who held to Calvinism prior to about 1640.[9] Skeats was an independent, having no Baptist affiliation, and no axe to grind.

Smyth died in Holland, forming no lasting church nor any church in England. It was his former friend and colleague, Thomas Helwys, who formed a church of Christ in London along Bible principles. Neither started the Baptist denomination, which came into being about three decades after their deaths. It is also true that churches of Christ were in London prior to the congregation of Helwys and elsewhere in Europe. The view left by historians and Baptists in particular is that no church of Christ existed prior to Alexander Campbell, and that Baptist churches originated with John Smyth. Other Baptist historians take a line of succession back to the church of the first century. Such is not true but revisionist history. On investigation, the Baptist Church in all of its various denominational forms was an apostate movement which came out of the churches of Christ in the 1640s, from which it spread abroad into the world.

There was no Baptist church of that name or denomination prior to the 1650s. Churches of Christ, founded on Biblical principles, preceded the Baptist church from where that denomination emerged, as can be confirmed with ease by the various confessions of faith, as published by the Baptists in last two hundred years.

This is Smyth's personal confession, never officially published. The original manuscript is held in the Mennonite Archives, Amsterdam. These are his twenty articles.

WE BELIEVE WITH THE HEART AND WITH THE MOUTH CONFESS:

(I) That there is one God, the best, the highest, and most glorious Creator and Preserver of all; who is Father, Son, and Holy Spirit.

(II) That God has created and redeemed the human race to his own image, and has ordained all men (no one being reprobated) to life.

(III) That God imposes no necessity of sinning on any one; but man freely, by Satanic instigation, departs from God.

(IV) That the law of life was originally placed by God in the keeping of the law; then, by reason of the weakness of the flesh, was, by the good pleasure of God, through the redemption of Christ, changed into justification of faith; on which account, no one ought justly blame God, but rather, with his inmost heart, to revere, adore, and praise his mercy, that God should have rendered that possible to man, by his grace, which before, since man had fallen, was impossible by nature.

(V) That there is no original sin (lit. no sin of origin or descent), but all sin is actual and voluntary, viz., a word, a deed, or a design against the law of God; and therefore, infants are without sin.

(VI) That Jesus Christ is true God and true man; viz.,

the Son of God taking to himself, in addition, the true and pure nature of a man, out of a true rational soul, and existing in a true human body.

(VII) That Jesus Christ, as pertaining to the flesh, was conceived by the Holy Spirit in the womb of the Virgin Mary, afterwards was born, circumcised, baptized, tempted; also that he hungered, thirsted, ate, drank, increased both in stature and in knowledge; he was wearied, he slept, at last was crucified, dead buried, he rose again, ascended into heaven; and that to himself as only King, Priest, and Prophet of the church, all power both in Heaven and earth is given.

(VIII) That the grace of God, through the finished redemption of Christ, was to be prepared and offered to all without distinction, and that not feignedly but in good faith, partly by things made, which declare the invisible things of God, and partly by the preaching of the Gospel.

(IX) That men, of the grace of God through the redemption of Christ, are able (the Holy Spirit, by grace, being before unto them grace prevement) to repent, to believe, to turn to God, and to attain to eternal life; so on the other hand, they are able themselves to resist the Holy Spirit, to depart from God, and to perish forever.

(X) That the justification of man before the Divine tribunal (which is both the throne of justice and of mercy), consists partly of the imputation of the righteousness of Christ apprehended by faith, and partly of inherent righteousness, in the holy themselves, by the operation of the Holy Spirit, which is called regeneration or sanctification, since any one is righteous, who doeth righteousness.

(XI) That faith, destitute of good works, is vain; but true and living faith is distinguished by good works.

(XII) That the church of Christ is a company of the faithful; baptised after confession of sin and of faith, endowed with the power of Christ.

(XIII) That the church of Christ has power delegated to themselves of announcing the word, administering the sacraments, appointing ministers, disclaiming them, and also excommunicating; but the last appeal is to the brethren of body of the church.

(XIV) That baptism is the external sign of the remission of sins, of dying and of being made alive, and therefore does not belong to infants.

(XV) That the Lord's Supper is the external sign of the communion of Christ, and of the faithful amongst themselves by faith and love.

(XVI) That the ministers of the church are, not only bishops, to whom the power is given of dispensing both the word and the sacraments, but also deacons, men and widows, who attend to the affairs of the poor and sick brethren.

(XVII) That brethren who persevere in sins known to themselves, after the third admonition, are to be excluded from the fellowship of the saints by excommunication.

(XVIII) That those who are excommunicated are not to be avoided in what pertains to worldly business.

(XIX) That the dead (the living being instantly changed) will rise again with the same bodies; not the substance but the qualities being changed.

(XX) That after the resurrection, all will be borne to the tribunal of Christ, the Judge, to be judged according to their works; the pious, after sentence of absolution, will enjoy eternal life with Christ in heaven; the wicked, condemned, will be punished with eternal torments in hell with the devil and his angels.

What Smyth meant by "grace prevement" I do not know. Whether this is active (Calvinism) or passive, in that "But God commendeth his love toward us, in that, while we were yet sinners, Christ died for us" (Rom. 5:8) and "For the love of Christ constraineth us; because we thus judge, that if one died for all, then were all dead: And that he died for all, that they which live should not henceforth live unto themselves, but unto him which died for them, and rose again" (2 Cor. 5:14-15). The idea in that time that salvation could be had through faith and obedience is at odds with the teaching of the world, as it is today.

Helwys took his congregation to London where he was an elder with Iohn Murton (John Morton). We know only a little about John Morton's early days. He first met Thomas Helwys in about 1606 at Gainsborough, England. The two would become lifelong friends and co-elders both in Holland and the church in London. Morton had been an elder of the Epworth congregation, at a young age, or his father was, sharing the same name.

John Morton had been an elder of the church in Holland along with fellow elders, who were most likely, Thomas Helwys, William Pigott and Thomas Seamer. These brethren had already resolved that a plurality of elders was the scriptural pattern and that the office of pastor was the same as elder.

We know these churches had (acapella) congregational singing and that women were allowed with the men to partake together of the Lord's Supper, held each Sunday. Later some Calvinist congregations that became Baptist would exclude women from congregational singing. Morton and Helwys were opposed to the idea of covenanting, which was popular amongst the separatists, stating the way into the church was via baptism.

The congregation had first met in Amsterdam, before moving to London. In London, it seems the congregation first met at Spittlefields, in about 1612 before moving to Newgate, home of the famous prison at London Bridge. Helwys died in prison by 1616 according to his brother, Geoffrey, fortunate to the extent that he did not have to suffer the flames. Morton, too, found himself in prison. It seems when Morton came out of prison, he was not only one of the elders, but the preacher for the congregation.

Morton opposed baptism by succession and a clergy, teaching on baptism that "we affirm that any disciple of Christ in what part of the world whatsoever coming to the Lord's way, he by the Word and Spirit of God preaching that the way unto others, and converting he may and ought also baptise them." Morton also stated:

> I say it is a mere fixation, there is not the least show in all
> the Testament of Jesus Christ, that baptising is peculiar
> only to pastors, which might satisfy any man of reason;

neither can it be proved that ever ordinary Pastor did baptise. And it is most plain, converting and baptising is no part of the Pastors office, his office is to feed, to watch, to oversee, the flock of Christ already the church, his charge is to take heed to the flock, and to feed the church, and to defend them in the truth against all gainsayers: Further than which, no charge is laid him by virtue of his office. That he may preach, convert and baptise I deny, not that another disciple may, but not either is required, or he doth perform it by virtue of his office; no proof for that imagination can be showed: and therefore it remains firm and stable, every disciple that have ability is authorised, yea commanded to preach, convert and baptise as well and as much (if not more) than a Pastor.

Morton also wrote regarding baptism and the church:

But first I will lay down a main foundation, which being sufficiently proved, the evident truth shall plainly appear: and this it is; that members and Churches of Christ, are so made: both by faith and baptism, and not by the one only, which being true; it will follow, that neither the church and members of Rome, are members of the Church of Christ, because Faith is neither required nor performed thereto; nor yet any profession of people, that separate from Rome as no Church of Christ, retaining Rome's baptism, and building new churches without baptism.

That the members and Church of Christ are so made by Faith and Baptism, even both, it is proved in Rom 11:20 &c., so that to be gathered into the name of Christ, by being Disciples and baptised, is, to be made members of his body (which is his Church) of his Flesh and of his bone: Thus Christ made Disciples, we must be the sons of God by Faith, and put on Christ by Baptism... and we are made partakers of Christ, by having the beginnings,

which beginnings are Repentance, Faith and Baptism,
other beginnings, or foundation can no man lay.

Thus it is clear these brethren maintained that any church member might preach, make converts and administer baptism and through baptism entry is into the church of Christ. The English of the above has been slightly modernised for clarity. The use of "Church of Christ" is found in the original. There is on my part no addition or omission, just the modernising of the English.

The Newgate congregation met close to St. Paul's, within half a mile from the Bell Alley congregation. They were about two miles from the Southwark congregation, which was across the river Thames via London Bridge, the only bridge in this time (all three being in what we now know as London). The latter Southwark church was the most liberal of the three, accepting into communion those who had been baptised as infants, though they taught believers' baptism. In the 1590s, several churches of Christ existed in London, but their locations remain a mystery (at this time) apart from Coleman Street and Bow Lane. In this period the sentence was death by burning for any member proved to belong to the church of Christ in England. Other earlier churches outside of London going back prior to the 1400s, and hence the reformation, were in fellowship with the London congregations. These congregations called themselves "Church of Christ" and opposed Calvinism, preaching and practicing baptism for the remission of sins using the formula "faith, repentance and baptism." John Morton, preacher and an elder of the church of Christ meeting in Newgate, died sometime between 1624 and 1626.

In the 1620s churches of Christ existed in London, Lincoln, Epworth, Sarum (Salisbury), Coventry, Tiverton (Devon), Warrington (Hill Cliff), Plymouth, Amersham, Olchon (Wales), Stoney Stratford, Eyethorn (which began in the 1590s) and Monksthorpe (Lincolnshire). Others would start or become known from the 1620s onwards, such as those in the Furness Fells and at Peterborough, Spalding, Holbeach, Uppingham, Nottingham and many other locations.

In about 1620, an attack was made on the churches of Christ which their enemies said "a great error held by them, that no infants dying in infancy are damned with the wicked in hell, which salvation they have by the merits of Chrift."[10]

A tract has come down to us from 1618 published both in the Holland and England, it is found in Crosby. A short paraphrase that states:

> Wherein it is clearly shown and out of good grounds demonstrated that baptism instituted and ordained by the Lord Jesus Christ, for those that believe and repent and was taught and used by his Apostles and observed by the primitive church. As also how that in process of time the baptism of children instead of true baptism was brought in and received, and by divers councils, Popes and Emperors commanded to be observed. Mark 16;16 He that shall

believe and be baptised shall be saved, But he that will not believe shall be dammed. [11]

ENDNOTES

I have used Thomas Crosby, who produced four volumes in his *History of the English Baptists*, published in London in 1738, 1739, and 1740. For Crosby the term *Baptist* simply referred to anyone who baptised by immersion, he did not use it to distinguish a denomination (preface, vol. 1). I have also referred Champlin Burrages's *The Early English Dissenters*, (Cambridge University Press, 1912).

[1] John T. Christian, *Did They Dip?*, 2nd ed. (1896) 86 ff.

[2] Christian, *Did They Dip?*. Estwep, *The Anabaptist Story* 222. Thomas Helwys, *The Mystery of Iniquity* (Grays Inn, London, 1612).

[3] Thomas Crosby, *History of the English Baptists*, vol. 1 (1738) 173.

[4] Crosby 174.

[5] Crosby 88.

[6] Crosby 99.

[7] Crosby 147.

[8] Herbert Skeats, *History of the Free Churches of England 1688-1891* (with a continuation by Charles S. Miall 1891) 18.

[9] Skeats 32.

[10] Crosby 142.

[11] Crosby 128ff.

14

DR. DANIEL FEATLEY (1578-1645):
Author of *The Dippers Dipt or the Anabaptists Dunckt and Plunged Over Head and Ears*

> But before all these, they shall lay their hands on you, and persecute you, delivering you up to the synagogues, and into prisons, being brought before kings and rulers for my name's sake (Luke 21:12).

Dr. Daniel Featley, Latinized as Danielis Featlei (also known under the pseudonym of Richard or Daniel Fairclough), was an adversary of the churches of Christ during the early to mid 1600s, writing against them. He was an Anglican theologian of considerable renown. He was born 1578 in Charlton, Oxfordshire and died on April 17th, 1645 in Chelsea, London.

It is from Featley, a witness to the existence of the church in the early seventeenth century, that we learn of some of its beliefs. He wrote about the church before and during the time some apostasied into Calvinism and later became the forerunners of the many Baptist denominations. He remains a valuable witness to the church in the early 1600s, despite his distaste.

403

Featley was a scholar of Corpus Christi College, Oxford, and probationer fellow in 1602, after which he went to the court of Henry IV of France as chaplain to the English ambassador. Featley was involved in the translation of the 1611 King James Version of the Bible. He served on the "First Oxford Company," responsible for the later books of the Old Testament, beginning with Isaiah to the end of the OT. Featley is listed under the pseudonym "Daniel Fairclough" in the list of translators. Aged 26, at the time, he was the youngest by far of the company, which may explain why he hid his identity.

For some years Featley was co-chaplain with Thomas Goad to George Abbot, Archbishop of Canterbury. Featley held the London rectories of Lambeth (1619), Allhallows, Bread Street (c. 1622), and Acton (1627), the last after leaving the archbishop's service in 1625.

Featley was also a chaplain in ordinary to Charles I (of England) and was appointed provost of Chelsea College in 1630. In 1641 he sat on a subcommittee to settle the many religious arguments and factions in the Church of England. In the course of this work, he was in disputation with four members of the church of Christ on October 17th, 1642, who he called "anabaptists," at Southwark (South London). This is commemorated in his book *The Dippers Dipt or the Anabaptists Dunckt and Plunged Over Head and Ears* (1645). At the time of the "disputation" in 1642, the majority of the churches of Christ were not Calvinist. Neither the Baptist Church denomination nor the description of men as Baptists had begun. Featley's antagonistic account of the Lord's Church offers a wonderful glimpse of the church in the 1600s, prior to the apostasy that led to the various Baptist denominations.

One of his adversaries he names as Cuffin, who was probably William Kiffin, who two years later was preaching at the church in Devonshire Square, where he served until his death in 1701. Kiffin was a wealthy London merchant of great standing in the community and with king Charles II. The king appointed him, viz., to public office, Alderman of London, Lord Lieutenant and magistrate, though he seldom exercised these offices. Kiffin associated in time with the churches that became Calvinistic, but was at first a member of the church of Christ meeting near the Tower of London. Kiffin was baptised in about 1639, three years before the disputation. The names of the other three are not mentioned in Featley's book. After the restoration of the monarchy in 1658, Kiffin was several times imprisoned for brief periods before becoming a friend of Charles II. In 1664, using his now restored influence, he was able to rescue twelve members of the church (non-Calvinistic) who had been convicted of heresy and sentenced to death for participating in an illegal conventicle (church).

Kiffin was one of the prime agents for spreading Calvinism into the Churches of Christ in the later part of the seventeenth century. He and others had a nationwide strategy. These congregations so converted later called themselves – Baptised Churches and their members Baptists. When Kiffin was baptised, the church was opposed to Calvinism and called "The Church of Christ" and its members "Christians."

Featley sat in the Westminster Assembly of 1643 and was the last of the Episcopal (Anglican) members to remain. For revealing its proceedings to Archbishop Usher, who was in league with the King, he was expelled and imprisoned in 1643. Even whilst in prison Parliament, now under control of the Calvinists (Puritans) could find no adequate defender of the faith in their own ranks and begged the imprisoned Featley to help them in their anti-papist campaign. Featley rose to the occasion despite being denied access to his library, which had been confiscated. Shortly thereafter he was allowed home to Chelsea on grounds of his ill health, where he died on April 17, 1645. Whilst in prison, Featley met the evangelist Henry Denne who too was imprisoned for preaching and baptising.

Contemporary picture looking from Southwark towards London and Bow Lane by Claes Van Visscher, 1616.

The "fovrth edition" of the *The Dippers Dipt or the Anabaptists Dunckt and Plunged Over Head and Ears* was printed in 1646 by Nicholas Bourn and Richard Royston, in Ivy Lane (London), one year after Featley's death and one year after the first edition appeared. It is this edition I have used and to which I refer, pictured below.

The work was written to oppose congregations who call themselves "Churches of Christ," meeting in England in the 1600s, who baptised by immersion for remission of sins; who were autonomous, being separate from the Church of England, ruled by a plurality of elders and deacons assisting. These congregations were Trinitarian, which was for a time denied by their enemies such as Featley.

Below , from the introduction.

The Dippers dipt.
O R,
THE ANABAPTISTS
DVCK'D AND PLVNG'D
Over Head and Eares, at a
Difputation in *Southwark*.

TOGETHER WITH
A large and full Discourse of

Their
1. Originall.
2. Severall forts.
3. Peculiar Errours.
4. High Attempts againſt the State.
5. Capitall puniſhments: with an Application to thefe times.

By DANIEL FEATLEY, *D. D.*

Valens & Gratianus ad Florianum Vicarium Afiæ.
Antiſtitem qui fanɛtitatem baptifmatis illicita ufurpatione geminaverit, facerdotio indignum effe cenfemus. Eorum enim damnamus errorem qui Apoſtolorum præcepta calcantes Chriſtiani nominis facramenta fortitos alio rurfus baptifmate non purificant , fed inceſtant facramenti nomine polluentes.

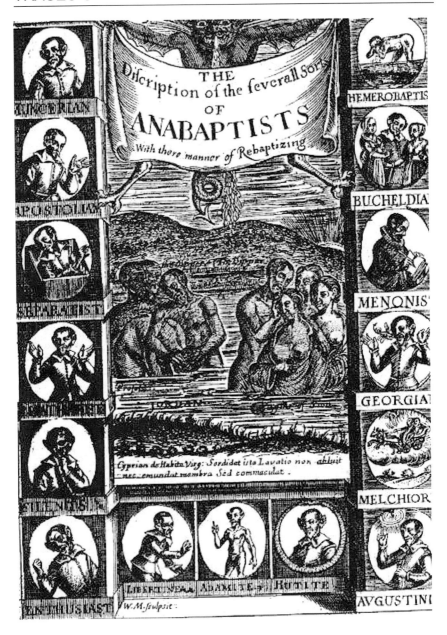

In the preface Featley complained with mordant irony of the various congregations, their meeting places and lay-preaching:

I am to tell ye, Christian Reader, this New Year of new changes never heard of in former ages, namely, of Haras turned into Aras, Stables into Temples, Stalls into Choirs, Shopboards into Communion Tables, Tubs into Pulpits, Aprons into Linen Ephods and Mechanics of the lowest rank into Priests of the high places... If ever Saint Jerome's complaint were in season, it is now: Physicians keep within the bounds of their Science; Smiths meddle with the Hammer and Anvil; the Linen Draper deals not in woolen cloth, nor the Woolen Draper in the Linen; the Carpenter takes not the joiners work out of his hand, nor the Joiner the Carpenters; the Shoemaker goes not beyond his last, nor the Taylor beyond his measure; namely the trade of Expounding Scripture is a mystery which every artisan arrogated to himself. The Physician here will be prescribing receipts, the Lawyer will be demurring upon dubia Evangelica, and every handicrafts man will be handling the pure word of God with impure and unwashed hands. This the prattling has wise, this the old dotard, this the wrangling sophister, in a word, these men of all professions, and men of no profession, take upon them to have skill in readily teaching that they never learned, and abundantly pouring out that which never infused into them.

From this remonstrance we learn that meetings were being held in all sorts of venues, such as barns and stables in which men, employed in various trades and able to preach, did so. In fact, just about everything Featley complains about is what is expected of Godly men. The church in the first century knew nothing of doctors or clergy, being made up of men of ordinary trades such as tent making (Acts 18:3) or fishermen (Mat. 14:18).

On page 20, Featley wrote regarding the Anabaptists:

> The third broached theirs in the year 1525, which was this; that baptism ought to be administered to none but such as can give a good account of their faith; and in case any have been baptized in their infancy, that they ought to be re-baptised after they come to years of discretion, before they are to be admitted to the Church of Christ.

To my knowledge, Featley used "Church of Christ" in all additions of the *Dippers Dipt*. Featley never retracted or sought to change this identity. It was not a printer's error, nor does it seem an error on the part of Featley. Historians opposed to the church such as Daniel Neal (1678 - 1743), who wrote his history of the Puritans, in four volumes between the years 1732 -38, did not find fault either. On the contrary Featley's statement agrees with the churches of Christ meeting in London in the 1530s, and in Kent. Such churches were also meeting elsewhere using the term church of Christ.

We can see that the church of Christ, according to the highly respected Anglican theologian, Dr. Featley, existed prior to the Church of England's reformation from the 1530s onwards. Methodism began over two hundred years later. The church of Christ predates John Calvin, who then was just sixteen years old in 1525, and the Presbyterian Church. The confirmation is just eight years after Luther started the Reformation in 1525. Such churches in England predate Luther. The continental Anabaptists began meeting in about 1526-7, which is after the church of Christ was mentioned by Featley. His statement implies the church of Christ had not just started, but was already in existence in 1525 and had come to the knowledge of the authorities by that date. Previously, such congregations had been prosecuted as Lollards, e.g., the church meeting in Tenderden, Kent in 1511.

In his *Dippers Dipt,* Featley makes sixteen distinctive Biblical points as is expected of the churches of Christ when complying with the scriptures:

1. Featley twice notes they used the identity church of Christ, on pages 5 and 20. At no point do they describe themselves by any other term than Christian. On page 124, Featley wrote concerning their name "how can they truly say that they are falsely called Anabaptists? If it be their nickname, what is their right name, whereby they may be distinguished from other Christians, Catholic or heretics?" Here Featley confirms that "Anabaptist" is a nickname and that they complained at being so called.

2. Featly attacks them for denying the Trinity, though they refute this by arguing that they believe the Father, Son and Holy Ghost are God. What they deny is the denominational Nicene Creed. Pages 2, 16.

3. These congregations deny circumcision is a precursor in the Old Testament to baptism in the New Testament, pointing out that if this were so, only male children could be baptised. Pages 6,7, 32,

35.

4. They ague that children do not need baptism to be admitted to the Kingdom, page 8.

5. They defend "lay-preaching", arguing all Christian men may preach and administer baptism and the Supper, denying any clergy-laity divide, pages 8,25,81. Featley complains concerning their preachers, "coach-men, weavers, feltmakers and other base mechanics and now, by some, thought able ministers and profound Doctors of the Church, and exercise, as they term it, not only in private conventicles (illegal meetings), but also in great churches, and public assemblies; to the great dishonour of God, profanation of his Ordinances, and scandal of the Reformed Churches," quoted from page 86.

6. They argue the Old Testament priesthood is abolished and now all Christians are in the priesthood, page 9.

7. They argue that the Ecclesia (the congregation) is the church and not the "steeplehouse", and may meet anywhere, page 10.

8. They defend the use of preaching before baptism, pages 14,15.

9. They deny the Church of England is a church of God. They also argue that the Church of Christ is the only church, and hence not a denomination, page 3.

10. They say there is no original sin, page 22.

414

11. They say that men have freewill, not only in natural and moral, but also in spiritual action, that man has freedom to choose or reject God's Grace whereby they may be saved (through baptism), pages 22,24.

12. They say that Luther's doctrine is worse than the Pope's, denying that they are Lutherans, page 22.

13. They do not use set forms of prayer, but pray from the heart for the occasion. They state the "Lord's Prayer" is a "pattern" for all prayer, and not to be "used as a prayer." Pages 58,59, 62.

14. Featley notes throughout The Dippers Dipt that they baptise by immersion. Featley argues that sprinkling and pouring may be used, which they deny arguing from the Greek that baptism is by immersion only, note page 25. They state that repentance and confession precedes baptism, page 29; that through baptism entry is into the church of Christ.

15. In his introduction to *The Dippers Dipt,* Featley states they pleaded for separation of Church and State.

16. Finally, these congregations held that the kingdom and the church are the same, page 8.

ENDNOTES

Primary source - Dr. Daniel Featley, *The Dippers Dipt or the Anabaptists Dunckt and Plunged Over Head and Ears,* 4th edition (Nicholas Bourn and Richard Royston., 1646).

15

CHURCHES OF CHRIST IN ENGLAND
IN THE 1600s

As I besought thee to abide still at Ephesus, when I went
into Macedonia, that thou mightest charge some that they
teach no other doctrine (1 Timothy 1:3).

The now forgotten tale of Thomas Lamb and the Bell Alley

Church of Christ and other London congregations in the 1600s

Panorama of London by Claes Van Visscher, 1616.

Thomas Lamb by trade was a "boiler of soap." He was a preacher
and one of two elders in the Bell Alley congregation in the 1630s
and 40s. He baptized many for the remission of sins in the "pool of
London," part of the river Thames near Traitors Gate, The Tower
of London. The other elder was Edward Barber, who was jailed for

eleven months in 1641 after being convicted for preaching against infant baptism. The crime was that as he was unlicensed as a preacher and preaching contrary to the Church of England's articles.[1]

The Tower of London and Traitors Gate.

The first we learn of "heresy" in Coleman Street, is in the pre-reformation 1400 and 1500s, when a small congregation made up of both working and profession classes (guilds) was then meeting in Coleman Street, London and another in Bow Lane, which is close by. There were more reports of "heresy" in Coleman Street, in the 1520s, when a leading figure in the Christian community, John Hacker, known as "old father Hacker," a water-bearer of Coleman Street and a convert of many years, who is mentioned in chapter 11, was arrested and, under examination, revealed the names of several congregations and members across southern England. The Coleman Street and Bell Alley Churches of Christ were pre-reformation, their roots being Lolloard in origin. At this time as elsewhere in London and throughout England existed churches of Christ. These congregations and their associates are pre-reformation, and hence not a result of the reformation but were motivated by a desire to restore the church to its Christian simplicity as found in scripture.

Great Bell Alley as it today, having suffered in the Great Fire of London in 1666 and more recently, the German Blitz.

About 1520, John Hacker was caught distributing heretical books at Burford. The books were Lollard materials and possibly some of Luther's books. In 1521, being then also involved with some Lollards from Buckinghamshire, he was by the authorities of the diocese of Lincoln compelled to abjure, under torture. Associated with him, and more prominent in the subsequent years, were John Stacey, also of Coleman Street, and Lawrence Maxwell, of Aldermanbury Parish. These two were prominent members of the Tilers' and Bricklayers' Company and had wide contacts both inside and outside London. Stacey kept an amenuensis (a man to prepare manuscripts by hand) in his house "to write the Apocalypse in English," the costs being met by John Sercot, a grocer.

Coleman Street, was located within a few yards of the Guildhall, a location that was destined for many years to become the centre of various "heretical sects." Hacker's associates had close connections with Christians in Colchester and Buckinghamshire, but its importance was in providing a ready-made organisation to promote the Bible, books and tract distribution in the late fifteen twenties.

Another of Hacker's disciples was the leather merchant John Tewkesbury, whom Bishop Tunstall persuaded to recant of heresy, but who went on to promote Tyndale's, *The Wicked Mammon*, copies of which he proceeded to sell to others. Robert Necton, another Londoner, sold books imported from Germany and Holland in and around London. He also had previous connections with the Lollards, accused before Bishop Longland of Lincoln in 1521. By the mid-twenties, the situation in the London diocese had become so notorious that Tunstall and his successor, Stokesley, were forced to attempt an extensive purge. Between 1527 and 1532, more than 200 heretics are alleged by Foxe to have abjured their heresy upon conviction in the diocesan courts. Of these people, about half came from the city and half from Colchester, Steeple Bumpstead, Birdbrook and other places in Essex.

Thomas Lamb, who was born in Colchester, a city in southeast England, is named after the ancient king, Cole, of nursery rhyme fame. We are fortunate to know a little about Thomas Lamb and his family. Lamb was arrested at Colchester for illegal preaching and brought to London to appear before the court of Star Chamber, his wife speaking on his, and their eight children's, behalf. The Anglican Archbishop Laud quickly resolved her outburst by having "the troublesome woman" removed. This was the first of his three jail sentences for his preaching and taking part in illegal conventicles (illegal church assemblies).

Lamb was arrested again and imprisoned, being released on bail on 25 June, 1640 with the condition "not to preach, baptise or frequent any conventicle." About the 15th October of the same year, Lamb was in Gloucestershire preaching and baptising converts.

Here he was opposed by the "Rev." Wynell. It was from Wynell's Church of England congregation in 1639 that Richard Baxter became acquainted with the Lord's Church. As a result, of this Baxter was sent to London to study under from Lamb. Lamb spent time in the west country and baptized many converts in the River Severn. He brought with him Clement Writer, who was also a preacher. Wynell says Lamb held his services in a private house "and by preaching there he subverted many, and shortly afterwards in an extreme cold, and frosty time, in the night season, diverse men and women were rebaptized in the great River Severn, in the City of Gloucester." These conversions took place in the early winter of 1640. In 1645 after the publishing of an "Ordinance of Parliament" against un-ordained preachers, the Lord-Mayor sent his officers to arrest Lamb who was preaching contrary to law. The congregation was furious that the authorities should break up their gathering on the Lord's Day. Some used some very rough language towards the constables. Lamb brought the affair to a peaceable end by undertaking to appear before Sir Thomas Adams, the Lord-Mayor at six pm. This was accepted. Adams, a royalist, had little sympathy with those seeking liberty in religious matters. Lamb and an assistant went to his lordship's house at the appointed time. Lamb argued they had broken no law for they were under the law of Christ. This was rejected and they were handed over to a committee of Parliament, which after hearing them, committed both men to jail. By the intercession of the brethren, they were released and found their liberty.

A story remains that once when Lamb was out evangelising in the village of Oldford (Nr Frome), Somerset, he baptised a lady in the river which the church there frequently used for the purpose. The husband of the lady, a man greatly opposed to the church took a "great stone", concealing it under his coat, his purpose to do "a great mischief" to Thomas Lamb. As baptising believers by unlicensed preachers was illegal, the husband ran little risk of prosecution for assault, even if a serious injury was to result. Had the women been baptised as an infant, as was likely, the offence of (re)baptism was even more serious. As Lamb stood with the lady in the river praying, speaking and preparing to immerse her, the husband was so moved that, hearing the gospel, he was baptised after her.

Despite the terror, torture and burnings, all the efforts of the Roman Catholic and later Protestant and Anglican churches could not extinguish the church of Christ. What led to its near extermination in the seventeenth century was not persecution, but apostasy from inside – the spread of Calvinism and the resulting Baptist movement and Quakerism. In pamphlets published in 1642, Lamb brought to the attention of the brotherhood the encroachment of Calvinism into the Lord's Church. This happened after John Spilsbury and others were ejected from the Church of England. Lamb was greatly opposed to the newly forming "Calvinistic" Churches of Christ and their scheme of "particular" redemption. He was one of the few brethren who withstood this new apostate movement. He wrote a pamphlet in 1642 entitled "A treatife of particular predeftination, wherein are anfwered, three letters, the firft, tending to difprove particular predeftination: the second, to shew the contradiction betwix Chrift's dying for all, and God's election of fome: the third, to prove, that the soul doth not come from the parent, and confequently that there is no original fin." He set out and showed how that redemption is limited to those who obey the gospel, though the offer of salvation is universal. Thus he denied universalism and limited atonement of the Calvinists.

John Spilsbury and his compatriots were Calvinists and independents. In 1638, they rejected infant baptism and were sprinkling believers. When they came into contact with the Lord's people (Kiffin), they learnt of immersion as the correct mode (1641), and also the name of the church, which they had adopted by 1643. By this date seven congregations and one French congregation of this new Calvinistic persuasion were meeting in London.

In 1643, Thomas Lamb baptised Henry Denne (born about 1599), who also wrote against this innovation in the Lord's church in a leaflet; *The Drag-net of the Kingdom of Heaven; or Christ's Drawing All Men*, 1646. Despite efforts through debate, leaflets and preaching, Calvinism became the doctrine of most churches of Christ from this time onwards. Calvinism was the popular doctrine of those opposed to the State church. People were comfortable with this teaching and brought it with them into the church of Christ.

These apostate churches of Christ with their Calvinism retained for awhile the Biblical identity "Church of Christ" and baptised for the remission of sins. They rejected for some time salvation outside of baptism, though taught a person had to be moved by the Spirit to be converted. By the 1660s, they had started to reject the Biblical name calling themselves first "Baptised Churches" and later "Baptist Churches." One step led to another, thus a new denomination was born, despite all the preaching and warnings against Calvinism.

Some churches rejected Calvinism, becoming Quaker. Others adopted universalism; some became members of the "General Baptists." A few, particularly in the North West of England retained the faith. At least one survived to join in fellowship with the American Churches of Christ in the 1840s. Later in life, Thomas Lamb was made a chaplain in the army of Oliver Cromwell. It is thought he died in 1672. About the year 1630, Thomas Lamb and his wife had a son who they named Isaac, who followed his father and assisted him in Cromwell's army. Isaac was made chaplain of the "Conftant Warwick," a British man-o-war at the age of sixteen. He often preached before Admiral Blake and, on one occasion, before both Admirals Penn and Blake. He baptised six of the ship's men in the sea on various occasions. Admiral Sir William Penn was a member of the church of Christ and father of William Penn, founder of the colony of Pennsylvania.

After the death of Oliver Cromwell and the failure of his son Richard, who fled to France, the monarchy was restored. The ship in which Isaac sailed was part of the fleet that picked up king Charles II in 1660 from France. Soon after he was stripped of his office as ship's chaplain due to the established church being Anglican which by force of law denied religious liberty. He became a preacher at Eastsmithfield (London) and often preached before three hundred. On one occasion, he was ordered by the authorities to stop preaching, to which he replied "Whether it be right in the sight of God, to hearken unto you more than unto God, judge ye." At this short rebuff, the authorities left without any more interruption.

On another occasion, seven Justices of the Peace, including Sir William Smith, Brown and Bury, arrived in their coaches on the Lord's day with a posse of willing helpers. They came prepared to break up the church fixtures, seating, pulpit, etc. Lamb having been previously warned of this had had the items removed. The posse was greatly disappointed, at which one of the justices exclaiming "his name ought to have been Fox, and not Lamb." He died on August the 20th 1691. The historian Crosby notes he was "a man of fweet temper, exemplary converfasion, and great ufefulnefs."

We learn the following from Ivimey who took this account from Dr. Some in 1589: "There were several Anabaptistical conventicles (congregations) in London and other places." It seems then that Christians had at this early period formed distinct churches both in London and in other parts of the country. Dr. Some adds, "Some persons of these sentiments have been bred at our universities." These Christians had pursued their principles to their legitimate ends, and had rejected infant baptism, and the other ceremonies of the church. The doctor, to expose these Christians, relates a story of one whom he calls T.L., "who at a conventicle in London took upon him to expound the scriptures, conceive long prayers on a sudden, and to excommunicate two persons who were formerly of that brotherhood, but had now left them." Who this T.L. was we know not; but it clearly appears that he was the preacher of the church, and that in their name, he declared that some persons who had left them were no longer of their communion. Likewise, his explaining the scriptures and praying without the use of a form, as commanded by the Lord. This was opposed to the repetitive prayers of the Anglican Church, contrary to scripture and the first century church. Is this "TL" Thomas Lamb? It seems far too early, but could it be his father? That Thomas Lamb came from Colchester is not a problem; in that part of Essex, churches of Christ had existed for some time, and would during persecution have been an ideal place to which to flee from London. In Bow Lane, in 1727, a congregation still met whose preacher, a descendent of the Lambs, was Thomas Lamb. In about 1640, at Bristol, a preacher, John Cann, stated that there are "many thousands in England that doe not hold communion with others, though they doe owne and practise believers' baptism, because they hold with it free-will and falling from grace."

Below is a private letter, signed "London, May 10, 1622. H.H." It was not intended to be published, and had it not been, we would not be aware of it today. The person who published this letter, replied to it in a work titled, "Anabaptist Mystery of Iniquity Unmasked, by J.P. 1623." It was certainly ungenerous that a private letter on a controverted subject should be sent to the press by an opponent who intended to write against it to unmask the "iniquity" it contained. The writer states that the Christians had separated from the established church, written many books in defence of their principles and had multitudes of disciples; that it was their custom to produce a great number of scriptures to prove their doctrines; that they were in appearance more holy than those of the established church; and that they dissuaded their disciples from reading the churchmen's books, participating in their assemblies, or conferring with their learned men. He adds that they "denied the doctrine of predestination, reprobation, final perseverance, and other truths."

The letter, according to Crosby (1738), was written by one who had recently been converted from the Church of England to a church of Christ in London. Rumours then abounded, and the Christian replied. The letter was passed around and ended up being made public. Membership in the church of Christ in this period frequently resulted in death in prison from starvation. The English below has been slightly modernized by me to make reading easier.

Beloved friends,

The ancient love that I have had towards you provoketh me to testify that I have not forgotten you, but a desirous still to shew my unfeigned love to you in any thing I may. I make no question but you have heard divers false reports of me, although among the same some truths; and that you may be truly informed of my state, I thought good to write a few words unto you, hoping that you will not speak evil of that which you know not, nor condemn a man unheard. The thing wherein I differ from the Church of England is; they say at their washing or baptizing their infants, that they are members, of Christ's holy church, children of God, and inheritors of the kingdom of heaven. This I dare not believe; for the scriptures of God declare, that neither flesh nor the washing of flesh can save. Flesh and blood cannot inherit the kingdom of God; for that which is born of the flesh is flesh, and we cannot enter into the kingdom of God except we be born again. They that have prerogative to be the sons of God, must be born of God, even believe in his name; and the washing of the filth of the flesh is not the baptism that saveth, but the answer of a good conscience towards God. If any man be in Christ, he is a new creature. The consequence of this is that infants are not to be baptized, nor can they be Christians but such only who confess their faith as the scriptures teach. [Matt. 28:19; Mark 16:5; John 1:12; 3:5; Gal. 6:5; 1 Pet. 3:21] from whence the word church is taken, can witness that it signifieth a people called out; and so the Church of Christ is a company called out of their former state wherein they were by nature, out of Babylon, wherein they have been in spiritual bondage to the spiritual antichrist, and from having fellowship in spiritual worship with unbelievers and ungodly men. From all, whosoever cometh, they are fit timber for this spiritual building, which is a habitation of God by the Spirit, and the household of faith. Those who thus come out of nature's Egyptian bondage, and the fellowship of the children of Belial, being new creatures, and so holy brethren, are made God's house or church, through being knit together by the Spirit of God, and baptized into his body, which is the church. This being undeniably the Church of Christ, infants cannot be of it; for they cannot be called out as afore said. Known wicked men cannot be of it, because they are not called out; nor antichrist's spiritual bondage cannot be of it, because that is a habitation of devil's, and all God's people must go out of that. [Acts 2:38,41; 8:12,37; 9:18; 10:47; 16:31; 18:8; 19:3; 1 Cor. 13:13; 2 Cor. 6:4; Gal. 2:20; Eph. 1:22,23; 2:22; Heb. 3:6; 1 Pet. 1:5; Rev. 18:2,4]

What can be objected against this? Are not all the sons of God by faith? If any be in Christ, or a Christian, must he not be a new creature? I pray you do not take up the usual objection which the antichristians have learned of the Jews; 'What tellest thou us of being made Christians only by faith in the Son, and so being made free? We are the children of Abraham, and of believers, and so are under the promise; I will be the God of thee and of thy seed. Thus are we and our children made free, whereas they neither do nor can believe in the Son.'

This is the Jewish antichrist fable: for Abraham had two

sons, which were types of the two seeds, to which two covenants were made. The one born after the flesh, typing out the fleshly Israelites, which were the inhabitants of material Jerusalem, where was the material temple, and the performance of those carnal rites which endured to the time of reformation. The other by faith typing out the children of the faith of Abraham, which are the inhabitants of the spiritual Jerusalem, the new testament state, in which is the spiritual temple, the church of the living God, and the performance of all those spiritual ordinances which Christ as prophet and king thereof hath appointed, and which remains and cannot be shaken or altered. [Gen. 17; John 8:3; "Rom. 4:8,9; 2 Cor. 5:17; Gal. 3:26; 4:22; 6:15; Heb. 9:10; 12:23]

Now if the old covenant be abolished, and all the appertainings thereof, as it is, being the similitude of heavenly things, even the covenant written in the book, the people, the tabernacle or temple, and all the ministering vessels, and a better covenant established upon better promises, and better temple and ministering vessels came instead thereof, procured and purchased by the blood of Jesus Christ, who is the new and living way; let us draw near with a true heart in full assurance of faith, sprinkling our hearts from an evil conscience, and baptized in our bodies with pure water; let us keep this profession of hope without wavering, and have no confidence in the flesh, to reap sanctification or justification thereby; but let us cast it away as dung and dross, for if any might plead privilege of being the child of the faithful, the apostle Paul might, as he saith. (See Phil. 3.) But it was nothing till he had the righteousness of God through faith: then was he baptized into Jesus Christ for the remission of his sins.

This covenant, which we as the children of Abraham challenge, is the covenant of life and salvation by Jesus Christ, made to all the children of Abraham, as it was

430

made to Abraham himself, to them that believe in him who raised up Jesus the Lord from the dead. As also the children of the flesh are not they: they must be put out, and must not be heirs with the faithful. If they that are of the flesh be heirs, faith is made void, and the promise of none effect. Therefore it is by faith, that it might come of grace, and that the promise might be sure to all the seed that are of the faith of Abraham, who is the father of all the faithful. They are his children: the promise of salvation is not made with both Abraham's seeds, but with his own seed, they that are of the faith of Abraham. [Acts 8:26,32,39; Rom. 4:14; 9:8; Gal. 3:7,9,29; 4:30; Eph. 4:28]

These things may be strange to those who are strangers from the life of God, through the ignorance that is in them, because of the hardness of their hearts. God hath written them as the great things of his law, but they are counted by many as a strange thing. Yet wisdom is justified of all her children; and they that set their hearts to seek for wisdom as for silver, and search for her as for treasure, they shall see the righteousness of these things as the light, and the evidence of them as the noon day. They that be wise will try these things by the true touchstone of the holy scriptures, and leave off rejoicing in men to hang their faith and profession on them; the which I fear not to supplicate God day and night on behalf of you all. To whose gracious direction I commit you, with a remembrance of my hearty love to everyone; desiring but this favour, that for requital I may receive your loving answer.

Yours to be commanded always in any children service.

London, May 10, 1622. H.H.

One of the most famous preachers of the time for the Lord's Church was Henry Denne (died 1661). Denne was educated at Cambridge University. He was ordained a minister of the Church of England by the Bishop of St. David's, Wales in 1630. He became minister at Pryton (Pirton), Hertfordshire, staying in that benefice about ten years. Henry Denne was at first a Calvinist but later converted to what was then termed incorrectly "Arminian" doctrine, of the opinion that "all men were put into the possibility of salvation through Christ" and "those that choose to perish do so at their own choice." He became disillusioned with the Church of England, rejecting Calvinism and infant baptism.

In 1641, Denne preached a sermon at Baldock, a short distance from Pryton. He here exposed the evils of the established church, his text being John 5:35. He focused on the pride and covetousness of the clergy, their pluralities, neglect of duty by non-residence, a common problem in that era, and other evils. He demanded restoration speaking against conformity. He said:

> I must call upon those in authority, to make diligent search after these foxes. If the courts had been so vigilant to find out these as non-conformable ministers, surely by this time the church would have been as free from them as the land from wolves. But they have preferred the traditions of men before the commandments of Almighty God. I tell you that conformity hath ever sped the worse for their sakes, who breaking the commandments of God think to make amends with conformity to the traditions of men.

After preaching at the "visitation" at Baldock, he realised he could no longer stay within the established Church (Church of England). He came into contact with Thomas Lamb (1642/3), the preacher of the Bell Alley church of Christ, Coleman Street, London. He resigned from the Church of England and, hence, his "living" at Pirton, and immediately became a travelling evangelist, working with and establishing congregations in Staffordshire, Cambridgeshire, Huntingdonshire, Lincolnshire, Kent and other places. A close friend objected to his new religion, and Denne was reported and arrested at Cambridge. His "crime" was preaching against infant baptism. He was sent to prison at Bishopsgate, London. During his time in prison, he met Dr. Featly, famous for *The Dippers Dipt; or the Anabaptists Duck'd, and Plunged Over Head and Ears, at a Disputation in Southwark.* Dr. Featly, when he realised the nature of the opposition declined any debate.

Released from prison, Denne became the preacher at Eltisley, about fifteen miles west from Cambridge. Eltisley, a village, was in this time a community who were mostly members of the church of Christ. Denne was in the unique position of being able to preach the Bible without compromise, in the Church of England, as a salaried licensed preacher. The congregation had both elders and deacons and was a major influence for evangelism in England.

In 1646, Denne was arrested again at Spalding, Lincolnshire

for preaching and baptising. Now with little money and with the country in civil war, he enlisted in the cavalry (parliamentary) and served several years as a cornet, the lowest rank of commissioned officer. We do not know if he saw any fighting. In May 1649 he took part in a mutiny, occasioned by his fellow soldiers' lack of enthusiasm concerning the campaign to Ireland. Denne and three others were court-marshalled and sentenced to be shot. He received his sentence without complaint. The other three, Tompson, Church and Perkins were shot. Denne was reprieved by Cromwell. Denne left the Army shortly afterwards. Cromwell dismissed "Anabaptists" from the Army because of pressure from the Scottish Government who were Presbyterian (Calvinistic) being opposed to freewill and anabaptism. Cromwell did not heed to pressure from the Scottish and English Puritans to clamp down on the church of Christ, who were allowed freedom to meet and evangelise.

To his friends, Denne was known as either Cornet Denne or Parson Denne (depending if he was serving in the army or preaching). When he took his uniform off to preach he was "Parson Denne" and when his uniform came back on, it was to his military title "Cornet Denne."

During a debate with a Dr. Gunning (St. Clement Dane's church, The Strand, London), which started after an unknown lady showed concern with the practice of infant baptism during 1658, the following exchange took place. Dr. Gunning, "Infants unbaptised where there is no desire of their baptism in their parents or friends shall be shut out of heaven." Denne, "If unbaptised infants be shut out of heaven, then God punisheth some creatures for that which they cannot help. Therefore unbaptised children are not shut out from heaven." Gunning, "I deny the consequence." Denne, "Then shutting out of heaven is no punishment." After this exchange the lady was baptised by Henry Denne. The previous year, Dr. Gunning, an Anglican, had been arrested by the Puritan authorities for celebrating Christmas with his congregation in St. Clement Dane's church. He was well known for his High Church Anglican views, under Puritan rule. Henry Denne preached and/or started churches of Christ at Rochester, Chatham, Canterbury, Ely, Eltisley, St. Ives, Spalding, Warboys, Whittlesey and Peterborough.

Lucy Hutchinson, the wife of Colonel John Hutchinson, Parliamentary Governor of Nottingham Castle during the Civil War, records in her "Memoirs of the Life of Colonel Hutchinson," how she and her husband came to adopt Christian views after reading literature confiscated from soldiers in the Castle. She speaks of the Presbyterian ministers' being unable to defend the baptism of infants "for any satisfactory reason but the tradition of the church ... which Tombes and Denne has so excellently overthrown." It is to this Henry Denne that the cause in South-East Lincolnshire is, to a large extent, indebted for its establishment.

In 1646, Denne preached several times in Spalding in the house of a merchant, John Makernesse. As a result, four were converted. They were Anne Stennet and Anne Croft, servants of Makernesse, and Godfrey Root and John Sowter. It was arranged that these four should be baptised at Little Croft a few days later, the baptism to take place at midnight to avoid the notice of the authorities. One of the women unwisely told a friend about the baptism who passed on the information to the magistrate. As a result, Denne was arrested and, according to the historian Crosby, was committed to Lincoln goal. The same magistrate was responsible also for the imprisonment of several other Christians. Nevertheless, in due course, Spalding became one of the more important Churches of Christ in the area.

John Bunyan and Henry Denne:
Controversy and the Church of Christ meeting in Bedford

John Bunyan (November 28, 1628 – August 31, 1688), a Christian writer and preacher for the Bedford Church of Christ, was born at Harrowden (one mile south-east of Bedford), in the Parish of Elstow, England. He wrote *The Pilgrim's Progress,* arguably the most famous published Christian allegory. The Church of England, who imprisoned him for twelve years, commemorates Bunyan in a Lesser Festival on the 30th August. Bunyan who preached against popish idolatry and worship of saints was given his own saints day by those who opposed him. John Bunyan died at 60, a year before

William III came to the throne in 1689 and granted limited religious toleration to dissenters.

Bunyan had clashed with Henry Denne, being doctrinally to the left of Denne. The church at Bedford in time became both liberal and Calvinistic. Bunyan was a tinker, a lowly esteemed trade. Because he had never been ordained in the Church of England, he earned the derogatory nickname as an itinerant preacher "the tinker."

When visiting Bedford, a short distance from Elstow, he heard of the "new Birth" after hearing some ladies talking of sin. Sometime later he was baptised, by immersion, in the River Great Ouse in 1653. In 1655, he became a deacon at the Bedford Church of Christ and also began preaching. Bunyan opposed the new sect called Quakers, as did Henry Denne. In time, the church at Bedford received into fellowship those baptised as infants and later, the church became congregational practicing infant baptism. John Bunyan was not a Baptist nor was the church of which he was a member. It was a church of Christ which in time fell into apostasy.

Before his final release from prison, for illegal preaching, Bunyan became involved in a controversy with two theologians of his day: Kiffin and Paul. In 1673, he published his *Differences In Judgment About Water-Baptism No Bar To Communion*, in which he took the ground that "the Church of Christ hath not warrant to keep out of the communion the Christian that is discovered to be a visible saint of the word, the Christian that walketh according to his own light with God." While he agreed that water baptism was God's ordinance, he refused to make "an idol of it" and he disagreed with those who would disfellowship those who did not adhere to water baptism. His position was on baptism influenced by reformed faith alone theology.

The prison on the bridge in Bedford, over the river Great Ouse, where Bunyan was held.

Bunyan clashed with Henry Denne and later his son, John Denne over baptism. There was though an occasion when Henry Denne came to the defence of John Bunyan. At this time Bunyan was a strong advocate of believers' baptism. In May 1659, John Bunyan preached in the tithe barn (near the village green) of his friend Daniel Angier at Toft, near Cambridge. Known as the "tinker," Bunyan's "holy orders" and hence his right to preach were always being questioned. Thomas Smith (the Keeper of the University Library, Cambridge), "attracted by the sound of devotion" walked in on the service towards the end of the sermon. Bunyan was preaching from 1 Tim. 4:16 and was actually stating that he knew most of his audience who were Anglicans were actually "unbelievers." When the preaching ended, Smith approached Bunyan and asked him what right he had to call the people of Toft "unbelievers" (half of whose faces Bunyan had never seen before).

Smith claimed that Bunyan was being uncharitable and as such was unfit to preach. Bunyan replied that when Christ preached from a boat to his hearers on the shore, he taught that there were four kinds of ground onto which the good seed of the sower fell and that only one of the four brought forth fruit. "Your position," said Bunyan, "is that he in effect condemneth the greater part of his hearers hath no charity, and is therefore not fit to preach the gospel." At this Daniel Angier rose to defend Bunyan and rebuke Smith, but Smith denied the layman's right to preach and asked Bunyan how he could answer the apostle's question "How shall they preach except they be sent?" Bunyan replied that the Church at Bedford had sent him, Smith responded "that the Church at Bedford, since they were only lay people, could not give the tinker that which they had not themselves."

Within a few weeks Smith had written and published a pamphlet entitled "A Letter to Mr. E of Taft (Toft) Four miles from Cambridge. To which No Answer hath been returned." Mr E. is presumed to refer to Mr John Ellis Junior, son of John Ellis, the Anglican minister of Toft. The pamphlet begins:

Sir,

1.Since you had not so much patience as to hear me t'other day, nor would suffer your daughters to tarry, I now make use of my first hour of leisure to write to you part of that which you might have heard me speak then hoping that you and they (whom I look on as having more breeding than any other, his Auditors that I saw) will not believe this, whom his Friends generally call the Tinker, upon his bare word, but like those noble Bereans, Acts 17.11 with readiness of mind search the Scripture whether those things were so.

2. I guess at the breeding of most of his followers by this passage; one of them, viz. Daniel Angier (who invites him to that Town, entertains him in his house, lends him his barn for a meeting place) when I charged him in that place with maintaining that God was body, (viz. that he had hands, feet, a face, &c. Like one of us) saying that he contradicted me in my Churchyard, after I had preached people when he saw his Ring-Leader T. would not defend it, that I lyed; whereas my whole Parish are ready to witness the truth of what I said.

440

3. But to the purpose, I shall in this paper follow that method which the T. commanded me (though I desire the contrary) shewing first his false doctrine and then prove 'tis a dangerous sin in him to preach (as he did publickly) and in the people to hear him...

All this your tinker hath been guilty of, and much more, for he hath intruded into the pulpits in these parts, and caused the people of your town to hate their lawful minister, but (as he told me) encouraged them to proceed as far as to cudgel him and break open the church doors by violence..."

Smith concludes:

And now, sir, let me beseech you for God's sake, for Christ's sake, for the Church's sake, for your reputation's sake, for your children's sake, for your country's sake to consider these things sadly and seriously, not to think a tinker more infallible than the pure Spouse of Christ, and to foresee what will be the sad consequences both to the souls, and bodies, and estates of you and your children in following such strangers." The pamphlet is written from "Caucat" (i.e. Caldecote) and dated May (1659). Caldecote is less than two miles from Toft.

Bunyan himself does not seem to have replied to this pamphlet, but there was a response from Henry Denne: who was a friend of Smith. He had known him at Cambridge University. For in a work known as *The Quaker No Papist* (London: Francis Smith, 1659) Denne wrote:

You seem to be angry with the tinker because he strives to mend souls as well as kettles and pans. The main drift

441

of your letter is to prove that none may preach except they be sent. Sir, I think him unworthy of the name of a tinker that affirms that any one is sufficient to preach the gospel without sending. By your confession the tinker thinks otherwise, and doth not deny what you labour to prove, and so you contend with a shadow. He proves his mission and commission from the Church at Bedford, you should also have proved that Mr. Thomas Smith hath a better commission from some other Church than the tinker either hath or can have from the Church at Bedford. You must give me leave to propound something for your consideration: Some shipwrackt men, swimming to an island, find there many inhabitants, to whom they preach; the heathen hearing are converted, and walk together in love, praising the Lord; whether the preaching of these shipwrackt men were a sin? Secondly whether it be not lawful for this congregation to chuse to themselves pastors, governours, teachers, &c. Thirdly, whether this congregation may not find some fitting men full of faith and the Holy Ghost to preach to other unbelieving heathen?

Henry Denne died during 1661. Upon his grave was inscribed the epitaph by a close friend: "To tell his wisdom, learning, goodness unto men, I need to say no more, but here lies Henry Denne."

His son John Denne started to preach the Gospel first from his house in Wilbraham, Cambridgeshire in 1675. He was once fined for preaching but, unlike those of his father, his views became more in line with the newly-forming General Baptist Denomination (which opposed Calvinism).

Henry Denne wrote at least seven books or tracts including:

1. *The Doctrine and Conversation of John the Baptist*, 1642, (This book has survived and a copy can be found at Cambridge University Library).

2. *The Foundation of Children's Baptism Discovered and Raised*; an answer to Dr. Featly and Mr. Marshal, 1645.

3. *The Man of Sin Discovered Whom the Lord Will Destroy With the Brightness of His Coming,* 1645.

4. *The Drag-net of the Kingdom of Heaven; or Christ's Drawing All Men*, 1646.

5. *The Levellers' Design Discovered*, a tract, 1649.

6. *A Contention for Truth*, in two public disputations at St. Clement's church between Dr Gunning and Henry Denne concerning infant-baptism. 1658.

7. *Grace, Mercy and Peace.*

In 1645 a member of the English Churches of Christ wrote to several churches of Christ in New England, America. John Tombes (1602-1676) was a clergyman in the Church of England, which caused controversy as he was determined to preach the truth on all matters, being a member of the church of Christ.

John Tombes refusal to baptise infants caused great controversy. The assembly of Divines, sitting in Henry the Seventh's chapel in Westminster during the 1640s, discussed further reformation of the Church of England. Further reformation in the church had been proposed to take the church back to first century apostolic teaching; the subject of baptism was discussed. "Mr. John Tombes (says Mr. Palmer) was among the first of the clergy of these times who endeavoured a reformation in the church by purging the worship of God of human inventions. He preached a sermon on the subject, which was afterwards printed by an order of the House of Commons." This exposed him to the rage of the church party at the beginning of the civil war in 1641. When some of the King's forces came into Herfordshire, he was obliged to leave his habitation and the church at Leominster and remove to Bristol. He soon afterwards fled from Bristol, and with great difficulty arrived in London, Sep. 22, 1643, from where he wrote his letter. He had lost his living with the Church of England but managed to find pulpits from which he could preach the truth.

The Church of England in this period had various parties prior to 1658 vying for power: the Puritans who were mainly Calvinists; and often Presbyterian (but not always as with Tombes). These were the true Protestants, and then there was the Anglican pro-Catholic party. After 1658, the Puritans were evicted from the Church of England, after which time the State Church was Anglican only and has remained so to this day. It has often been pointed out that in doctrine the Church of England is Arminium, in theology, Calvinistic and in traditions and ceremonies, Catholic. It should be pointed out that since the Puritans, the pro-Bible party, was evicted, it is incorrect to refer to the Church of England as a protestant church. It is not, it is Anglican.

In 1659 Tombes wrote:

To the Christian Reader.

Many are the things at this day charged on Antipoaedobaptists in their Doctrine and Practise, which have been proved to be unjustly imputed to them, by many large Treatises extant in print. For a more facile understanding of the truth than by reading larger Tracts, is this Compendium, in a manner of a catechism composed and published in this time, wherein others of different judgment, have thought fit to declare their way to the world, which is done, not because the disagreement in other things is either small, or of particular persons (whose cause is to be severed from that which is commonly held) and therefore requires not a distinct Confession or Declaration from that which is by others published. Which I have thought necessary to be done because of the importance of restoring right baptism, the Doctrine of which is one article of the foundation of Christianity, Heb. 6.2. whereby we put on Christ, Gal. 3.27. united to his Members, Ephes. 4.5. conformed to Christ, Col. 2.12. Rom. 6.3,4,5. required with faith to salvation, Mark 16.16. with repentance to remission of sins, Acts 2.38. with express profession of the Baptized's faith required, Acts 8.37. upon manifestation of conversion, Acts 10.47. Acts 11.17. as the duty of the Baptized, and not a meer Priviledge, Acts 22.16. most solemly administered in the Primitive times, with strict examination and greatest engagement of persons baptized, accounted the chief evidence of Christianity, of as much or more moment than the Lord's Supper; insomuch that some conceived from

Heb. 6.4. that falling away after it irreparable. But the pretended Baptism of Infants, as now used slightly and profanely done, quite different from Christ's Institution and the Apostles practice by Ministers and people in so wholy and carnal manner as that, it is upon and with gross untruths and perverting of holy Scripture, obtruded on unwary souls with a pretence of a Baptismal Vow, which is a meer fiction, and so many ill consequents both in Christian conversation and communion and church-constitution and Government, that were men sensible to their evil as they should be, they would tremble at such mockery of God, and abuse of so holy an Ordinance of God's worship and men's souls by it, and with such arrogant presumption in avowing such a manifest invention of men as God's precept. And to speak truth, if the History of this corruption were fully cleared, it would be found that the undue Ministration of this Ordinance was the inlet to the Antichristian darkness and tyranny which overspread and oppressed the Christian Churches. The aim of the composer of it is the manifestation of the truth, wherein doth he rejoyce, and desires thou mayest rejoyce with him. His motion is that of the Apostle, Phil. 3.15,16. As many of us be perfect let us be thus minded, and if ye be otherwise minded, God shall reveal even this unto you. Nevertheless whereunto we have already attained, let us walk by the same rule, let us mind the same thing.

Farewel.

We learn from Thomas Crosby that in 1645, John Tombes, learning of problems that the churches in New England were having with infant baptism, wrote to them a letter of encouragement enclosing further advice.

A "Mr. Emlin" was a paid minister of one church of Christ at Boston and another church existed elsewhere that was baptising believers. An argument had developed with other churches over the matter of infant baptism and help was needed. Information to refute those baptising infants in other churches was sent.[2]

We can learn much from the letter; that churches that were established adopting the Biblical identity, had elders and baptised believers. We may questions the title "reverend brethren," the title in this time inferred respect. That Tombes knew and was associated with Henry Denne is of interest as we know much of what the churches Denne was associated with taught.

1. They denied Calvinism.

2. They did not use the identity "Baptist Church" but "Church of Christ.'"

3. They partook of the Supper weekly on the first day.

4. They had when possible a plurality of elders and deacons.

5. They baptised by full immersion believers for the remission of sins - The "confession" of 1660 (London) states "but all who come not first to repent of their sins, believe on the Lord Jesus, and so baptized in his name for remission of sins... we utterly deny." In article XI the confession confirms that mode of baptism is to "dip."[3]

6. They did not have separate priesthood.

7. They taught the triune Godhead.

8. They taught the church is the called out of God.

9. They taught the word only in establishing doctrine.

10. They taught Free Will, a dangerous doctrine in the early seventeenth century.

11. They considered themselves to be in the Kingdom.

For Crosby the term "baptist" simply meant a person who baptises a beliver by immersion. It had in this time period no denominational connotations as it would with the emerging Baptist movement.

> *To the elders of the church of Christ in New-England, and to each particular by name: To the Pastor and Teacher of the Church of God at Boston, there, these present.*

> *Understanding that there is some disquiet in your churches about paedobaptism (infant baptism), and being moved by some that honour you much in the Lord, and desire your comfortable account at the day of Christ, that I would yield that a copy of my examen of the master Marshall his sermon of infant baptism might be transcribed, to be sent to you; I have consented thereto, and do commend it to your examination, in like manner, as you may perceive by the reading of it, I did to master Marshall. But not doubting that you will, as in God's presence, and accountable to Christ Jesus, weigh the thing; remembering that our Lord Christ, John V11. 24. Judge not according to appearance, but judge righteous judgment. To the blessing of Him who is your God and our God, your judge and our judge, I leave you and the flock over which the Holy Ghost has made you overseers, and rest.*

> *Your brother and fellow servant in the work of Christ, John Tombes.*

"From my study in the temple in London, May 25th, 1645.

John Tombes at that time was preaching at the Temple, an old church in London. The Church of England forced him to leave his office there because of the controversy over baptism.

At least one congregation of the churches of Christ was established within the Indian community in the 1640s. When evangelising amongst the native indigenous population of North America, the Indians were surprised that baptism (purification) of infants was not practised by the church of Christ, who baptised believers' only. Pagans worldwide practiced infant purification. In pagan societies, the baptism of infants for removal of sins was universal.

The Mayflower arriving in America in 1620 brought among the Pilgrim Fathers members of the Bell Alley and Southwark Churches of Christ (London). The captain of the Mayflower, Christopher Jones was from Southward. Whilst the majority of the Pilgrim Fathers were Puritans not converted, they did know the truth of believers' baptism. Within a few years of arriving a church of Christ independent from other churches had been established in New England. Regrettably, these churches fell first into Calvinism, and later turned Baptist. But in origin, they were churches of Christ.[4]

The Mayflower left from Plymouth, England, which in 1620 had a small church of Christ. The congregation was associated with some of the Pilgrim Fathers during their stay at Plymouth. It must be understood that the majority of the passengers were Calvinistic and were opposed to the church of Christ.[5]

Broadmead, Church of Christ, Bristol. Founded 1640

Founded in 1640, the members met regularly for worship, at first without a paid preacher. During 1642, John Tombes preached for the congregation before being forced to flee to London.

The Broadmead congregation is typical of the many churches of Christ that appeared in the early 1640s across England. The traditional view is that the church of Helwys (London, Newgate) established many other congregations in a short period of time. But Helwys' congregation was severely persecuted and its members risked prison and confiscation of property. Helwys himself died in prison, yet it is assumed, despite these severe, almost impossible conditions, Helwys was able with a few friends to establish his denomination, the General Baptists (a name unknown to Helwys or anyone else in this period) and numerous more congregations throughout England.

Bristol had by the Middle Ages become a wealthy city with an independent middle class. It was from Bristol in 1497 that John Cabot set out, under the patronage of King Henry VII, on one of the most remarkable voyages in the history of maritime discovery. The significance of the voyage of the "Matthew" is that it took John

Cabot to the mainland of North America and eventually led to the migration of many English-speaking people to the countries of that continent.

By the late 1300s, Bristol and the surrounding area had become known to the authorities as a centre for Lollardy or heresy, which continued into the 1500s, who were in fellowship with others in Holland and throughout England. John Purvey, who was the New Testament translator of the Wyclif Bible, preached at Bristol, but was prosecuted in August 1387 by the Bishop of Worcester. In 1390, he was in prison for heresy. Ten years later, in 1400, he renounced his Lollardy at St. Paul's Cross, London. The archdeacon of Canterbury admitted him to the vicarage of West Hythe, Kent. Purvey resigned Oct. 8th 1403, and was again in prison in 1421 for heresy from where he possibly died.

During the 1460s, James Willis, a Bristol weaver by trade and a well known preacher, was prosecuted for attacking the practice of pilgrimages, the sacraments, worship of images, and the papacy. He moved to London to continue preaching there, where he was arrested, charged, prosecuted, found guilty and imprisoned. William Tyndale was a regular open air preacher in the city on the college green. Simon Fish, previously mentioned, came from Bristol.

In 1577, John Northbrooke, "preacher of the Word of God" at Bristol, published one of England's earliest condemnations of stage plays, interludes, "jugglings and false sleyghts," and other pastimes. Our duty, he says, requires us to "apply al and euery of our doings to ye glory of God," but instead "we kepe ioly cheare one with another in banquetting, surfeiting and dronkennesse; also we vse all the night long in ranging from town to town, and from house to house, with mummeries and maskes, diceplaying, carding and dauncing." Thus, "we leaue Christ alone at the aultar, and feed our eyes with vaine and vnhonest sights." Festival and holy days contribute to this spirit of dissipation, for by them "halfe the yeare, and more," is "ouerpassed…in loytering and vaine pastimes…restrayning men from their handy labours and occupations."

Northbrooke's views represent a fundamental rejection of the cultural traditions that dominated English life until the sixteenth century. Nowhere had these traditions been better exemplified than in the town in which Northbrooke served his ministry, Bristol.

Bristol had benefited by some degree of religious tolerance. The survival of Lollardy into the seventeenth century from the middle ages testifies of this. John Canne, author of the "authenticated version" of the Bible, which appeared in 1647 at Amsterdam, under the title, *The Bible, With Marginal Notes, Shewing Scripture to be the Best Interpreter of Scripture,* preached in Bristol. When Canne was baptised is uncertain, but it was before 1640. He was in Bristol in 1640 preaching in "public places" and was declared to be a "baptized man," or an "immersed man" as that phrase was used.

Crosby wrote in the 1730's of Canne and that the church at Southwark (London) "was constituted about the year 1621." Then he says the first preacher was a "Mr. Hubbard, or Herbert" and that "he was succeeded by Mr. John Canne who, it appears from the records of the church in Broadmead, Bristol, was a 'Baptist,' and the first person who preached the doctrine of believers' baptism in that city" (Bristol).

At this time Calvinism was not present in the church of Christ, so, from the start the Broadmead Church would not have been Calvinist, though it is not denied it turned to Calvinism later, and from there, became Baptist as it is today.

The Broadmead record says:

> At this juncture of time the providence of God brought to this city one Mr. Canne, a baptized man; it was Mr. Canne that made notes and references upon the Bible. He was a man very eminent in his day for godliness, and for reformation in religion, having great understanding in the way of the Lord.

> Mrs. Hazzard, who was the wife of the Broadmead parish priest, found him and fetched him to her home. Then the Records say: He taught the way of the Lord more perfectly, and settled them in church order, and showed them the difference betwixt the Church of Christ and anti-Christ, and left with them a printed book treating of the same; and divers printed papers to that purpose. So that by this instrument Mr. Canne, the Lord did confirm and settle

them; showing them how they should join together, and take in members. So the congregation was established.

In 1645 the congregation agreed to the following, as they sought to establish a New Testament Church:

> That they would in ye strength of Christ, keepe close to His Holy Scriptures, ye word of God; and ye plaine truths and ordinances of ye Gospel, of Church Fellowship, breaking bread, and Prayers; And to Subject to one another, according to ye Discipline and admonition by ye Rules of Christ, in ye New Testament, or ye Scriptures.

In 1651, Mr. Ewins, who had been a minister in the Church of England, became their preacher. Under his ministry the church prospered. In addition to the Lord's-day exercise, they met on Thursday evenings in private houses for free conference on the Scriptures and mutual exhortation. These meetings were found very profitable in teaching the word of God.

In 1656, Denis Hollister, an enemy of the church of Christ, published a tract that was widely distributed. Entitled "The Skirts of the Whore discovered, and the Mingled People in the midst of her, in a letter sent by D. Hollister to the Independent Baptiz'd People, who call themselves a Church of Christ in Bristol, but are found to be a Synagogue of Satan." It was sent together with another letter to J. Ewens.

A reply was made to Hollister in a tract by one of the elders, Robert Purnell (and others) entitled "The Church of Christ in Bristol recovering her vail out of the hands of them that have smitten and wounded her, and taken it away. Being a ... vindication from a false ... imputation cast upon her by D. Hollister, formerly a Member of her but now an Apostate... as appears by a late pamphlet put forth by him, called, The skirts of the Whore discovered ... Likewise a word by T. Ewen, unto what concerns him in the said pamphlet, and also to the later part of another Book, called, Satan enthroned, etc."

At this time the church was under the protection of Oliver Cromwell and Parliament. But with the restoration of the monarchy, things would change for the worse. In 1661, their troubles began. On the 27th of July in that year, brother Ewins was apprehended while preaching contrary to the Act of Uniformity. He was released on the 25th of September following, and immediately recommenced his work. Next year, he endured another short imprisonment after being caught preaching. A heavier trial came upon them in 1663. Brother Ewins and several others were arrested on the 4th of October and indicted at the quarter sessions for riot. Upon conviction various fines were imposed (Ewins was fined £50), and the parties were sentenced to lie in prison till the fines were paid. So the prison became the "parsonage" till the following September, when a compromise was effected and, on payment of part of the fine, the prisoners were released. Brother Ewins had not been idle, however. The people were accustomed to gather around the prison, where he preached to them from the window of the room on the fourth storey which he occupied. "The word of the Lord was precious in those days."

Hitherto they had met in a "chapel called the Friars" but now they were compelled for a time to worship in private houses. The constables frequently disturbed them, and many were imprisoned and fined. Sometimes, when they learnt that the bishop's officers were coming they evaded them by taking refuge in a cellar, and sometimes by climbing into a garret (attic). Still they resolutely kept up their assemblies. "In the year 1665," they say, "we had many disturbances, and divers imprisoned, but the Lord helped us through it." Their remarkable firmness was shown by a resolution passed that "those who absented themselves from worship through fear should be dealt with as disorderly members."

In 1666, plague broke out in Bristol, and a stop was put to the persecution because of the need for the authorities to use available resources to deal with the emergency. There was peace for four years. In 1667, the Church obtained another "public meeting place." It was "a large warehouse, up one pair of stairs." Brother Ewins died April 26th, 1670. In the following month, the constables made their appearance, and some members of the congregation were arrested for being part of an illegal conventicle. The magistrates fined them without their being imprisoned. This persecution was repeated several Lord's-days. In order to secure a successful prosecution, it was required the preacher to be arrested with the congregation. The building was modified by breaking a hole in the wall, so that the preacher could stand in a room of the adjoining house and preach without being seen. Thus their enemies were baffled when the opposition becoming more violent, they adopted another course. They nailed up the doors of the meeting-house; and "we were fain," the record states, "to meet in the lanes and highways for several months."

Another short interval of tranquility was enjoyed. They invited Brother Thomas Hardcastle, who had been preaching in London, to become their preacher. He was in prison when the invitation reached him. After his release, he visited the Church and subsequently accepted the offer in 1671. In that year, they procured "the meeting-house at the lower end of Broadmead, where the Quakers had formerly met; it being four great rooms made into one square room, about sixteen yards long and fifteen yards broad." There bro. Hardcastle preached upwards of three years without any disturbance. In 1671, the church had three elders, Thomas Ellis, Edward Terrill and Richard White. Robert Simpson, William Dickason and Thomas Rieves were deacons.

In 1674, there came a new Anglican bishop to Bristol, "one Guy Carleton" — "though aged and gray, a violent man against good people that separated from that which he called the Church." . . . "He resolved to destroy all our meetings, and said he would not leave a track of a meeting in Bristol; but would make us all come to Church, as he called it." With him was leagued George Hellier, a lawyer, who took up the trade of an informer, and found it more lucrative than his profession. He spent the Lord's-days in going from one meeting-house to another in search of prey. His chief object was to seize the minister, partly in the hope of thereby suppressing the meetings, and partly for the sake of the heavy fine. Bro. Hardcastle was apprehended Feb. 4th, 1675, and imprisoned for six months. But the meetings were not discontinued, although arrests took place nearly every Lord's-day. In order to protect the preacher, a curtain was prepared which when drawn, separated a portion of the room. About fifty members could sit behind the curtain, the preacher being placed among them, undistinguished. Care was taken that a number of "women and maids" should sit on the staircase, "so that the informers could not quickly run up." By this contrivance, whenever Hellier and his minions were approaching, notice was given, the curtain was drawn, the service ceased, and the whole congregation, according to a prearrangement, commenced singing a psalm. When the informers entered at such a time, they were utterly confused. It was impossible to tell who had been preaching; singing psalms was no crime. But "justice had fallen in the streets," and they rarely failed to arrest someone from the congregation and procure the infliction of fines upon them for being part of an illegal conventicle.

Bro. Hardcastle was released from prison at the end of six months; but, on the second Lord's-day after his release, he was apprehended while preaching and sent to jail again. During this second sentence of imprisonment, he wrote a weekly letter to the Church, which was read at the Lord's-day meetings. These letters have been preserved. They are admirably adapted to the instruction and comfort of a people in such trying circumstances. And they were much needed. Towards the end of the year, the meetings were "grown very poor and lean, through fines, imprisonments, and constant worrying of us every day." On one occasion, the bishop himself was among the constables. From the beginning of 1676 to the middle of 1680, there was a lull in the storm. bro. Hardcastle died in 1678, and was succeeded by George Fownes in September, 1679.

Interruption of their worship resumed in July, 1680, and continued at times through that year and the next. In December, 1681, bro. Fownes and a large number of the brethren were seized, sentenced and imprisoned. He preached to them there. Twenty-four of them were brought up at the quarter sessions, and granted bail for their appearance when called on to answer an indictment for a breach of the peace, with which they were most unrighteously threatened. Bro. Fownes was detained, but the brethren were determined to test the legality of his imprisonment, and procured a writ of *habeas corpus*, by which means his cause was taken to the Court of King's Bench in London. He was ultimately discharged, although he was still prevented by the operation of the Five Mile Act from preaching in the meeting place. The Five Mile Act, or Oxford Act, or Nonconformists Act 1665, was an Act of Parliament of England, with the lengthy title "An Act for restraining Non-Conformists from inhabiting in Corporations." It was one of the laws that sought to enforce conformity to the established Church of England. It forbade preachers from living within five miles of a parish from which they had been banned, unless they swore an oath never to resist the king, or attempt to alter the government of Church or State.

The years 1682 and 1683 were the darkest times. Members of the church of Christ held their meetings in private houses, in the fields, or in the woods, wherever they could best escape the vigilance of the Church of England and its agents of terror. Mayors, aldermen, and constables could hardly have gone to Church at all in those years, for all their time was spent in hunting after Dissenters' meetings on the first day of the week. A few brief extracts from the Bristol records will show how the brethren fared.

> 1682. Jan. 29. — The Church met at four venues. Many of them went in the afternoon on Durdham Down, and got into a cave of a rock towards Clifton, where brother Thomas Whinnell preached to them. March 12. — Met in the fields by Barton Hundred, and brother Samuel Buttall of Plymouth preached in the fore-part of the day,

and brother Whinnell in the evening. It was thought there were near a thousand persons in the morning. March 19. — Met in the lanes beyond Baptist Mills. April 13. — Met in the rain in a lane. April 20. — A day of prayer, from nine till five in the evening, at Mr. Jackson's, over the Down, in peace. May 4. — Information was brought to a petty session for Gloucestershire, against brother Jennings, for preaching in the lanes, and a warrant granted for levying five pounds, or else goods, or person. June 11. — Brother Fownes being come from London, but not daring to come into the city because of the Corporation Act, met with us, and preached in Kingswood, near Scruze Hole, under a tree, and endured the rain. July 2. — Brother Fownes preached in another place in the wood. Our friends took much pains in the rain, because many informers were ordered out to search; and we were in peace, though there were near twenty men and boys in search. July 16. — Brother Fownes first, and Brother Whinnell after; preached under a tree, it being very rainy. August 20. — Met above Scruze Hole, in our old place, and heard brother Fownes preach twice in peace. Brother Terril had caused a workman to make banks on the side of the hill to sit down on, several of them like a gallery; and there we met also on the 27th, in peace. On both days we sang a psalm in the open woods. On the 7th of December we met for our lecture at bro. Shuter's, on Redcliffe Hill, in peace, taking a great deal of care in going and coming, the women wearing neither white aprons nor patterns.

1683. Jan. 21. — We met at eight in the morning, and though there were seven on horseback and twenty on foot to seek after us, we escaped, having broken up at ten. March — This week about 150 Dissenters were convicted by our recorder, on the statute of 23rd Eliz., for £20 a month, for not coming to church. March 25. — Brother Fownes, though very ill, went to the meetings in the wood; but after three quarters of an hour we were surrounded by horse and foot, the former in ambush. Mr Fownes was arrested, and sent to Gloucester jail for six months. April 22. — We went out at four in the morning, and were in peace. November 14. — A day of prayer, having some hours together in the wood, between London and Sodbury Road: the enemy came upon us unawares, and seized about eight persons; but the brethren escaped to admiration. The bushes were of great service to us. A number of the sisters were taken: they got Justice Fitz-Herbert to come, and upon examination he could get little out of them, and could not learn who was the preacher; so they were let go. December 20. — Watkins, the marshal, and others, went with warrants from Justice Herbert to brother John Morgan, in Temple Street, and took his yarn and what goods they could find, for seven pounds ten shillings. And the day before took away Margaret Seymour's trunk and clothes, with about thirty pounds, for seven pounds odd money, for being at our meeting in the fields. December 30. — Being a hard frost, and snow on the ground, we met in the wood, and though we stood in the snow the sun shone upon us, and we were in peace.

1684. March 4. — We took our sad state into consideration; and brother Terrill signified, that our duty lay in three things: — 1st. To watch over one another, that none draw back to the world's worship. 2nd. That every one sanctify the Lord's-day. 3rd. That we endeavour to edify one another as members, and also do what we can for others' souls. And, considering what is above, and that writs are daily expected to levy £20 a month, £240 per annum a man, upon us, for not coming to church, or imprison us if it be not be paid, there being thirteen brethren present, we agreed to have circular meetings at five places, where the brethren were to exercise their gifts, and twice in a day, at nine in the morning, and at one in the afternoon. These five places were. — 1st, brother Dickson, or Davis; 2nd, brother Clark or Robert Lewis; 3rd, brother Whinnell; 4th, brother Ellis or J. Coirnhs [Cornish]; 5th, brother Terrill. And also three places for prayer and repetition; viz. brother Gwilliam's, brother Bodenham's, brother Reeve's. And because some might be sick or otherwise detained, we appointed six or seven to a place, and the first four were to be taken in, and that those that were shut out were to go to the places of repetition. And none were to go to a place but once a day, and not to the same place every Lord's-day; but round, so they came to the same once in five weeks. And by this means near one hundred might hear every Lord's-day, and in a few weeks have the benefit of all the Church's gifts. And besides, brother Whinnell would repeat again at some house in the evening, and on week-days at other places. Thus we kept within the law, which allowed four besides the family. And on the ninth of March we began this circular meeting. April 10. —Brother Warren was fined £10 for a riot, being at a meeting near Roe Gate, and fees 47 shillings, which he paid in the hall at Gloucester. But Lugg was forsworn in it, for he swore it was on the 27th, and it was on the 29th day that the meeting was. Old brother Cornish was bound to appear again next sessions, and several others. Some were fined 40 shillings and their fees, and released. Sister Fowles was put in prison at Gloucester. Some were fined five marks, as bro. Jos. Wey; some £5, as the justices pleased, and to lie in prison till paid. About this time Pug Read died miserably, being an informer about twenty years old: had his skull broke, as was said, by one of his companions; he was one that broke into bro. Terrill's house. September 16. — Several of our brethren, brother Hunt, William Dickason, & co., and many more, were summoned by the apparitor to the bishop's court, for not receiving the Lord's Supper. October 7 — Nearly twenty more friends were indicted for eleven months' not coming to church. Brother Fownes being brought into court, was by Powell, the chairman, called a ringleader, turbulent, seditious, and told he must find six hundred pounds' bail to appear next sessions at Bristol, and be of good behaviour, or lie in prison. October 10 — New mayor and sheriff being chosen, James Twyford, sheriff, threatens to find out our little meetings, and he would be like death, spare none.

1685. January 13. — At the quarter sessions, brother Fownes was treated as before, and Justice Powell, the chairman, told him, Sir Richard Hart, of Bristol, should say he was a dangerous man. So they still kept him there at Gloucester, prisoner. On the 29th of November, 1685, brother Fownes, died in Gloucester jail, having been kept there for two years and about nine months a prisoner, unjustly and maliciously, for the testimony of Jesus and preaching the Gospel." He was originally committed for six months, but they would not release him unless he would give bond for his good behaviour, which meant, that he would not preach again. This, of course, he would not do."

Thus the enemy prevailed, and the servants of God were brought low. Truly, they were "perilous times." The church in time converted to Calvinism, the greatest enemy in the 1600s, and from there in time became part of the Baptist denomination. Churches of Christ, along with the Quakers and Presbyterians were persecuted, the Presbyterians, being the larger party, offered some respite when joining together, and this meant the churches of Christ taking a denominational stance, taking on Calvinism, becoming a protestant sect. What protection it offered is to some degree questionable. The law showed little mercy, but working together would have allowed funding for lawyers and assisting brethren in prison .[6]

William Kiffin was a native of London. He is well known today as being one of the originators of the Baptist movement. He was born in 1616. When he was nine years of age, he lost both his parents to the Plague, which at that time raged violently in London, in June 1625, and was himself "left with six plague sores" upon him, so that "nothing but death was looked for" by his friends. He became proficient in business, becoming one of the London "merchant-princes."

He was deeply interested in religion and attended many of the puritan Church of England congregations in London. It seems his baptism took place in early youth. Where he was baptised remains unknown, but we do know he was a member of the Church of Christ meeting in a house at Tower Hill. This congregation was not Calvinist. It would seem it was here Kiffin was baptised.[7]

By 1640, he was a member of an independent church where John Spilsbury was a preacher. This was the Jessey Church, with many of its members known today as the Pilgrim Fathers, having fled to America in 1620. Whilst Kiffin was a member, the congregation split over the question of baptism. Kiffin and others formed another congregation where believers' baptism was practised. Kiffin was now preaching occasionally.

Early in 1641, Kiffin was arrested at Southwark (South London) on a charge of organising an conventicle or illegal congregation (the former Jessey church) and committed by Judge Mallet to the White Lion prison, bail being refused. Mallet was himself committed to the Tower in the following July, whereupon Kiffin obtained his release. On 17th October 1642, he was one of four disputants, defending believer's baptism, encountered at Southwark by the Anglican divine, Daniel Featley. The White Lion was the borough prison for Southwark, and as with other prisons was privately owned and run for profit. Life could be acceptable if the prisoner had money; if not, it was very hard. Wealthy prisoners had access to a shop and food which was prepared for them, and the crucial privilege of being allowed to leave the prison during the day. Prisoners with no access to funds could starve to death. The various churches were kept busy providing food and comfort for the brethren in jail. Prisoners were required to pay their keep, and even faced punishment through lack of food when they could not. As most prisons were for debtors, such unfortunate folk could find themselves in an impossible situation where the only respite was death. It was only in the 1800s that various prison reforms were carried out including prisons being run by the state.

Kiffin and Spilsbury were among the signatories of the 1644

Confession of seven Calvinistic churches of Christ in London. Kiffin's wealth as one of London's leading merchants was put to use, fighting legal actions and assisting brethren in prison, and also in funding preachers of the Calvinistic churches, which is reflected in their organization and leadership.

Kiffin became one of two elders and preacher of a congregation he formed in Devonshire Square, London. Here on 1 March 1667, they had their own dedicated meeting-house.

King Charles II, seeking a loan of forty thousand pounds, a fortune in the seventeenth century (and still a great deal of money today), approached Kiffin for a loan. Kiffin believed the king would not repay so he responded by offering the king a gift of ten thousand pounds (in lieu of the loan). Charles accepted, Kiffin later boasted that he had saved thirty thousand pounds. Kiffin's life was not easy. His eldest son William died on the 31st August 1669, aged 20. His second son died at Venice, and was supposed to have been poisoned by a Roman Catholic priest after a dispute over scripture. Harry, another son, died on 8 Dec. 1698, aged 44. His daughter Priscilla died 15 March 1679. She had married Robert Liddel.

Kiffin worked with brethren on both sides of the Church, which had divided over Calvinism. He joined in evangelistic campaigns in Kent with brethren opposed to Calvinism.[8] As late as 1660, Kiffin, Henry Dene, Thomas Lambe, John Spilsbery and others published a book *The Humble Apology Of Some Commonly Called Anabaptist*, in the belief of themselves and others of the same judgment with them (London: Printed by Henry Hills 1660).[9] Despite his association with the churches of Christ, Kiffin was one of the founders of the many Baptist denominations, a movement that came out of the Churches of Christ in the seventeenth century.

In Baptist histories, Kiffin is cited as signing the 1644 Calvinistic Confession of Faith, although the Calvinism is an extremely mild type. These brethren held to preaching the word, being evangelistically minded, and to listeners believing, repenting and being baptised for the remission of sins, whereby they were added to the church of Christ. They used verses such as Mark 16:15-16, Matthew 28:19, Acts 2:38 applying those verses to evangelism. Whilst Calvinism was a problem for the churches of Christ in the 1640s, it was of a mild type. To what degree it was promoted among the members is uncertain. The Particular Baptist congregations that were Calvinist was applied by Baptist historians later to the signers of the 1644 and later confessions.[10] Certainly there was a worldly advantage in being seen to side with Calvinism in a Calvinistic country, as England was in that time when persecution was rampant and friends too often too few.

The following is the title page of the 1646 confession,
showing the identity, Church of Christ.

A CONFESSION OF FAITH

Of seven Congregations or Churches of Chrift in L O N D O N, which
are commonly (but uniuftly) called Anabaptifts.

PUBLISHED

For the vindication of the Truth, and information of the ignorant ; likewife for the taking off of
thofe afperfions which are frequently both
in Pulpit and Print unjuftly caft upon them.

*But this I confeffe unto thee, that after the way which they call herefie, fo
worfhip I the God of my Fathers, beleeving all things that are written in
the Law and the Prophets, and h.ve hope towards God, which they them-
felves alfo allow, that there fhall be a refurrection of dead both of the juft
and unjuft.* Acts 24. 14, 15.

For we cannot but fpeak the things that we have feen and heard, Acts 4. 20.

*If I have fpoken evill, bear witneffe of the evill ; but if well, why fmiteft thou
me ?* John 18. 23.

*Bleffed are yee when men revile you, and fay all manner of evill againft you
falfly for my fake. Rejoyce, &c.* Matth. 5. 1. 12. & 19. 29.

The fecond Impreffion corrected and enlarged.

Publifhed according to Order.

London printed by *Matth. Simmons*, and are to be fold by *John*
Hancock in Popes-head Alley. 1 6 4 6.

469

There were within the Church of Christ some with considerable influence. John Milton (1608-1674) was for a time such a member. In time he tended towards Arianism (denying the deity of Christ). Milton was both an accomplished scholarly man of letters, polemical writer, and an official serving under Oliver Cromwell who had an international reputation during his lifetime. He sought freedom of the press and religious liberty. His influence with parliament was considerable on behalf of the church.

Cromwell's home at Ely.

Milton believed in and defended believers' baptism. In *Paradise Lost* (Bk 12) he wrote "To teach all nations what of him they learned and his salvation; them who shall believe, baptizing in the profluent stream, the sign of washing them from guilt of sin to life pure, and in mind prepared, if so befall, for death, like that which the Redeemer died." His widow was a member of the Church of Christ at Nantwich, Cheshire, where her body was interred in the meeting house.[11] Under the protection of Oliver Cromwell with the influence of Milton, there was a respite of the bloody persecution under the Church of England and Monarchy for about fifteen years from the mid 1640s to 1658. After the restoration of the monarchy, the persecution started in earnest.

The last member of the church to be burned alive in England was Elizabeth Gaunt, on October 23, 1685. By all accounts she was a wonderfully charitable lady, frequently engaged in visiting the poor, particularly those in jail who needed help.

In 1683, the Rye House Plot was hatched. It was an attempt to assassinate King Charles II and his brother James, Duke of York who after Charles was heir to the throne. The plot was undertaken by some members of the Whig party. The plan was to assassinate Charles II and his brother as they passed by Rye House. The house was owned by a well-known Republican, Richard Rumbold. The design was to conceal a force of 100 men in the grounds of the house and ambush the King and the Duke on their way back to London from the races at Newmarket.

Although the plot was abandoned, they were betrayed to the

government. James Burton, one of the men implicated, pleaded with Elizabeth Gaunt to hide him from his pursuers for the sake of his family. Believing that it was what God would expect, she not only helped him escape but gave him her savings. A reward was offered for the capture of Burton.

The government issued a proclamation that any suspect who gave evidence leading to the arrest of other participants who took part in the plot would be granted immunity from prosecution. James Burton saw this as a way to save his skin. He made a deal with the authorities; he would testify against Elizabeth, who had saved his life if they would grant him the promised immunity. The government agreed to this, and, as the philosopher David Hume wrote, "He received a pardon as a recompense for his treachery and she was burnt alive for her charity."

"My fault," wrote Elizabeth, shortly before her death, "was one which a prince might well have forgiven. I did but relieve a poor family and I must die for it." And die she did. She died bravely, at Tyburn (London, near to Marble Arch). She was the last person burned alive in England for treason. William Penn, founder of Pennsylvania, was at the scene and saw her die. He recorded some of the details stating that when she calmly disposed the straw about her in such a manner as to shorten her sufferings, all the bystanders burst into tears.[12]

Born at Aldwincle in Northamptonshire, 1616, Charles Fleetwood was the third son of Sir Miles Fleetwood, a prominent official at the hated Court of Wards and Liveries (abolished in 1660). He attended Emmanuel College, Cambridge, and then trained as a barrister at Gray's Inn. In 1652, Fleetwood married Cromwell's daughter Bridget, the widow of Henry Ireton. In 1655, he was promoted to the rank of Major-General. After the Restoration of the Monarchy in 1660, Fleetwood was unable to hold any future position in the army, public office or position of trust. He lived quietly at Stoke Newington in Middlesex until his death in October 1692. Fleetwood and his wife became members of the Church (I do not know when) along with other high ranking officers that included Major-General Harrison, Major-General Ludlow, and Colonel Hutchinson.[13]

Various acts of parliament were introduced to oppose the Church of Christ and the Presbyterians, making it illegal, among other things, to preach against infant baptism, to rebaptise a person baptised (as an infant) and preaching the necessity of believers' baptism. The act was passed May 2nd 1648 and amended March 1653. Other acts banned lay-preaching. The Conventicle Act of 1664 forbade religious assemblies of more than five people outside the auspices of the Church of England. This law was part of the program of Edward Hyde, 1st Earl of Clarendon, to discourage nonconformism and to strengthen the position of the Established

Church. These prohibitions forbade preaching within five miles of the established church and led many to vacate their parishes rather than submit to the new Episcopal authorities. Just as the ministers left so too did the congregations, following their old pastors to sermons on the hillside. The Act of Uniformity, 1662, required the use of all the rites and ceremonies in the Book of Common Prayer in church services. This resulted in those congregations who obeyed the Five Mile Act breaking new laws. The Five Mile Act or Oxford Act, was an Act of the Parliament of England passed in 1665 with the long title "An Act for restraining Non-Conformists from inhabiting in Corporations." It was one of the English penal laws that sought to enforce conformity to the established Church of England. It forbade clergymen from living within five miles of a parish from which they had been banned, unless they swore an oath never to resist the king, or attempt to alter the government of Church or State. These two acts (and the following repercussions) led to congregations going into hiding and/or meeting in rural locations.

St. Paul's Cathedral and the church yard, where Christians evangelised right under the noses of the authorities.

The following pictures are of the Christian Meeting House disguised as a barn, at Monksthorpe, Lincolnshire with the outdoor baptismal pool where a church of Christ met in the seventeenth century.

ENDNOTES

I have used original mss and books held at the Cambridge University Library and the British Library London to confirm the accuracy of the information presented. I have also relied on Crosby and Ivimey.

[1]Thomas Crosby, *The History of the English Baptists*, vol. 1 (1738) 219.

[2]Crosby, vol. 1 120.

[3] William L. Lumpkin, *Baptist Confessions of Faith,* 6th print (1989) 226-8.

[4] Herbert S. Skeats, *A History of the Free Churches of England, from A.D. 1688 – A.D. 1851* (1868) 52. Walter Wilson, *Dissenting Churches*, vol. 4, 122. Thomas Crosby, *The History of the English Baptists*, vol. 3 (1738) 39ff.

[5]My source for Denne and Lamb: Thomas Crosby, *The History of the English Baptists* (1738). The introduction of the *Records of the Churches of Christ gathered at Fenstanton, Warboys and Hexham*, edited for the Hanserd Knollys Society, by Edward Bean Underhill, 1854. John Mocket Cramp, D.D., *Baptist History: From The Foundation Of The Christian Church To The Close Of The Eighteenth Century* 1871. The Tombes letter is reproduced from Thomas Crosby, *History of the English Baptists* vol. 1 (1738) 121-2.

[6]Sources used for the Broadmead Church:

J. M. Cramp, *Baptist History: From the Foundation of the Christian Church to the Present Time* (1871). Cramp replaces "church of Christ" with "Baptist," but allowing for his prejudice and plagiarising Edward Underhill, he remains as a useful resource. Edward Terrill, *The Records of a Church of Christ, Meeting in Broadmead, Bristol, AD 1640 to AD1688,* edition by Nathaniel Haycroft, M.A. (1865). Edward Bean Underhill, ed., *The Records of a Church of Christ Meeting in Broadmead, Bristol, 1640-1687* (1847).

J.G.Fuller, *THE RISE AND PROGRESS OF DISSENT IN BRISTOL; Chiefly in Relation to the Broadmead Church: with Brief Accounts of the Church Meeting in King Street, and of the Community of Friends,* Including Notices of the Early History of Castle Green, Bridge Street, and Lewin's Mead (1840).

John Tombes, B.D, *Jehovah Jireh: or Gods Providence in Delivering the Godly.* Opened in two sermons in the citie of Bristol on the day of publike thanksgiving in that citie, March 14, 1642, for the deliverance of that citie from the Invasion without, and the Plot of Malignants within. ... With a short narration of that bloody and abominable plot.

John Tombes, *A Plea for Anti-Paedobaptists, Against the Vanity and Falsehood of Scribled Papers,* entituled: *The Anabaptists anatomiz'd and silenc'd in a publique dispute at Abergavenny in Monmouthshire. Sept. 5. 1653, betwix't John Tombes, John Cragg, and Henry Vaughan touching Infant-Baptism* (Henry Hills: London, 1654) 44.

Robert Purnell and others, *The Church of Christ in Bristol Recovering Her Vail Out of the Hands of Them That Have Smitten and Wounded Her, and Taken It Away.* Being a ... vindication from a false ... imputation cast upon her by D. Hollister, formerly a Member of her but now an Apostate ... as appears by a late pamphlet put forth by him, called, The skirts of the Whore discovered ... Likewise a word by T. Ewen, unto what concerns him in the said pamphlet, and also to the later part of another Book, called, Satan enthroned, etc." (London, 1657) 40.

Denis Hollister, "*The Skirts of the Whore Discovered, and the Mingled People in the Midst of Her,* A letter sent by D. Hollister to the Independent Baptiz'd People, who call themselves a Church of Christ in Bristol, but are found to be a Synagogue of Satan ... Together with another letter ... to J. Ewens, ... and likewise an answer to 16 antiqueries, etc." (London, 1656). Crosby *History of the Baptists* (1738).

[8] William Kiffin, a member of the Churches of Christ that denied Calvinism, *Remarkable Passages in the Life of William Kiffin,* ed. William Orme (1823) 15.Kiffin is considered father of the "Particular Baptists," that is, the Calvinist party. What Baptist historians fail to mention is where and when he was converted. The evidence points that he was not a Calvinist in belief at first, being a member of the Church of Christ meeting near the Tower of London . Edward Bean Underhill, ed., (for the Hanserd Knollys Society), *Records of the Churches of Christ gathered at Fenstanton, Warboys and Hexham* (1854) 223. Herbert S. Skeats, *A History of*

the Free Churches of England, From A.D. 1688 – A.D. 1851 (1868) 122.

[9]Underhill 101.

[10] Adam Taylor, *The History of the English General Baptists* (1818) 189.

[11]Cramp and Crosby.

[12] Thomas Armitage, *History of the Baptists* (1887) 540.

[13]Cramp 328.

[14]Skeats 42.

16

EXCERPTS OF A CHURCH OF CHRIST'S MINUTES IN THE 1600S

His lord said unto him, Well done, good and faithful servant; thou hast been faithful over a few things, I will make thee ruler over many things: enter thou into the joy of thy lord (Matthew 25:23).

Pictures of the former Roman Catholic chapel in St. Ives, Cambridgeshire, which sits on the bridge over the river Great Ouse. For a few months in the 1650s a Church of Christ met here where Henry Denne preached.

The following excerpts are taken from the minutes of the Warboys and Fenstanton Churches of Christ meeting in the 1650s. The records are from 1644 to 1720, encompassing the period which started when the church was opposed to Calvinism through to being Baptist. They give an insight into the day-to-day dealings and concerns of the church at that time. During the protectorate, when England was a republic, Oliver Cromwell allowed considerable liberty of worship. This allowed congregations to keep detailed records without fear of prosecution. After the death of Cromwell, the monarchy was restored in 1660 with Charles II taking the throne. From that time until the Act of Toleration of 1689, the persecution and terror would return. Many Christians died in prison where they were left to languish, away from the public spectacle and sympathy which the burnings produced.

What is known as the Glorious Revolution took place in 1688. King William III (William of Orange) and his wife Queen Mary II, a daughter of James II, were asked by parliament to take the joint sovereignty over England, Scotland, Ireland and Wales. Their joint reign began in February, 1689, when they were called to the throne by Parliament, replacing James II, who was "deemed to have fled" the country. On 24 May 1689, the Act of Toleration was passed by the English Parliament. The Act granted freedom of worship to Nonconformists who had taken the oaths of Allegiance and Supremacy and formally rejected transubstantiation, *i.e.* those who dissented from the Church of England such as Baptists and Congregationalists, but not Catholics or Quakers. It allowed Nonconformists their own places of worship and their own teachers and preachers, subject to acceptance of oaths of allegiance. It expressly excluded Catholics and non-Trinitarians and continued the existing social and political disabilities of Dissenters, including their exclusion from political office and universities.

Dissenters were required to register their meeting places and were forbidden from meeting in private homes. Any dissenting preacher had to be licensed; it was a great step forward in religious liberty.

The John Denne mentioned is the son of Henry Denne. Both, it seems, were elders. James Disbrowe was a deacon and a wealthy land owner.

The record of the Church of Christ first cited deals with the problem of those who made a business of begging money from congregations and the problem of whether children and marriages should be registered, with the Church of England, their enemy:

> *On the 26th day of the seventh month, (1652) at a meeting held at Caxton Pastures, county Cambridge, where the elders, deacons, and brethren were assembled together in the name of our Lord Jesus Christ,*

> *Brother Maile stood up and declared that there were many persons that had not yet been admonished; and some had been admonished and reproved, but as yet do remain perverse and obstinate; and others that have professed their willingness to walk in the ways of God, yet no fruit hath appeared in them, "so that we cannot apprehend anything in them but hypocrisy and dissimulation; wherefore, my advice is that, in the firstplace, we take some order for the proceeding against such persons*

according to the mind of God revealed in the scriptures."

Then, upon due consideration, it pleased the elders, deacons, and the whole church to agree and consent unto these ensuing things, viz:

First, That it is the duty of persons that are in want truly to declare their condition to the church, or to the deacons.

Secondly, That after due examination had of the condition of any brother by the deacons of the church, they are to declare it to the congregation, or at the least to two or three of them, of whom (if it may be) one to be an elder.

Thirdly, That the deacons shall give nothing, at any time, or to any person, without the consent, at the least, of two or three of the congregation, of which (if it may be) one to be an elder.

Fourthly, That if any one belonging to the congregation have any in want that are nearly allied to them, that is to say, of their near kindred, as husband or wife, father or mother, son or daughter, grandfather or grandmother, uncle or aunt, nephew, &c, they shall, to the utmost of their abilities, relieve them, and not suffer them to be burdensome to the church.

Fifthly, That if the congregation are not able to relieve those that are in want amongst them, but are forced to send to other congregations for help, yet they shall not send any person in want, neither with nor without a letter, to gather their liberality for himself; but they shall send a man that is not in want, of whose fidelity they have had experience, that he may receive their liberality, and also bring it to the congregation.

Sixthly, That if any person in want shall come of his own accord from any congregation unto us for relief, we will not relieve them, unless we are sent unto by the hands of an able and faithful brother, as aforesaid.

Seventhly, That no person shall, at any time, be relieved by the congregation but such as, to the utmost of their abilities, do use all lawful means for their subsistence.

Eighthly, That the deacons shall give up their accounts every half-year, at the least.

Ninthly, That all those children that are born of any belonging to the congregation, shall be registered.

Tenthly, That all those that are married in the congregation, shall be registered.

Agreed upon and ordered, that these things, and all other acts of the congregation, shall be recorded.

John Denne, James Disbrowe, Jo. Gilman, Edmond Maile.[1]

On Christmas day, which they clearly did not celebrate, brethren visited with the widow Sanders and disfellowshipped her.

On the five-and-twentieth day of the twelfth month, John Denne, and James Disbrowe, according to former order and appointment, did go to Sutton, in the county of Bedford, to the widow Sanders; to whom, after salutations, we spake, saying: "The congregation having formerly sent unto you and having received your answers, and unto you, and having received your answers, and finding them to be erroneous, have now sent us to you to know whether you have repented of your evil, and are willing to be guided by the scriptures, and to walk in the observation of the ordinances of God." She said, "Indeed I have almost forgotten what I declared unto you." Then we repeated them unto her, which things she hearing, she stood to maintain, and multiplied many words to no purpose (which are too tedious here to relate), declaring, as she said, her experience of God; how God had carried her out of one dispensation unto another, and now He had brought her out of those fleshly ordinances which we walk in, and truly she would not be brought back again to them.

We desired her to use fewer words, and to prove what she said by the scriptures. She said, "I believe the manifestation of the Spirit is as sure a rule for me to walk by, as the scriptures are for you." We denied it, proving that that cannot be so safe a rule, because there are many false spirits, 1 John iv. 1. "Wherefore we are commanded to try the spirits, 1 John iv. 1, and the only way of trial is the scriptures, Isa. viii.20, and therefore the scriptures are the safest rule to walk by, 2 Peter i. 19, and we desire to be guided by it all our days." Then she said, " I can prove what I say by the scriptures ; but that will not give you satisfaction." Then we replied, saying, "How do you know? doth your conscience tell you that your proofs are so weak that they will not satisfy ?" She answered, "No; I believe they are strong enough." Then she instanced in this, Am not I better to thee than ten sons? 1 Sam. i. 8. "So," said she, "God hath told me that he is better than all ordinances, and that now I must worship him out of ordinances." We answered, saying: "We confess that God is above all ordinances, yet he is found in them; but that scripture which you have mentioned speaketh of no such thing; and if it did, yet it is too weak to prove what you would have it." Which we made manifest by several demonstrations from the scripture; whereupon she was exceeding angry, saying : "I said I should not satisfy you." And many other angry words did she use, exclaiming against many persons, And when she had ended her exclamations, we did reprove her for her faults, declaring our sorrowfulness for her, in that she refused to be guided by the scriptures and to walk in the observation of the ordinances of Jesus Christ. Here she interrupted us, saying: "I do and will refuse." Whereupon, with much sorrowfulness for that sinful expression, we did excommunicate her for these ensuing reasons, viz.:

First, For forsaking the assembly of the saints.

Secondly, For denying to be guided and ruled by the holy scriptures.

Thirdly, For charging God with dissimulation and injustice, saying, that God commands one thing, and secretly intendeth the contrary.

Fourthly, For slighting and despising all the ordinances of God, calling them fleshly ordinances.

Fifthly, For despising and contemning the reproof and admonition of the church.

John Denne.[2]

The issues below concern general misbehavior and the disfellowshipping of John Eppings and his wife for having their children "sprinkled" in the Church of England.

On the 19th day of the fifth month, at a meeting held at Papworth Everard, Hen. Denne stood up and said: "Brethren, at the last general meeting at Caxton, you were pleased to appoint bro. Gilman and myself to go to George Mitchell to admonish him of his faults. But we accidentally meeting with him at Eltisley, on the 17th day of this present month, took then occasion to speak unto him, according to your command. But our admonitions and reproofs would take no place; for he replied that what he had said was true, and he said he would come and make it appear before the congregation. Then we desired him to appoint the time when he would come. He said he could not tell. Yet, afterwards, he promised to come that day six weeks, which will be on the eight and twentieth day of the sixth month at the farthest." Whereupon the congregation, being willing to manifest all patience towards him, resolved to wait till the expiration of that time, that so they might hear his answers.

Afterward, Edmond Mayle stood up and said: "Brethren according to your former order, on the 10th day of the fifth month, brother Marriatt and myself did go to Sutton, in the Isle of Ely, to John Eppings and his wife, to whom we began to speak, saying: "You have been formerly admonished by messengers from the congregation, but despised their admonitions, therefore, they have now sent once more unto you by us, to see if you have repented of your evil which you have committed in forsaking the congregation, sprinkling your children, &c." They answered, that they believed they had not sinned in sprinkling their children. We replied, saying: "You have sinned greatly in doing that for which you have no rule in the scripture, and therefore it is an addition to the word of God." Then they said that they did believe that there were other people that do not walk in the way which we walk in, that are the people of God. We told them that we would not judge others; but we desired to know how we should know them to be the people of God. They answered that all people walked in the ways of God. Then we proved the contrary by the scriptures, and declared unto them how dangerous their condition is and from what they are fallen, and exhorted them to return from whence they are fallen and repent. And, indeed, many arguments we used, but they would not move them to repentance. For they replied that they could do nothing but what God acted in them, and as for that way which we walk in, they said they found no love to it. Then, taking into our serious consideration,

First, How that they have forsaken the congregation.

Secondly, Joined themselves with the church of England.

Thirdly, Forsaken and despised the ordinances of God.

Fourthly, Sprinkled their children.

Fifthly, Affirmed that all persons walk in the way of God, and that God acts all actions in all men. Sixthly, And despised all the reproof and admonition of the church; — we did deliver them unto Satan, declaring that the church would have no communion with them.[3]

In this appeal, Henry Denne requests that he is allowed to carry on the Great Commission, and the situation of James Disbrowe, a deacon, is discussed as he has left the area and is unable to remain in that office. The term "dismiss" allows him to join another congregation, no longer being a member at Fenstanton.

> On the three and twentieth day of the eighth month, at
> a general meeting at Fenystanton, Hen. Denne began to
> speak, saying: "Brethren, I desire you to consider the word
> of Christ, saying, Go ye therefore and teach all nations,
> baptizing them in the name of the Father, Son, and Holy
> Spirit; teaching them to observe all things whatsoever I
> have commanded you, and lo! I am with you always, even
> to the end of the world, Matt, xxviii. 19; which last words
> are often used by us, yet I think not too often. But I desire
> that we may seriously consider the former, viz., Go, teach
> all nations, baptizing them, &c. [or], as Mark saith, Go,
> preach the gospel to every creature; and so, whether we
> are not as much bound to observe them as any. And if it
> appeareth that we are, then I pray consider whether we
> are not in a great fault, in being so negligent in sending
> forth persons to divulge the gospel, in those many places
> that are ignorant thereof. Truly I conceive that we are
> much to blame, and especially seeing there [are] many
> towns hereabouts that have no teachers; and who can tell
> but that the Lord may work in this opportunity." Then
> the congregation, taking these things into consideration,
> acknowledged that they were in an evil, and resolved to
> amend; and, accordingly, did appoint a meeting on the
> eight and twentieth day of this present month, at Papworth
> Everard, to confess our faults and humble ourselves
> before our God, that we might find mercy according to his
> promise, saying, If ye would judge yourselves you should
> not be judged by the Lord, 1 Cor. Xi.

> Afterward, the condition of James Disbrowe, a deacon,
> was declared, viz., that he having removed his habitation,
> and thereby being far distant from us, is not able to supply
> the office of a deacon, wherefore he desired a discharge.
> Whereupon the congregation ordered him to give up his

accounts and to pay in the money that he had in his hands, which when he had done, the congregation, considering the ground of his desires, were pleased to dismiss him.[4]

The issue of Calvinism, other problems and the destitute sister Whittock are discussed.

On the fourth day of the tenth month, at a general meeting held at Caxton Pastures, the congregation taking into their serious consideration the condition of many persons, John Denne declared the condition of Mary Whittock, saying: "Brethren, Here is our sister Whittock, who is destitute of harbour, and her mother being very sick, and her children small, and the ways dirty, she is not able to travel from place to place as she hath been accustomed; therefore I desire that we may take her condition into consideration, and use the utmost of our endeavour to provide her harbour for this winter time. I hope none will be against it, knowing that he which hath pity upon the poor lendeth unto the Lord; and whatsoever he giveth, it shall be repaid. She was at Royston, but the town would not suffer her there to abide. Therefore, on the thirtieth day of the ninth month, my father and bro. Gilman brought her in their cart from thence, since which time I have given her harbour. But, indeed, this place is not convenient for her, because she cannot go any whither, either for her own relief, or her children's." Then Henry Denne declared that she was at Melbourne, and the townsmen forced her to depart; and that from thence she went to Royston, and the town would not suffer her to continue there. Then it was objected that it would be the same here. It was answered, that for the preventing of it we must give security to the town that she shall not be chargeable to them, which was consented unto. And thereupon the congregation, being willing to manifest their love towards her, and their care of her, did appoint Edmond Mayle, Tho. Phillips, and

Robt. Cole, to use the utmost of their endeavours for the providing a house for her.

Afterwards, Hen. Denne spake, saying: "Brethren, it came into our minds from something that was spoken on the first day of the last week from those words, 'Contend earnestly for the faith;' and from the consideration of the armour of God, part of which is the preparation of the gospel of peace, that it would be good and profitable for the strengthening of the weak, and for the edification of the whole body, if that the great differences about religion were all drawn up, and that all things that are brought either on the one side or on the other out of the scriptures were set down under that controversy, and a copy thereof delivered to every part of the congregation; that so every member may become acquainted with the objections of our adversaries, that thereby they may be able to answer; and this thing coming then into our minds, it was agreed that it should be propounded this day unto your consideration, which I have now done." Then the congregation seriously weighing the thing, and considering that it would be very profitable for the acquainting the saints with the objections of our adversaries, that so they may not come upon us unawares, and for acquainting the saints with the scriptures, that so our spiritual weapons may be always ready against our adversaries, did conclude that it should be done; and thereupon the greatest controversies were nominated, which were as followeth:

First, Whether Christ died for all men, or only for some particular persons?

(Calvinism)

Secondly, Whether baptism belongeth to believers or to infants?

(Church of England)

Thirdly, Whether God be the author of sins?

(Predestination and freewill)

Fourthly, Whether the ordinances of God, as prayer, exhortation, baptism, breaking of bread, &c. are ceased, or do yet continue?

(Quakerism)

Fifthly, Whether there be a possibility for believers to fall away? and referred to several persons, viz. the first to Hen. Denne; the second to John Denne; the third to Edmond Mayle; the fourth to Richard Ellegood; the fifth to John Blowes; that they might draw up all that is said on eitherside and present it to the congregation.

After this, John Denne spake, saying: "Brethren, I considering lately the records of the congregation, I found that when those people at Over, in the county of Cambridge, were admonished by messengers from the congregation, the widow Binns, being one of them, was demanded why she joined with the church of England in their public worship? Her answer was that Mr. Pope was a great friend of hers, and she did it to please him. Now for this she never gave satisfaction, which I conceive she ought to do, if you do apprehend it to be a sin." Then, upon consideration, it was concluded to be a very heinous sin; and, thereupon, Edm. Mayle, Tho. Coxe, and Rich. Ellegood were appointed to go unto her and to reprove and admonish her, and if she doth not repent, to proceed according to the rules of scripture.

On the 15th day of the eleventh month, at a general

meeting held at Fenstanton, Edmond Mayle, Tho. Coxe, and Rich. Ellegood declared that, according to the former order of the congregation, they had been with the widow Binns, of Over, and that now she was with the assembly to speak for herself. Whereupon it was declared to her that the congregation did conceive that she had sinned very heinously in joining with the church of England. She said she did not join with them. We told her she went to their assemblies, and therein she joined with them. She confessed that she went to their assemblies, but she did it to please the world, to please Mr. Pope, and to try the spirits. It was replied that she had tried the spirits before, and therefore we did believe the greatest reason to be, that she might please Mr. Pope and the world, which we did apprehend to be an abominable sin, according as it is written: "Who art thou that fearest man, and forgettest the Lord thy maker?" and, therefore, she was sharply reproved by the congregation and exhorted to repent. Then she alleged that she was forced so to do for the maintaining of herself and children. We replied that that was not the way to be maintained, but if it were, she ought not to have used it; for shall we do evil that good may come of it? God forbid. Then after many other wrords(sic) she confessed that she had done evil, and said that she was very sorry for it. Whereupon the congregation did willingly accept thereof and did receive her; and to manifest their love gave unto her seven shillings to satisfy her necessities. Afterwards, the condition of our sister Whittock was taken into consideration; and we, taking notice thereof, upon diligent search found that the best way for the satisfying her necessities, was to provide her a stock to trade withal, as formerly she was accustomed; and thereupon [we] gave unto her twenty shillings, and concluded that a letter should be sent to Melbourne and Royston, to desire them to do something for her.

After which, brother Tiffins and his wife's absenting themselves from the congregation was taken into consideration; and after some debate, it being concluded to be contrary to the will of God, Tho. Phillips and Christopher Marriatt were appointed to go unto them, to reprove and admonish them.[5]

Good news of evangelizing from Henry Denne.

On the 27th day of the ninth month, Hen. Denne declared the proceedings at Hawson, as followeth:—

Brethren,—Concerning the success that the Lord gave to brother Marriatt and myself, it hath been already given in writing, and therefore I shall say nothing of it; but at the latter end of that relation there was mention of a promise that I should go to Hawson the next first day, and accordingly on the nineteenth day of this present month I went thither; and on the next day, it being the first day of the week, the priest and the chiefest men of the town sent to me to come and preach in their public place. Whereupon I went, intending to have spoken there unto the people; but as soon as I began to speak, the rude multitude gathered together, and would not suffer me to speak; they being suborned by those which sent to me to preach, as it did most evidently appear afterwards, and that as well by the confession of some of those rude persons as by other demonstrations. Whereupon I departed from them, and spake in a private house.

Many people came unto us, and those which were our great enemies (yet so rational that they abhorred such dissimulation as appeared in those forementioned persons) came and heard, and indeed many of them seemed greatly to be affected with that which was spoken. Afterwards I was desired to go to Great Shelford the next day, and accordingly I did; but Satan having stirred up the priest, a Justice of the Peace, and several others against us, thereby hindered many from coming to us; yea, many of those which sent for me durst not come to us, only they sent their servants and children. The people seemed generally to be affected with the truth, and two of them, viz., Francis Holmes, and Mary Green, went along with me to Hawson the next night, it being the two and twentieth day of the month, and were baptized.

Also one King propounded himself to be baptized; but he desired liberty to hear the priests of the Church of England as often as he should think fit. I demanded of him, whether he thought they were the ministers of Christ, or of anti-Christ, for if they were the ministers of Christ, why, then, would he separate from them? But if they were the ministers of anti-Christ, why would he join with them? He then confessed that they were the ministers of anti-Christ; but he said, that they preached many good doctrines. I replied, the devil did so, as when he said that Jesus Christ was the Son of God. Then, after many words, he said that he hired a farm of Mr. Bendich, and if he should know that he was baptized he would turn him out. I told him that the earth was the Lord's and the fulness thereof, and wished him to trust God, and he would be a better landlord than Mr Bendich. Then he said he would consider of it, and so departed.[6]

The disciplining and excommunication of John Langhorne.

On the 26th day of the twelfth month, at a general meeting held at Caxton Pastures, these ensuing things were declared and taken into consideration:

John Denne stood up and said: "Brethren, according to your former order, brother Gilman and myself, on the eighteenth day of this present month, went to Potton, in the county of Bedford, to reprove those persons that have forsaken the congregation and denied the faith. Where, first, after we perceived we could not get them together, we went to John Langhorne, and after some salutations we spake unto him, saying: "The cause of our coming at this time is this; the congregation, taking into their serious consideration how that many persons who formerly joined with us are now turned back, denying the faith, despising the ordinances of God, and followed after vanity, have resolved, according to their duty, to reprove and admonish all such persons, and if they do not repent, to proceed according to the will of God in separating them from the body of our Lord Jesus Christ. And, accordingly, we two were appointed to come unto you, to reprove you for your heinous faults, viz. for denying the faith, and despising the ordinances of God, &c. He said he had been reproved already. We told him it was true he had been so, yet that we might fulfill the will of God we do it again; and withal did earnestly desire him to consider from whence he was fallen and repent. Then he could not believe that Christ died for all. We answered and told him that he did once believe it; but now he said he was better enlightened; and, moreover, he said he was gone beyond those low ordinances which we practice. "For a man," he said, "must not always dwell upon one thing." Then we laboured to prove by the scriptures that the ordinances of God were not low. He confessed that it was true by the letter; but it was the spiritual meaning he said that we must look to; and therefore he said he could not believe as we believed. We told him we did not blame him for not believing as we believed, but for denying the faith which formerly he professed. Then he said: "I believe you hold that God hath given power to all men to believe, but if you do I shall deny it; yet, nevertheless I would, if I were nigh, come and hear you, for I can hear any;" and many other words were spoken which are too tedious here to relate. Whereupon, taking into our consideration his heinous crimes, in:

First, Denying the faith:

Secondly, Forsaking the church of Christ and joining with the Church of England:

Thirdly, Despising the ordinances of God:

Fourthly, condemning all the reproof of the church:

We excommunicated him.[7]

John Blowes was a character causing problems for the churches, as we shall read. He preached, so he must at one time have been held in high regard. He travelled, and on one occasion left debts with the brethren in London. He also loved football which got him into trouble. He was baptised on the 3rd May 1652 and the last he is recorded as being disfellowshipped.[8]

After [this] the matter of John Blowes was taken into consideration. And he being present, he declared that according to the advice of the brethren, he went to London, and that he had given full satisfaction to all his accusers. The congregation hearing this, desired a certificate from the brethren at London. Whereupon he produced this ensuing writing, viz: "These are to certify the brethren at Caxton Pastures, that brother Blowes hath paid the money due to John Thompson, Simon Parratt, and Roger Stampe, and hath given full satisfaction for all things they have charged against him. "Roger Stampe." This note being read and taken into consideration, it was asked why John Thompson and Simon Parratt did not subscribe it, seeing they subscribed his accusation. He answered, that he did not speak with John Thompson, and that Simon Parratt refused to set his hand to it, because John Thompson was not present. It was then demanded, why he did not speak with John Thompson. He answered, that he endeavoured twice to speak with him, but could not. Whereupon there was much debate upon the matter; but at length it was resolved, that the foregoing writing was not a sufficient testimony, because, First, It was not adjudged safe to receive the testimony of one person; Second, It was not thought possible that he should give satisfaction, and not see his accusers. These things considered, John Denne was appointed to write to London touching the business, and in the meantime the matter was deferred until we should hear from thence.

After these things, and the observation of some ordinances of God, praise was rendered to the Lord, and so the assembly were dismissed.

On the four-and-twentieth day of the eleventh month, at a general meeting of the congregation held at Caxton Pastures, after prayer and supplication to the God of heaven, and some words of doctrine and exhortation, John Denne spake, saying: "Brethren, you were pleased to appoint me to write a letter to London, touching the business of John Blowes. According to your order I did write to brother Loveday, an account whereof I think meet to give you. The letter was as followeth:

Beloved brother,—After salutations due unto you in the Lord Jesus Christ, wishing the increase of grace, and the knowledge of God to be granted to you; these are to acquaint you that when I was last with you, I received an information by several members of your congregation, especially by Roger Stampe and Simon Parratt, touching the behavior of John Blowes, when he was with you at London, by whom he was then accused of great evils, viz., First, Of idleness in his calling, not providing for necessary uses. Second, Whereas by this means he became indebted to some persons, yet he took no care to pay; insomuch that bailiffs were employed to arrest him, to the dishonour of God. Notwithstanding which, he did not [at] all endeavour to prevent the ensuing danger. Third, Some brethren perceiving this, and being tender of the honour of God and his good, did voluntarily disburse the money for him; to whom, notwithstanding, he showed such ingratitude, that he altogether neglected the repaying of the money, and also endeavoured (as was supposed) to defraud them; in that he endeavoured privily to depart from his lodging. But being discovered, and asked for the money, he told them that he intended to lodge in "Whitechapel, at the sign of the Heron", to which place if they came next morning they should have their money. To which place he never came, but went another way. Fourth, They accuse him of lying very heinously, not regarding his promises and engagements. The substance of these things being set down in a letter to us, subscribed by John Thomson and Mary his wife, Roger Stampe and Simon Parratt; which things we considering, and knowing how dangerous it is to suffer a brother to go on in sin, and also to heal a wound slightly, of which the Lord complains; we thought it our duty to tell him of these things. Which accordingly Ave did, showing unto him his error, and exhorted him to confess his faults, and to bring forth fruits meet for amendment of life. But he greatly justified himself. Whereupon our advice was, that he would come to London, and clear himself before his accusers. And if he should give ample satisfaction to you, we (being certified thereof by sufficient testimony) should be satisfied. This he altogether refused whilst he was with us; but afterwards went up, and being returned, brought us this enclosed note, which did not satisfy us; because, first, We judged it not safe to receive the testimony of one; especially when other of his accusers refused to subscribe, as Simon Parratt did. Second, we think it not possible that he should give satisfaction, when he himself confesseth he did not see all his accusers. Which things considered, I was appointed to write to you, and you are hereby desired to make inquiry of the business, and to send us word as soon as you can. For the matter is in suspense till we hear from you. For if he hath given full satisfaction, as he pretends, it will suffice. Yet we suppose that the payment of the money without humble confession of transgression, since there hath been so great an aggravation of offences, will not be sufficient. But I need not direct you in this thing, the wisdom which you have received from above being sufficient to which I shall leave you at this time, hoping that you will not be negligent, either in inquiring or sending to us concerning this matter. And now, commending you to the Lord, I shall remain,

Your brother in the Lord,

John Denne.

Caxton, 24th day of the 10th month, 1657.

This letter, I sent; but have not yet received any answer. The congregation hearing this approved thereof; and further resolved to wait until they received an answer to the letter, before anything should be concluded of.

501

On the seventh day of the first month 1658.

After this John Denne spake, saying, Brethren, I formerly acquainted you with a letter which I sent to London by your appointment, touching John Blowes. I have now received an answer thereunto from brother Loveday, Which is as followeth:

Dear and faithful brother in the Lord, whose prosperity in soul and body I much desire, and the rest with thee. These are in answer to a letter received concerning John Blowes. The brethren that formerly complained of him, are not satisfied with him, as appeareth by their paper here enclosed, and by them signed. For it is one thing to pay them what was owing to them, and another thing to show humiliation for former evils. Therefore I leave it to your Christian wisdom to consider. I fear much he is not as he ought to be. So praying that God would give wisdom to us, to separate the precious from the vile, I shall cease at present to write, and remain, your loving brother, and fellow labourer in the gospel.

Dated, London, Feb. 2nd, '57.

Sam. Loveday.

I received a letter enclosed, which was subscribed by John Thompson and Simon Parratt, which specified as much.

The congregation hearing this, adjudged John Blowes to be in a great fault; not only for his former evils, but also for dealing so hypocritically, in pretending he had given satisfaction when he had not, it being now found to the contrary. For which he was sharply reproved in the name of our Lord, and exhorted to repent. At the first he justified himself, but at length he confessed his sin in every particular. Upon which there was some debate what to do; but at length it was advised, that he should specify the same in a letter to London, subscribed by himself as a testimony of his repentance. This he promised to do. Whereupon it was referred to John Denne to view what he should write, and to make account thereof to the congregation. After these things, praise was rendered to the Lord, which, with the administration of some ordinances, being finished, the assembly was dismissed.

On the eighteenth day of the second month, at a general meeting of the congregation held at Caxton Pastures.

Then John Denne spake further, saying; "Brethren, you were pleased to appoint me to view what should be written by John Blowes to London. According to your order I did, which writing I suppose will be satisfactory. It was as followeth:

To brother Thompson and his wife, and to brother Parratt, and to brother Roger.

Brethren,—These few lines are to let you understand, that God hath been pleased to make me truly sensible of those many evils which have been by me ungodly committed, and by you justly charged against me; which particulars are these :

First, Neglecting my calling.

Secondly, Neglecting to pay the money due to my landlady in Shadwell.

Thirdly, Neglecting to pay the money due to you, and also my breach of promise.

Fourthly, My not making you acquainted with my departure from your house. All which particulars I humbly confess, that God may have the glory, and that the shame may light upon me, to whom it is due. So desiring you would forgive me, and that you would be assistant to me with your prayers to God for me, that I may not be overtaken in the like temptations, I rest,

Your unworthiest brother,

Joh. Blowes.

The congregation hearing this were satisfied therewith, and received him again into fellowship. But not for long, soon John was in trouble, this time for playing football.

On the thirtieth day of the fifth month, Robt. Jackson informed us that John Blowes was not only absent from us, but that he was this day at a great foot-ball play, he being one of the principal appointers thereof. This being heard, it was concluded a great evil that he should not only be absent from the meeting, but also be instrumental in the appointing such a foolish and wicked matter, and that upon a day which he knew to be set apart by the church for fasting and prayer. Whereupon John Denne was ordered to reprove him for it, and also to certify him, that it was desired that he should be present at the next general meeting, to give an account thereof.

After these things, praise was rendered to the Lord, and so (the day being spent) the assembly were dismissed.

On the two and twentieth day of the sixth month, at a general meeting of the congregation held at Fenystanton, after prayer and supplication to the God of heaven, and some words of doctrine and exhortation, the brethren were generally reproved for their negligence at the fast day. After which, John Denne certified the congregation, that according to order, he did reprove John Blowes for his evil, in being absent from the congregation upon the fast day, and being at a foolish foot-ball play, he being one of the principal appointers thereof; and that John Blowes stood to justify his actions; and moreover that he was now present to answer for himself. Whereupon it being adjudged a great evil, he was sharply reproved; nevertheless he stood to justify his action to be no evil. But it being plainly proved to be a great evil, at length he confessed it, and promised to abstain from the like for the time to come; whereupon some debate was had about the matter, after which it was resolved that, seeing thereby he had:

First, Dishonoured the Lord; Secondly, Grieved the people of God; Thirdly, Given great occasion to the adversaries to speak reproachfully—he should not be suffered to preach, until further fruits meet for repentance did appear. After these things, and the observation of some ordinances of God, as breaking of bread, &c, praise was rendered to the Lord, and so (the day being spent) the assembly were dismissed.[9]

On the two and twentieth day of the fourth month, 1655, according to former order, the elders of several congregations met at Cambridge. After discussing several matters, John Denne spoke concerning John Matthews, who had converted to Calvinism. John was also one of several preachers for the congregation:

Brethren, I think it requisite to declare at this time the proceedings with John Matthews, which proceedings, although they are partly known to some of you, yet for the satisfaction of all, I shall speak; and so much the rather, because he was a person of such eminency amongst us before his departure from us into Ireland, where he remained some time. But at length, coming over to visit his friends, we had thereby an occasion to speak with him. Which accordingly we did, and after some salutations we told him that we had heard that he had altered his judgment, and forsaken that truth which formerly he professed. He answered, yea, he had altered his judgment, and forsaken that which we profess, and was likewise formerly professed by himself; but it was not the truth, but error. We told him, that he had once owned it to be the truth; and not only owned it, but likewise preached it publicly to the world. At which time, the Spirit and power of God was so manifested in him, that none of the adversaries durst open their mouths to oppose, and therefore we demanded why he disowned it now. He answered, first, that it was true he did once both own it, and preach it; at which time, he confessed, that the power of God was manifested in him to admiration; insomuch that not one of the adversaries durst open their mouths to oppose. Secondly, he answered, that the reason why he disowned it now, was because he was persuaded within himself that it was false. We replied, that out of his own mouth he should be judged; for he had confessed before us, that when he preached that which he now denieth, the spirit and power of God was mightily manifested in him, even to admiration; and if [it were] so that that was the Spirit of God, then this must needs be a false spirit that is contrary thereunto. He then answered, that he thought at that time it was the Spirit of God, as we do; but now he believed it to be a false spirit. We replied, that the effects did evidently prove it to be a true spirit, and likewise the scriptures would manifest the truth of the doctrine which he then preached. He answered, that the scriptures would manifest the contrary. Whereupon we entered into a large conference about the matters in controversy; until at length, he told us that it was in vain to multiply words about the matter, for he knew what we could say, he being once as ready as we to say the same things. Whereupon, we did, in the name of our Lord Jesus Christ, reprove him for his sin, exhorting him to consider from whence he was fallen, and repent and turn unto the Lord, if peradventure the thought of his heart may be forgiven him, But he refused to hearken to our words. Wherefore we exhorted him to consider what he did, and to beware of despising the reproof and admonition of the saints. And so we parted at that time. The things affirmed by him contrary to the doctrine believed by us, and formerly preached by him, are as followeth, viz: First, That Christ died only for his elect, even such as either do, or shall believe on him. Secondly, That God hath from the beginning chosen a certain number of persons to himself, to which persons he cometh with such a compulsive power that they cannot resist. Thirdly, That God hath from the beginning pre-ordained a certain number of persons to condemnation, from which persons he withholdeth all manner of power, so that there is not any possibility of their believing. For which things, at another time, our bro. Mayle, accompanied with some of the brethren, did reprove him the second time; but he refused to hearken. Whereupon, the third time he was reproved and exhorted to repent by our brother Mayle and myself, in the presence of many of the brethren; but he refused to hearken unto us, persisting stubbornly in his opinion. Whereupon it was resolved, that the next first day the business should be declared in the presence of the congregation. It was likewise resolved,

507

that I should come unto Fenystanton upon that day. These resolutions were declared unto him, and he was desired to be present at the assembly of the congregation upon that day; he promised he would be present. Whereupon, the first day being come, I went to Fenystanton. And the congregation being assembled we went to prayer, after which a word of exhortation was spoken by our brother Mayle, and afterwards a word of exhortation was spoken by myself; yet all this time he came not. Wherefore we sent for him, but he came not at present; but at length he came to us; at which time we did reprove him for denying the faith which once he professed, and for labouring to destroy it in all places where he came. But he refused to hearken to us; whereupon we earnestly desired him to consider from whence he was fallen and repent; but he contemned all our words. Wherefore we desired to know whether he desired any further consideration upon the matter. He answered, no; he would not consider of it any more. Whereupon we, knowing how he denied the faith which formerly he professed, and also laboured to the utmost of his power to destroy it in all places, and likewise despised and contemned all our words of reproof and admonition, and finding no hope of recovery but a stubborn persisting in his evil: — we delivered him unto Satan.[10]

The following is from the introduction of the Warboys congregation, that first met in 1644.

Mystery, Babylon, or the great whore, spoken of by the blessed apostle John in the Revelation, with whom the inhabitants of the earth have committed fornication, had so deceived the nations of the world, that although something had been done in this nation by way of reformation, yet so great was the darkness, that few knew in what manner churches ought to be gathered and governed, according [to] the scriptures and practice of the holy apostles and churches in their time. It pleased God about this time to stir up some in this town to search the scriptures; and by the Lord's providence, one Henry Denne, an able and learned teacher, did by preaching and writing, manifest the great love of God the Father to mankind, in giving his only Son, the Lord Jesus Christ, to die for every man; and further declaring that whosoever did believe in him and repent of their sins, ought to be dipped in water (which is baptism), and from thenceforth to walk all their days in obedience to the holy scriptures; declaring such to be the church of God. And by the preaching of the said Henry Denne, many in this county received the faith, of whom some were of this town; who, considering that lest Eusebius Hunt, parish teacher of Warboys, should be offended at it, thought good to acquaint him with it; and finding an opportunity when he had sprinkled an infant, one William Dunn told him he had no ground for so doing in the scriptures, but it was a tradition of man, desiring him to take it into consideration and leave it. Eusebius Hunt said, he would dispute it. Whereupon Henry Denne being sent for, came to Warboys, accompanied with sundry of the brethren; and Henry Denne preached in the public meeting places, who confirmed them much in the truth of the gospel. Afterwards Henry Denne was desired to come again, who, after a long dispute with Eusebius Hunt, Henry Denne demanded whether he judged it best to sprinkle infants, or let them alone. Eusebius Hunt answered, to let them alone. Henry Denne said, surely we are to do the best way. William Dunne, with the rest, being resolved to join with Henry Denne, acquainted him of their mind, who exhorted them not to delay [the] time of their baptism. Not long after, these, by name, were baptized; William Dunn, John Richards, John Ward, John Kidson, William Askew.[11]

The following is a letter from the church at Canterbury dealing with the success of Henry Denne, now working for them, but supported by the brethren at Caxton and elsewhere. Interestingly for us, the brethren sign themselves as being "In the kingdom." At this time they were not waiting for the kingdom as Calvinists and premillennialists do.

To the church of God in Caxton.

Beloved Brethren, — We salute you in the Lord. "We being sufficiently informed of your faithfulness and love to the truth, in your willingness to promote the publishing and spreading of it, as appears by your readiness in sending our beloved brother Denne to the ministerial performance of that great work, both to us and others:—we thank the Lord who hath put that earnest care into your hearts, desiring from our very souls that both you and we, and all that do love our Lord Jesus Christ in sincerity, may abound yet more and more in every good word and work to the praise of his grace, both to the truth and to the lovers of it. Now, dear brethren, forasmuch as we do not expect our brother Denne's coming to Canterbury to us (although we hear that by the great and special hand of God he is returned to you again, for which we desire to be very thankful to our God who hath been so very gracious unto him and all his relations), because he was not his own, and could not make any promise of coming again unto us, though he knew all our desires, by reason he knew not the mind of the church for the future, so that we have been in suspense between hope and fear all the time of his absence; and not the church only, but many more also in and about this city, which of enemies are become friends to the truth, they being very much affected with him for the truth's sake. Now, brethren, in order to his coming to Canterbury to do the work of the Lord, we have, in all Christian humility, sent you these lines, whereby we do earnestly entreat you (being absent as though we were present), that for the honour of God's name, and the truth, and the good of many poor souls, which may be as much eclipsed if he come not again as it was advanced by his being there amongst us; we have many more reasons to move you to a free condescension to this weighty matter, viz, that the truth hath lain hid these many years in this place, being trodden under foot, and so clouded by reason of a mixt party that had all owned once but were turned out of the way, most of them into the mystery of iniquity. Only some few that did all this time own the principles of the doctrine of Christ, but what for want of inward and outward abilities they were not able to do much more than they did, especially having so great discouragements by the departure of so many from the truth. And having no officers to deal with them according to the word, we were looked upon all alike, as men destitute wholly of the truth; and by this means, according to the apostle Peter's word, the way of truth had a very evil report. But now the Lord hath been pleased to open a door both to you and us, blessed be his name, that we have good ground to hope [it] will prove effectual to many; because he hath been pleased to magnify his grace, and to make his truth honourable in the eyes of many in the world. And therefore, now is the time; let us up, and be doing. And the Lord will be with us in taking away that thick darkness which hath covered the truth, but is now a breaking forth like the sun from under a cloud. Another reason why we desire our brother Denne to be a labourer in this work in this place is, because of his wisdom and understanding, that our God hath furnished him withal in the mysteries of the gospel; and it is our duty to use all possible means we can that we may gain the more. And we judge him to be able, by sound doctrine, both to exhort and to convince the gainsayers; for here are many unruly and vain talkers, and deceivers of minds, especially they called Ranters, whose mouths must be stopped. And our brother Denne hath been an instrument in the hand of God, for the snatching of some of them as firebrands out of the fire already, which we hope will be close walkers with God. We might add many more reasons, but we shall forbear; knowing that a word to the wise is enough. All which considered, we judge that you cannot reasonably deny our desires for our brother Denne's coming to Canterbury; but rather to appoint and send him to stay with us as long as the Lord shall please, here being very great need of him. Thus hoping that you will rightly weigh this matter in the balance of the sanctuary and right reason, we shall say no more to it; building upon all your faithfulness to us and the truth as it is in Jesus. Brethren, we beseech you for the Lord's sake that you join together with us in prayer to God, both for us and all saints, that we may be kept by the mighty power and Spirit of God through faith unto salvation, and blameless as the sons of God, shining as lights in the world, brighter and brighter, unto the perfect day of Christ's coming.

The love of God the Father, and the grace of our Lord Jesus Christ, with the comfortable communion of the Holy-Spirit, be with you and all that love him, even for evermore. Amen.

By this, our dear brethren, you may fully know that the affections of us all are as formerly; and that we are unprovided of one to go in and out before us.

Your ever loving brethren and companions in the kingdom and patience of Christ Jesus: —

Rich. Beacham, Jonas Cooke, Tho. Beacham, John Wigmore, Tho. Jarman, Joh. Skillett, Daniel Jarman, John Smith, Joh. Ratcliffe, Rich. Gouldhack,

Joh. Miles.

From Canterbury, this 11th of the ninth mouth, 1654. [12]

About the year 1652 a congregation was started in the Army stationed near Edinburgh (Scotland). Many soldiers, some of high rank, members of the church, were in Cromwell's army. This may help explain why Cromwell's army had such a good reputation for discipline. This congregation met weekly, but changed locations, one week at Leith and the other at Edinburgh. Leith today is part of Edinburgh, but then distinct communities. Major General Robert Lilburne in 1652 was in command of the army in Scotland. He was also a member of the church of Christ.

Thomas Disbrowe, who was a member of the church at Fenstanton, was related to James Disbrowe, a deacon of the church (was Thomas his son?). James was younger brother of Major-General Disbrowe, brother-in-law of Oliver Cromwell. Thomas Disbrowe in 1655 was stationed in Scotland and requested to join the congregation meeting in Leith and Edinburgh. Fellowship between the congregations meeting in Cambridgeshire and those to the north is confirmed by the evidence of this correspondence.

On the thirtieth day of the tenth month, at a general

meeting of the congregation held at Caxton Pastures, after prayer and supplication to the most high God, and some words of exhortation, a letter was read which came from our brother Thomas Disbrowe in Scotland, which was as folioweth, viz:

Beloved brethren; grace, mercy, and peace be multiplied unto you, from God the Father, and from our Lord Jesus Christ, the Father of mercies, and the God of all comforts, who comforteth us in all our tribulations, that we may be able to comfort them which are in any trouble, by the comfort wherewith we ourselves are comforted of God. I thank my God upon every remembrance of you, and always and at every time making request for you, that you may be kept together in grace and truth, and that your love may abound more and more, in all knowledge and in all judgment. Beloved brethren, I would that you should understand, that although at my first coming into Scotland, I was much troubled in being deprived of the sweet and comfortable society of the people of God, yet remembering the promises of God, that they are all yea and amen to them whose minds are stayed upon him, it did strengthen me very much, causing me to wait patiently, until God should manifest, more comfort to me. Which now he hath done in due time; for there are several persons come to Leith and Edinburgh, with whom I may have comfortable society. The man that brought me first to know them, was a countryman of ours. His name is Thomas Gates. He lived at Ellington in Huntingdonshire. The people are most of them soldiers, of a regiment that is but lately come to Leith, and they are permitted to meet at the Tolbooth at Leith one first day, and at the Tolbooth at Edinburgh another first day. Now, brethren I would entreat you that you would certify under your hands that I was received into fellowship, according to gospel order, with you. I also think it necessary to put you in remembrance, that you would not be unmindful of me in your prayers to God, that I may be grounded and settled in the hope of the gospel. Salute all the friends with you. And the very God of peace sanctify you all, and present you blameless at the coming of our Lord and Saviour Jesus Christ. The grace of our Lord Jesus be with you all. Amen.

Your loving brother,

Tho. Disbrowe.

Leith, the 3rd day of the 9th month, 1655.

This letter being read and taken into consideration, it [was] ordered that an answer should be sent thereunto, with a letter of testimony, according to the desire of our brother. Which accordingly was done; copies whereof follow:

A copy of the letter sent to our brother Tho. Disbrowe.

The brethren in and about Caxton and Fenystanton, to our beloved brother in the Lord, Tho. Disbrowe, do wish grace, mercy, and peace, from God the Father, and from the Lord Jesus, the Son of the Father, in truth and love.

Dearly beloved brother, we received your letter, dated the third day of the ninth month, which hath caused much joy and rejoicing in our spirits, being bound to return thanks to God in thy behalf, for the manifestation of his divine love to thy soul, in that time when thou wert deprived of the society of the saints. For of a truth this was even to try thee, that the trial of thy faith might be much more precious than gold that is seven times refined. Wherefore,

515

beloved brother, we beseech thee to mind the dealings of God towards thee. Lay them up in thy heart. Meditate upon them continually, that thereby thou mayest be kept steadfast and immoveable in the ways of our God; which is the earnest and continual prayer of thy brethren in the Lord Jesus Christ; and likewise that thou mayest be filled with the fruits of righteousness and holiness, being strengthened by the Spirit of our God, until thou comest to the measure of the stature of the fulness of Christ. But now, brother, since the Lord hath caused thee at length to enjoy that which thou didst so much want and so earnestly desire, even the society of the saints, we desire thee to prize the mercies of God. Oh! let the consideration of them draw forth thy soul to praise Him more and more, and to wait upon Him with constancy, knowing that He will never leave nor forsake those that trust in Him. Brother, we have thought meet to satisfy thy desires, in sending thee a letter of testimony, to certify the brethren that thou art a member of the church of Christ. The Lord be with thy spirit.

Farewell.

Thy brethren assembled in the name of our Lord Jesus Christ.

Caxton,

The 30th day of the 10th month, 1655.

A copy of the letter of testimony.

The brethren in and about Caxton and Fenystanton, to all the churches of Christ whom this may concern, wish grace, mercy, and peace, from God the Father, and from the Lord Jesus Christ, the Son of the Father, in truth and love.

Dear and holy brethren, we commend unto you our beloved brother Thomas Disbrowe, he being a member of the church of our Lord Jesus Christ, received by us, according to the order of the gospel. Wherefore we beseech you to receive him in the Lord, as becometh saints, and to assist him in whatsoever business he shall stand in need of you; and we shall account it as done unto ourselves. Farewell.

Your brethren in the Lord Jesus Christ.

Caxton.

The 30th day of the 10th month, 1655.[13]

ENDNOTES

[1]Edward Bean Underhill, ed. (for the Hanserd Knollys Society), *Records of the Churches of Christ gathered at Fenstanton, Warboys and Hexham* (1854) 18-19.

[2]Underhill 42.

[3]Underhill 58.

[4]Underhill 71.

[5]Underhill 82.

[6]Underhill 81.

[7]Underhill 86.

[8] Underhill 253.

[9]Underhill 229 ff.

[10]Underhill 149.

[11]Underhill 267.

[12]Underhill 105.

[13]Underhill 163. Also see David Douglas of Hamsterley, *History Of The Baptist Churches In The North Of England From 1648 To 1845* (1846) 33-34.

17

CHURCHES OF CHRIST IN ENGLAND IN THE LATE 1600s AND THE PORTSMOUTH DEBATE

> But sanctify the Lord God in your hearts: and be ready always to give an answer to every man that asketh you a reason of the hope that is in you with meekness and fear (1 Peter 3:15).

> Let your speech be always with grace, seasoned with salt, that ye may know how ye ought to answer every man (Colossians 4:6).

The Great Debate, held at Portsmouth and the decline of the church of Christ due to apostasy from Calvinism and Quakerism

The seventeenth century closed with a then famous debate at Portsmouth, on the south coast of England. The debate is fascinating, held at a time when religious liberty was beginning to be allowed. This was due to the Act of Toleration, May 24th 1689, that granted limited freedom of worship to nonconformists. When soldiers would be present to prevent disorder and rioting as required by the terms of licence for the debate.

The account of the debate is from J. Jackson Goadby's 1871 work, *Bye-Paths in Baptist History*. Goadby was a General Baptist whose

518

congregation dates back to the churches of Christ of the seventeenth century. Goadby's account is remote from the debate by two hundred years, his sources unknown today, which we at best must consider second or third hand. To him we must rely for information and his biases, demonstrated on more than one occasion, are obvious, as we shall see. Nonetheless, Goadby's account is a marvelous view into a debate just prior to most churches of Christ turning Baptist.

Samuel Chandler, a Presbyterian minister of Fareham, established a fortnightly lectureship at Portsmouth. In his lectures, he defended infant baptism, speaking out harshly against those who practised believers' baptism. His remarks were reported by a person long forgotten, who wrote down what Chandler had said. This was relayed to Thomas Bowes, preacher at the church of Christ in Portsmouth.

At the next lecture, a number of persons were present who held to believers' baptism. Thomas Bowles accused Samuel Chandler of preaching false doctrine, proposing a debate, which was accepted. The only condition laid down by Chandler was that his opponent "should be a man who understood the laws of disputation." The Presbyterians then applied to the town magistrates to obtain a licence from the King "publicly to vindicate the common cause of the Reformed churches and settle the wavering in the belief and practice of those truths which tend very much to the advancement of early piety and religion." The licence was granted. Both sides looked to the ablest of champions for their cause.

Bowes conferred with Mr Webber, the Particular Baptist minister of the town. A debate was arranged between the parties. William Russell, M.D., the well-known church of Christ preacher from London, was chosen to defend believers' baptism. Assisting Russell in the position of "junior counsel" and "moderator," were John Williams, of East Knowle, and John Sharpe, of Frome, both Particular Baptist ministers. The Presbyterians selected Samuel Chandler, Mr. Leigh, of Newport, and Mr. Robinson of Hungerford. The debate was held in the Presbyterian meeting house February 22, 1698 or 1699. The governor and lieutenant-governor, the mayor and magistrates of Portsmouth were present. The military were also there at the command of the King's licence to insure orderly conduct and peace. The debate continued nine hours. The debate came to an end between six and seven o'clock p.m..

A few days later, an article was published in the *Postman* newspaper, from the pen of Colonel John Gibson, the Lieutenant-Governor:

> Portsmouth, Feb. 23rd Yesterday, the dispute between the Presbyterians and the Anabaptists was held in the Presbyterian meeting-house. It began at ten o'clock in the morning, and continued till six in the afternoon, without intermission. The theme of the dispute was; the subject of baptism, and the manner in which it is to be

performed. Russell and Williams were the opponents for the Anabaptists, and Mr Chandler and Mr Leigh for the Presbyterians; Mr Sharpe was moderator for the former, and Mr Robinson for the latter, Mr Russell opposed infant baptism with all the subtlety and sophistry of the schools; and it was answered with good reason and learning. Upon the whole, it was the opinion of all the judicious auditory, the Presbyterians sufficiently defended their doctrines, and worsted their adversaries, when they came to assume the place of opponents.

Another article was in the *Flying Post,* which was, according to Goadby, one sided and unfair. Dr. Russell published an account of the debate which brought an answer from the Presbyterians. The debate and these various articles and replies occasioned much bitterness. During this period, many churches of Christ had either taken onboard reformed doctrine, becoming Baptist, or, as in the case of the Portsmouth brethren, were soon to follow. As Protestants, they were seeking fellowship with others who held to reformed doctrine. This would result in a dislike of debating with those whom they considered brethren.

William Russell's account, as recorded by an unknown acquaintance, and was planned with the Presbyterians for publication, who pulled out of the venture to publish the debate. As noted above, this record is preserved by the Rev. J Jackson Goadby in his *Bye-Paths in Baptist History*, 1871. I have retained the punctuation.

> The debate began somewhere between nine and ten in the morning, continuing for about nine hours, without

cessation. Mr Chandler commenced by delivering a "prologue," and repeating questions to be disputed, namely, 1/ Whether according to the commission of our Lord and Saviour Jesus Christ, adult believers are the only proper subjects of baptism, and not infants? 2/ Whether the ordinance of baptism, as appointed by Christ, is to be administered by dipping, plunging, or overwhelming only, and not otherwise? They affirm, and we deny.

Dr Russell, after a few preliminary questions and answers, leads off the debate. He affirms that Christ nowhere requires any of His ministers to baptise infants, and therefore the baptism of infants is not according to his commission. Mr Chandler replies, "If you will allow good consequences drawn from Scripture, I will deny your minor." "Then you must suppose that Christ hath required some of His ministers to baptise infants," said Dr Russell. Mr Chandler's answers, "We do distinguish between consequential truth and express words." "So do we," answers Dr Russell; "but I hope our Lord's commission about holy baptism is delivered in express words, and not in consequentials. The term of my argument is very lax; I do not say there 'command', but 'required' and if you prove the baptism of infants anywhere 'required' by Christ, it is sufficient."

Mr Leigh here interposes to ask if the doughty champion of the Baptists "will allow good Scripture consequences in the case, or whether he expects plain Scripture words?" "If you can prove without express command, prove, that is, that Christ 'required' it, that will suffice; but," adds the doctor, "you must remember that you are to prove it according to Christ's commission (for those are the terms of the question), and I believe you will find it a difficult task to do that by consequence.' 'What! From the commission?" asked Chandler in amazement; whereupon the Presbyterian moderator, Mr Robinson, declares that Dr Russell must prove his position by a universal negative. Nothing loth, the doctor asks that Mr Chandler should deny some part of his argument, a thing he had not yet prevailed upon him to do, and presently says "if the requiring of infant baptism be anywhere recorded in Holy Scripture, either Mr Chandler, or some other person, is able to show it. But neither Mr Chandler, nor any other is able to show it; therefore, it is not anywhere so recorded in Holy Scripture." Mr Chandler, being thus pinned in a corner, seeks to escape by "denying Dr Russell's minor;" upon which the doctor appeals to the Presbyterian moderator, that he (the moderator) had asked for "an universal negative," that one had now been given, and that Mr Chandler was therefore bound, in all fairness, to give a single instance where it was so written that infants should be baptised. Conscious of his own mistake, the moderator replies "Suppose Mr Chandler cannot given an instance, nor anybody in the company, you cannot thence infer that none in the world can." But this evasive answer calls for a biting reply from Dr Russell. "What is this," said he, "but in effect to give away your cause, when so many men of parts and learning are here present? If you all refuse to give a single instance, the people will think that you have none to give."

The doctor, begging the audience to notice that his first argument stands until the instance asked for is given, now marshals his second, which is as follows: "If infants are not capable of being made disciples of Christ by the ministry of men; therefore they cannot possibly be subjects of baptism intended in Christ's commission." A dispute at once followed as to whether Dr Russell meant by 'making disciples, actual and complete disciples,' Mr Leigh (Presbyterian) urging, 'I thus distinguish: infants may be entered into the church in order for learning, etc., and they are disciples before baptism; yet, in a more visible sense, they are made disciples by baptism." This does not satisfy Dr Russell; "infants have, as infants, no knowledge of good and evil, and therefore they are not capable, while they are infants, to be made disciples by the ministry of men." Chandler here complains that Russell "tricks all the while; that what he (Chandler) means by infants being disciples, is their being solemnly invested by baptism;" But Russell declares he is discussing "perquisites for baptism," and was not speaking of "investiture." A second time the debate falls into dispute about "complete" discipleship; and Chandler, confessing that infants were not, as infants, capable of that, Russell claims to have maintained his second argument. "It is now, therefore, high time I descended into a new one."

The "new argument" should be specially observed, from the shuffling method by which Mr Leigh sought to meet it. "If the Apostle Paul did declare all the counsel of God, and kept back nothing that was profitable for the Church of God, and yet did never declare the baptism of infants to be a Gospel institution, according to Christ's commission, then it is no Gospel institution, nor any part of the counsel of God, nor profitable for the Church of God; but the Apostle Paul did declare all the counsel of God, and kept back nothing that was profitable for the Church of God; and yet did never declare the baptism of infants to be a Gospel institution, according to Christ's commission; therefore it is no Gospel institution, nor any part of the counsel of God, nor profitable for the church of God." Mr Leigh's method of replying to this argument is, by suggesting that Paul, wrote divers Epistles upon many subjects; that evidently some leaves were cut off from one of his Epistles, that to the Ephesians; and that, for anything that Dr Russell might know contrary, Paul might have advocated infant baptism in one or other of these missing leaves! The doctor replies to Mr Leigh's miserable shift by asking him pointedly if he believes with the Assembly of Divines, that the Scripture of the Old and New Testaments are the only rule to direct us in matters of worship; and by demanding that Mr Leigh, or some of his friends, should produce these six missing leaves of the Epistle of Paul (of which he had never before heard), and prove they really were written by Paul; and then, if such a thing as infant baptism were contained in any of them, he would allow it. "Hereupon Mr Leigh was angry;" and no wonder. He still, however, reiterated his statement in another form. "Paul's writings are not the hundredth part of what Paul preached; we cannot suppose that in these six chapters to the Ephesians, he could contriver to put down the whole of his preaching in them." Here Dr Russell sarcastically twits Leigh with favouring the Popish notion of the value of tradition, in his talk about Paul's sermons, "not written." "I have heard," he says, "of some unwritten traditions that are locked up in the Pope's breast, to be delivered out as he finds occasion to serve a turn; but I never knew that the Presbyterians were ever entrusted with any such treasure!"

Triumphing over his opponents in his third argument, Dr Russell now adduces his forth; "Christ's commission doth show who are to be baptised; but it doth not show that infants are to be baptised; therefore infants are not the subjects of baptism, according to Christ's commission." Mr Leigh objects; again cites his former statement, that children are included in the term "all nations;" and a second time repeats the opinion, that there is no necessity for persons to be disciples, in the doctor's sense, before they are baptised. Then Dr Russell, a little piqued by the stale repetition, replies, "I will read my Master's commission;" and forthwith slowly reads Matthew 28:19

"Go ye therefore, and teach all nations, baptizing them in the name of the Father, and of the Son, and of the Holy Ghost."

Here the Presbyterian moderator bawls very loudly, saying, "Mr Williams, will you suffer him to preach?" But the doctor is not to be put down by clamor, nor yet by the insinuation that he is going to preach Arminian doctrine, and so offend his Calvinistic colleague, Mr Williams. "What" said Dr Russell to the Presbyterian moderator, "do you talk of preaching? Are you afraid of the commission? Are you not in danger earning Tertullian's reproach of one of the Fathers, that he was Lucifuge Scripturarum ect., as Tertullian called heretics, Lucifuge Scripturarum, because they would not be cured of their errors; so are such men also afraid to bring their hearts to the test of the Word, because they would not be cured of their false presumptions, flying from the light of the Scriptures, as bats from the light of the sun?" And declares that if his opponents, who are sticklers for the Institutes of the Genevan Reformer should oppose what he (Dr Russell) had said, they would at the same time oppose Calvin himself, who had not only declared that there was no mention made of infants in the commission, but had further said, that we might well apply these words to little infants: "If any will not work, neither shall he eat (2Th 3:10), and so keep them from food until they starve!"

This apt question from Calvin displeased the Presbyterian moderator, who asked, in querulous tones, "what have we to do with what Mr Calvin says?" To which the doctor slyly rejoins, "I did not know but you might have had a veneration for Mr Calvin; but seeing it otherwise, I will thus argue from the commission:" And then proceeds

526

to give his own view of it. A squabble presently arises between Mr Leigh and the moderator of his party; and Dr Russell thinks that the two had better change places; Mr Leigh becomes moderator and Mr Robinson disputant. After this escapade on the moderators part (who seems to have been very unfit for his responsible post), the wordy war proceeds, Russell affirming, Leigh denying, now in one way now in another, that the commission only warrants the baptism of believers.

Mr Leigh touches by-and-by upon dangerous ground. He argues that "if believing be previous to baptism, it must be necessary to salvation; and so you must say, that all not believing are damned; and so all infants are damned." Russell declares that this is a *non sequitur*, as he has already shown that infants are not at all intended in the commission; "but," be solemnly adds, "as touching infants, I am far from believing that God hath decreed them as such, to eternal damnation, I will rather believe that all infants dying in their infancy, are elected than conclude any of them are dammed." He asks, moreover, that as he has so freely expressed his opinion upon this subject of infant salvation, the Presbyterians should be equally outspoken concerning their opinions on the same subject. But he asks in vain!

Mr Williams (Particular Baptist), next suggests Erasmus' reading of the commission "Go, teach all nations, and when they have learned, did them;" but the Presbyterian moderator again forgets his duties, and appeals to the audience: "You see, sir, this gentleman grounds his opinion upon the authority of Erasmus, who is well known to have been between a papist and a protestant," chimes in Mr Leigh. But both Russell and Williams argue that, whatever his opinions, Erasmus was not to be despised

527

for his skill about the etymology of a Greek word; and it was his judgment, as one of the best scholars of his time, and to his authority, that led to his being quoted; "but" says Russell, with some exhibition of temper, "anything serves your turn at a pinch."

Mr Leigh again makes an unfortunate slip, which Dr Russell, as a controversialist, quickly takes up, and makes merry over, namely, unspeaking about eunuchs and "the eunuchs children." Russell at once recollects an amusing story of another Presbyterian minister who had made the same blunder, and cannot forbear telling it with the evident gusto of an "M.D. of the famous University of Cambridge."

Mr Williams, the "junior counsel," now relieves Dr Russell of the leading part in the debate. He (Mr Williams) argues, that since infants are incapable of denying themselves Christ, they are incapable of being made disciples of Christ. Of course, Mr Leigh, who has been left by Mr Chandler to do the hardest part of the work, objects to this, and asks "if infants are not as capable of believing in Christ, as of coming to Christ; and yet they were said to come when their parents brought them." Mr Williams denies the parent's faith was imputed to the children, as Mr Leigh suggests. Again a rather dangerous concession was made by the leading Presbyterian disputant; Mr Leigh said, in effect, that infant baptism might be practised in the apostolic or early times, though no instance was recorded in the New Testament. At this Dr Russell wakes up again and asks if he (Leigh) will grant that no case is recorded in the New Testament? "We will suppose it" he replies "but not grant it." "O yes," adds the doctor, "you suppose it but cannot prove it; for you are not so free of your concessions." This stirs up Mr Leigh's anger, and he replies with tartness, "It is not recorded in the New Testament what you practise; namely, that grown children of believers were baptized, I challenge you to give one instance of any one, born of believing parents, baptized at age." Dr Russell here repeats his former challenge, for a single instance in the New Testament of any one infant that was ever baptized; and as Mr Leigh presses for an example of a child of believing parents who was baptized, he refers to Constantine, whose mother Helen was a Christian, and declares that he does not recollect a single instance of any one of the Fathers, or eminent bishops of the Church during the first five hundred years of the Christian era, who were baptized until they were between twenty and thirty years of age; and if any of his opponents know an instance to the contrary, he shall be glad if they will quote it. "What do you tell us of Fathers?" Asks Mr Leigh: "We are not bound to abide by their testimony." "Well then," asks Mr Williams, "was not the mother of our Lord a believer when Christ was born?" Mr Leigh is angry that such question should be asked; and declares, with some exhibition of impatience, "that everybody knows that she was." "But do you believe it?" rejoins Mr Williams, following up the advantage he has gained by this adroit question. "Yes, I do believe it: What then?" "Then, this," replies Mr Williams, "here is an instance for you, from Scripture, of a child believer, that was a believer before he was born; and yet he was not baptized till he came to years; and this we can prove."

A general titter ran through the crowded assembly at the skilful manner in which Mr Leigh was caught; and Mr Leigh grew pale and troubled, as a man might be expected to do under such uncomfortable circumstance; but he presently recovered his self possession, and replied, "Our discourse was grounded on the commission; now was this before the commission, or after it?" A skilful parry, but losing its effect through coming rather as an after-thought than as a prompt and instantaneous reply. Of course, Dr Russell now came to the rescue of his "junior," showed that Mr Leigh was mistaken, and that he really had received "a pertinent answer already, every way suitable to his question." There must have been more laughter among the audience at this point, since Mr Leigh "made no more reply." He is nothing daunted, however; and proceeds to show that, in his judgment, "infants are visible Church members," the proof-passage being the words of Christ, "suffer little children to come unto me, and forbid them not, for of such is the kingdom of heaven." Mr Williams' reply to this is, that infants are neither members of the universal Church, nor yet of a particularly constituted church, and therefore they are not members of the visible Church at all. His opponent does not notice his argument, but again declares that infants are part of a nation, and therefore might be baptized. Mr Williams answers, "Though children are part of a nation, yet not of the nation modified by Christ's commission."

Upon this the Presbyterian moderator rather rudely calls the attention of the audience to the fact that Mr Williams "has no academical learning;" Mr Williams rejoins with a touch of sarcasm, "I am warned by that word to have a care of vain philosophy;" and at once asked "what was the antecedent to the relative them in the commission?" The moderator now found it wiser to be silent; but both Dr Russell and Mr Williams answered for him, "all nations discipled." They both again asked for a single instance of infant baptism from the Word of God; and no reply being forthcoming, Dr. Russell said, "If infants are capable of being made disciples of Christ by the ministry of men, without the use of reason, then the beasts of the field are also capable; but the beasts of the field are not capable; therefore infants are not capable."

This reply greatly agitated the irritable Presbyterian moderator. He stood up and threw himself about, making a noise like one in a delirious paroxysm, and bade the people take notice that Dr Russell had ranked their infants among the brute beasts; and that, if they became of his opinion, they must look upon them as dogs, or cats, or hogs etc., with much more of the same sort of rhetoric, endeavouring all he could to enrage the multitude of unthinking persons against him, and put the people into confusion. "Hold, hold" cries Dr Russell, "Mr Robinson, I have already told you how great an esteem I have for your little infants... I now bring this illustration to show the absurdity of your opinions: Suppose there were twenty or thirty new born infants in a room, and you should choose out of the most able and learned persons amongst you to preach to them, in order to make them disciples, according to Christ's commission, I believe he would have no better success than St. Anthony had, as the story goes, when he took upon him to instruct the pigs; or, as some others have done, even Popish saints, who have taken upon them to preach to the fowls of the air etc." His remark about the beasts, is, after all, he says, not such an out-of-the-way "conceit," since the Romish Church baptises bells, which are certainly passive in their baptism, and on that account, says Augustine, "the fittest subjects since children show their resistance by crying!" "And now," said he, "I demand of any of you to take off the retortion, and show the disparity if you can."

A general silence ensues, which is at length broken by the undaunted Mr Leigh, who exclaims, "It is time to proceed to the other question: Whether the ordinances of baptism, as appointed by Christ, is to be administered by dipping, plunging, or overwhelming only, and not otherwise." Dr Russell meets this by saying: "The Holy Scriptures shows us the right way of baptising as appointed by Christ, but it doth not show us that it ought to be done by sprinkling; therefore sprinkling is not the right way of baptising." This did not satisfy Mr Leigh who at once exclaimed; "Sir, you must bring in that dipping is absolutely necessary; what do you talk of sprinkling for?" Here is another opportunity for a smart retort, and Dr Russell could not resist it; "I hope you are not ashamed of your practice; but if you will disown sprinkling to be the right way of baptising, I am contented. I will not then insist upon it." Mr Robinson, the moderator, felt the force of this retort; and as Mr Leigh was silent, Mr Robinson said; "We are not discoursing upon that now; you are to prove dipping to be the only way; and you must and shall is for the king, and not for Mr Robinson."

The debate then turns to the meaning of the Greek word (Baptizo) translated *baptize*, and Mr Chandler, who had been silent during the greater part of the day, now opens his lips. He confesses that *baptize* means to dip, but it means also to *wash*; and declares that there is great probability that many in the Scripture times were baptised by pouring a little water on the face. Dr Russell meets his new antagonist by quoting what "Astedius saith in his *Lexicon Theologicum*," showing that it was only in a secondary and remote sense that the word *baptize* can mean "to wash;" and quotes, in confutation of the other part of Chandler's statement, the baptism of Christ by John, and the Eunuch by Peter, where both administrator and "person baptized" went into the water.

A good deal of confused jangling and noise followed Russell's reply, when a new opponent suddenly starts up, a Presbyterian minister, who thinks that had been little said to purpose; whereupon Russell at once says that, on the contrary, he thinks a good deal has been said, and I will dispute it over with you, *de novo* (from the beginning). The Presbyterian minister shrugged his shoulders at this unexpected challenge, declared, that, "he did not feel very well;" and, in fact, declined to pick up the gauntlet.

The debate came to an end between six and seven o'clock. Mr Leigh returned thanks to the governor and mayor for their civility, which the Baptists very promptly endorsed. Two "scribes" were employed to take short-hand notes of the debate, but when the "Baptist Scribe" went to the Presbyterian "Scribe" in order to compare notes, the Presbyterian declined, pleaded he had never been engaged in such a work, and his account was very imperfect, nor was a copy of his "imperfect" work ever seen.

A great deal of bitterness was caused by the debate, which was felt for some time afterwards. The purpose in taking on Protestant beliefs was to find friends in a world of religious persecution, not make enemies. The debate had made enemies which for many of the period was counterproductive. Debates of this type would cease as the "Baptists" slowly moved towards the denominational and reformed position. It would not be until the Restoration Movements in Great Britain and America that such debates would start again along with the revival of the nineteenth century church of Christ.

The Act did not give complete freedom. For example the Act of 1688 was "An Act for the Amoving Papists and reputed Papists from the Cityes of London and Westminster and Ten Miles distance from the same." There was another act against Roman Catholics in 1701 and 1716. It was not until 1778, almost ninety years after the Act of Toleration, was freedom granted to Roman Catholics and others. The Act of Toleration was really freedom for Protestants which resulted in many churches of Christ taking a denominational stance, calling themselves Baptist and becoming Calvinist. Whilst in the words of William Howitt in reference to the Church of England, "the blatant beast muzzled but still mischievous." As such it was not religious freedom. A heavy price was paid by anyone not an Anglican or Protestant.

The newly forming Baptist denominations were desperate to be of the world. This would offer schooling, access to finance and improved status in society. They sought fellowship with the Presbyterian party who in turn based their confession of faith on the Westminster Confession (Church of England).

It is interesting to see how biblical churches over many years slowly became a denomination—The Baptist Church, a protestant denomination. They rejected penance, etc. (Anglo-Catholic), but firmly turned to reformed doctrine.

Despite the grievances, the recounted debate above did not result in the animosity of that held with the Presbyterians, on the same subject, about forty-five years earlier. In 1643, Benjamin Cox, a Church of England Bishop's Son and the preacher of the church of Christ at Bedford, after debating, was sent to jail. In 1643 it was illegal to preach against infant baptism and preach believers' baptism. The opponents and subject was the same "infant baptism" at Coventry with the Presbyterians. Who won the debate we do not know, but the Presbyterians having initially encouraged the debate called for the constabulary, who had arrested Benjamin Cox, which promptly finished the debate. He was ordered to leave Coventry, he refused to go, and was immediately sent to jail. He was released shortly afterwards after agreeing to leave the city.[1] Such was the oppression of that time. Had he refused to leave, he would have been left to starve in jail.

In 1657, the church at Bedford appointed John Bunyan, who frequently clashed with Henry Denne, as a preacher. The Bedford church became more prone towards Calvinism (as did others), Bunyan himself disagreed with salvation at the point of baptism allowing for the baptism of infants, saying of believers baptism "I will not make an idol of it." In 1673, Bunyan published his *Differences In Judgment About Water-Baptism No Bar To Communion,* in which he took the ground that "the Church of Christ hath not warrant to keep out of the communion the Christian that is discovered to be a visible saint of the word, the Christian that walketh according to his own light with God." While he owned "water baptism to be God's ordinance," he refused to make "an idol of it," as he thought those did who made the lack of it a ground for disfellowshiping those recognized as genuine Christians. Kiffin and Paul published a rejoinder in *Serious Reflections* (London, 1673), in which they ably set forth the argument in favour of the restriction of the Lord's Supper to baptized believers, and received the approval of Henry D'Anvers in his *Treatise of Baptism* (London, 1674). The result of the controversy was to leave the question of communion with the unbaptised an open one. Bunyan's church admitted pedobaptists to fellowship and finally became pedobaptist (Congregationalist).[2]

By the beginning of the seventeenth century, churches of Christ existed throughout England and in Europe. By the end of the century, most were overtaken by two errors, the first, the Augustinian theology of the Reformers, which resulted in Lutherism and Calvinism, the second the more problematic—denominationalism. The term "Baptist" was coined by the apostate churches of Christ, who sought a new name, after they had declared themselves Protestant in the late 1670s. At first they called themselves "baptised congregation" which became "baptised church" and later Baptist church. Not all the churches of Christ agreed with this, but those who termed themselves Protestants associated with the Presbyterians and a new denomination was born – the Baptists.

Augustine's introduced the doctrine of original sin, infant baptism and predestination into the developing Roman Catholic Church, beliefs which were founded on paganism. From there it continued into all the reformation churches. Modified further into Calvinism, it was then adopted into the church of Christ making such congregations Baptist. The Roman Catholic Church kept Augustinian theology restricted to original sin and infant baptism, through which faith could enter the child. But as previously mentioned, the state (national) churches which the reformation produced, whether Catholic or Protestant, were founded together on Augustinian theology despite the Protestants claim of *sola scriptura*. As previously stated, you cannot restore that which did not previously exist. The Roman Catholic Church was never the church of the New Testament.

Protestantism, with the denial that baptism saves, the one man pastor system, associations, which in many ways were a type of presbytery, the academy (bible school), along with a new denominational name—The Baptist Church. Many of those Baptist denominations are happy to advertise they hold to "reformed doctrine." Something their forbears opposed, denying they were Protestant.

Bible schools in themselves are not wrong, but, when error enters such institutions, a medium for rapidly disseminating error exists. Both sides of the churches of Christ had their institutions for teaching by the 1660s.

What destroyed many churches of Christ was not persecution,

which it had suffered for centuries, but error from inside the church. Paul's warning to the Ephesian elders leaves a message they should have heeded and remains relevant today. "For I know this, that after my departing shall grievous wolves enter in among you, not sparing the flock" (Acts 20:29). When the churches departed from scripture, the council of God, to the teaching and ordinances of men, grievous wolves entered in.

There were three clear divisions by the end of the seventeenth century: the first, those who argued the gospel agency (the Spirit working through the word) who retained the identity "Church of Christ." Secondly, those who adopted the mid-way position of Arminianism, which is a light version of Calvinism. The second (of the two) are known as General Baptists because, in spite of their weak Calvinism (Arminianism), they held to a possible redemption of all mankind. The Calvinists, the third division, were known as the Particular Baptists. After 1890 many General Baptist congregations, by then known as the New Connexion, joined with the majority of Particular Baptists in the Baptist Union.

One church of Christ, at Kirkby, and a second in St. Ives, Cambridgeshire remained to join in fellowship with the Restoration Movement in the nineteenth century. The St. Ives congregation became in the 1960s part of the United Reformed Church. The story of the Kirkby congregation is in the next chapter.

According to Herbert Skeats, there were no "Baptists" in England holding to Calvinism prior to about 1640 (page 32). Skeats was an independent dissenter with no Baptist affiliations, having no axe to grind.[3] Skeats confirms that Baptists existed (those who practised believers' baptism), but not those of the Calvinistic (reformed) party.

Thomas Crosby, who I have quoted earlier, wrote in 1738. He interviewed those witnesses who knew first-hand of the changes that had taken place that led to the Baptist denominations.

> It may be proper to observe here, that there have been two parties of the English Baptists ever since the beginning of the reformation; those that have followed the Calvinistical scheme or doctrines, and from the principal points therein, personal election, and have been termed Particular Baptists; and those that have professed the Arminian or remonstrant tenets; and have also from the chief of those doctrines, universal redemption, been called General Baptists.[4]

Crosby distinguishes a third group, "There were likewise many Baptists in England who did not choose to assume either name, because they receive what they think to be truth, without regarding with what human schemes it agrees or disagrees."[5]

Controversy was not limited to Freewill, Arminianism and Calvinism, arguments over which first started in about 1644. Other issues vexed the brotherhood from the 1650s causing division. These included foot-washing, the laying-on of hands, singing (many congregations did not sing. This started as a precaution to avoid notice by their enemies and in time became, for some, a doctrine), fellowship meals. Modern issues such as divorce and the instrument did not cause major upset due to few brethren divorcing and the unacceptability of the instrument in the denominations. Family ties being much stronger, less money being available and short life expectancy meant that divorce was largely unheard of. The instrument had not in that time found its way into use in independent congregations, so was not an issue.

Several movements that caused division inside the church of Christ, taking entire congregations, include congregationalism which led to the Baptists (Calvinistic variety), Seekers, Ranters and Quakers. In 1677, the Calvinist party proposed a "Confession of Faith, put forward by the elders and brethren of many congregations of Christians (baptized upon Profession of their Faith) in London and the Country."

This confession is noteworthy; the Calvinists call themselves "Christians" who are "baptized upon Profession of their Faith." They no longer identify themselves as "Churches of Christ," as presumably, it was too contentious. The introduction reads:

> ...with many others whose orthodox confessions have been published to the world, on the behalf of the protestants in diverse nations and cities; and also to convince all that we have no itch to clog religion with new words, but readily acquiesce in that form of sound words which hath been, in consent with the holy scriptures, used by others before

us; hereby declaring before God, angels, and men, our
hearty agreement with them, in that wholesome protestant
doctrine, which, with so clear evidence of scriptures they
have asserted.

This confession is in agreement with the protestant religion present in England, at the time Presbyterian or Congregational. These they now regard as brethren, though not in agreement over some issues such as baptism. It is divisive from their former brethren who held to believers' baptism. They still hold to baptism as being for the "remission of sins," but also to the Calvinistic scheme of redemption. This confession, though not signed by all the Calvinistic congregations, is a significant step towards the founding of the various Baptist congregations and agreement with reformed and Catholic theology of depravity, requiring supernatural agency (the Holy Spirit) working in addition and apart from the word, rather than the Spirit working through the word (gospel agency).[6] Just how Protestant this confession is will be revealed later in this chapter. Some from the Arminian party responded with a similar confession in 1679, addressed as "An Orthodox Creed or a Protestant Confession of Faith." Again, the identity "Baptist Church" is not used but they acknowledge being part of the Reformed religion.[7] The 1677 confession is also known as the 1689 confession.

Slowly the Baptist denomination was appearing. Prior to these two confessions, although there were churches of Christ in error, there was no Baptist church. Even with these two confessions, only the foundations are being formed of what in the next century would become numerous Baptist denominations.

As noted in Henry D'Anvers' work, *A Treatise of Baptism*, 1674, "Protestants," when mentioned, are seen as a distinct group, separate from the church. D'Anvers was an evangelist of a church of Christ, a congregation in Staffordshire, when he wrote the book.

Henry Denne, in his work *Antichrist*, which sets out his argument against Daniel Featley, makes an interesting point:

> But before I leave this argument, I deem it necessary, to give you the meaning of the text which is wrestled by the doctor – except a man be borne againe of water, and of the spirit, he cannot enter into the kingdome of heaven. I did make bold to tell the doctor to his face, that the protestants doe not understand this text of baptism. Which thing he confeffed, and said that the protestants, out of their zeale againft the papifts, did goe too farre on the right hand in the meaning of the text. How farre hee hath wandred on the left hand, let all be judge.
>
> Cardinal Bellamin confeffeth that the protestants doe not make ufe of this Text as not acknowledging the necessity of baptism unto salvation, which this Text feemeth to hold forth.

Denne's comments confirm that he was not Protestant or Roman Catholic, that there were churches of Christ who did not hold to either scheme in the 1600s. The "doctor" is Daniel Featley, an Anglican theologian who defends infant baptism. The Protestants are clearly another group who, like Featley, and the papists, teach error. Denne also states the kingdom is the church, another doctrine Protestants have a problem with. He also says "we deny the minor proposition, and say that by denying them baptifme, we doe not at all exclude infants from the Kingdome of Heaven: But we say Children are as free from sinne, as fully in the favour and grace of God as before baptifme as after."[9] Denne denies both the Catholic and Protestant teaching on depravity (original sin and predestination). Henry Denne in 1658 wrote of the "protestant church", clearly showing the absurdity of the claims of both Protestants and Catholics regarding forgiveness of sins. Denne and his brethren were not Protestant or Catholic but members of the church of Christ founded on Biblical precept.[10]

The majority of modern Baptist historians go back to two beginnings, neither of which they can agree upon. The oldest was that of the Thomas Helwys' congregation in London about 1611, which was distinctly opposed to Calvinism and infant depravity and to Augustinian theology of the Roman Catholics and Reformers. They used the identity church of Christ and baptised by immersion for the remission of sins. Baptists, who recognise this as being the first Baptist congregation, then attack the Restoration Movement. They should take a step back and check what Helwys taught and practised, for these people, except in minor beliefs, stand with the

Restoration Movement of America and England of the late 1700s and early 1800s. Helwys was active two centuries before Campbell, to use Baptist terminology, a "Campbellite" two centuries before the Restoration Movement.

Another movement that was to split the church of Christ was congregationalism which later influenced the forerunners of the Baptist denominations. From the start the movement, which goes back to the late 1580s, had come out of the church of Christ. John Penry, an Oxford and Cambridge graduate, was involved from the start, but later withdrew, being an active preacher within the churches of Christ.[11] The two notable founders were John Greenwood and Robert Brown. Their congregational theology was Calvinist, but they rejected the Presbyterian plan following the Biblical congregationalism (autonomy) as practised by the churches of Christ. The movement was popular in Norwich and Colchester where the churches of Christ had existed for generations. They retained infant sprinkling, learned from the Calvinists, rather than believers' baptism by immersion. Many of the Pilgrim Fathers were congregational, but that is another story for investigating further. The congregational plan had been widely promoted by the London churches of Christ. When modified with infant baptism and Calvinism, it resulted in congregationalism. From the start, there was enmity between the two groups.

The Congregationalists in 1596 produced a "True Confession" setting out their beliefs. In about 1616, Henry Jacob set up a congregation in Southwark, London. It was congregational but with close ties to the Church of England. In 1622 Jacob left London for the American colonies. The congregation was established by John Lathrop from about 1624. After a spell in prison for "heresy," Lathrop followed Jacob to America in 1634. By 1637, Henry Jessey was the preacher, the congregation now meeting within the City near the Mansion House, close to the the Bow Lane and Bell Alley churches of Christ. In 1640, the congregation split amicably because of its size. At this time Samuel Howe, a preacher of a small church of Christ, joined with Jessey's congregation. Jessey himself had become involved with the churches of Christ, and with Howe's assistance, was trying to resolve the matter of infant and believers' baptism and Calvinism. In about 1642, a preacher of the church, Hanserd Knolleys, refused to have his child baptised. William Kiffin, a prosperous merchant, was an active member of the congregation and supported Knolleys in what was becoming a major source of contention within Jessey's congregation. Kiffin himself had been baptised into the church of Christ. This resulted in a major conference of London Independent congregations in 1643-4. The result of this conference was the creation of a new Independent congregation in London under William Kiffin. The congregation was formed on Calvinistic principles, infant baptism and teachings from the churches of Christ who practised believers' baptism. Jessey's congregation too was now practising believers' as well as infant baptism. Using the 1596 "True Confession," the seven congregations working together modified it to produce the famous "Baptist" 1644 confession (the word Baptist was not used by these brethren). The confession was sent to Daniel Featley, possibly the most well known Anglican theologian of the time and also to a parliament with Presbyterian leanings (Calvinist).[12]

This resulted in Calvinists, who were infant baptisers, apostates from the churches of Christ, working together with Anglicans and a Presbyterian Parliament, to produce a confession of faith. The only person missing was the king, Charles I executed in 1649, when the monarchy was abolished. A confession suitable to parliament, the Calvinists and the Anglicans (via Featly) was produced in 1646, known much later as the second Baptist confession of faith. Its title is *A Confession of faith of Seven Congregations or Churches of Christ in London.* By this time infant baptism had been dropped and believers' baptism by immersion for the remission of sins, as practised by the (non-Calvinistic) churches of Christ, instituted. These confessions, today called Baptist, although Calvinist in origin, they are congregational and denominational. These confessions would be used to subvert many churches of Christ from freewill to

Calvinism.

Baptists do not like reproducing the title page of this confession. That it does not use the name "Baptist" but "Churches of Christ" is something they apparently do not wish to be too well known. I am aware that originals of the 1646 confession can be found at Cambridge University Library (where the copy I refer to is kept), Trinity College, Cambridge, The British Library, Gould Collection, Oxford and The Bodleian Library, Oxford. That is five original copies in existence which means reproduction should present no great problem for what we are told is such an important confession.

The Calvinist Church of England produced the Westminster Confession of Faith in 1646. In part, the 1646 Baptist confession allowed for the Westminster Confession, but the "second" 1677 "London Baptist Confession of Faith" which did not use the word "Baptist," and was actually the third, not second, was based on the Westminster Church of England (Calvinist) confession.[12] The Baptists Confession of Faith used a Church of England Protestant confession, dated from 1646, and modified for their use. The 1644 and 1646 confessions too were modified from the Congregationists, Presbyterians and Anglicans. The desire to be part of the Protestant religion was there from the start, and became a denomination that in time would wear the name "Baptist." The Biblical name "church of Christ" would become too controversial.

After the death of Oliver Cromwell, in 1660 Parliament offered to restore the monarchy if Charles II would agree to concessions for religious toleration and a general amnesty. Charles II agreed to the proposals and the Church of England would from that time be Anglican. Many Calvinists were leaving, with many emigrating to the American colonies.

The 1689 Confession, the Westminster Confession, and Savoy Declaration are considered to be the most important Reformed Confessions made in the English-speaking world. There is no doubt that the 1689 confession relied heavily upon the drafting already done in writing the two other confessions (1646 & 1644), but this is not to understate its importance and influence in Baptist churches who held to reformed theology.

The Particular Baptists were quick to develop churches in colonial America, and in 1707 the Philadelphia Baptist Association was formed. This association formally adopted the 1689 confession in 1742, after years of tacit endorsement by individual churches and congregational members. With the addition of two chapters (on the singing of psalms and the laying on of hands), it was named *The Philadelphia Confession of Faith*. Further Calvinistic Baptist church associations formed in the mid-late 18th century and adopted the confession as "The Baptist Confession." The 1689 confession remains to this day a very important document for all Reformed

Baptist churches internationally, allowing them to have an historical confession of faith, but one based on a protestant denominational confession, viz., the Church of England 1646 confession.

From 1646, there are two clear parties within the churches of Christ in London: the Calvinistic party, which had apostatised from the existing churches of Christ; and those remaining faithful, possibly no more than three congregations in London but many outside. The Calvinistic party from the outset turned to world and denominations for acceptance and support. Romans 12:2 states, "And be not conformed to this world: but be ye transformed by the renewing of your mind, that ye may prove what is that good, and acceptable, and perfect, will of God."

James McGoldrick asks in his work *Baptist Successionism* "are Baptists Protestants?" and then affirms that such is the case. He argues successfully that their confessions and catechetical instructions are in theology Protestant. From this argument alone we can conclude the Baptists cannot be earlier than the Protestant Reformation, as they are Protestants.[13] Therefore, those congregations that called themselves churches of Christ, baptising by immersion repentant believers for the remission of sins, existed prior to the Baptists. They cannot be Baptist, as the world understands the Baptists today (those who hold to reformed theology). When Baptists claim successionism, they have but two options: to go back through time

to the churches of Christ; or, with their infant baptisers of the first
Baptist churches of the 1640s, to go back through the Church of
England to the Roman Catholic Church.

The predominant theology of the 1600s in England was
Calvinist. With a confession acceptable to Parliament, owing to a
denominational stance designed to please the Presbyterians, the new
movement was popular and evangelised well, not only establishing
new congregations, but turning existing congregations to the new
teaching. In practise there was little difference between the existing
congregations, preaching the gospel and adding members by
immersion for remission of sins. But the underlying theology was
Calvinist, but only of a moderate type that allowed evangelism.

Existing churches did not recognise the new faith, and those
who were baptised in the Calvinistic churches wishing to join the
existing churches were required to be baptised again. Sometimes
enmity was considerable, at other times members from both sides
were found cooperating.

Baptists who seek their origin have claimed, incorrectly, that
it was this group who reintroduced baptism by immersion for
believers. While they originally practised infant sprinkling, which
the Calvinists introduced into Britain (the Catholics and Anglicans
dipped infants prior to the 1640s), they learned of believers' baptism
(by immersion) from the existing non-Calvinistic churches of Christ

in London.

A strange irony for a group tied down with reformed theology was the retention of Baptism by immersion for remission of sins, as learned from the existing churches of Christ. Many Baptist groups to this day still baptise for remission of sins whereby entry is made into the church while retaining their Calvinistic theology.

Although some readers may object to my claims for the origin of the Baptist denominations, I rely on historical fact. Those Baptists opposed to what they call "Campbellism" must consider that Baptist origins are almost identical with those of the Restoration Movement. If "Campbellism" is error, so were those who existed prior to the Baptist denominations. The judge must be scripture. If "Campbellism" studied in light of scripture is correct, then it is the Baptist churches that lie in error, being apostate to the churches of Christ which existed prior to the sixteenth and seventeenth centuries, from whence the Baptist originated.

I have very briefly outlined the origins of the Baptists, as this book is not a history of the Baptists, but traces of God's people through the ages. A comprehensive history of the Baptist Church would be out of place here other than to establish their origin in the churches of Christ. I shall conclude here with Paul's statement in Galatians 4:16 – "Am I therefore become your enemy, because I tell you the truth?"

If the onslaught of Calvinism into the church were not enough, the next error was that of George Fox and Quakerism. Fox's uncle, Pickering, was a member of the church of Christ, and from this Fox became familiar with the various congregations. The Quakers built on the Seekers, who had been active from the 1620s and also caused problems within the church. Evidence is lacking as to how great a threat they were. The Quakers on the other hand are well documented; they turned entire congregations to the new belief and hence, presented a major problem.

As late as 1785, some congregations were still advocating the Gospel agency in conversion.

> On regeneration by the Holy Spirit. We believe that, as the scriptures assure us, we are justified, made the children of God, purified and sanctified by faith: That when a person come to believe in Jesus (and not before) he is regenerated or renewed in his soul, by the Spirit of God, through the instrumentality of the word, now believed and embraced. (Quoted from the "General Baptist, New Connexion" articles of faith).

They were still preaching the need of baptism for remission of sins as a requirement to entering the church.[14]

A member of one of the congregations of this group was William Whiston, who is best remembered today as an assistant to Sir Isaac Newton and author of A New Theory of the Earth From its Original to the Consummation of All Things (1696), an articulation of creationism and flood geology which held that the global flood of Noah had been caused by a comet. He obtained the praise of both Newton and Locke, the latter classing the author among those who, if not adding much to our knowledge "At least bring some new things to our thoughts." Whiston was accused of Arianism (a denial of the deity of the eternity of Christ, or his deity). Whiston had a happy family life and died in Lyndon Hall, Rutland, at the home of his son-in-law, Samuel Barker on 22 August 1752. For his Arian belief, he was dismissed from his professorship at Cambridge University. In 1745, Whiston was a member of the church of Christ at Morcott in Rutlandshire, a congregation which held a thoroughly orthodox view of Christ and His deity. Presumably by then Whiston had given up his Arian views, if indeed he ever held to such.

Today Whiston is best remembered for his 1732 translation of Josephus. At an earlier time, he was a preacher in the Church of England, during which time he was asked, regarding children, "would it not be better if baptism were deferred until after instruction?" To which Whiston replied, "I honestly confess, that I myself should have thought so, but I am no legislator; and submit to what I take to be a law of Christ." Afterwards he reflected on the matter, coming to the conclusion he was in the wrong church, and, in 1742, was baptised into the church of Christ, five years before his death.[15]

Whiston's close friend, Sir Isaac Newton (one of the greatest physicist who ever lived), declared it was "his conviction that the Baptists were the only Christians who had not symbolized with Rome." William Whiston, who records this statement, was the successor of Newton at Cambridge University, and lectured on Mathematics and Natural Philosophy before his dismissal noted previously.[16]

Newton never made a public declaration of his faith, but in view of the above, we can ask, was he a Christian? We do not know, but this statement points in that direction. There was a church of Christ meeting close by in Chesterton during Newton's time (there was nothing to stop him being a member).

Baptist historians in their books and websites too often remove the name "Church of Christ" from their sources, replacing the Bible name with either "Baptist church" or just "church." Both are a falsification of history. They have also neglected to mention the beliefs of those congregations prior to the 1650s; beliefs that identify not with the Baptists, but the churches of Christ in the nineteenth century revival, known as the Restoration Movement.

From the late 1600s and early 1700s, the Calvinistic Baptists became known as the Particular Baptists, then later just as Baptist. The one-man pastor system, the Lord's Supper held monthly, the associations becoming a type of presbytery, the denomination increased and divided to where it is today. As Calvinism became ingrained, the need to evangelise ceased. Evangelism is pointless when God determines through predestination who is and who is not saved. The Great Commission and Calvinism are opposed being contrary.

ENDNOTES

My source for the debate is: Rev. J Jackson Goadby, *Bye-Paths in Baptist History* (1871). Goadby was an English General Baptist historian.

[1] Regarding the act of Toleration, I've quoted from William Howitt, *Howitt's History of Priestcraft*, 8th ed. (1846) 195 ff. Cox from Thomas Crosby, *The History of the English Baptists*" vol. 1 of 4 vols. (London, 1738) 219.

[2] Bunyan, *The New Schaff-Herzog Encyclopedia of Religious Knowledge*, vol. 2.

[3] Herbert S. Skeats, *A History of the Free Churches of England, From A.D. 1688 – A.D. 1851* (1868) 32.

[4] Crosby 173.

[5] Crosby 174.

[6] William L. Lumpkin, *Baptist Confessions of Faith*, 6th print (1989) 235ff. It follows on the 1644 and 1646 confessions. It was not signed by many congregations, including those in the north of England.

[7] Lumpkin 297.

[8] John T. Christian, *Did They Dip?* (1896) 133.

[9] Henry Denne, *Antichrist* (1645)18-19. On page 8 Denne clearly states Baptism is "unto us Remission of Sins" and quotes Acts 2:38. The position he held (the biblical position) was called by adversaries "blood washing" because they rejected the Catholic holy water which had the power to remove sin holding that baptism works through the blood of Christ quoting Rev 1:5 And from Jesus Christ, who is the faithful witness, and the first begotten of the dead, and the prince of the kings of the earth. Unto him that loved us, and washed us from our sins in his own blood. The "confession" of 1660 (London) states "but all who come not first to repent of their sins, believe on the Lord Jesus, and so baptized in his name for remission of sins… we utterly deny" In article X1 the confession confirms that mode of baptism is to "dip," Lumpkin 226-8. The Calvinistic party (forerunners of the Baptists) in there "second" confession are explicit in stating "baptism is for remission of sins" Lumpkin 291.

[10] Henry Denne, *Grace Mercy and Peace* (1658) 43. Edward Bean Underhill,,

ed. (for the Hanserd Knollys Society), *Records of the Churches of Christ gathered at Fenstanton, Warboys and Hexham* (1854) 394.

[11]*A History of the Baptist Confessions* starting with the congregational 1596 being the basis of the 1644. Consequent confessions can be found in *Baptist Confessions of Faith*, William L. Lumpkin, 6th print (1989) 79.

[12]Lumpkin 241

[13]James Edward McGoldrick, *Baptist Successionism: A Crucial Question in Baptist History* (1994)136ff.

[14]Lumpkin 344.

[15]Adam Taylor, *The History of the English General Baptists* (1818) 428.

[16]John T. Christian, *A History of the Baptists*, vol. 1 (1922) 84. Also see chapter 11. Newton never made a public declaration of his faith, but in view of the above, we can ask, was he a Christian? We do not know, but this statement points in that direction. There was a church of Christ meeting in Cambridge at Hog Hill (now Downing Street or Downing Place), during Newton's time. This is where Robert Robinson preached in the mid 1700s. He was a local businessman and farmer at Chesterton and his quoted in chapter one of this book.

18

THE NORTH OF ENGLAND, TOTTLEBANK, ULVERSTON, FURNESS FELLS AND LATER CHURCHES OF CHRIST

Whosoever transgresseth, and abideth not in the doctrine of Christ, hath not God. He that abideth in the doctrine of Christ, he hath both the Father and the Son (2 John 1:9).

When Lollardy reached the north of England we do not know. Richard Wyche, as previously mentioned, had been active in the north prior to 1402. One of the towns he would have passed through, or, close to, Bedale, North Yorkshire, close to the Great North Road (London to Edinburgh), was a known source of Lollard belief. Here England is almost at its narrowest point; the journey from Bedale, through Wensleydale (part of the Yorkshires Dales), to Kendal, is fifty-four miles. The Lollards were active along this route and into the Furness Fells, where the abbot of Furness Abbey in the 1500s had confiscated Lollard books. Another source of Lollardy in the Fells was Hawkshead, a village later reported to have an "Anabaptist" congregation in the 1670s. From Kendal to Barrow-in-Furness, a port on the western side of North England, is another journey of forty-four miles.

The terrain, the fells and dales, is of high hills and mountains. Although beautiful today, it was then, bleak and sparsely populated especially in winter, where families and groups could live as Christians, away from the prying eyes of the authorities. Life was hard in the north, but safer than in the south and other locations nearer London where persecution was constant.

Kirkstone Pass, North West Cumbrian Fells

Lollardy was reported in the 1500s in Kendal and Richmondshire, in the Yorkshire Dales, mentioned by Margaret Spufford and Arthur Dickens. That we know little about this "heresy" is probably a mercy, if from this we many induce they were not persecuted to the point of extinction.[1]

In 1419 in Kirkby Stephen, about twenty-four miles from Kendal, Thomas Seggeswick was charged with being an accomplice of Lord Oldcastle and Lollardy though no further details are known. He was also described as a common cutthroat, but if this name calling were the case, a common thief was of no concern to the goverment.[2]

In York in 1533, a Dutchman called Lambert Sparrow was arrested, charged with heresy and tried in York, where he confessed the following beliefs: that the sacraments of the altar were bread and not Christ's body (a typical Lollard belief); that there is no temple of God except a man's body and soul; no priest can make one water holier than another; no priest or bishop can assoil any man of his sins; every man ought to be baptised in common water and any man may baptise another; there is no such thing as hallowed ground, no bishop of man can make one place holier than another; there is no purgatory; burial may be undertaken by any man; there should by no pilgrimages to holy places; matrimony is sufficient without solemnisation in church; pardons and blessings by priests have no value; men should not pray to saints. He further stated the supper is a memorial, that the drink and bread need not be taken in hallowed places. He was made to swear that he would not keep or sell any books including those of Luther, yet his beliefs were not Lutheran but in agreement with scripture.[3]

The York brothers, Edward and Valentine Freeze, provide a link from the north to the churches of Christ in London and the South East. Both died for their faith. The younger, Edward, lived in Colchester, which for a long time had been a source of "heresy."

He was arrested, charged with heresy, found guilty and sentenced to imprisonment at Fulham Palace, where he was fed bread made partly with sawdust. When his wife, who was pregnant, visited him she was kicked by the porter and died of her injuries. He was then moved to the Lollards Tower, where "being so manacled his flesh grew higher than the irons." His brother, Valentine, appealed to the King, and subsequently Edward was not fed for three days. He died mentally ill. Valentine, took a great risk getting a file into prison for Andrew Hewitt, a tailor, who was incarcerated with John Frith. They were burned together on 4 July, 1533.[4]

Frith was either a member of the church of Christ meeting in Bow Lane, or was a travelling preacher there and at other congregations. Edward was burned, with his wife in York, shortly afterwards. Andrew Hewitt was in prison for heresy; that they were close suggests that Hewitt too held Lollard views, in England to be called Anabaptism. Hewitt was from Faversham, Kent, only thirty-five miles from where Frith was born at Sevenoaks. It was area where the church was every active.

The history of the congregation at Hillcliffe, Warrington, (now Baptist) goes back before the reformation. Dr. Hans Grimm in his small book *Tradition and History of the Early Churches of Christ In Central Europe* (on page 19), writes "But even as late as 1390 A.D. a New Testament church in Celtic Hill Cliff in Wales built a room for worship with a great basin for immersion of adults in baptism of confession of faith." Originally concealed on the side of a hill, in woodland, a place of safety for worshipers who could with ease flee if soldiers were to arrive. No early records exist. The earliest deeds state that the chapel was for use of the people known as "Anabaptists." The Church of England at that time was only too happy to throw into prison anyone teaching the Gospel. Warrington, about two miles to the north, was in the county of Lancashire. When persecution arose in one county, the congregation in Warrington would worship at Hillcliffe or the Hillcliffe congregation could worship in Warrington, thereby avoiding the jurisdiction of those seeking to make arrests for heresy.

The chapel as it was and is now

Today, the church is in the county of Cheshire. It is towards the bottom of a sharp inline from which the town gets its name—"Hillcliff." Hillcliff is south of Warrington which is on the ancient south-north western road leading originally from Gloucester to Dumfries, Scotland. The chapel and burial ground are shown on a map dated 1643.

Goadby mentions a tradition that the Lollards built the chapel, confirmed by an ancient baptistery carved from stone, which was rediscovered in 1841 when work was started in modernizing and extending the chapel. In 1594, a Mr. Weyerburton, or Warburton, a minister of the church, died. He was succeeded by a Mr. Dainteth, who died in 1602. It is said the earliest evidence for the existence of Hill Cliffe is found on a stone in the burial ground bearing the date

1357. Another stone has been found with the date 1414, another has 1523, another 1599. The dates on the greater number of stones are lost to the ravages of time. The following are copied from stones in the burial ground as reported in other histories:

HERE LYS Ye BODY

OF ELIZABETH PYCROFT WHO

DIED DECEMBER 6,

1522

———

HERE LYETH THE BODY OF

WILLIAM BATHO OF CHESTER

WHO DIED NOVEMBER 13TH IN YEAR

1584

The Hill Cliff congregation had a full-time preacher and evangelist in 1594, but his name is unknown. Christians (Anabaptists) in Cromwell's army worshipped at the chapel in 1646. Later the church took on Baptist doctrine as did other similar congregations. Hill Cliffe is possibly the oldest surviving non-establishment congregation in Britain.[5]

Another early church of Christ is that of Barnoldswick. The

563

author of the *History of the Baptists of Barnoldswick*, and its preacher when writing the book, claims the congregation started in about 1500, which is entirely possible. The following few pages are excerpted from his book, now out of copyright. It is a fascinating account going back to the days when they were Lollards through to becoming Baptists,

> When the church was established is uncertain, if we accept the definition of a church as being 'a congregation of faithful men in which the true word of God is preached and the sacrament duly administered according to Christ's ordinances.' Then there was a church here as early as A. D. 1500, for at that time there were at least six eminent Baptist families in and around Barnoldswick, namely: The Mitchells, Higgins, Edmondsons, Hargreaves, Barretts and Greenwoods. These families were branded as Dissenters, and several of their members subsequently became prominent officials of the church. The Mitchell family up to very recently was actively connected with the church, and descendants of some of the other families still live here. The first emphatic reference to the church as a properly organised society is dated 1661. In that year certain property consisting of a messuage, barn, croft and garden, which had been held in trust by three of the members named Christopher Edmondson, Henry Higgins and Matthew Watson, was conveyed to one John Taylor another member. He in 1694 transferred it to David Crossley the minister of the church, who in 1705 transferred it to an elder of the church, named John Barrit, who ultimately bequeathed it to the Society as a meeting house for the perpetual use of the Baptists at Barnoldswick. That identical property still remains in the possession of the church.[6]

A later preacher of the congregation was David Crosley, who was born at Heptonstall, in the neighbourhood of Todmorden, in January 1669. He is important to us as we will meet him at the church of Christ in Tottlebank. The following account is from Evan Lewis.

> Crosley was brought up from childhood by his aunt, who was a very pious woman. As soon as young David learnt to read, his aunt used to engage him in reading the scriptures and printed sermons for him, a practice which the lad evidently appreciated, and which proved a great blessing to him. By this devotional exercise he acquired considerable acquaintance with the Scripture, so that like Timothy, 'from his youth up he knew the Holy Scriptures,' and at the early age of twelve was converted.
>
> The reading of the sermons too, had a beneficial effect upon him in another direction, for at a very early age he manifested intense love for preaching. Being a youth of singular intellectual ability he would compose sermons, and when asked by his aunt to read for her, would, under the pretence of reading a published sermon, recite his own from memory, and then coolly ask her opinion of it. He was a mason by trade, and worked at his vocation during the day, and went about the neighbourhood preaching the gospel at night, and was, together with his cousin William Mitchell, the honoured instrument in introducing the Gospel into Bacup. He was in a twofold sense a born builder; in the higher sense according to the grace of God given him he was a wise master builder, a workman that needed not to he ashamed. The walls of Jerusalem were broken down, and the altars of Jehovah forsaken, and the Master called for him 'to build the ruined places, and plant that, which was desolate,' so that soon after beginning to preach, he laid aside his trowel and hammer and with intense devotion consecrated himself to the ministry.

On one occasion Crosley was engaged to preach the morning sermon at Mr. Pomfret's meeting house in Gravel Lane, Spitalsfields, July 28th, 1691, when he delivered a most remarkable sermon entitled "Samson a Type of Christ." The sermon created considerable interest and by special request was published. In the preface to the reprint of that sermon fifty-three years afterwards, he gives an interesting account of the circumstances of its composition and publication. He says: 'The day after I was engaged to preach that sermon, I was invited to dine with Mr. Strudwick (the gentleman with whom Mr. John Bunyan died) at the foot of Snow-hill. He was a wholesale grocer in whose dining room opposite to where I sat at dinner, was a piece of Turkey Tapestry hanging, wherein was wrought the figure of Samson and the Lion, which he slew by the vineyard of' Timnath, when he went to marry the Philistine woman (Judges xiv) At first I looked upon it, only to gratify my curiosity; but presently considered I was not viewing an ordinary landscape, but scripture history, which perhaps might not only entertain the eye, but also afford speculation of a much sublimer nature. I began to frame ideas in my mind, which in due time were productive of the several observations and improvements contained in the discourse; and being, but in the twenty-second year of my age, and not having the aid of books, nor accustomed to the use of notes, it may well be supposed I had a working head, and I hope a heart full of earnest breathings, and frequent ejaculations heavenwards for fresh anointing, and an illuminated understanding in what was before me, that those pleasing conceptions, which my mind so abounded with, might not (however recent) prove raw and undigested when published in the ears of a polite auditory. And how it was approved and received, it is not for me to say. It has already and perhaps yet does speak for itself. But so it was, a gentleman bookseller, unknown by person to me, before I came down from the pulpit, spoke to the congregation, and proposed that, as the discourse had been so pleasing to him, and as he conceived, it had to the whole congregation, and the argument in his apprehension being both singular and profitable, he was minded, if those who had heard it thought fit to encourage in and that he could prevail with me to write it out, to be at the charge of printing it himself, and if they that were able would buy, he would give to them that were not. The proposal at first was very surprising to me, being far from supposing anything of mine could be fit for such a publication. But the congregation was so unanimous and importunate to have what was proposed go forward, that I could not gainsay it, whereupon with the assistance of some that had taken the sermon in short-hand, I wrote it out and in a few days after, it came out in print to the number of one thousand copies which went off with such expedition that in a little more than half a year's time the impression was sold off, which must needs be owing to the agreeableness of the argument, the author being not only young but in a manner wholly unknown except to a few.

In the year 1692, he returned to Bacup to labour with his cousin William Mitchell at the meeting house erected for them both 'to pray, preach and worship in' During the same year he went to Bromsgrove, in Worcestershire, where he was baptized August 6th, 1692, by a Mr. Eccles, and where he remained but a short while. The church at Bromsgrove gave him a letter of recommendation to preach where he wished. 'To what place he went after leaving Bromsgrove has been until now a mystery. Ivimey, who in his history of the Baptists, records Crosley's life, lost sight of him for about three years. Hargreaves, in his appendix to the life of Hirst, says, 'whether he now returned to Bacup and continued there until 1695, cannot now be ascertained.' Parry, in his history of the Rossendale Baptists, states,

'David Crosley after his baptism at Bromsgrove returned, it is presumed to Rossendale, where he remained until 1695' He no doubt did visit Bacup after leaving Bromsgrove, for he signed a trust deed there in 1693. Still there is the period between that date, and his settlement at Tottlebank in 1695 to account for, and we have found the missing link in some old documents dated 1694, 1695, and 1703; two of which bear his own signature, and all of which affirm that David Crosley was pastor of this church. Why he chose Barnoldswick as a sphere of labour we cannot tell, unless the Crosleys of Stock, Salterforth, and Barnoldswick were his relatives, and he was attracted hither by them. When he came to Barnoldswick, he found an organized society worshipping in a barn, but in a low, depressed, lifeless condition. He energetically set to work to arouse the church from its lethargy, and having in a short while done so, he proceeded to secure more suitable premises. This he did by purchasing the adjoining cottage, and then converting it into a meeting house. The following is an extract of the Indenture confirming the purchase:

This Indenture made the three and twentieth day of April in the sixth year of the Raigne of our Gracious Sovereigne Lord and Lady William and Mary by the grace of God of England, Scotland France and Ireland and King and Queene Defenders of the faith, etc. Between John Taylor of Barnoldswick in the County of York yeoman on the one party, and David Crosley of Barnoldswick aforesaid Clerk on the other party. Witnesseth that the said John Taylor as well for and in consideration of the whole and just sum of thirty-four pounds of lawful English money to him in hand by the said David Crosley at or before the sealing and delivery hereof well and truly payd. The receipt whereof he the said John Taylor doth hereby acknowledge thereof and of every part thereof fully and clearly and absolutely, acquit, exonerate and discharge him the said David Crosley, his heirs executors, administrators and assigns and every of them for ever by these presents, and also for divers other good causes and valuable considerations, him thereunto moving. He the said John Taylor hath granted bargained and sold ... and confirmed by these presents for and from him the said John Taylor, doth grant, bargaine sell alliene unto the said David Crosley, all that messuage or dwelling house wherein the said John Taylor now liveth, together with one little barne and one croft on the backside of the said barne and two gardens, etc, In witnesse whereof the partys to these presents to the parto of these indues, interchangeably have set to their hands and seals the day and year first above written. JOHN TAYLOR.

King James II's Declaration of Indulgence was proclaimed April 1687 authorising protestant dissenters to perform their worship openly. It had by this time wrought some amount of tolerance although James was a disguised papist, and his edict but a beguiling bait, and though the trumpet gave an uncertain sound, yet the Baptists here prepared themselves for battle. David Crosley converted the cottage he had purchased into a chapel proper, with pulpit, pews and forms.

There in the humble thatched sanctuary surrounded by gardens, fields and woods, laboured this eminent and youthful servant of Christ, declaring the way of life to the scattered ones who came to worship from Malham, Colne, Sutton, Bolland, Cowling Hill, Thornton, Earby, Salterforth, Gisburn, and Bracewell. His labours were greatly blessed. The church was revived and strengthened under his ministry. This handful of corn in the land, and upon the top of the mountains, sown by God's diligent labourers, fell into good ground and sprang up in different fields to beautify and replenish the moral wastes of Craven.

On January 7th, 1695, David, Crosley purchased from one William Mitchell, a piece of land adjoining the meeting house called the Parrock for the sum of £25 for the use of the minister and the church. Having built a flourishing church spiritually and financially strong, he departed to another sphere of active service. He was a veritable itinerant, and there was still more land to be possessed, hence in May 1695, he accepted an invitation to the pastorate of 'The Church behind the sands' or Tottlebank in Furness, and removed thither.

Mr. Crosley's removal was a great loss to this and other Yorkshire churches, and efforts were made to induce him to return. At an associated meeting of pastors and elders convened at Barnoldswick at that time, it was proposed "That a letter from this association be drawn to the said church representing the great and many fould inconveniences, disadvantages and distractions that will in all probability follow in case of his (Mr. Crosley's) removal in all or most parts of the country where we of the association are concerned."

For five years after Mr. Crosley's removal the church had no pastor, but was evidently well managed and supplied either by its own members or itinerating preachers, for during 1697 and 1698 above twenty members were added to it. The church however desiring a regular ministry, according to primitive custom, appointed to the office of teaching-elder, one of its members named James Howarth. Under James Howarth's ministrations the church continued to prosper, so that in 1705 it consisted of seventy communicants, which was a large number at a period so remote, in a place so obscure, and under circumstances so unfavourable.

Eight years after his removal to Tottlebank, Mr. Crosley relinquished his ownership of the meeting place at Barnoldswick, by selling it for the nominal sum of £14, and placing it in the trust of five of the church members, as the Extract of the Deed certifies. 'This Indenture made the Twenty Second day of April. In the Second Year of the Raigne of our most gracious Sovereign Lady Ann by the Grace of God of England, Scotland & France & Ireland, Queen Defender of the faith etc. And in the year of our Lord according to the account and computation of the Church of England ; One Thousand Seven Hundred & Three. Between David Crosley of Marsh Grange in the County of Lancaster, Minister of the one parte and John Barrit Senior, of Wood End in the parish of Barnoldswick in the County of York, Yeoman. William Mitchell of Barnoldswick aforesaid in the said County Yeoman. Martin Dickonson of Parke within the said parish & County, Yeoman, & John Hargreaves of Beatswell (or Bracewell) within the said County of York Yeoman of the other parte. Witnesseth that the sd David Crosley for & in consideration of the whole & just sum of fourteen pounds of lawfull money of England hath granted, bargained, aliened, sold and confirmed unto them the said John Barritt, William Mitchell, Martin Dickonson, John Hargreaves All that one Chappele or Meeting house, erected by the said David Crosley for Divine Worship. And also all the seats, pews, & forms placed therein together with all hereditaments whatsoever to the same belonging, being part of a dwelling house lately purchased by the said David Crosley of one John Taylor, and now in the tenure of James Haworth being Minister there for the time being etc. And lastly it is Covenanted, concluded and justly agreed upon by them the said parties

571

to those presents, and hereby declared (provided that Libertie of Conscience hereafter be restrained) and that the above hereby granted Chappell or meeting house for Divine service shall by reason thereof be demolished or happen to be converted into a dwelling house, it shall not be see done, but with the advice of the said David Crosley And likewise if the said feofee in trust be determined to sell the said meeting house, then the said David Crosley or his heirs shall have the first intelligence thereof and three months tyme allowed to consider and give in his or their Answer whether they will buy it or noe. In Witnesse whereof the parties above named, have to these present indentures interchangeably sett their hands & seales the day and year first above written DAVID CROSLEY.'

In the year 1705 Mr. Crosley removed to London, to the pastorate of the church formed by and previously under the pastoral care of the celebrated Mr. Hansard Knollys, but he remained there only a few years. His last days in London were very unhappy, consequent on a serious charge that was preferred against him, and which caused his return to Rossendale. The associated churches were troubled about him, but impartially subjected him to rigid discipline.

Mr. Crosley died at Tatop farm near Goodshaw, March 7th, 1741, in the 76th year of his age, having preached the Gospel for 57 years, and having through loving, faithful services rendered untold benefit to the churches of Christ in various parts of England.[7]

It seems the congregation went through some difficulty, for we learn from Lewis:

The Church having been restored to an active, aggressive

and organised state, it was deemed necessary to review the doctrinal foundations of the Church and draw up for future guidance a Confession of Faith. Such a solemn and important task required special preparations hence at a meeting held August 11th 1743, John Greenwood Deacon proposed, the pastor seconded, and the members unanimously agreed. "That a meeting should be observed, the first Thursday in every mouth, by prayer, fasting (often) and preaching on proper subjects; and the whole church summoned and exhorted to attend to it duely." In pursuance hereof the following texts were preached on viz., Ezek. 43-10, 11, 12, Sept. 1st and Octob. 6th ; Math. 18-20, Nov. 3rd, Jan. 5th, Feb. 9th. ; 1 Pet. 2-5, Mar Ist.; Sam. 3-40, Apr 5th, 1744; 2 Chron. 29-10, 11, May 4th; Neh 9-38, June Ist. And several Lord's days both before and after, the subjects treated on had an eye to it, e.g. Zech. 8-21, Apr 22; Isa 44-5, May 6th and 20th ; Psal 50-5, June 3rd; 2 Cor 11-2, June I7-July 1st.

BARNOLDSWICK, June 1st, 1774. WE the Church of Christ at Barnoldswick in the County of Yorke having in several meetings consulted the affair and come to an unanimous conclusion that it is our Duty and Interest in a solemn manner to review the Foundation on which we are builded as a religious Society; and to Renew the Covenant of our Communion with God, and one with another: and having also taken several preparatory steps towards the performance of this good work ; and being now met together in order to complete the pious design; we think it is proper for us: 1. To Recite the reasons that have induced us to it. 2. To give a brief Summary of our Faith. And 3. To Report the Covenant by which we are joined together.

First. The principal Reasons that have induced us to this work, are such as these that follow, 1. It is undeniably

573

evident that every regular Church of Christ for the manner of its constitution, is founded upon a solemn Covenant: for there is no other medium, by which a free and voluntary Society can be incorporated, but which carries in it the nature of a Covenant. A Contract, or Agreement, freely enter'd into and mutually confirmed, in such a way & manner, as is directed and warranted by the Laws and agreeable to ye nature of the Society whether it be Civil or Sacred: Hence the manner of entering into Church fellowship, under ye New Testament is expressed by persons first giving their own selves to the Lord, and unto us by the Will of God: 2 Cor, 8-5, and the Will of God in this case (here referred to) is declared by the prophet Isaiah, Chap 62-5 & 44-5. When, speaking by the Spirit of Prophecy, concerning the Church of Christ under the New Testament, he saith, As a young man marrieth a virgin, so shall thy Sons marry thee : which, we all know is done by the mutual consent and solemn Covenant; and, one shall say I am the Lord's; and another shall call himself by the name of Jacob ; and another shall subscribe with his hand unto the Lord, and surname himself by the name of Israel ; teaching us, that is in the days of Nehemiah (chap 9 & 10) so in the days of the Gospel Church-Covenants should be written and subscribed with the hand, and that so to do, is to seek ye Lord after the Due Order ; the want of which may cause the Lord to make breaches upon us, 1 Chron. 15-13.

2. Though we hope, that this church in its first gathering did, herein follow in the footsteps of the flock, yet to our unspeakable loss, these footsteps of theirs do not now remain to be reviewed by us: for the Foundations of the first building (ie church) here have been unhappily destroyed ; all accounts of these matters before the year 1711 have been cut, or torn out of our church Book, when or by whom, we do not know: so that, for these many

years, this tottering Tabernacle, bath stood, like a building without a Foundation, having neither Confession of Faith nor Covenant of Communion, prefixt to the names in the Church Book : and though several attempts have been made to supply these defects ; yet either through want of wisdom to conduct them; or, of Unanimity to execute them, they have failed of due success: so that, without some thing of this kind being done by us, in a better manner than in any thing we have yet done, that is Extant; we can neither satisfie our selves that we have done our duty nor can we shew the Forms of the House to those that shall enquire after them; nor can those who shall come after us, find any certain accounts of our Faith & Order for their Instruction and Imitation: so that Necessity is laid upon us to do this.

3. Our present Circumstances call loudly upon us, to set about this good and necessary work, without any further delay: for those who first engaged in the work of the Lord, and joined themselves in Church-fellowship and by whom the Foundation of the Lord's House was laid in this place, after they had served their own Generation are most of them long since gone to rest from their labours; and none of the present members have either seen a Confession of the Faith in which they sat down; or signed the covenant of their Communion and it is to be feared that many of them are too much in Darkness & Ignorance concerning them both; so that there is some resemblance between our present case and that of the Church of Israel, whom God by the Charter of a solemn covenant, incorporated at Mount Sinai, but when most of that Generation was dead (though the covenant of their communion had been duly executed, and remained extant amongst them, which is more than can be said of ours: yet) Moses by divine direction renewed the Covenant with the survivors, before his death in the land of Moab, Duet.. 29, 30, 31

chapters. And afterward when that Generation was worn out, his honourable successor Joshua, found it necessary & adviseable after his example to repeat the practice before his death, as we read in Josh. 23, 24 chapters.

4. Many that belong to us, are grossly negligent in filling up their places with us; and seem to have lost the sense of their obligation so to do: and a general coldness, a sinful indifferency, and want of lively communion with God, and one with another, hath long prevailed amongst us all: which renders it necessary for us to set about some method for a reformation and revival, and when we look into the sacred records, we cannot but observe That those happy instruments of God's honour, and the Church's Good; who set about the blessed work of reforming and reviving religion have in all ages pitched upon and practised the Renewing of Covenant as a good and necessary step towards it: so did the pious and reforming kings of Judah (whose names are recorded with immortal honour, and whose actions are written for our Learning as) Asa 2 Chron. 15. Hezekiah 2 Chron. 29. Josiah 2 Chron. 34, 29, etc. 2 Kings 23, 1, etc. And so did the returning captives, under the conduct and direction of their pious governor Nehemiah 9 & 10 chapters. And (omitting many other instances that might be named) to come nearer to our own times, that pious work of Renewing Church Covenants which was set on foot, with so good Success by the Reforming Synod of New England, in the year 1679, is well worthy of our serious observation, and conscientious imitation, as related by ye excellent Dr. Cotton Mather's History of New England Book V.

And now, when the Lord Jesus hath somewhat against us because we have left our first Eve; should not we also, remember from whence we are fallen, and repent, and do our best works: lest He come unto us quickly, and remove

576

our candlestick out of his place: and if we ask-How shall we do this? His answer is, Go thy way forth by the footsteps of the flock, and act herein as they have left you an example.

5. If the forms of the House of God, respecting Faith & Order had been better observed and preserved by us than they have been; so that both had been produceable at this day in their due order, which now they are not; yet, even in that case it is evident to demonstration from the nature of the thing itself, that the frequent Renewing of the Foundation and at proper seasons. The solemn Renewing of the Covenant of Communion, is both necessary and useful to preserve our Constitution in its purity; and to keep the sense of our obligations warm upon our minds to revive the love of our espousals; to prevent irregularities and corruptions from breaking in upon us, to recover us from relapses, and guard us against declentions and apostasy: so that if there had been no other reasons for setting about this work at this time, it is a point of spiritual and necessary prudence and good husbandry, which alone ought to be a sufficient inducement to engage in it.

6. The happy experience which others have had of the good effects the great benefits and advantages of this practice, ought to be improved by us both for arguments and encouragements to follow their worthy and commendable example. It is very engaging and affecting to observe, how in most instances above mentioned, the people concerned were melted into humiliation warned with a lively sense of religion, armed with fresh resolutions against sin and wickedness, and for God & Holiness, and filled with ravishing joy and consolation, in the believing expectations of enjoying more of the favour and presence of God with them and of hearing him say unto them From this day will I bless you. O what good Impression are these and if preserved by walking worthy of them for the

future. What glorious effects would they produce? And surely God never said to the seed of Jacob ~ Seek ye me in vain. And Dr. Mather tells us that thousands of Spectators will testifie that they never saw the special presence of the Great God our Saviour more notably discovered than in those solemnities wherein the Churches of New England renewed their Covenants, and he adds very remarkable was the Blessing of God that followed it: not only by a great advancement of Holiness in the Churches that engaged in it, but also by a great addition of Converts unto their holy fellowship. May the Lord thus visit us with his Salvation, and remember us with the favour he bears unto his people, that we also may see the good of his Chosen and may Glory with his Inheritance-Amen.

Secondly. To give a brief summary, or Confession of the Faith upon which we are builded together as a Church, under the blessed name of Christians ; the general name of peaceable Protestant Dissenters, and the particular name of Baptists; our consciences, enlightened and directed (we trust) by the Word and Spirit of God, obliging us to worship the living and true God, after the way which some call Heresie yet, believing all things which are written in ye Law and the Prophets, the Gospels, the Acts and the Epistles of the Apostles which Holy Scriptures of the Old and New Testament, and them only we declare to be the Divine Rule and Certain Standard of our Faith and Practice: so in Faith and Worship we build only on the Foundation of the prophets and Apostles. Jesus Christ himself being the Chief Corner Stone, in whom we desire that this building may be fitly framed together; may grow into an holy temple in the Lord, and may be for an habitation of God through the Spirit.

Nevertheless, we being willing to manifest our Consent and Agreement in Faith and Doctrine with others our

Christian Brethren and Churches of Christ in their summaries of heavenly Doctrine and Confessions of Christian Faith as founded upon and contained in ye Holy Scriptures we declare that our faith is that same for substance with what is delivered in the 39 Articles of the Church of England except the 34th the 35th and the 36th and part of the 20th and part of he 27th and understanding the 3rd of Christ's continuing in the state of the dead and under the power of Death until the 3rd day, and the word penance in the 33rd for a proffession of true repentance, accompanied with proper Thts, and by the judge there mentioned, the whole church.,

The same, for the most part with that of ye Church of Scotland, called the Assemblies Confession: More nearly the same with that Declaration of the Faith and Order of the Congregational Churches agreed upon by their Elders and Messengers at the Savoy in the year 1658 reprinted 1729. And without exception the same, both for Faith and Order, with a Confession of Faith set forth in 1689 signed and Assented to, by more than 100 Ministers & Messengers of baptized churches in England and Wales (Denying Arminianism).

Thirdly To repeat the Covenant by, which we are joined together. We a small handful of the unworthy dust of Zion : usually assembling for the worship of God at Barnoldswick, and in obedience to the command of God and conformity to the example of our Lord Jesus Christ, and of his faithfull followers recorded in the New Testament upon Proffession of Repentance toward God; and of Faith toward our Lord Jesus Christ; Baptised with water in the name of the Father and of the Son and of the Holy Ghost, being now met together with one accord to make a fresh surrender of our selves to the Lord, with deep humiliation for our past sins & earnest supplication to God for pardoning mercy and quickening grace: and as a proper means to awaken our drowsie souls to a lively sense of our duty and to revive the languishing work of religion amongst us, we have unanimously agreed this day, to renew the solemn Covenant of our Communion with God, and one with another; and so to say with our hearts, we are the Lord's and to subscribe unto him with our hands in manner following, namely:

We this day avouch the ever blessed Jehovah Father, Son and Holy Spirit the one only true and living God, for our Covenant God and All-sufficient portion, and give up ourselves to him alone for his peculiar people in a perpetual Covenant never to be forgotten. "We receive and submit to the Lord Jesus Christ as our alone Saviour, Prophet, Priest and King, in whom done we trust for Wisdom and Righteousness Sanctification and Redemption. We devote and Consecrate ourselves, as living Temples to the Holy Ghost, our Sanctifier Guide and Comforter; whose gracious operations and heavenly Conduct, we desire daily more and more to feel and follow.

We take the Holy Scriptures of the Old and New Testament as the only ground and rule of our Faith & Practice; desiring in all things to be conformable to the Holy Will of God therein revealed: according to the tenor whereof we now Covenant with God, each for ourselves, and jointly together through and by the help of his Spirit and Grace assisting us to worship God in Spirit and in Truth, to observe all his commandments and keep his ordinances as he hath therein delivered them to us: to be subject to divine order and discipline, which Jesus Christ our only King and Law giver, hath appointed in his church: and not to forsake the assembling of ourselves together, for the worship of God in his appointed seasons; but to continue in our relation one to another, and fill up our places in the House of God and maintain his worship therein, to the best of our Capacity until death, or evident calls of divine providence shall separate us one from another, to love one another with pure hearts fervently; and endeavour to keep the unity of the Spirit in ye bond of peace; for the honour of our God, and our mutual good and edification. We will also make it our care to walk before the Lord in our own houses with perfect hearts; and to uphold ye worship of God therein, by prayer to God, and reading the Holy Scriptures, that so, the word of God may dwell richly in us. And as we have given our children to he Lord by a solemn dedication; so we will endeavour to teach them ye way of the Lord, and command them to keep it; setting before them an holy example, worthy of their imitation, and continuing in prayer to God, for their conversion and Salvation.

We will also endeavour to keep our selves pure from the sins of the times and places wherein we live, and so to be holy in all manner of conversation, that none may have occasion given by our unholy lives to speak evil of God's holy ways. And all this under an abiding sense that we must shortly give up our accounts to him that is ready to judge the quick and the dead.

Unto which solemn covenant we set our hands in the presence of ye all seeing heart-searching God. This first day of June in the year of our Lord one thousand seven hundred and forty four. This covenant and Confession was signed by Alvery Jackson, pastor, and one hundred and six members. Each member either writing the name or affixing a mark.[8]

581

The church had not formerly adopted the Baptist confession of Faith until 1774. It had previously signed a Calvinistic Confession in 1719 along with Tottlebank.[9] As this would have been the same confession signed later in 1774, there may have been dissention over Calvinism between those dates by the congregation. Without further information, we can only guess of the discussions and heated debates that would have taken place.

There was a church of Christ, meeting at Preston Patrick, South of Kendal, whose members became Quakers after the preaching of George Fox in about 1652. Another congregation at Firbank Fell converted to Quakerism in the same year. The graveyard of the chapel remains, the latter destroyed in the nineteenth century. The Firbank Fell congregation, which turned to Quakerism, is usually identified as the start of the Quaker movement.

Ken Chumbley stands where George Fox preached,
converting the congregation to Quakerism

The site of the former chapel, a grave stone remains and church yard wall.

A member of the congregation and one of their elders was Francis Howgill, a local farmer. He lived near Grayrigg, north of Kendal, a local man as implied by his name "Howgill," the name of the hills in which he lived. The Howgills lie east of Kendal, mostly within the boundaries of the Yorkshire Dales. Howgill, like the congregation, was converted to Quakerism with his fellow elder John Audland, a linen draper. This was one of the first mass conversions of an entire congregation to Quakerism and a pattern that would follow in future. We do not know when these congregations started, but they were sufficiently established to come to the attention of George Fox. The Quakers at Preston Patrick by the 1700s had their own licensed chapel, that at Firbank no longer being used. They also had another at Brigflatts, which is close to, but more accessible than Firbank.[10]

Now to the Church of Christ at Tottlebank. After the restoration of the monarchy in England and Scotland in 1658, the persecution of Christians by the Anglicans and government began again in earnest. To avoid persecution, Roger Sawrey left a church of Christ in London, where George Coackine was an elder, to seek freedom of worship in the mountain fells of what is today the Lake District. Roger Sawrey "departed this life to be forever with ye Lord August ye 6th 1699."

The house where the Tottlebank brethren first met.

The chapel built by the Tottlebank brethren,
a minutes' or so walk from the house

He met two dissatisfied Church of England clergymen, William Campbell and George Malcolm. Roger Sawrey, a former officer in Cromwell's army, was known as "praying Sawrey" due to his piety. There was locally at least one other church of Christ meeting in "Cumberland" prior to the Tottlebank congregation. As George Lurkham, one of the founders of the Tottlebank congregation, was a pastor of the other older congregation. Tottlebank at that time period was in Lancashire, not Cumberland. The older congregation, established in 1648, was at Broughton, fifteen miles to the north, where Roger Sawrey had been a member after leaving London. After the "Five Mile Act" this congregation would have been forced to cease meeting. The act was repealed in 1689. George Lurkham was also involved in the church of Christ meeting at Cockermouth, close to Broughton, which also predated the Tottlebank congregation having started in 1651. Cockermouth too would have ceased to meet because of the Five Mile Act. The closure of these two congregations resulting in the Tottlebank church coming into being. Cockermouth and Brougham congregations were reinstated later.

Broughton is a village in Cumberland lying about three miles to the west of Cockermouth. It lies also at nearly equal distance from Maryport, on the Irish Channel. It is situated in beautifully level, yet slightly undulating and fertile country, having the sea on one side, and the bold and splendid scenery of the lofty Cumberland and Westmorland mountains on the other; the land of the lakes, the lake poets, of Skiddaw and Helvellyn. The origin of the Baptist Church in this village is now hidden in obscurity. Tradition, however, according to the account of its late minister (Mr. S. Huston), places it in 1648.[11] At this time the Broughton and Cockermouth congregations were mixed in regard to baptism, baptizing both infants and believers. Prior to Tottlebank's coming into existence, the two parties divided over baptism, Cockermouth becoming congregational.

Thomas Larkham (Lurkham) was father to George Lurkham and the preacher at a church of Christ in Tavistock, Devon (South England). Gabriel Camelford was a former preacher/minister in the

Church of England ("CoE"). At that time, prior to the restoration of the monarchy, the CoE allowed different parties. Today, the CoE is Anglican only. Arguments may be made that as Camelford was from the CoE, he would have practised infant sprinkling along with worship at the altar, clerical dress and positions, etc. Such arguments are entirely void. It was possible to preach the truth in the CoE, though it caused much debate and argument. John Toombes and Henry Denne had for periods preached for the Church of England the true faith whilst members of the church of Christ. In the 1600s ,what is now the tourist area known as the Lake District, an English national park, was largely unknown. To the south is Morecambe Bay, passage to Furness being possible across the sands at low tide. The area is made up of mountains and lakes in one of the wettest parts of England. Scattered communities of little wealth meant there was little opportunity for clergy seeking financial recompense in this harsh mountainous rural environment. Before the act of Uniformity (1662), non-conformist ministers were able to preach the truth. The churches they preached from were stripped of their ecclesiastical furniture; the organs were removed along with the altars and stained glass windows. The Lord's Supper was served from kitchen tables and the clergy did not wear the surplice (clerical gown).[12] Infant baptism could be dismissed as papist and believers' baptism practised. Elders could oversee autonomous congregations.

To overcome this, Charles II and parliament reinstated the Anglican faith with the force of persecution for those who objected.[13] Another was the church at Eltisley near Cambridge where Henry and John Denne preached. The congregation was made up entirely of those who had rejected infant baptism and the Church of England system.

One such minister in the north was Gabriel Camelford, who was rector of Staveley in Cartmel, then in Lancashire but now Cumbria. The congregation was fortunate in their seclusion. Camelford was able to preach Christianity with little hindrance. The congregations in Cartmel and neighbouring Furness were able to support their ministers after the act of conformity. Little real persecution took place in these valleys. In 1662 Gabriel Camelford was ejected from his "living" at Staveley. About this Robert Halley wrote: "It has been disputed where was formed the first congregational church in England. Islington, Yarmouth, Southwark, Dukinfield have claimed the honour. Among the fells of Furness was founded the first Christian church in England. By Christian I mean here not congregational, not Presbyterian, not Episcopal, not Baptist, but simply Christian in its unrestricted sense - Christian not sectarian, Catholic not denominational, a church of people acknowledged as Christians and nothing else. A poor ejected Minister from over the sands had the wisdom and grace to form such a church, and the poor mountaineers of his neighbourhood had the piety firmly to adhere to it and long sustain it." [14] Dr. Halley was wrong. Such churches in the Furness Fells pre-existed the Tottlebank congregation. The heritage of these congregations led in time to the work in Ulverston.

The Church at Staveley in Cartmel

Camelford would become the minster at Tottlebank, a few miles from Staveley in Cartmel. His reputation as a Christian and evangelist would be felt for decades after he died. Although the Church of Christ in Tottlebank may have been located away from any town to conform to the law under the Five Mile Act, it was well known. From this work many other congregations of Christ started in the Furness Fells.

589

Tottlebank in 1695 had four elders, Roger Sawrey, David Crosley, William Braithwaite and William Robinson.[15] In 1840 the new minister, Thomas Taylor, introduced the Baptist belief of holding communion monthly. Previously, it had been held each Lord's Day. Differences over doctrine had been causing problems between the brethren at Kirkby and Tottlebank going back to 1824, when there had been a separation. The final act of separation was in 1879, when the brethren at Kirkby demanded the deeds of their meeting place from the brethren at Tottlebank, which were handed over for a nominal sum of ten pounds. The old property was sold and a new one built which remains to this day.[16] Under Cromwell the Presbyterians in the Church of England had introduced "communion Sunday." From there it found its way into the later Anglican Church and Baptists, who were only too keen to join with the Presbyterians in taking the Lord's Supper monthly, and, of course, in taking on reformed doctrine.

There is some confusion as to where the congregation stood in regard to baptism and Calvinism (the predominant theology for independents in that period). I shall try to settle this matter. The 1890 Ordinance Survey map marks the building as "General" Baptist. There must have had very good reason to do so. When they first used the title "Baptist church," they were of the "Particular Baptist," that is, of the Calvinistic persuasion. Accordingly the building should be listed as either "Baptist" or "Particular Baptist." There is no reason for the General Baptist identification to be used unless they were, what is now termed, of the General Baptist denomination.

The Tottlebank confession is of the type associated with the Six Principle General Baptists.

> Therefore leaving the principles of the doctrine of Christ, let us go on unto perfection; not laying again the foundation of repentance from dead works, and of faith toward God, Of the doctrine of baptisms, and of laying on of hands, and of resurrection of the dead, and of eternal judgment (Heb. 6:1-2).

Their confession reads:

> First according to the apostles Heb. 6:1 the six principals therein told 1. Repentance from dead workes. 2. Faith towards God. 3. The doctrine off baptism as at water and of the spirit. 4. and off eternal judgement and besides these God hath taught us first to bottome all our workes on a principle off love to God and desire off his glory for his love to us.

The term "Six Principle General Baptists" was coined later, but suits our purpose of identifying their beliefs and background - i.e., of the church of Christ, which had an Anabaptist, Lollard and pre-reformation background, though they never used the terms Anabaptist or Lollard. They became Calvinistic (Particular Baptist) in 1719 when they signed the "Baptist" Confession of Faith,[17] and called themselves the "Baptist Church" in 1765.[18]

The book of the church begins:

This booke is for the use off that Church of Christ in Broughton Ffurnessfells and Cartmel whereof Mr. Gabrill Camelford is teaching elder. 18th day of the sixth month called August 1669. A Church of Christ was founded in order and faith drawn together in the fellowship and order of the Gospel of Jesus Christ. All the house of William Rawlinge off Tottlebank in Doulton in Furness there weare present, and assisted Mr. George Lurkham pastor off a Church of Christ in Cumberland and Mr. Roger Sawrey of Broughton Tower, a member of Christ and off that particular Church in London of which Mr. George Coackine is teachinge elder. The persons joyninge themselves at this tyme.

The term "teaching elder" is used where one of the elders is responsible for teaching and may have been a paid position. "Particular Church in London" is reference to an individual church, not doctrine (particular election vs. general election).

As such they should be classed as restorationist, not reformed or protestant and certainly not Anglican or Catholic. They would have practised believers' baptism by immersion for remission of sins whereby one entered the church of Christ. The "The doctrine off baptism as at water and of the spirit" is a rejection of infant baptism and supernatural regeneration due to the power of the water. Regarding the "spirit," the General Baptists (though they did not use that term in that period) taught that the spirit operates through the word in conversion. The laying on of hands again does not impart anything supernatural but, from their perspective, follows the ordinances of Christ.

The picture too often painted of the 1669 confession is that it is congregational, rather than Baptist (using modern secular terms) since as the "we can agree with them with us is a dore wide enough, to entertain every sonn of the Lord of glory", which is open communion and opposed to the Calvinistic scheme, rather than congregational. Open communion is defended by 1 Corinthians 11:28-29 "But let a man examine himself, and so let him eat of that bread, and drink of that cup. For he that eateth and drinketh unworthily, eateth and drinketh damnation to himself, not discerning the Lord's body;" which places the responsibility on the individual rather than the congregation. Some of the first Baptist churches in the USA were "Six Principle General Baptists" – churches of Christ that denied Calvinism.

They also sang psalms:

> Further wee doe believe that in his church prayer, spirituall praise is to be used with readings of the scriptures with preachinge and hearinge the same singinge of psalms as also administration off water baptism and the Lords supper, these are all part off religiouse worship, to be performed by Christs prescription amonge his people to the end of the world.

Congregational singing was a major point of contention in the mid 1600s onwards, not resolved until the 1700s.

George Fox clashed angrily with Gabriel Camelford, who was

to become the "teaching elder" of Tottlebank. Camelford lived in Staveley, near Lakeside (South Windermere), Fox calling him "priest Camelford". Margaret Fell, a Quaker, wrote to Francis Benson in 1655, "If ever yee owne the liveinge God or his people yee must deny Camelford and if yee owne Camelford then yee deny God." The wife of a local judge and local dignitary, Fell married George Fox after she became a widow in 1658. Her wealth helped considerably in the promulgation of the Quakers. The Quakers were converting entire congregations of churches of Christ which caused much consternation. We are told on one occasion Gabriel Camelford threw George Fox over a wall, but did not cause any permanent injury. The Commonwealth survey of 1650 said that Camelford was "a godly and painful man in his calling." Edmund Calamy (died 1666) wrote of Camelford, "a useful preacher in this remote corner."[19] The brethren in the Ulverston and Newby Bridge area, after the Five Mile Act (see chapter 15) was imposed, started to meet at Tottlebank in a house still standing, forming a "Church of Christ." The minute book is dated 1669. Later, they built a chapel at the same location, hidden in the Furness Fells. The congregation grew and a second work was planted in Broughton-in-Furness, the chapel being on the road to Coniston. Another congregation was started at Ravensglass and another started at St. Mary's Well in a cottage at Kirkby-in-Furness. The Kirkby congregation grew and other churches of Christ started from there. Today in the Furness Fells, two churches of Christ remain whose origins predate the Restoration Movement and Reformation. The details of their origin are long forgotten. Other denominational churches in the area have the same origin.

David Crosley became the preacher at Tottlebank in 1695 and an elder in 1696, along with Roger Sawrey, William Braithwaite and William Robinson. Crosley was a Calvinist and later closely involved with the "particular churches" in London, which were the forerunners of the Baptist denomination. Today, the Tottlebank house and chapel are owned by the Baptists who still meet there. As churches of Christ, following the Biblical pattern, they were part of a fellowship going back many centuries.

Crosley left Tottlebank to a "pastorate" at Curriers Hall, London, and to drink and engage in other "indiscreet behaviour" which led to his disfellowship. He redeemed himself later with the Tottlebank brethren but never paid back the £5 he owed them, a large sum in those days. In 1670, William and James Towers were elected deacons at Tottlebank.

Frederick Overend, pastor of the Ebenezer Baptist Church, Bacup wrote a book on the history of the seventeenth century churches of Christ in Lancashire prior to their becoming Baptist. The book was published in 1912 and relied on the letters of two evangelists, William Mitchel and David Crosley, who were active in the late 1600 and early 1700s. Crosley was born in 1669 and Mitchel in 1662, Crosley died in 1744. The letters had not been published at the time Overend undertook his research so offered new insight into the churches of Christ in the seventeenth century. Overend had obtained copies of the letters from a Dr. Farrar of Hall Garth, Carnforth. Though written from an early twentieth century Calvinist Baptist viewpoint, his work offers an insight into the early Baptist church and its predecessor, the churches of Christ. The title of the book is *History of the Ebenezer Baptist Church Bacup. Together with an Historical Account of the "Church of Christ in Rossendale,* based on the Mitchel and Crosley Letters, hitherto unpublished. He notes that the dissenters, whom he calls "Protestant Dissenters"— though he does not qualify the use of "Protestant"—who called themselves "Church of Christ", and from elsewhere we known they denied being Protestant.[20] He writes:

> In 1705, though the generosity of Mr. Robert Litchford, another meeting house was provided for the Rosendale Church of Cloughfold. When the "Church of Christ in Rosendale" was transformed into a Baptist Church, the old meeting house at Bacup continued to be one of its chief meeting places and centres. In process of time, Barnoldswick, Tottlebank, Bacup, Cloughfold, Rodhill End and Stoneslack, Heaton, Rawden, Gildersome, and some other branches of the great confederacy became distinct Baptist Churches.[21]

Overend notes that these churches did not originate within the Baptist movement but wrote:

> The Rosendale Church, when Mitchel died, was in the process of transformation into a Baptist Church. The Baptist leaven, through the preaching of Crosley and Mitchel, was doing its sure work, and in the course of a few years from the time of Mitchel's death it is probable that the "Church of Christ in Rosendale" had become distinctly Baptist in its constitution and practice. The traditional date of the completion of the transformation is 1710, a date probably as near as any that could be fixed. From that time the great Church and its many branches must be regarded as Baptist.[22]

Regarding the identity of the Rosedale Church Overend wrote:

> It is uncertain at what time the designation "The Church of Christ in Rosendale" ceased to be used. We have seen that in the dismissions to Rawdon, Heaton and Gildersome the title was in use in 1715. We get glimpses of Baptist history in 1718, when a group of Churches formed themselves into a Baptist Association.

The Church at Tottlebank was part of this association.[23]

It will be asked, who were these "Protestant Dissenters" before they became Baptist? Overend states they were independents and Anabaptists.[24] The Anabaptists baptised for the remission of sins and upheld freewill denying Calvinism. Nowhere does Overend state they were of the Presbyterian party (Calvinist infant sprinklers). From other sources we known these brethren were following the biblical pattern and not at first Baptist principles.

From a letter sent by the "The Church of Christ in Rosendale" on January 1st, 1695/6 we learn a little of the organisation of the church. The heading is "To the beloved Brethren in Yorkshire, the Elders, Deacons and Brethren of the Church of Christ in Rosendale send greeting."[25] On page 81, Overend notes that pastor, elder and bishop are the same office and founded on New Testament principles, this being the organisation of the churches of the Rosendale circuit.

Overend notes that Crosley and Mitchel were itinerant preachers and evangelists, not pastors.[26] Overend refutes other Baptist histories that claim David Crosley and John Bunyan were acquainted to the point Crosley was one of Bunyan's evangelists having trained under him. Crosley was born in 1669. Bunyan died in 1688. Crosley did not start to preach until after the death of Bunyan, though he did on one occasion preach in the meeting house at Bedford where Bunyan had been the evangelist.[27]

Close by to Tottlebank, another congregation started in 1678 at Sunny Bank, Torver, about twelve miles distance.[28] The following account given of the formation of this church is paraphrased from David Douglas' *History of the Baptist Churches in the North of England from 1648 to 1845*:

> In 1678, June 15, a church was formed at Torver, and afterwards known as the church at Hawksheadhill, in Furness-fells, Lancashire, by the joint efforts of Messrs. Ward and Blenkinsop. Mr. Ward, it seems, had to visit this district once in eight weeks to fulfill his duties as a

mining superintendent in Torver and Muggleswick. Mr. Blenkinsop was minister of Great Broughton, but as his name is mentioned in connection with Mr. Ward's, in 1674, in the revival of the church at Hexham, it is likely, that he supplied frequently at Broughton at this time. Mr. Camelford's name does not appear in the incorporation of the church, nor yet that of Mr. Larkham, but as autonomous congregations this should not lead to any conclusions of fellowship. The following is the account given of the formation of this church, from an old copy of its original formation in the possession of Mr. Harbottle of Accrington, Lancashire, whose father, Mr. Thomas Harbottle, was pastor at Hawksheadhill: 'In the year of our Lord 1678, and on the 15th day of the 4th month, it having pleased God, by his special grace, to call a people, and raise them up for himself, in measure out of the world, and put them into his holy fear and service, in and about Torver, in Lancashire, who have, the day and year above written, in the presence of and before John Ward and Robert Blenkinsop, messengers and elders, from the church of Christ, in Derwentwater-side, in and about Muggleswick park; first giving up ourselves to the Lord and to one another, according to the will of God, promising by help of divine grace, to walk as becometh saints, in the order of the gospel, testifying the same by subscribing their names, John Dickeson, John Rawlinson, Thomas Braithwaite, etc., up to thirty one, including not only the original members, but all those added till Feb. 10th, 1723.'[29]

The term "messenger" at that time means no more than evangelist, the term messenger is found in Philippians 2:25 in the King James Version.

The Sunny Bank Chapel still stands in an isolated position in the hamlet of Sunny Bank, Coniston, a short distance from Torver. It is somewhat forlorn, having ceased being used for worship in 1940. Unique as (possibly) the oldest original dissenting meeting house in the UK, it has never been subject to major updating apart from minor renovation. The baptismal pond remains, cut into the hillside close to the chapel, the wooden steps that the candidate and baptizer would have used to enter the water together, having long disappeared. Trees surround the building from which a short mud path leads to the road. In 1709 the congregation moved to a new building between Torver and Coniston at Hawkshead Hill, where a Baptist congregation still meets.[30]

Views of the Sunny Bank chapel

Interior view

The baptismal pool

The pool with the building.

In 1701, the brethren at Tottlebank purchased land at Whallenrigg, Broughton. It was purchased on their behalf by Hugh Towers, one of the founding brethren at Tottlebank. It was "to be built upon to worship and serve God in." The land cost two pounds. The Quarter Sessions Records, at Lancaster 1703 state "Certifies the Court that a house newly erected at Whallenrigg... is appointed and set apart for a publick Meeting House of Protestant Dissenters..." It became known as Scroggs meeting house, on the Broughton to Conniston Road (via Torver). Scroggs is marked on The Ordinance Survey Map of 1847 as a "Baptist Church in ruins."[31] It is now used as a shelter for cattle. The table went to Wall End at Kirkby and the Bible to a family at Ulpha.[32]

Scroggs meeting house

From 1826, the brethren at Kirkby were entirely isolated as they knew of no other churches of Christ anywhere, apart from those in the Furness Fells.

The meeting house of the Kirkby (Wall End) Church of Christ

A.C. Watters in his *History of British Churches of Christ* wrote

> In the then remote peninsula of Furness there was a church
> at Kirkby, meeting in a chapel which was probably built
> in 1826, and the church must have been in existence for at
> least some years before that. It was not discovered by the
> main body of "Churches of Christ" until 1854.

Watters continues:

> In a yet unpublished history of the *Churches in Furness*
> Principal William Robinson (himself a native of the
> peninsula) wrote, "This church undoubtedly owes its
> origin to a group of Churches of similar, though no
> identical, faith and order which began their troubled
> history in the troubled days after the Restoration of
> Charles II. There were at least four of these churches and
> three have now ceased to exist. The fourth – Tottlebank

– is now in the Baptist Union. Fortunately it possesses a minute book going back to its foundation in 1669. The Church Minute Book contains a full Confession of Faith, and it is interesting to note that the Church had the following marks usually associated with the Reformation of the Campbells –

1. It was named "The Church of Christ."

2. Only believers' baptism by immersion was practiced.

3. The Lord's Supper was the chief service of worship each Sunday and only baptized communicants were allowed.

4. The government was congregational and there was liberty of ministry. Elders and deacons were ordained, and one elder served as Teaching Elder and was supported by the Church."[33]

The Kirkby congregation continued to increase. In 1874 they numbered 38, by 1876, 101. In that year the present meeting house was built. From the work at Kirby, other congregations were started in the area.

The work in Barrow-in-Furness was established in 1864, by a group of Whitehaven fishermen who moved to Walney Island, just off Barrow-in-Furness. Later they moved into the town centre. In 1915, the present building was bought from the Railway Mission. This consisted of the Church and a small kitchen/boiler room and an outside toilet and coal shed. In 1972, a small extension was built to provide a Community Room, kitchen and toilets. In 1981 the Church, along with the majority of the Churches of Christ, joined the United Reformed Church. Others of unknown dates include Langdale, Broughton Mills and Swarthmoor.

The meeting place in Ramsden Road

The Lindale Church of Christ was founded in 1873, the meeting house built two years later, it is now a private house.

Askam Church of Christ was founded in 1878, the building is now owned and used by the Roman Catholics.

Dalton Church of Christ was founded in 1891. The congregation ceased as a church of Christ in 1971, at the end of its 80th Anniversary year, with its members moving in to share with the former Congregational Church to form the new Dalton United Reformed Church. The building is now used by the Seventh Day Adventists.

Great Urswick Church of Christ was founded in 1911.
The congregation is now United Reformed.

The Ulverston church of Christ was founded in 1876 from the work at Lindale. At some point they acquired a meeting house in the Ellers, Ulverston. It was here that Joseph Crosthwaite was one of the elders. In 1891, his son, Walter Crosthwaite, was baptised. The late American brother, John Allen Hudson, in his book *The Churches of Christ in Great Britain* (1948), said that brother Walter Crosthwaite "saved the cause of our Lord from complete defeat in Britain."[34] It was from Walter Crosthwaite that the work of training evangelists to prepare the church for the latter part of the twentieth century was undertaken. Brother Crosthwaite was born in Ulverston on October 30th, 1873.

609

The following is the Meeting House of the Church of Christ in the Ellers, Ulverston, which was demolished many years ago. It is to the left of the Coal Merchant. The building was acquired after 1883. In the picture on the left is Brother Joe Rockliff, the other brother is unknown, but it has been suggested he may be either Joseph or Walter Crosthwaite. Walter died on May 23, 1961. Clearly the brother in the picture is too old to be Walter, therefore if it is one of the Crosthwaites, it is Joseph.

The fellowship to which Joseph Crosthwaite belonged was the churches of Christ which are known to have existed in the Furness Fells of Northern England in the 1600s, and those churches were in fellowship with other churches of Christ, which went back many years earlier.

From the account written by the father of Walter Crosthwaite, published in "Notes on my life," in *Scripture Standard* of August 1955: "In January, 1876, I joined the Church of Christ meeting at Lindale, having previously belonged to the Baptists at Ulverston." He explains how he came to leave the Baptists for the church of Christ:

> I attended the discussion on baptism between the "Rev" L. O. Lewis, Vicar of Lindale-in-Furness, and Mr David King of Birmingham, held on the 8th, 9th 14th and 15th of December 1875. That, and conversations I had with John Coward, William MacDougall and several other brethren forced the truth upon me, causing me to see clearly that I was not on New Testament ground in many things, therefore I was forced to move. On the 12th day of March, 1876, I had a conversation with two friends of mine who had been formerly connected with the Baptists. They said they would like to meet according to the teaching of the New Testament. I invited them to go with me to Lindale, and they would see our form; and also hear bro. Evans give his finishing discourse on "The Tabernacle." They did so and were delighted. Bro. Evans advised us to meet at once, he believing us to be men of stability. Therefore we met for the first time in Ulverston to 'break bread' in the house of sister Sarah Woods on the 19th day of March, 1876. There were present four brethren and three sisters... The Church continued to exist amidst many trials from false and unfaithful brethren up to March 20th, 1881, when it was decided that after March 27th we meet with the brethren at Lindale, about three miles off. We continued there up to April 1st, 1883, upon which day we met again in Ulverston, and hope we will never have to give up till the Master comes to call his people to Himself – Joseph Crosthwaite. [35]

Later the Ulverston congregation moved to Union Street in about 1925, the congregation cease to meet there in about 1984. They had begun using instrumental music, having divided for that and other reasons, in the late 1920s. They sold the building, it housed an Assembly of God congregation, being about twelve in number.

Walter Crosthwaite

The Union Street Church of Christ building in Ulverston, built in 1925. The congregation ceased meeting in 1984.

The Mill Street Church of Christ building, in Ulverston.
They are still meeting and remain acapella.

The interior

The baptismal pool

Other churches of Christ in the UK started independently of the American Restoration Movement. The church first met in Kirkcaldy in the late 18th century as a missionary outreach from the original "Scotch Baptist" Church in Edinburgh. The first members of the church in Kirkcaldy came from Edinburgh sometime between 1784 and 1786. By the time the first elders were appointed in 1798, they were renting a meeting place in Kirk Wynd. By 1819, this building had become too small, so they built the Rose Street Chapel which could seat at least 200. In 1847, Alexander Campbell came to the Rose Street Chapel to meet all three Kirkcaldy congregations (Rose Street, Links Hall, and the Assembly Rooms).

The church of Christ meeting in Morrisons Court, Glasgow, was established somewhere between 1772 and 1782. They had 180 members in 1818. The church of Christ assembling in Leith Walk, Edinburgh, was planted around 1798. In 1818, they numbered 250, including three elders and four deacons. The church of Christ at Tubermore, Scotland, first met in May, 1807. The church of Christ, Manchester, England, was established in 1810 with only three members. Elders and deacons were appointed in 1817. The Stephen Street congregation in Dublin was established in 1810 and consisted of 100 members in 1818.

Archibald Watters in his 1948 *History of the British Churches of Christ* states that the first of these to know anything about the

"Campbellite Movement" was the church in Dungannon, Ireland, which in 1825 entered into correspondence with Alexander Campbell. In 1830, the church meeting at Auchtermuchty, Scotland (formed 1807), came to know of Alexander Campbell, one of its leaders visiting America in 1834 to meet the leader of the Restoration Movement.[36]

The Cox Lane, Denbighshire, congregation, under the leadership of John Davies, began meeting in 1809 and were overjoyed to learn in 1835 that over 15,000 people in America shared their views, and soon began corresponding with Campbell and others of like mind in England and Scotland. Through the influence of Campbell's written word in the pages of Jones' *Millennial Harbinger,* many of the Scots Baptists began to break away to form "Church of Christ" congregations. Perhaps among the first of these was the church in Nottingham under the leadership of James Wallis.

In 1837, in the home of John Black of Hatton Garden, London, a small group was meeting on the first day of the week, on New Testament principles. John Black died in 1857. In 1842, David King, possibly the most able of British evangelists in the nineteenth century, was baptised by bro. Black. King's wife, Louise, followed shortly in baptism. By 1848, they had a hundred members meeting in Providence Chapel, Elstree Street, St. Pancras Road. In this building, Alexander Campbell preached several sermons in his visit to London in 1847. On the eighth of October, 1871, they met in Hope Chapel which they had raised the funding to build. The chapel is in the Prince of Wales Road, Kentish Town, London, where the congregation still meets. J.B. Rotherham, author of the *New Testament Critically Emphasised,* was involved for a time with the congregation.[37]

From this time onwards, churches of Christ grew in Britain and in fellowship with those in the USA. The Restoration Movement has been blessed with men of great ability and understanding of the scriptures. Free from persecutions to contend with, able men with a level of knowledge surpassing that of previous generations were able to evangelise and plant churches. For those seeking to come to a knowledge of the truth, the resources and help available are mighty indeed.

Archie Watters in his *The Story of the Churches of Christ in Great Britain* wrote that it "…is of particular value in correcting an error which has persisted for some time that the movement is peculiarly American. Alexander Campbell was at considerable pains to point out the fact that the movement was as much native to Britain as America."[38]

ENDNOTES

[1]Margaret Spufford, *The World of Rural Dissenters, 1520-1725* (Cambridge University Press, 2008)42. Arthur Geoffrey Dickens, *Lollards and Protestants in the Diocese of York 1509-58* (Published for the University of Hull by the Oxford University Press, 1959) 2.

[2]John A. F. Thomson, *The Later Lollards 1414-1520* (Oxford University Press, 1965) 194.

[3]Thomson 19.

[4]Dickenson 30. John Foxe (1517-1587), *Acts and Monuments of the Christian Church*, vol. 2, 9th ed. (1684) 255.

[5]W. A. Jarrel, *Baptist Church Perpetuity-Or-The Continuous Existence Of Baptist Churches From The Apostolic To The Present Day Demonstrated By The Bible And By History* (1894) 339. J. Jackson Goadby, *Bye Paths in Baptist History* (1871) 21-23. J. M. Cramp, *Baptist History* (1871) 205.

[6]"Rev." Evan R Lewis, *History of the Baptists of Barnoldswick* (1893) 1.

[7]Lewis 4ff.

[8]Lewis 45ff.

[9]M. F. Thomas, *A History of Tottlebank Baptist Church* (1999) 16.

[10]Michael R. Watts, *The Dissenters: From the Reformation to the French Revolution*, 203. "Rev." Benjamin Nightingale, *Early Stages of the Quaker Movement in Lancashire* (1921)12-14.

[11]David Douglas Hamsterley, *History Of The Baptist Churches In The North Of England, From 1648 To 1845* (1846) 3.

[12]Daniel Neal, MA., *The History of the Puritans or Protestant Non-Conformists, from the Reformation to the Death of Queen Elizabeth.* In four volumes. 1733. Consult the second volume in regards to the communion table, surplices etc.

[13]E. H. Broadbent, *The Pilgrim Church* (1931) 249.

[14]Robert Halley D.D., *Lancashire: Its Puritanism and Nonconformity*, vol. 2 (1869) 205-9. Halley was principle of the (congregational) New College, London.

[15]Foster Sunderland, *A Brief History of the Tottlebank Baptist Church, The Oldest Baptist Church in Lancashire* (when Tottlebank due to boundary changes came under Cumbria) (n.d.,between 1957 and 1974) 9.

[16]Sunderland 17-18.

[17]Thomas 16.

[18]Thomas 16.

[19]Nightingale 16-17.

[20]Frederick Overend, *History of the Ebenezer Baptist Church Bacup.*

*Together with an Historical Account of the "Church of Christ in Rossendale,"
based on the Mitchel and Crosley Letters*, hitherto unpublished (The Kingsgate
Press, 1912) 63.

[21]Overend 63-64.

[22]Overend 117.

[23]Overend 125-6.

[24]Overend 121-2.

[25]Overend 84.

[26]Overend 58.

[27]Overend 28-29.

[28]Hamsterley 95

[29]Hamsterly 101.

[30]John Dawson, *Torver, The Story of a Lakeland Community* (1985) 113.

[31]Sunderland 6.

[32]Thomas 12.

[33]Archibald C. Watters, *History of British Churches of Christ* (1948) 17.
[34]John Allen Hudson, *The Church in Great Britain* (1948) 250.

[35]"Notes on my life," *Scripture Standard*, August 1955: Given by a member
of the Ulverston Church.

[36]Watters 28-29.

[37]Derek L. Daniell, *The Kentish Town Messenger*, n.d. leaflet. Hudson 66.
Louise King, *Memoir of David King* (n.d. 19th century) 7.

[38]Watters preface.

Other sources:
Centenary of Church of Christ Kirkby in Furness (1976).
*Church of Christ at the Christian Meeting House, Wall End, Kirkby-in-
Furness, Cumbria* (n.d.).

19

SUMMARY

Am I therefore become your enemy, because I tell you the truth? Paul of Tarsus (c. 5 BC-67AD) from his Galatian epistle, 4:6.

It is dangerous to be right in matters on which the established authorities are wrong. Voltaire (1694-1778)

Some may think it strange that churches of Christ, holding to the same doctrinal position of the Restoration Movement, existed prior to Alexander Campbell and Barton Stone. We should not think it strange that people in bygone times should understand scripture alike. The whole Roman Catholic system, with its Augustinian theology, is based on the pagan belief in original sin with the pagan priesthood and ceremonies. The Protestant Reformers took this a further stage forward in justification through faith alone, whilst discarding the excesses of Romanism, seen, e.g., in the pope, purgatory, pilgrimages and confession.

Once the belief in original sin or human depravity is denied, believers' baptism makes sense. A study of scripture quickly reveals that baptism is for the believer by immersion for the remission of sins.

The Romish Church has always had a problem with the Blood of Christ taking away sin. Their baptism works through the supernatural power of Holy Water along with the exorcisms of the priest to remove original sin. Holy Water can still be found in the denominations minus the exorcisms. The Greek Orthodox as does the Roman Church retains exorcism in baptism. As the child ages, he will need to attend confession and work his way to heaven through good works such as monetary donations and pilgrimages.

After death, the soul has to work its way through purgatory with the prayers of the living for the dead. Those objecting to this error knew that sin is redeemed through the Blood of Christ for the repentant sinner. Thus, they preached that the Blood of Christ, through baptism, takes away sin, quoting Mark 16:16 and Rev 1:5. These people, separated from the world, were called falsely Lollards, Waldensians, Pelagians and a host of other names. They were burned as heretics and witches in a holocaust of 200,000, killed for simply obeying Christ by people who claimed to be Christians.

Using sources contemporary to those who lived in bygone ages along with modern research, we can conclude that several heretical groups, whose members wore the name Christian and the church – the church of Christ, existed before, during, and after the protestant reformation, and later, in the mid nineteenth century, joined in fellowship with the Restoration Movement. It is claimed by reformed historians, but without proof, these heretic groups retained infant baptism. Why should those people opposed to the Romish Church retain its corner stone – infant baptism?

With the Reformation, there was to be no respite. Old Catholic was now New Protestant; the burnings continued but a new derogatory name was invented – Anabaptist. The Protestants have always had a problem with forgiveness of sin in baptism, a change in scripture proof came about to address this. Out went Rev 1:5 as a proof text, the Blood of Christ was no longer in dispute, and in came Acts 2:38 (Baptised for remission of sins). These hardy evangelists still used Mark 16:16.

The areas in England and Europe where the Waldensians were active was later where the Lollards preached and met. Later still, where the Lollards were there were now Anabaptists and these were in areas where the General Baptists met later. As previously noted, none of these people used these names.

Later, the General Baptists would develop doctrines that denied Biblical truth becoming Arminian in doctrine, but these later people do not concern us. It is wrong though to call those Christians who rejected predestination, faith alone and human depravity by a name they never used.

One problem is how the origin of the Baptists is dealt with. My belief is that they are dated too early at either 1612 or 1638. A more accurate date would be from 1678 when some congregations decided to be known as Protestant. At that point, they had taken on reformed theology and identified themselves with the Protestants. They were now a denomination.

Baptists often take the churches of Christ to task calling them "Campbellites"; they would be better employed reading their own histories, for their descendants held to the same views as Campbell, by many centuries, before Campbell was born. The problem for the Baptist historian is the pre-reformation origin of the European churches of Christ, who are labelled in Baptist histories as Baptist, a name they never wore.

When the Restoration Movement started in Great Britain and America a legacy from earlier churches of Christ was there. The Bible was easily available and legal to own. Freedom of religion and conscience had been established. Knowledge of believers' baptism and congregational autonomy still existed within some denominations; all these had been fought for by Christians in the fifteenth through to the seventeenth centuries.

Dr. Hans Grimm in his small work, *Tradition and History of the Early Churches of Christ In Central Europe*, claims he and his family were members of the church of Christ in a tradition independent of the American and British Restoration Movements. The same is true of the churches of Christ in the Furness Fells of England, whose tradition predates the Restoration Movement. No one should think of the Restoration Movement as a denomination, but as the church of Christ, whose sole guide in spiritual matters is the Bible, and this includes rejecting Augustine, which includes Catholicism, and Reformation theology, including Luther and Calvin.

Through the ages, Christianity has been a hijacked religion, "Beloved, when I gave all diligence to write unto you of the common salvation, it was needful for me to write unto you, and exhort you that ye should earnestly contend for the faith which was once delivered unto the saints" (Jude 3). The faith was once delivered; that means it cannot be added to, or taken away from. From the pagans taking over of the apostate Christian religion which developed into the Roman Catholic Church, and later, into the Reformed Churches, we now have Islam knocking at the door. Their claim is that the Bible has been falsified and theirs (like the Roman Catholic Church) is the true faith.

On one side, we have the liberals who would introduce homosexual priests and female bishops, and on the other side, Islam who would have us believe the Bible is false and their prophet Mohamed superior to Christ. Before, during and after the Reformation, churches of Christ stood on the radical left. Today such belief has a person labeled right wing Christian fundamental. At one time the Church of England sought the death penalty by burning members of the churches of Christ for their views of freedom of conscience and freedom of worship. Today, the Church of England will oppose the church of Christ as fundamental. How society has changed over the last four hundred years – Isaiah wrote (5:20) "Woe unto them that call evil good, and good evil; that put darkness for light, and light for darkness; that put bitter for sweet, and sweet for bitter!"

The pagan/Romish system of the church is of a congregation divided into two parts, the un-godly and the clergy. Anyone studying the scriptures knows this to be untrue. The congregation, the church of Christ, is a people called out of the world, i.e., the ecclesia, made up of Godly people separated from the world. The Biblical church denies infant baptism where all are added, without choice into a national church. The Biblical church of Christ, the Lord's Church, was never and never will be a national church.

Paul wrote in Galatians 1:6-9:

> I marvel that ye are so soon removed from him that called you into the grace of Christ unto another gospel: Which is not another; but there be some that trouble you, and would pervert the gospel of Christ. But though we, or an angel from heaven, preach any other gospel unto you than that which we have preached unto you, let him be accursed. As we said before, so say I now again, if any man preach any other gospel unto you than that ye have received, let him be accursed.

Most, if not all of the innovations found in the denominations not only stem from Augustine, but also from the pagan system that existed in the first century – another Gospel. When the Emperor Constantine legalised Christianity in 313, the path was set for a national church. Infant baptism, altar worship, the choir, clergy (or separate priesthood), holy ground (buildings on sanctified ground), holy water, popes and pontiffs and more all existed when Paul wrote the above passage. If such is acceptable in Christian worship, why then are they not mentioned in scripture? Of course, the Bible cannot list everything thing we are not to do, but list only that which is acceptable to God which excludes the above. The faith was once given and it is that faith which Christians are told to "contend" for. The faith we find today in the denominations is another faith, which is not the faith practised in the first century, the faith found in scripture and hence, not the faith of Christ.

Paul stated in Colossians 2:20-23:

> Wherefore if ye be dead with Christ from the rudiments of the world, why, as though living in the world, are ye subject to ordinances, (Touch not; taste not; handle not; Which all are to perish with the using;) after the commandments and doctrines of men? Which things have indeed a shew of wisdom in will worship, and humility, and neglecting of the body; not in any honour to the satisfying of the flesh.

And again in Romans 12:2: "And be not conformed to this world: but be ye transformed by the renewing of your mind, that ye may prove what is that good, and acceptable, and perfect, will of

627

God." How can we "prove what is that good, and acceptable" when we are "conformed to this world?"

From the fourth century, scripture was interpreted through Augustinian theology and social needs of contemporary society. It is no different today; Augustinian theology has been built upon since the Reformation. The denominations are conformed to the world and to idolatry. Paul urges "Wherefore, my dearly beloved, flee from idolatry (1Cor. 10:14)." The idolatry Paul spoke of has now hijacked Christianity! The church of Christ, the Lord's Church, is founded on scripture alone without the theology and idolatry of the Church Fathers. It has been persecuted, but has not persecuted. It has been denied, but does not deny Christ. It does not conform to the world, though the worldly denominations are so conformed. The evidence as laid out in this small book is that such congregations pre-dated the protestant reformation by several centuries; in fact, the first church of Christ met on the first Pentecost after the Resurrection at Jerusalem.

An example of conforming to the world is found in the Anglican (and other) denominations where female bishops, homosexual priests and living together outside marriage and defended for Christians. All disagree with scripture, but the excuse is made that the scriptures need to be interpreted through contemporary values – thus clashing with Paul's writing in 1 Corinthians 10:14.

Another example of failing to understand Biblical doctrine is that of female priests. There has been considerable controversy over female priests in the Anglican and other denominations, yet in the first century all Christians were priests. The first epistle of Peter describes all Christians as a "royal priesthood": "But ye are a chosen generation, a royal priesthood, an holy nation, a peculiar people; that ye should shew forth the praises of him who hath called you out of darkness into his marvelous light" (1Pet. 2:9). The controversy, therefore, cannot be over female priests, but female clergy. In the first century church there was no clergy-laity divide, the divide being introduced in the late second century which followed the pattern of pagan temple worship. Of course, the Old Testament priesthood had a clergy, but the law was nailed to the cross so does not apply to the New Testament (Col. 2:14).

David King (1819-1894) wrote of this, the following taken from his memoirs published by his wife (pages 249-251):

> Thus the tribe of Levi was called the *inheritance* (or clergy) of the Lord, while, reciprocally, He was called their inheritance. In every church in which a *clergy* is recognised, there, as a consequence, is the *laity.* The word *laos* is found in the New Testament over one hundred and thirty times, and is translated *people.* Were we now lifted out of the Dispensation of the Spirit, and carried back to that of the Law; nothing would be more appropriate than the terms *clergy* and *laity,* the one designating the *priests,* and the other the *people* and distinguished from the priesthood. But no trace of such distinction is found

in the present economy - it belongs not to the church of Christ. Not that *laos* is not used in the New Testament to denote the people, in contradistinction to the Church of God, which is the *Royal Priesthood,* and the only one now acknowledged. It is used (as we use the word *people*) to designate the nation under the law, the unconverted masses, and the church of Christ. But whenever it is applied to the church it expresses the *whole body* and never stands for an unpriestly or unclerical portion thereof - as, *"A holy nation, a peculiar people"* – "A peculiar *people* zealous of good works." So, too, *kleeros* (which occurs in the New Testament some thirteen times) is never used to distinguish a section, or class, of God's people from the many, or other portion of the Lord's church. In Ephesians 1:11, the whole church is said to *"have obtained an inheritance"* in Christ, or, expressed literally, "to have been taken as His *inheritance, lot* or *clergy."* So that the Lord's people are, as a whole, the Lord's *clergy,* and the only clergy he has. Bishops, elders, pastors, are not designated clergy, otherwise than as the poorest and most illiterate of the flock are so designated; every one of whom is a clergyman, or a clergywoman, in the only sense in which the term can be applied to any. Peter wrote to the elders, saying, *"Feed the flock of God, which is among you, taking the oversight, not by constraint, but willingly, not for filthy lucre, but of a ready mind; neither as being lords over God's heritage."*

Here, *heritage* is a translation of *kleeros,* and the whole Church is designated God's clergy, over which the elders are forbidden to constitute themselves lords. Every member of the people, or *laity,* of Acts xv:14, Rom. ix:26, 2 Cor. vi:16, is one of the *clergy* of 1 Peter v:3. There is, then, no clerical caste, or order, in the Church of God - all the laity of God are the clergy of Christ; and by this standard we determine the Greek Church, the Roman

Church, the Anglican Church, the Mormon Church, etc., to appertain to the apostasy, and to have no claim to be received as that institution set up by the authority of Christ and designated the Church of God.

David King (1819-1894)

So what is the issue pertaining to female priests? It is Paul's statement found in 1 Timothy, chapter 2 verse 12 – "But I suffer not a woman to teach, nor to usurp authority over the man, but to be in silence." Those who wish to interpret scripture through contemporary society will argue this is temporary, for that time. But Paul continues in verses thirteen and fourteen "For Adam was first formed, then Eve. And Adam was not deceived, but the woman being deceived was in the transgression." Paul takes this back to the beginning, that man should have pre-eminence and take the lead. It is not a local custom, for there were females in the pagan priesthoods. It was a command for all time and in the words of Jesus, "Teaching them to observe all things whatsoever I have commanded you: and, lo, I am with you always, even unto the end of the world. Amen" (Mat. 28:20). The objection may be that the teaching of Jesus is limited to His time on earth, the gospels. The teaching of Jesus continued through His apostles. Luke wrote accordingly, "The former treatise have I made, O Theophilus, of all that Jesus began both to do and teach" (Acts 1:1). Jesus had said in John 14:26:, "But the Comforter, which is the Holy Ghost, whom the Father will send in my name, he shall teach you all things, and bring all things to your remembrance, whatsoever I have said unto you." Paul's inspired instruction remains in force today, "But I suffer not a woman to teach, nor to usurp authority over the man, but to be in silence."

The history of the Christian church is often viewed as a cruel, bloody religion, a history of persecution. Those that persecuted so often committed their crimes against Christians, and when the persecutors of innocents claimed to be Christians, they had hijacked the name Christian, a name they had no right to be called.

The Christianity of the first century was a religion based on reason, "Come now, and let us reason together" (Isa 1:18a). Luke wrote in his history of the early church, "These were more noble than those in Thessalonica, in that they received the word with all readiness of mind, and searched the scriptures daily, whether those things were so" (Acts 17:11). It was a religion of peace, not violence and coercion. Paul wrote, "and let us not be weary in well doing: for in due season we shall reap, if we faint not. As we have therefore opportunity, let us do good unto all men, especially unto them who are of the household of faith" (Gal. 6:9-10). Peter said, "But sanctify the Lord God in your hearts: and be ready always to give an answer to every man that asketh you a reason of the hope that is in you with meekness and fear" (1 Pet. 3:15).

Today churches of Christ are seen as being on the Christian fundamentalist far-right, whereas the same belief just a few decades ago placed them on the radical left. What has changed is society. Prior to the American Restoration Movement, such churches met in Great Britain and Europe, autonomous and independent of each other. During the early 1800s, fellowship between the various congregations in countries where they met was established.

Such churches are not founded on man-made doctrine or succession, but the"seed" principle found in Matthew 13:3-23:

> And he spake many things unto them in parables, saying, Behold, a sower went forth to sow; And when he sowed, some seeds fell by the way side, and the fowls came and devoured them up: Some fell upon stony places, where they had not much earth: and forthwith they sprung up, because they had no deepness of earth: And when the sun was up, they were scorched; and because they had no root, they withered away. And some fell among thorns; and the thorns sprung up, and choked them: But other fell into good ground, and brought forth fruit, some an hundredfold, some sixtyfold, some thirtyfold. Who hath ears to hear, let him hear. And the disciples came, and said unto him, Why speakest thou unto them in parables? He answered and said unto them, Because it is given unto you to know the mysteries of the kingdom of heaven, but to them it is not given. For whosoever hath, to him shall be given, and he shall have more abundance: but whosoever hath not, from him shall be taken away even that he hath. Therefore speak I to them in parables: because they seeing see not; and hearing they hear not, neither do they understand. And in them is fulfilled the prophecy of Esaias, which saith, By hearing ye shall hear, and shall not understand; and seeing ye shall see, and shall not perceive: For this people's heart is waxed gross, and their ears are dull of hearing, and their eyes they have closed; lest at any time they should see with their eyes, and hear with their ears, and should understand with their heart, and should be converted, and I should heal them. But blessed are your eyes, for they see: and your ears, for they hear. For verily I say unto you, That many prophets

and righteous men have desired to see those things which ye see, and have not seen them; and to hear those things which ye hear, and have not heard them.

Hear ye therefore the parable of the sower. When any one heareth the word of the kingdom, and understandeth it not, then cometh the wicked one, and catcheth away that which was sown in his heart. This is he which received seed by the way side.But he that received the seed into stony places, the same is he that heareth the word, and anon with joy receiveth it; Yet hath he not root in himself, but dureth for a while: for when tribulation or persecution ariseth because of the word, by and by he is offended. He also that received seed among the thorns is he that heareth the word; and the care of this world, and the deceitfulness of riches, choke the word, and he becometh unfruitful. But he that received seed into the good ground is he that heareth the word, and understandeth it; which also beareth fruit, and bringeth forth, some an hundredfold, some sixty, some thirty.

Churches of Christ do not deny the Elect; they oppose the predestination of individuals but preach the church of Christ as the predestined eternal plan of God. As such they hold to the Elect, but through freewill and hence free choice of the individual.

The means of evangelism was the gospel agency in conversion; there was no supernatural conversion. Those of the Calvinistic persuasion teach of supernatural conversion of an elect few. Jesus said, "And I will pray the Father, and he shall give you another Comforter, that he may abide with you forever; Even the Spirit of truth, whom the world cannot receive, because it seeth him not, neither knoweth him, but ye know him; for he dwelleth with you, and shall be in you" (John 14:16-17). Jesus speaks of "the Spirit of truth, whom the world cannot receive." The inference must be that those outside the Christian faith "cannot receive" the Holy Spirit. The "Comforter" in John 14:26 is the Holy Ghost (or Spirit) "But the Comforter, which is the Holy Ghost." Paul wrote to Timothy, "Who will have all men to be saved and to come unto the knowledge of the truth" (1 Tim. 2:4). Jesus said, "For God so loved the world, that he gave his only begotten Son, that whosoever believeth in him should not perish, but have everlasting life" (John 3:16). These verses refute the Calvinistic view of Holy Spirit conversion or limited atonement. Salvation is for all who hear, obey and remain faithful unto death (Rev. 2:10). We do find, of course, the supernatural assisting the evangelists in the first century, e.g., in the conversion of Cornelius. But this was to assist the Jewish Christians in understanding that the gospel was for gentiles as well (Acts 11:16-17), that they were to go out into all the world (Mark 16:15).

Paul wrote of the word: "Preach the word; be instant in season, out of season; reprove, rebuke, exhort with all longsuffering and doctrine" (2 Tim. 4:2). "So then faith cometh by hearing, and hearing by the word of God" (Rom. 10:17). James wrote of the word and salvation, "Wherefore lay apart all filthiness and superfluity of naughtiness, and receive with meekness the engrafted word, which

636

is able to save your souls" (Jam. 1:21).

Faith only (or faith alone) proponents will object. The only place where "faith only" is mentioned in the scriptures is found in James 2:14-24:

> What doth it profit, my brethren, though a man say he hath faith, and have not works? Can faith save him? If a brother or sister be naked, and destitute of daily food, And one of you say unto them, Depart in peace, be ye warmed and filled; notwithstanding ye give them not those things which are needful to the body; what doth it profit? Even so faith, if it hath not works, is dead, being alone. Yea, a man may say, Thou hast faith, and I have works: shew me thy faith without thy works, and I will shew thee my faith by my works. Thou believest that there is one God; thou doest well: the devils also believe, and tremble. But wilt thou know, O vain man, that faith without works is dead? Was not Abraham our father justified by works, when he had offered Isaac his son upon the altar? Seest thou how faith wrought with his works, and by works was faith made perfect? And the scripture was fulfilled which saith, Abraham believed God, and it was imputed unto him for righteousness: and he was called the Friend of God. Ye see then how that by works a man is justified, and not by *faith only*.

The New Testament does teach man is "justified by faith." In Romans 3:23-25 justification is through faith in His blood,

> For all have sinned, and come short of the glory of God; Being justified freely by his grace through the redemption that is in Christ Jesus: Whom God hath set forth to be a propitiation through faith in his blood, to declare his righteousness for the remission of sins that are past,

637

through the forbearance of God.

In Titus 3:5-7 is by the washing of regeneration (baptism) that we are justified by His grace:

> Not by works of righteousness which we have done, but according to his mercy he saved us, by the washing of regeneration, and renewing of the Holy Ghost; Which he shed on us abundantly through Jesus Christ our Saviour; That being justified by his grace, we should be made heirs according to the hope of eternal life.

God justifies through these means, by Christ (Rom. 3:24), His blood (Rom. 3:25), by knowledge (Isa. 53:11), baptism (Tit. 3:5), grace (Tit. 3:7), faith and works (Jam. 2:14-24).

The Biblical plan of salvation is the gospel agency. The sinner hears the gospel, believes the gospel and in baptism has his sins forgiven. Jesus said in handing out the Great Commission, "And he said unto them, Go ye into all the world, and preach the gospel to every creature. He that believeth and is baptized shall be saved; but he that believeth not shall be damned" (Mark 16:15-16). Another account is found in Matthew 28:18-20:

> And Jesus came and spake unto them, saying, all power is given unto me in heaven and in earth. Go ye therefore, and teach all nations, baptizing them in the name of the Father, and of the Son, and of the Holy Ghost: Teaching them to observe all things whatsoever I have commanded you: and, lo, I am with you always, even unto the end of the world. Amen.

Peter in the first gospel sermon proclaimed, "Then Peter said unto them, Repent, and be baptized every one of you in the name of Jesus Christ for the remission of sins, and ye shall receive the gift of the Holy Ghost" (Acts 2:38). The gospel plan is seen when Crispus was baptized, "And Crispus, the chief ruler of the synagogue, believed on the Lord with all his house; and many of the Corinthians hearing believed, and were baptized" (Acts 18:8). Justification by grace alone through faith alone in Christ's righteousness alone is a doctrine of the Protestant Reformation; it is fifteen hundred years too late, being "another gospel," not that preached in the first century.

The church of Christ (Rom. 16:16) was promised by the Christ (Mat. 16:18), "And I say also unto thee, that thou art Peter, and upon this rock I will build my church; and the gates of hell shall not prevail against it." The promise looked to the future, in Acts 20:28 we find the church established which was purchased with His own blood; "Take heed therefore unto yourselves, and to all the flock, over which the Holy Ghost hath made you overseers, to feed the church of God, which he hath purchased with his own blood." Christ is the Saviour of the body, the church, "For the husband is the head of the wife, even as Christ is the head of the church: and he is the Saviour of the body" (Eph. 5:23). It is in the church that where the saved are found, added to the church through baptism, "For as many of you as have been baptised into Christ have put on Christ" (Gal.

3:27).

Another false doctrine is that of the thief on the cross, it is ecumenical and recent; it denies baptism is required and surprisingly, is promoted by many Baptists along with several denominations. As a new doctrine, we must consider the words of Paul found in Galatians 1:6-8. This false doctrine is another gospel. Those who advocate this new error claim without evidence the thief was not baptised for the remission of sins. They state this not knowing the scriptures, for Matthew said concerning John's baptism, "Then went out to him Jerusalem, and all Judaea, and all the region round about Jordan" (Mat. 3:5). Mark said "John did baptize in the wilderness, and preach the baptism of repentance for the remission of sins" (Mark 1:4), and Matthew "And were baptized of him in Jordan, confessing their sins" (Mat. 3:6). Those who push the Thief on the Cross doctrine cannot state the thief was not baptised for the remission of sins as Jerusalem, and all Judaea, and all the region round about Jordan had gone to John; the thief most likely was one of these people. Even if he was not baptised (for the remission of sins), he died under the old covenant before the Christian dispensation had begun. Today John's baptism is no longer valid as it looked towards the cross, but baptism in Christ today is still for remission of sins (Acts 2:38). Salvation requires obedience, which is more than a faith without works, "And being made perfect, he became the author of eternal salvation unto all them that obey him" (Heb. 5:9), and "For the time is come that judgment must begin at the house of God: and if it first begin at us, what shall the end be of them that obey not the gospel of God" (1 Pet. 4:17). Another argument presented by those who promote the thief on the cross doctrine is that as he died at the crucifixion, he died in the new (Christian) dispensation. The new dispensation did not start until after the Resurrection at Pentecost. Peter said "The like figure whereunto even baptism doth also now save us (not the putting away of the filth of the flesh, but the answer of a good conscience toward God,) by the resurrection of Jesus Christ" (1 Pet. 3:21). This baptism that "saves" is "by the resurrection of Jesus Christ" which was three days after His death, thus it excludes the thief who died under the Old Covenant. That the thief died before the resurrection to use as evidence for or against baptism is ridiculous, yet this is done time and again. The thief on the cross didn't even comply with the first prerequisite of salvation, as evidenced by Romans 10:9-10 (That if thou shalt confess with thy mouth the Lord Jesus, and shalt believe in thine heart that God hath raised him from the dead, thou shalt be saved. For with the heart man believeth unto righteousness; and with the mouth confession is made unto salvation). He could not confess any belief in the resurrection since it had not as yet happened. Dying before the gospel was fulfilled puts this man under the Old Testament law where Jesus had the power to forgive sins. It

641

does not place him under the New Testament.

After the Resurrection the Lord became High Priest in Heaven, a position he could not hold on earth as he was of the tribe of Judah (Heb. 7:14). Christians are priests which they could not be under the Old Covenant, "Ye also, as lively stones, are built up a spiritual house, an holy priesthood, to offer up spiritual sacrifices, acceptable to God by Jesus Christ" (1 Pet. 2:5). Christ is High Priest, a position he did not hold at His death.

> Now of the things which we have spoken this is the sum: We have such an high priest, who is set on the right hand of the throne of the Majesty in the heavens; A minister of the sanctuary, and of the true tabernacle, which the Lord pitched, and not man. For every high priest is ordained to offer gifts and sacrifices: wherefore it is of necessity that this man have somewhat also to offer. For if he were on earth, he should not be a priest, seeing that there are priests that offer gifts according to the law: Who serve unto the example and shadow of heavenly things, as Moses was admonished of God when he was about to make the tabernacle: for, see, saith he, that thou make all things according to the pattern shewed to thee in the mount. But now hath he obtained a more excellent ministry, by how much also he is the mediator of a better covenant, which was established upon better promises. For if that first covenant had been faultless, then should no place have been sought for the second. For finding fault with them, he saith, Behold, the days come, saith the Lord, when I will make a new covenant with the house of Israel and with the house of Judah: Not according to the covenant that I made with their fathers in the day when I took them by the hand to lead them out of the land of Egypt; because

they continued not in my covenant, and I regarded them not, saith the Lord. For this is the covenant that I will make with the house of Israel after those days, saith the Lord; I will put my laws into their mind, and write them in their hearts: and I will be to them a God, and they shall be to me a people: And they shall not teach every man his neighbour, and every man his brother, saying, Know the Lord: for all shall know me, from the least to the greatest. For I will be merciful to their unrighteousness, and their sins and their iniquities will I remember no more. In that he saith, A new covenant, he hath made the first old. Now that which decayeth and waxeth old is ready to vanish away (Heb. 8:1-13).

Those who push this ungodly doctrine of the "thief on the cross" look for an exception to prove the rule, but the rule, i.e., the New Covenant, came into force after the Resurrection. Having had several debates with Baptists over the "thief on the Cross," they claim to have direct revelation from the Holy Spirit thereby making Scripture a dead book. We are witnessing a return to the days of the reformers when ex-cathedra statements are forced on others without peace and love. Baptists (and others who promote the thief) need to look to their own histories; from the people they claim to be Baptists in bygone ages, for they taught a baptism of remission of sins whereby the person was added to the church of Christ, "Know ye not, that so many of us as were baptised into Jesus Christ were baptised into his death" (Rom. 6:3) and "For as many of you as have been baptised into Christ have put on Christ" (Gal.

3:27). We put on Christ through baptism and without baptism we do not belong to Him, who purchased our salvation through His blood (Acts 20:28). We need not go back two thousand years to be saved, by being nailed to a cross; baptism is what the Lord requires. The "thief on the cross" doctrine is mans' doctrine, a false doctrine; we need to be engaged with the doctrine of Christ, if we return to the Old Covenant under which the thief died, we also return to blood sacrifice and stoning.

Another oft repeated error and recent doctrine not dissimilar to the "thief on the cross" is that called the "sinner's prayer." Two scriptures used to promote this is Romans 10:13, "For whosoever shall call upon the name of the Lord shall be saved," and Acts 2:21, "And it shall come to pass, that whosoever shall call on the name of the Lord shall be saved." When Paul called upon the name of the Lord, he was baptised, "And now why tarriest thou? arise, and be baptized, and wash away thy sins, calling on the name of the Lord" (Acts 22:16). We are baptised in the name of the Lord, "Go ye therefore, and teach all nations, baptizing them in the name of the Father, and of the Son, and of the Holy Ghost" (Mat. 28:19).

Paul wrote of the one faith in Jesus Christ "Now I beseech you, brethren, by the name of our Lord Jesus Christ, that ye all speak the same thing, and that there be no divisions among you; but that ye be perfectly joined together in the same mind and in the same judgment" (1 Cor. 1:10). In his letter to the Ephesians, he developed this injunction further, "Endeavouring to keep the unity of the Spirit in the bond of peace. There is one body, and one Spirit, even as ye are called in one hope of your calling; One Lord, one faith, one baptism, One God and Father of all, who is above all, and through all, and in you all" (Eph. 4:3-6), a message that has been preached for two thousand years in the churches of Christ.

Jesus proclaimed, "And I say also unto thee, That thou art Peter, and upon this rock I will build my church; and the gates of hell shall not prevail against it" (Mat. 16:18). Paul stated, "Salute one another with an holy kiss. The churches of Christ salute you" (Rom 16:16). A need to return to Gospel preaching is required in a world ignorant of Jesus and His plan for mankind. The world needs turning upside down with preaching, a return to the Jerusalem gospel "And when they found them not, they drew Jason and certain brethren unto the rulers of the city, crying, these that have turned the world upside down are come hither also" (Acts 17:6). For "baptism doth also now save us" (1 Pet. 3:21).

Index

Dates are from *The Oxford Dictionary of The Christian Church*, by F. L. Cross and E.A. Livingstone, 1993

A

Abbey of Tewkesbury 283
Abbot, George, Archbishop of Canterbury 101, 405
Abbot Mellitus 83, 84
Accusations against Christians 179
Act of Toleration 348, 482, 518, 534
Act of Uniformity 455, 474
Albigenses 124, 136, 146, 233, 237
Albigensians 135
Alexandria 48, 104
America 83, 100, 101, 102, 103, 104, 106, 107, 108, 109, 110,
    111, 112, 115, 116, 117, 120, 121, 155, 240, 375, 443, 449,
    451, 465, 533, 544, 545, 548, 617, 618, 624
Amersham 401
Amesbury 91
Ammonius, Andreas 327
Amsterdam 203, 240, 381, 382, 385, 386, 388, 394, 398, 452
Anabaptist Mystery of Iniquity Unmasked 427
Anabaptists 9, 126, 135, 137, 144, 148, 149, 151, 152, 153, 154,
    158, 175, 179, 199, 207, 208, 209, 220, 221, 222, 228, 229,
    231, 239, 240, 241, 246, 249, 250, 260, 282, 310, 315, 317,
    318, 319, 320, 321, 322, 323, 324, 349, 360, 362, 369, 372,
    377, 378, 379, 391, 403, 405, 408, 412, 413, 415, 433, 434,
    478, 520, 521, 561, 563, 597, 623
Anglesey 62
Antwerp 14, 254, 289, 300, 329
Apostasy 1, 5, 19, 30, 34, 47, 55, 149, 405, 422, 437, 518, 577,
    631